P9-DER-259

# sudden *glory*

BEACON PRESS

*Boston*

laughter

as

subversive

history

# sudden *glory*



barry sanders

BEACON PRESS
25 Beacon Street
Boston, Massachusetts
02108-2892

Beacon Press books are published under the auspices of the Unitarian Universalist Association of Congregations.


Printed in the United States of America

99 98 97 96 95
8 7 6 5 4 3 2 1

Text design by Diane Jaroch
Composition by Wilsted & Taylor
Printed on recycled paper

Library of Congress Cataloging-in-Publication Data

Sanders, Barry, 1938–
Sudden glory: laughter as subversive history / Barry Sanders.
p. cm.
Includes bibliographical references and index.
ISBN 0-8070-6204-9
1. Wit and humor—History.
2. Laughter—History.
I. Title.
PN6147.S26 1995
809.7—dc20
95-5720
CIP

*For Jeanne Sanders and Grace Zury:*

*Back to breath, back to laughing breath once more*

And we should consider every day lost on which

we have not danced at least once. And we should

call every truth false which was not accompanied

by at least one laugh.

—Nietzsche, *Thus Spake Zarathustra*

**contents**



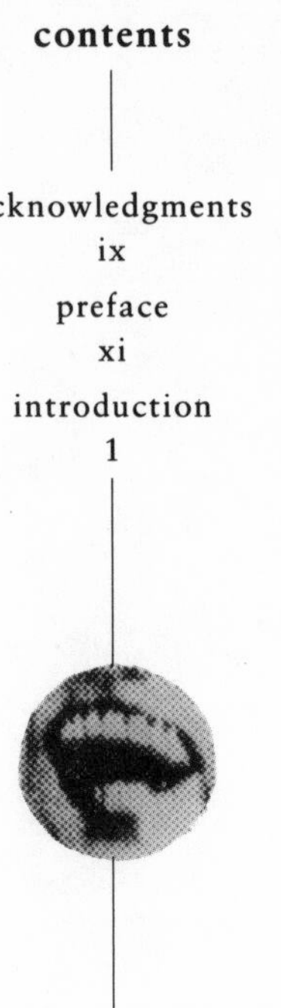

# *acknowledgments*

*What* a delight to have an editor with a sense of humor! Thank you Deanne Urmy for hand and heart. Once more with feeling: Thank you Grace for turning my outbursts into ideas. Kali and Erik heard pieces of this book out loud maybe one time too many. All three suffered my indulgences. Thanks to Bert Meyers for telling me to write this book; to Chuck Young for his help in the ancient world. To the librarians of the Huntington Library, especially to Ginger Renner, for allowing me to hold captive a good portion of their holdings. And always, to Miriam Altshuler: thanks again for believing.

# *preface*

*In* the nineteenth century, the Russian philosopher A. I. Herzen made the following tantalizing statement: "It would be extremely interesting to write the history of laughter." I don't know if Herzen meant to be ironic or not, for the history of laughter can never be written. It can only be reconstructed. The history of *attitudes* toward laughter, however, can be written.

The laughs have long since disappeared into the ether: The evidence has evaporated. While theories of laughter have come from those in positions of authority, the laughs have come most powerfully, and thus most threateningly, from those who have occupied the underbelly of history, from those who have remained as historically anonymous as their laughs. I want to resuscitate them and their laughter. So I ask you to listen in particular to those who have been denied access to writing—not only the peasants of every livery, but especially the women of every class—who have remained closely attuned to the heartbeat, the impulse, of vernacular speech. Every time someone like Plato advises against laughing to excess because it violates decorum or morality, imagine scores of common citizens cracking up for just those reasons. No sooner than the law tightens its rope, some smart alec will twist a noose into a loophole and make a clean getaway, laughing all the way to the border. The escape raises problems for the reader of this book, problems I can describe best through analogy.

In *The Little Prince*, a book that generations of adults have read to their children, the narrator makes a delightfully innocent drawing of a boa constrictor, misshapen because it has just devoured, in one great gulp, an elephant. The Little Prince gets his first dose of adult stupidity as grown-up after grown-up mistakes the drawing for a rendering of a fedora. The drawing teaches an important lesson: As educated, sophisticated adults, we can eventually learn to see the invisible in the visible, but only by exercising our imagination so vigorously that we rid ourselves of expectations and prejudices, that is, by turning naive once again and adopting a spirit of play. And to make that point, St. Exupéry, the author of this "kid's book," knows he must turn the tables and "kid around" with his readers.

The drawing provides other lessons. First we understand that the slippery, potentially lethal in society threatens to swallow in one gulp the benign and plodding who stand in the way—no matter their size. Although historically those in central positions of authority have devoured those who reside at the margins of society, if you look hard you can still make out their distinctive outline. And if you listen hard you can hear their plotting and scheming—a faint but joyous giggle just below the surface of the aboveground history. That underground, telluric giggle—"rough music," as E. P. Thompson calls it—is best imagined as an ongoing carnival, a festival of fools, organized by peasants, of the sort that constantly threatened to flip the medieval world topsy-turvy by sending boys to the throne as bishops, and by handing women the scepter as rulers of the realm. It is not so strange to read history in this oblique way. In his beautiful description of the erotics of reading, *The Pleasure of the Text*, Roland Barthes writes: "[The text] produces, in me, the best pleasure if it manages to make itself heard indirectly; if, reading it, I am led to look up often, to listen to something else."

In an odd book entitled *All about Strange Beasts of the Past*, Roy Chapman Andrews offers this description of the great wooly mammoth, which reverberates with meaning for this study of laughter: "The word *mammoth* is derived from the Tartar word *mama* meaning 'the earth'. . . . From this some mistakenly came to believe that the great beast had always lived underground, burrowing like a big mole. And they were sure it died when it came to the surface and breathed air." I want to unearth the great wooly *mama* and, after all these centuries, coax her out into the open and let her breathe some fresh air. I am convinced she will not die exposed to the bright light of day. With fresh air in her lungs, I would like to hear her speak out loud. With the help of some even fresher air, I would like to hear her laugh out loud.

The difficult question is, How to read? Or more to the point, How to listen? And just where do we find that "fresher air"? The answer lies, I think, in according sentences the proper reception, in adopting the right attitude—inclining toward each and every word. We have to invite words, with all their lexical untidiness, into our most private chambers. We have to become generous and expansive, hospitable to them all. As contemporary readers, so far removed from our subject, both in temperament and time, we fumble for meaning. We must bring foreign words to our home ground and try to make sense of them. We must read as translators. "A master translator," as George Steiner aptly says, "can be defined as a perfect host." It is just this nonmaterial definition of *host* I am after—the state of mind willing to entertain the wildest, most unruly of ideas.

From time to time this book abruptly halts its narrative and turns to etymology. I see these moments as times of sheer hospitality, when the story relaxes a bit and takes a breath. I want to approach each word, particularly the technical jargon of joking and laughter, as if it were a stranger whom I am delighted to meet: What's your name? (Perhaps even your maiden name.) Where are you from? What have you seen? Who was your teacher? Your playmates? Your parents? I invite each word to take off its outer wraps and loaf a bit, for only with pleasure, and a good deal of good-natured conversation—talking directly to the ghosts of history—can we ever hope to understand so elusive a subject as laughter.

In some pieces of amber found under water, tiny bubbles of air trapped hundreds and hundreds of years earlier have been suddenly released. I have often wondered how that air would smell. What effect would it have on the stuff we now breathe? Could one sense, let's say, the spirit of the Renaissance in one single atom of $O_2$? Like amber, words contain meanings trapped ages ago; we blithely wear them, like so much decoration, unaware of the truth that might be caught at their core. We use them without testing their true weight. To break each word open and liberate old meanings is like breathing ancient air or listening to ancient music. To try to reach even an approximate understanding of the past means reading in a new way, what I term reading *ponderously*, from a marvelously rich Latin root, *pendere*, which means "to depend," like a pendant, "to hang suspended," and "to carry weight." To read ponderously is to treat each text gravely—to accord it weight—but out of a sense of play and a feeling of grace. As historians, we dangle in front of evidence and the truth dangles before our eyes, like a precious gem. We hang suspended for the longest time, waiting to make up our minds: Do we buy it or not?

The New Historians—*annalistes* like Marc Bloch, Fernand Braudel, Philippe Ariès, and Le Roy Ladurie—resemble archaeologists in their incessant dig to uncover the peasant voice. They have primarily scoured the public records offices, sifting through arrest records of the poor and the persecuted, reading each page of testimony for evidence of the folk *mentalité*. But the houses of words—the *Oxford English Dictionary*, the French *Littré*, the Paully-Wissowa, and so on—themselves contain startling testimony, for peasants were also sentenced *there*, through each and every word. Coaxed a bit, each word gradually gives up its history. Opening its covers, the historian enters the dictionary as a vast playground for the imagination.

I am unconcerned with comedy—with the worlds of Old and New Comedy, with Dante's divine versions or Shakespeare's romantic ones. Those genres have been studied not only by literary critics, but by anthropologists and folklorists, psychologists and historians, political theorists, and then some. I want to pay especial attention to laughter and to what, for me, prompts it in a satisfying, interesting, and most literate way: jokes. To get the story of laughter told, this book roams widely, like the Great Wooly itself, from the land of Canaan, to ancient Greece and Rome, around Europe, lingering in England on October 25, 1400, the date of Chaucer's death, chiseled into his stone in the Poet's Corner of Westminster Abbey. To understand fully Chaucer's staggering effect on the history of laughter, the concluding chapters take up the crushing political pressures leveled against laughter in the Renaissance, and the resulting criminalizing of laughers during the Enlightenment. I examine monstrous and grotesque laughter in the next to the last chapter, and end with a personal account of a joker who radically changed contemporary comedy—Lenny Bruce.

In every other historical subject, the reader must be on constant guard not to mistake contemporary definitions for historical ones. This holds true even for an activity that seems so unmistakably clear as "reading." But when Charlemagne uses the phrase, "I have read," for example, he most often means that Bishop Alcuin, his spiritual advisor, has recited out loud to him. There is no mistaking the sound, however, whatever its implications, of a hearty laugh; and no one can laugh for you. "We must go on reading," the historian Keith Thomas advises, "until we can hear the people not just talking but laughing."

sudden *glory*

# *introduction*

## I

In the beginning was the Laugh. That is how the world comes to be, according to an Egyptian alchemical papyrus dating from around the third century B.C. God utters not one word, not a single syllable, in the act of Creation. For the Egyptian Creator, words and sentences will come much later. "Let There Be" resounds with too much authority. The first Egyptian god knows another, more lively and basic way into Creation. He confronts Chaos and laughs it off, delivering a world of joy and exuberance into the light: "When God laughed, seven gods were born to rule the world. . . . When he burst out laughing there was light. . . . When he burst out laughing the second time the waters were born; at the seventh burst of laughter, the soul was born."* Compared to this god's bellowing laughter, the *afflatus serpentis*, the envious hiss of the serpent, sounds like an old tire giving up its air. Two different cosmogonies, two different kinds of air. Whenever an ancient Egyptian laughed, he or she automatically cleared the air, and joyously recreated the world anew.

Jews and Christians also view God's breath as holy, but an air of solemnity hangs about him. One hears little, if any, laughter. In Judaic tradition, God exhales into a handful of earth and brings Adam into a fully spirited life. (Adam's name in Hebrew, *Adamah*, means "earth." Did the sober God of the Jews start out much more playfully, perhaps laughing Adam, that lump of clay, into existence?) After Adam disobeyed God for a taste of the forbidden fruit, however, God retaliated by cursing Adam at his most vulnerable spot: with shortness of breath. God demanded that, at the end of their days, Jews return their breath, or *ruach*, back to him. Breath marks our coming and our going; we come in with an inhale and depart with an

*Quoted in Theodore Hopfner, *Griechisch-ägyptischer Offenbarungszauber*, Studien zur Palaeographie und Papyruskunde, no. 21 (Leipzig, 1972), p. 618.

exhale. By returning this precious gift, the cycle of life continually turns, ensuring that God, in his infinite wisdom, will always have the last laugh.*

Christians participate in their own version of this airy cycle. Medieval spires reach high into the heavens, conduits through which God fills every cathedral with his divine breath—an act of holy inspiration. Priests keep the precious stuff in circulation by blowing puffs of that rarified air into the mouth of each novitiate during Mass, in an act called the Conspiratorial Kiss. Without participating in this priestly conspiracy—*con-spiratio*, "breathing together"—Christians must live out their days forever dispirited, never really knowing the taste of Eternity.

Breath is the basic miracle of life. Circulating throughout the body, it has been called many things—*prahna, spiritus, ruach, afflatus, pneuma, anima*—but whatever the name, it has always been regarded as sacred stuff. The whole of civilization rises out of thin air, every creation made possible by this most insubstantial, invisible gas that fills our lungs. Without air, of course, there is no laughter. So the history of laughter requires sleuthing at a most abstract, ethereal level, and the task of this book requires the tracing of the most abundant, unseen, and intangible element in the universe—air. The problem is compounded, moreover, because the air of laughter is of a special kind.

Most of us know this gaseous stuff from our high school chemistry classes. As with every other element, science has grabbed the air we breathe, set it in a niche on the periodic chart, and charged it with an exact atomic weight. Solidly in place, it has been reduced to a chemical notation, $O_2$, and dubbed oxygen, "the acidifying one." When organic matter decays, molecules of oxygen become liberated, as if the soul of the plant or animal has suddenly been released from bondage, free once again to float around the atmosphere.

* In certain cultures, like the Trobiand Islanders', the gift must always move; it must always be passed on. The ultimate gift we can pass on, of course, is life itself—through offspring—as we ourselves "pass on." Perhaps "passing on" refers to God as the true Indian-giver, who demands that we return his gift of air.

But laughter is much too lofty to be classed along with the ordinary air that fills and exhausts our lungs. In the history of laughter, breath does not constitute life's essential miracle; breath merely primes the pump.* The earliest philosophical documents in the West, three or four hundred years before the birth of Christ, tell of another, more vital inhalation of air that every infant enjoys shortly after birth. This other kind of air sounds a lot like the breath of the ancient Egyptian Creator.

This air has eluded the grasp of science. It does not behave like oxygen. Too unpredictable to be captured in a single definition, too unruly to be reduced to a chemical notation, this air stands in the same relation to $O_2$ as water stands to $H_2O$. It cannot be filtered or purified, conditioned, or even polluted. Angels and witches travel through this stuff; halos radiate in it; auras refract an eerie glow through it. While this air may appear to be the equivalent of "God's breath," in ancient Greece and Rome it does something radically different from quickening life, or even sustaining life. This air ensouls life. A gift from the Olympian gods, it prompted ancient philosophers, like Aristotle, to create a new category by which humans could be differentiated from all other animals. More than that, this air marked the distinction between human existence and human be-ing, for it was precisely this air that activated a person's soul.**

## II

Throughout time and across various cultures, infants signal their arrival into life by crying. But in the ancient world, the infant also announces that

*The phrase "As I live and breathe" presents a puzzle. It hints at two distinct kinds of breath, as if living and breathing were discrete events. One way, at least, of making sense out of that strange idiom is to read it against the history of laughter, where living and breathing truly mark two distinct functions.

**Once more we can wonder, Does God enliven Adam with one or two breaths? Genesis records no instance of Adam laughing. More of God's sober nature? Who knows? But it certainly contributed to Adam's predicament: He lacked the option of laughing off Eve's invitation. Laughter might have provided him the perfect, nonverbal way of getting off the hook. Creating life out of a rib might be viewed as a metaphoric rendering of Creation out of laughter: Creation out of a cosmic tickle. (Interestingly enough, the ribs protect the thoracic area, the region of circulation and respiration. Breath is most concentrated beneath the ribs.)

it has caught a second wind, which it makes evident in the most wonderful way: by laughing. This more excitable, hotter, laughing air miraculously transforms each infant from a human into a human being by filling out its soul with risible air. What does *person* mean (*per-sonare* in Latin), after all, but a "sounding through"? What can be more consonant with life than the sound of laughter? Through laughing, the *anima* became animated. Because of that, the simple act of laughing is fraught with significance, for it marks the beginning, in the ancient world, of each person's spiritual journey. Unlike Judeo-Christian breath, this laughing air is a gift from the gods that signals one's victorious passage from this world to the next. For example, in apotheosis literature—the literature that describes a person's release from earthly existence—when a person expires, the soul ascends, buoyed aloft by this laughing gas. On reaching the eighth or ninth celestial sphere—the traditional resting place of the soul, its *patria*—the soul looks back down on earth and sets every earthly woe into proper perspective, with a knowing, disembodied laugh. In particular, the voyager laughs at his or her own cadaver lying, so pitifully, far below, the laugh signaling a newly acquired liberty. Thus, when Chaucer's Troilus dies after a protracted and painful love affair, "His lighte gost ful blysfully it went/Up to the holughnesse [hollowness] of the eighte spere/ . . . And down from thennes faste he gan avyse/ This litel spot of erthe, that with the se/Embraced is, and fully gan despise/ This wrecched world, and held al vanite/To respect of the pleyn felicite/That is yn hevene above" (*Troilus and Criseyde* 5, ll. 1808–17).*

Cicero maintains that whether the soul is composed of fire or air—both consort intimately with risibility—the soul's essence is nevertheless divine and desires to return to its heavenly home, to "pleyn felicite," as soon as it can. There, it takes up residence in the peculiar kind of air it so longs for: "No sort of speed can match the speed of the soul. If it survives [death] unadulterated . . . it is of necessity carried away so rapidly as to pierce asun-

*In a medieval commentary on Pompey's flight in Lucan's *Pharsalia*, Pompey laughs at the "vanity of his tomb" because of the sudden and surprising realization that he has actually ascended into heaven.

der all this atmosphere of airs, in which clouds, storms and winds collect. . . . When the soul has passed this tract and reaches to and recognizes a substance resembling its own, it stops amongst the fires which are formed of rarified air and the modified glow of the sun and ceases to make higher ascent" (*De oratore* 2). Cicero's "clouds, storms and winds" can be read as the atmosphere of earthly toil, which produces one kind of laughter. But "rarified air and modified glow," what might be called a spiritual tranquility, produces a higher, more satisfying laugh—an Olympian laugh. If the history of fleshly existence can be described as a journey from ashes to ashes, or from dust to dust, then the soul roams from air to air, or from fire to fire.

An infant's first laugh occurs early: Ancient sources point to the fourth or fortieth day following birth. The exact day mattered greatly, since that moment forever inspirited the life of the newborn. For Aristotle, this moment so radically separated humans from all the other animals that he used it to define human essence: *animal ridens*, the "creature who laughs." Of all the creatures in the animal kingdom, humans alone possess the remarkable ability to laugh. Very little distinguishes us from other animals, finally, except language and laughter. For the ancients, however, only laughter grants humans their unique, spiritual life. It is this risible air, rather than mere respiration, that leaves on each and every person an indelible trace of immortality.* At the beginning of what we like to call "western" civilization, then, humans do not require divine intercession. They laugh themselves into being. At their days' end, they laugh themselves into heaven. What a joyous self-sufficiency!

We should not forget, however, that this gift of laughter descends

*The Tanya, an eighteenth-century Belorussian guide to Hasidism—a sect of Judaism—postulates the presence of two souls in each person, animated, one is tempted to conclude, by two distinct breaths: "One, the 'animal soul' from which proceeds all of what is called 'human nature'; the other, 'the divine soul,' which exists before it enters a body, survives it after death, and enables humans to rise above their 'natural' inclination in the service of God." Read against the background of laughter and risibility, the use of the verb *rise* takes on additional meaning. See Adin Steinsaltz, *The Long Shorter Way: Discourses on Chasidic Thought* (Northvale, N.J.: Jason Aronson, 1988), p. 5. The Kabbalah also postulates two souls in every Jew.

from the gods, who laugh so wholeheartedly and enjoy it so much that they generously bestow the blessing on all those lowly mortals who toil away beneath them. (Even in the Old Testament, joyous laughter can only be handed down to the Hebrew people as a gift—and a rare one at that—from Yahweh.) A rowdy bunch, those Greek gods. They laugh so often and so derisively that many classical scholars have expressed shock over their behavior. C. M. Bowra found it so offensive he had to develop a theory to explain it away. He argues that their laughter "is not one of scepticism but of a belief which is so sure of itself that it is not afraid of ridiculing what it believes."*

*Ha ha ha* can only feebly approximate what the gods had in mind. For one thing, *ha ha ha* records only exhalation. In truth, laughter is closer to a long series of *ahas*—rapid-air breathing, or, as the yogis prefer to call it, rapid-fire breathing. When we say a writer has found his or her voice, we refer to a normal kind of breath—respiration. But when we say that a poem works magic, we mean something more godlike and fiery; we aim to recognize that the poet has found an extraordinary second wind; that the poet has been taken over by *enthusiasmous*—has become "god-possessed"—and that the poem explodes through the ludic power of laughter, scattering joy and inspiring everyone within earshot.

## III

Laughter is such a basic, universal, and useful response that it is difficult to conceive of any group of people—anywhere or any time or any place—not laughing. We commonly speak of a person's "sense of humor," acknowledging just how basic laughter is, by ranking it along with the traditional five

*Bowra, in *The Greek Experience*, says that the gods have no fear of contradicting themselves, of falling into a foolish consistency that hangs onto beliefs for dear life. Perched high on Mount Aetna, they can see infinite possibilities, notice all connections. From that perspective, they can pick out similarities between the most seemingly disparate things. Laughter, like metaphor, breaks down categories and permits an easy flow between ideas and objects. Jean-Paul Richter, a nineteenth-century philosopher, puts it more poetically in his *Golden Age of Classic Christian Art:* "Joking is the disguised priest who weds every couple."

senses. A certain nineteenth-century, self-styled anthropologist, B. F. Hartshorne, thought otherwise. In an article describing the Weddas, a group off the coast of Ceylon, that appeared in the March 1876 issue of the *Fortnightly Review*, he reached this startling conclusion: "Every conceivable incitive to laughter was used in vain. When asked whether they ever laughed, they replied, 'No, what is there to laugh at?' "

The reader immediately smells a rat. The Weddas must have been playing a trick on that strange academic in their midst, a practical joke, for his conclusion seems so obviously naive. Perhaps they simply refused to laugh whenever he observed them; and when he left the island, they laughed in delight at having pulled the wool over his myopic eyes. Perhaps laughter was a personal affair for the Weddas, a taboo activity in front of strangers. Something, surely, will explain away the Weddas' sober response, for while it is easy to conceive of straight-faced, serious folk, it would be difficult, if not impossible, to imagine any group totally devoid of laughter. Surely, everyone laughs at something, for laughter, as Aristotle rightly argues, is so characteristically a human activity.

Test that belief against those historical constructs, the Neanderthals. What could the earliest *Homo sapiens* have possibly laughed at? Obviously, they did not tell mother-in-law jokes or crack one-liners. But we can easily imagine those prehistoric creatures guffawing over each other's mistakes. A cave dweller, for far-fetched instance, trips over the edge of a mastodon rug, sending huge swells of guttural laughter washing over the entire tribe. Later, whenever that clumsy Neanderthal passed other members of the tribe, they laughed again, remembering him as the One Who Slips on Skins.*

Most laughter springs from that same Neanderthal example: the unexpected, the momentary surprise, prompted by a sudden slip of the body,

*Commenting on a 1968 exhibit of Ice Age art at the Museum of Natural History in New York, the anthropologist Randall White, curator of the show, observed: "They also had a sense of humor. There is a bas-relief here of a bison behind the bent-over figure of a man who is about to get it in the rear end" (Gayle Young, "Ice Age Cro-Magnon Man Finally Gets Some Respect," *Los Angeles Times*, November 23, 1986, pt. 1, p. 2).

or the tongue, which delights us for a whole range of reasons.* First, a person who stumbles or stutters surprises us by re-presenting the mundane in an absolutely fresh way. The stumbler permits us to see the grammar of walking, just as the stammerer allows us to hear the grammar of speech. In a sense, both take back what we take for granted in the everyday.**

Through a sudden break, the stumbler simply interrupts the stream of everyday activity. In an instant, he or she makes us witness to the truth about even a simple act like walking—that we fall and catch ourselves with each step we take. The philosopher Henri Bergson describes this break in the continuity of our movements as a "certain mechanical inelasticity, just where one would expect to find the wideawake adaptability and living pliableness of a human being."† Bergson's theory rests on the belief that we expect a continuous flow of graceful movements from people—especially in such pedestrian acts—so that when a person stumbles, unintentionally totters, or even falls, we laugh at his or her surprising "inelasticity"—at the inability to fulfill the promise of grace immediately, even automatically. How odd the person seems, how absurdly mechanical. Has the puppeteer relaxed his grip? The sight of such a creature gives us pleasure that runs so deep we even laugh when that inelasticity results from a permanent disability.

We have all seen deformed people walking down the street, their arms dangling by their sides like a pair of broken wings, and have suppressed the urge to giggle or even laugh out loud. Even when we are absolutely convinced the person is crippled, we still feel that demonic urge slowly taking charge. What an awful feeling, we mutter to ourselves—how much we hate ourselves for having it. This insidious laugh also springs from our own well-established expectations about human behavior that have been so terribly

*It is virtually impossible, for example, to tickle oneself—to give oneself a ribbing—since ticklish laughter must be triggered by surprise. And no matter how sneaky or speedy, one can never surprise oneself.

**Both *stumble* and *stammer* derive from the same Germanic root.

†Henri Bergson, *Laughter: an Essay on the Meaning of the Comic*, trans. Claudesley Brereton and Fred Rothwell (London: Macmillan, 1921), p. 10.

shaken—what is the cripple, after all, but a continual stumbler? Thomas Hobbes, in a famous phrase, fills out the reasons we laugh, and as we shall see, the question perplexes philosophers all through history. In his *Leviathan*, Hobbes explains our fascination with the handicapped as springing, oddly enough, from a rush of exhilaration and a feeling of our own well-being: "Men experience the passion of a sudden glory by some sudden act of their own, that pleaseth them; or by apprehension of some deformed thing in another, by comparison whereof they suddenly applaud themselves. And it is most evident to them that are conscious of the fewest abilities in themselves; who are forced to keep themselves in their own favour, by observing the imperfections of others."* Pleasure—downright satisfaction—comes at the expense of some other, less fortunate soul, because we realize we are somehow better, or better off. Little people, the insecure, laugh the loudest: The smaller the ego, the higher the rise to "sudden glory." To say it the other way around: A small ego fires off a very powerful laugh of derision.

But why should we feel such profound elation from mere surprise or status, particularly when it arises from another's pain? I spend time with the question here, in the introduction, because it lingers behind virtually every discussion of laughter throughout history. The question is not only a knotty one, but the answer is also slightly troubling. We laugh at what the stumbler or cripple reveals. And here, as we come to the third and most important reason for derisive laughter, we can begin to understand why people in positions of authority find laughter so offensive and threatening. By breaking the gestures of continuity and rhythm, both stumbler and cripple break something much more fundamental—the powerful and persistent grip that civilized behavior tightens around each and every one of our lives.

In Henri Bergson's view, when a person navigates awkwardly, he or she exposes humankind's true nature by forcing attention on "something mechanical encrusted on the living," as with the walker, say, descending the

*Thomas Hobbes, *Leviathan; Or the Matter, Form, and Power of a Commonwealth, Ecclesiastical and Civil* (London: Routledge, 1907), p. 33.

stairs in Duchamps's revolutionary modern painting.* In my view, just the opposite occurs. Stumbling does not create the *homme-automate*, but the re-laxed man. The stumbler shatters the gestures of elegance and continuity and opens a crack, enabling us to glimpse beneath the facade of our socialized, civilized, and regulated lives. The Puritans heaped on piles and piles of decorum to help stanch those laughing breaks. Those breaks provide a vision, for the briefest moment, a glimpse of who we really are—not a robot, but just another animal, albeit with more intelligence and consciousness. Certain moments, like this one, arrest our attention so thoroughly we find ourselves, to quote Wallace Stevens, confronting an essential truth, that "we are condemned to be that inescapable animal, ourselves."

All those rules, those laws and regulations, all that training—the whole enterprise disintegrates before our eyes. We are left to fall back on our own inner senses, free to revert to pure impulse and gratification, wholesale liberty unbound by rules: a fleshy anarchy of the soul. And that vision both teases us and pleases us; it enables us to declare, under our breath, "Oh, what a joy. What a relief, not to be so damned conscious, so self-aware, for one blissful minute." We can see—in a safe, contained way—how loosely civilization actually holds our lives. No wonder that visionaries like William Blake believe that humans trip into a true religious state, for no appropriate gesture can give shape or higher meaning to a stumbling step; every fall "falls" outside the world of gesture. Every fall is a "free" fall.

The history of the human race records, in great part, humankind's desire to rise above this falling self, to get as far away from our oafish origins as possible by stylizing our behavior through gesture—not only with great artistic works, but with the articulated gestures we call manners and through which we conduct our daily affairs. Without these civilized gestures, as King Lear painfully discovers, we confront the world as "bare forked animals."** Every toddler records the way adults stammer and stum-

*Bergson, *Laughter*, p. 37.

**The earliest cave drawings, in France and Spain, already show this impulse toward stylization over 35,000 years ago. Even the prehistoric eye longs for something more than "the naked

ble into their humanness, falling down and getting back up with a few tears, and then finally standing upright, laughing with delight at such a nervy defiance of gravity.* The account of Adam and Eve's expulsion from the Garden of Eden—a story I turn to in the body of this work—bears an eerie resemblance, in all its scariness and anticipation, to an infant's first, tentative steps. The Bible describes the expulsion not as a simple casting out from Paradise and into mortality, but as a falling into experience, as if standing on one's own two feet required a concerted effort, a sustained risibility, against the downward pull of gravity. But, then, how better to counter gravity than with levity? How better to rise above the grave than through laughter?

Outside the Garden, Adam and Eve must struggle to regain their grace. I know of no more elegant and poignant rendering of this monumental chore than Masaccio's fifteenth-century fresco, *The Expulsion of Adam and Eve from Earthly Paradise*, in the Brancucci Chapel of Santa Maria del Carmine in Florence. Masaccio's fresco shocks the viewer into an understanding, arrests the attention the way traffic accidents stop us, against our will, in mid-gaze. Likewise, Masaccio seems suddenly to have frozen Adam and Eve in their steps, stopped them dead in their tracks, as they pass reluctantly under the portals of the Garden; the archangel Raphael hovers above them, pointing the way into the world with one of the sternest index fingers in the history of Western art. (The sternness of that damning finger recalls the gentleness of God's creative finger on the ceiling of the Sistine Chapel.) Not only does this primal couple desperately need a sense of direction, they appear to be shouldering the weight of the Word. What distinguishes their new, postlapsarian selves from their earlier blessed state is gesture. They must now attempt to incorporate—to embody—their embarrassment and impudence. Like a medieval version of a cave painting, Masaccio's fresco

truth." The word *gesture*, from Latin *gerare*, "to carry," also yields *geste*, "story," and *jest*, "funny story." Each gesture carries a little story, a kernel of our comic nature. Each gesture arrives laden with meaning and humor, on the verge of dropping its freight and revealing its total meaning.

*You think you've got it licked until you try life in another medium, say underwater with a scuba tank, or on a frozen pond with skates. It takes a lot of practice, and a lot of spills, before you can cut a graceful figure eight on an icy floor.

shows a deliberately stylized Adam and Eve.* Adam awkwardly laces his fingers over his eyes (*embarre*, "embarrassment") while Eve covers her private parts (*pudendum*, "impudence"). Each of them is shown with arms and legs grotesquely distorted, as they struggle toward the appropriate gestures in their estrangement.

They are hiding. But from whom? Obviously, no other person sees them. But the painting assumes an observer, for Adam and Eve have called *observation* into being. Embarrassment posits its own witnesses, just as all gestures assume a community of observers. So even though Adam and Eve try to hide, they cannot prevent themselves from being observed—and interpreted. Adam and Eve are just dying to find the right gestures; that is the anguish Masaccio finds in the biblical story. But at this liminal moment—at the threshold of their break from innocence—they can only adopt an awkward attitude: a disposition and posture in a space and time that, for them, have become circumscribed and limited by death.

This is a religious picture, not a funny one. Masaccio's fresco reaches to the heart of the human condition. Adam and Eve set out for the wilderness, like groping kids, and every gesture—each footfall—they must figure out, reconstruct, as they make their way toward what the sixteenth century calls *civilité*. In the world of the Renaissance, as Erasmus says in a short treatise on decorum titled *De civilitate morum puerilium* (*On Civility in Children*), manner shapes all reality, but most important it shapes "outward bodily poetry." And since inside and outside mirror each other in this period, awkward physical movements reflect a soul devoid of grace, just as too much giggling indicates a soul run amok.

In a flash, then, the stumbler pulls aside the thin cloak of *civilité*, revealing humanity in its gestureless state. Stumblers cause us to laugh in delight, in perceiving our own fleshly essence, at reviewing our unadorned animal na-

*In Italian, Masaccio means "scatterbrain," what we today would call a "nut." Friends must have been taken with Masaccio's sense of humor, his joking around, and his benign distractedness. It's interesting to think that his joking and lightheartedness, and not his seriousness, led him to this monumental portrait of pain.

ture. We are called back into the Garden. How can there be gestures in Paradise, a place that knows only spontaneity, action freely expressed? One might argue that only inside the Garden of Eden can we experience our true nature, in that idyllic place where we are free to act without the restraints of shame or embarrassment, where we are free to *be* ourselves. Little kids who spin madly about and finally fall, giggling all the way down to the ground, their arms and legs turning every which way, have abandoned themselves to the same giddy state. How delightful to be so out of control—so safely, so playfully out of control. Our own delight in stumblers derives, not from their failure to find the appropriate gestures as they paw the air, but from the privilege of witnessing the sudden, exhilarating absence of all gesture.*

Maintaining behavior stylized through social gesture requires effort; we must actively work at being graceful—not to eat like pigs, rage like lions, or sneak around like sly and crafty foxes. We must be wary not to falter. We must hold ourselves erect: Bearing is all. Laughter thus arises, not merely from the delightful image of our unrestrained selves, but from the sheer relief that for the moment we can "let our hair down"—surely an animal image—and relax. At the same time, however, we also know that such exposure lays us wide open to judgment and possible ridicule. Stumblers and cripples often feel belittled; that's Hobbes's point. So, if anyone has to fall, we would rather it be the other person, not us.

Indeed, if our clumsy stumbler did not pull up lame, or never faltered or fell, we would trip him up anyway, because it makes us feel superior. In competitive society, stumblers and fallers guarantee our own social well-being; they assure us of a higher rung on the social ladder. We measure our own carefully articulated manners against their failures; they let us know,

*The stumbler and the joker, as narrators of an incident—performers—are related both in terms of etymology and in terms of time. The stumbler always falls behind, while the joker, in fooling around, pulls us out of the busyness of the moment. Out of exasperation, we sometimes urge the joker to quit fooling *around* and to *get on* with it. This relationship—time and laughter—is touched on in one of the most refreshing modern theories of laughter, one worked out by Helmuth Plessner, who believes that laughter is a liminal expression between consciousness and unconsciousness, between the physical and the psychic (*Lachen und Weinen* [Bern: Francke Verlag, 1961]). Dropping off to sleep and dropping down from dizziness both play at the edges of consciousness, where gesture and the clock quit ticking.

not only who we are, but where we stand. In the modern world, we periodically envy those with more money or more status and pray for their downfall, their ultimate demise. Feeling that things are out of balance, we aim to get even, to set the pans of justice level again: What joy to see the other guy knocked down a peg or two! That desire to push our neighbor off balance is hinted at in the earliest philosophical discussions of laughter and will eventually fuel the development of the aggressive, hostile joke, with its punishing and often painful punch line, a blow to the victim's most vital parts—usually the ego—when he or she is least suspecting it.

Ironically, though, laughter will turn out to be not merely the only, but perhaps the best, protection against envy. The gods may even have meant laughter as our natural line of defense: against illness, boredom and most important, against the colonization of the spirit. That funny grouch Mark Twain fired off salvos of laughter his entire life: "For your race, in its poverty, has unquestionably one really effective weapon—laughter. Power, money, persuasion, supplication, persecution—these can lift a colossal humbug—push it a little—weaken it a little, century by century; but only laughter can blow it to rags and atoms at a blast. Against the assault of laughter nothing stands."* Nothing stands, not even more laughter. The aphorism "fighting fire with fire," as we shall see later in this history, can be effectively turned to fighting laughter with laughter.** The cripple can turn around and cripple the bully with a crisp one-liner or two.

Surely, a loud laugh was the first shot heard 'round the world. A hearty laugh can reach metaphoric gale speeds, knocking down silly arguments and bowling over solid opponents foolish enough to stand in its way. Laughter certainly can put on a ferocious face. Think how arrogant a laugh can sound. How absolutely disarming. Without a word, a laugh can punch holes

*Mark Twain, *Letters from the Earth*, ed. Henry Nash Smith (New York: Harper and Row, 1962), p. 258.

**How appropriate that *guff*, "nonsense" or "bull," and *guffaw* both echo something so innocent as the sound of a puff of air. Hot air meets hotter air. Caustic laughter meets caustic laughter, a way of fighting fire with fire.

in the biggest bully's threats or cut the biggest creep down to size. Most of us learn, early on, what tremendous power we can unleash with one good belly laugh. Dangerous stuff, this laughter business. As recently as July 1989, the editor of an underground magazine in Czechoslovakia was sentenced to two and a half years in prison for incitement against the state, "which meant that he had dared crack jokes about *perestroika*." The Western report concludes: "still, as in *The Joke*, Milan Kundera's novel of twenty-two years ago, the price of jest is jail. Jokes aimed at *perestroika* are evidently as liable to offend as jokes in favor of it." In the same month, in Baja California, a journalist was murdered, many think for his long-standing practice of making jokes about local, powerful politicians. Experience tells us that we must modulate our own laughter, for prolonged fits of it can sometimes restrict breathing until we find ourselves struggling for air. And no one wants to die laughing.

But people risk it anyway, for laughter lightens the burden of reality. Laughter offers relief, at least for the moment, by allowing some breathing space, enabling the laugher to step back, to remove him- or herself temporarily, and to comment without uttering a single word, like a bear signaling displeasure with a growl, merely through the force of its own breath. That laugh holds the hope of political liberation; it suggests that the world does not have to be accepted at face value. Instead, it can be laughed off, turned aside, and kept at bay, transforming hard and fast rules, instantly and miraculously, into something plastic and flexible—into fluidity.

*Humorous* is, after all, a liquid term.* But people can laugh off an experience only when they gain enough distance—step back far enough—to see the silly and the absurd in the everyday, when they begin to say no and start to make choices. From this perspective, the laugher can reenter reality more confidently, for the object of fear has been disarmed. The movement

*Confronted by problems, we can reach solutions—liquidity—in different ways. English offers a range of them. We can see them as *humorous*. We can of course shed *tears* over them. We can talk and talk about them, reaching a kind of *fluency*. We can drink our cares away with *alcohol*. We can *derive* (from *river*) inspiration from some source. Finally, we can buy our way out—with enough *currency*, with a cash flow swift enough, and with assets liquid enough to wash our problems away.

assumes the rhythm of an emotional inhale and exhale, as if the simple act of breathing provides the model for dealing with all of experience: a form of meditation. Mikhail Bakhtin, the Russian antiformalist critic, describes this peculiar kind of respiration, in which the world seems to be inhaled and exhaled:

> Laughter has the remarkable power of making an object come up close, of drawing it into a zone of crude contact where one can finger it familiarly on all sides, turn it upside down, inside out, peer at it from above and below, break open its external shell, look into its center, doubt it, take it apart, dismember it, lay it bare and expose it, examine it freely and experiment with it. Laughter demolishes fear and piety before an object, before a world, making of it an object of familiar contact and thus clearing the ground for an absolutely free investigation of it. Laughter is a vital factor in laying down that prerequisite for fearlessness without which it would be impossible to approach the world realistically. As it draws an object to itself and makes it familiar, laughter delivers the object into the fearless hands of investigative experiment—both scientific and artistic—and into the hands of free experimental fantasy.*

Bakhtin's comments carry wonderfully liberating implications, particularly for the scientist. Even the person of science, Bakhtin implies, must be willing to play, if he or she hopes to uncover meaning. This means that, like the artist, the scientist must always remain open to surprise.

But caution is in order, for laughter has the power to remove a person altogether, by lifting him or her straight up. The film *Mary Poppins*—despite all its Disney corn—achieved great popularity in part because it dramatized laughter's great metaphoric, levitating power. Excited, rarified air makes people feel light-headed—so light-headed that after a time they begin to imagine themselves bouncing and bobbing off the ceiling. That is what it means to be risible. Only levity has sufficient power to defy gravity. The laughing Buddha is fat just to show that even the most massive bulk can lift off the ground—with a big enough laugh. The bigger the Buddha, the louder

*Mikhail M. Bakhtin, *The Dialogic Imagination: Four Essays*, ed. Michael Holquist and trans. Caryl Emerson and Michael Holquist (Austin: University of Texas Press, 1981), p. 23.

the laugh. That's what we always laugh off—gravity; the weight and pressure of life (*gravitas* means seriousness), until we feel light enough, finally, to rise above our problems (*levitas* means lightness). The sky's the limit.*

## IV

The grid of gender has been laid over so many things it prompts one to ask if laughter, too, might not be gendered. Intuitively, it wouldn't seem so. Certainly, breath itself has escaped the clutch of gender: all of us—men *and* women—take in the same $O_2$, in the very same way. Shouldn't breath's second cousin, laughter, escape as well? After all, laughter obliterates national lines and language differences; a Frenchman's guffaw sounds just like a Spaniard's. As Samuel Johnson remarks in his essay "On the Difficulty of Defining Comedy," "Men have been wise in very different modes, but they have always laughed in the same way." Sociologists and anthropologists have observed, however, a key difference between men's and women's laughter. In Western cultures, at least, women tell fewer jokes than men. Not that women do not have a sense of humor, or cannot tell stories, social scientists argue, but they have been socialized into a quieter, more passive and retiring role than men. Telling jokes requires a degree of aggression—sometimes masked and sometimes not so subtly disguised. These distinctions stand out fairly clearly. But the anthropologist's gaze has missed other, less apparent reasons for the difference in men's and women's laughter. While those reasons require magnification to make them visible, they provide a historical explanation for the gendered differences in joking.**

*The close historical connection between jugglers, tumblers, tight-wire walkers—acrobats of all kinds—and jokers points to their shared ability to break the bonds of gravity. When the juggler or the joker moves center stage, audiences can expect the miraculous.

**Virtually all critical studies of women's literature—providing they cover a wide variety of genres—pay attention to humor, rather than to laughter. They concentrate on literary form—the tall tale, character sketch, and so on—and not on oral performance. So, for example, Nancy A. Walker, in *A Very Serious Thing: Women's Humor and American Culture* (Minneapolis: University of Minnesota Press, 1988), concludes that nineteenth-century American humor is characterized by a male fondness for the tall tale, and that "women have not written the traditional tall tale" (p. 44). But Walker misses an essential point: Women may have shared that same fondness but were unable to break into print. See especially her chapter 2, "The Male Tradition and the Female Tradition," pp. 39–72.

For more than one thousand years, from the sixth to the seventeenth centuries, aristocratic families in England and western Europe educated their sons in grammar schools, where they were taught a linguistic artifact known as Learned Latin. No one outside of school ever spoke a single word in this language. It was never heard on street corners or in drawing rooms, never found utterance in baby talk, in the language of love, or even in the marketplace. Daily life found expression in the vernacular, Romance languages. Stories could be told *only* out of school. Learned Latin might be heard in school, but only in sentences shaped by formal rules of rhetoric. Men in the universities committed its rules of grammar and correct usage to memory; they learned it by practicing the art of rhetoric, and practiced it by learning strategies of debate. Royal, legal, and religious charters assumed official status only when they were drafted in Learned Latin.

While writing in general provides more objectivity than speaking, by further separating the knower from the known, Learned Latin created an even greater objectivity, as Walter Ong argues, "by establishing knowledge in a medium isolated from the emotion-charged depths of one's own mother tongue, thus reducing interference from the human lifeworld and making possible the exquisitely abstract world of medieval scholasticism and of the new mathematical modern science which followed on the scholastic experience. Without Learned Latin, it appears that modern science would have got under way with greater difficulty if it had got under way at all."* In this atmosphere, Learned Latin immaculately conceived its insulated, carefully modulated world.

Only a few cloistered women managed to write anything in this elevated, uncontaminated language. The overwhelming bulk of women lived surrounded by the clutter of the vernacular—amid the racket of baby talk, immersed in the hurly-burly of conversation. More than men, women faced off in gritty negotiations in the give-and-take of the local marketplace. For women, life was marked by the spontaneity of oral discourse, in sentences less

*Walter Ong, *Orality and Literacy: The Technologizing of the Word* (London: Methuen, 1982), p. 114.

affected by the syntax of the schools—Learned Latin—and thus structurally less formal. Women thus remained more attuned to rhythm, measure, and periodicity, and felt more at home with the fits and starts, the interruptions and improbabilities of discourse. They remained more in touch with the plasticity of language, as well, for rules of pronunciation and spelling and standards of correctness do not obtain in orality. But more important, this linguistic flexibility must have given to women a more flexible attitude toward the world in general, and thus allowed them to remain more open to playfulness and the possibilities of change, to stay more adaptable than men, who were being inculcated in the strict rhetorical training of the grammar schools.

Barred from acquiring formal rhetorical skills, denied access to writing, and prevented from occupying positions of social, commercial, or religious power, women found their voices in their own intimate female conversations. Those voices were at times understandably angry, maybe even angry as hell, at those in power—namely, men. Women circulated their own aggressive, amusing little stories in tightly knit social circles. Some of these stories were no doubt true, others probably embellished or trumped up and blown way out of proportion—filled with hot air?—and the bulk of them were about men. No wonder that by the late Middle Ages men found women's talk dangerous enough to dismiss it as idle chatter, to disparage it as banal by redefining it as gossip. But while gossip may have lowered their voices, women refused to be silenced.

I can think of no more appropriate dramatization of this historic episode than Petruchio's attempt to tame Kate, Shakespeare's quick-witted, loose-tongued shrew, a task we can understand as impossible once we realize that *shrew*, the name for the animal, derives from *shrewd*. A shrew can no more be domesticated than a shrewd woman. Kate can only hope to reach the life she so desperately desires by pretending to be domesticated—hence her shrewdness, and hence Shakespeare's. Read this way, the play's most famous request, "Kiss me, Kate," resounds not only with a harsh alliteration, but also with a crafty irony, for when she agrees, she can only give Petruchio a conspiratorial kiss—a conspiracy known only to her.

Patricia Meyer Spacks, who has written the only book-length study of gossip, tries to reinstate gossip's place in history both as a pleasurable and politically potent activity: "From outside . . . gossip often looks dangerous. It ferrets out secrets, harms other people, reveals human nature's worst propensities. Within the group of participants, gossip can feel otherwise. Freed from ordinary social inhibitions, seeking no material benefits, proceeding by established rules, forging bonds within their group, talkers pursue a game which, like all absorbing games, expresses impulses and satisfies needs."* Historically, most men have pushed gossip to the margins, as a secret, spiteful, and harmful activity. Spacks's description brings gossip back closer to the truth, as a political response—a playful but potent political resistance to the clearly articulated, firmly established voice of power.

Denied training in the art of formal rhetoric, women could not slug it out with men on equal linguistic footing. Instead, women developed their own domain of discursive power by telling pointed stories, filled with punch and bite, in that clandestine pastime called gossip. In this light Roger Abrahams, who has studied gossip cross-culturally, finds significant analogies between, say, gossiping in the West Indies and aggressive joke-telling within that same culture. Even in widely diverse cultures, gossiping resembles a more intimate and personal form of joke-telling. Hélène Cixous, the French feminist critic, has written an essay about the nature of women's talk entitled "The Laugh of the Medusa," an image that corroborates Abrahams's findings. Cixous claims that, from a distance, women in intimate, secret discourse appear to be mere playful, joking creatures. But come closer and you may find yourself the victim of a venomous bite from one of those many barbed tongues.**

This gendered distinction in joke-telling has worked its way into the English language. The words *grammar* and *glamour* share a common Latin

*Patricia Meyer Spacks, *Gossip* (New York: Alfred A. Knopf, 1985), p. 29.

**Hélène Cixous, "The Laugh of the Medusa," trans. Keith Cohen and Paula Cohen. *Signs* (Summer 1976): 245–64. Nancy Walker observes that "the common theme of women's desire to claim autonomy and power is central to American women's humor" (*A Very Serious Thing*, p. 4). Why expect anything different from a more secretive, humorous form of humor, gossip?

root meaning "magic," but they have branched off and developed along separate gender lines. Grammar has to do with working magic by casting correctly structured sentences, and glamour with working magic by casting a playful eye. One is literate, the other physical; one is considered profound, the other provocative. One is encouraged as a sign of intelligence, the other only when it is convenient, being generally regarded as a poor substitute for intelligence.* Cixous has reunited the two words in her Medusa, who gives a "come hither" glance, followed quickly by a don't-you-dare rebuff. As if that were not enough, her Medusa adds insult to injury by laughing the whole thing off.

While women were not permitted to attend grammar schools before the end of the sixteenth century, they surrounded themselves with a home-bred but little noticed kind of linguistic instruction. The blabbing of babies, like the babbling of Mnemosyne, the mother of the Muses, provides subtle instruction in the great pleasures of social intercourse—the luxuries of talking. The baby acts as the muse of the mother. Raising an infant is never one-sided—in the Middle Ages or in the modern period—for the baby, in its limited but utterly sophisticated way, socializes the parent in what it means to grow up. Through cries and smiles, the infant shapes the behavior of its parents to suit its needs for food and comfort. The psychologist Harriet Rheingold casts this interaction in the strongest terms: "That particular facet of socialization called parental behavior—caring for the infant in a responsible fashion—is taught to them by the infant. . . . The specific proposition is that he teaches them what he needs to have them do for him. He makes them behave in a nurturing fashion. . . . Of men and women he makes fathers and mothers."** The infant recalls the process of growing up for its parents, but in particular it schools that parent most intimately connected with infant care, the mother. And it undertakes that task from the moment of its birth, through its own quirky brand of communication.

*A similar pairing exists in French, in the etymological connection between *le chanteur* and *l'enchanteur*, "singer" and "magician."

**Harriet L. Rheingold, "The Social and Socializing Infant," in *Concept of Development*, ed. H. W. Stevenson (Monograph of the Society for Research and Child Development, 1967), pp. 782–83.

Infant blather, that tiny rivulet of consciousness, noisy with unfamiliar sounds, flows without carrying along with it one pebble of a recognizable word. Each utterance, however, comes rolling along with meaning—through intonation, rhythm and relation—a primitive grammar that would make even Noam Chomsky smile. Every mother understands that private language, knowing in an instant what her baby needs from listening to its goos and gahs. She can distinguish questions from statements, needs from wants, and respond in turn with just the right sentence and caring response. This language is diametrically opposed to Learned Latin: It is never written, has no formal grammar or rules of spelling, could never serve rhetorical precision. No one teaches it; it is acquired without tuition. Even for orality, infant blather seems strange in its evanescence, lasting but one to two years before it evolves into something approximating conversation. This is small talk in its most elemental stage: The deepest, most emotional, life-and-death transactions are negotiated in this innocent jabber.

The infant "informs" the mother by "telling" her what it wants, keeping her in tune with the rhythm of sentences, with breathing, and with loose and goofy constructions kept lively and animated through giggles and laughter. The baby, that is, keeps the mother fluid (the hip phrase suggests she "go with the flow"). The mother must remain flexible, willing to respond spontaneously, try different solutions to make her baby comfortable, offer her breast at a moment's notice—the most fundamental *solution*—until the infant gets on "schedule." It is the mother who comes to understand best of anyone the true meaning of that phrase "kidding around." By allowing the roles to reverse, she can feel like a kid again—through playfulness.* And, if she wants to understand her offspring, she has to enter its world with her whole being.

*Even though the door of writing slammed shut in the face of women, they banged so hard against it that in the tenth and eleventh centuries they were able to publish a few lullabies, an onomatopoetic word that mimics the sound a mother croons—*lu lu lu*—to send her child off to sleep. Lullabies were so important to women, they were willing to risk it all to preserve them in print. Lullabies and that other medieval nursery song, the lay—which may itself mean "to play"—provide at least a small testament that women's rhythmic roots lay deep in a playful orality. Most important, it allows us to see that women kept the soul of literature breathing for centuries.

In a much more modern context, the child psychiatrist D. W. Winnicott, in a brilliant book,

This interdependence between mother and child may sound terribly modern, but as early as circa 30 B.C., the poet Virgil described this very same connection, in his Fourth Eclogue: "Incipe, parve puer,/risu cognoscere matrem,/matri longa decem tulurent/fastidia menses./Incipe, parve puer:/ Cui non parentes/nec deus nunc mensa,/dea nec dignata cubili est" (Begin, little infant,/knowing your mother with a laugh,/who for ten long months/ has suffered discomfort./Begin, little infant:/Those parents who have not laughed/the god disdains from his table,/and the goddess refuses her bed). For Virgil, the infant plays the decisive role in the fortune of the family, for without the infant's gift, both parents face the prospect of a mere humdrum life. Laughter, offered to its new household by the infant (in gratitude to its long-suffering mother), works magic, transforming the most basic of drives, like eating and copulating, into inspired dining and lovemaking.

Beyond that, Virgil's seemingly innocent little poem takes us to the religious heart of laughter, for the newborn infant creates the possibility of ecstasy (*ex-stasis*, "moving out of this spot"). Parents, who begin to laugh, suddenly find themselves whisked off to this new, higher level of existence. Pleasure falls like a thin veil over the poem. For what business do we mortals really have with the gods and goddesses? We can only stare in awe, pray in supplication; we can only allow ourselves to be drawn into *their* influence. And so the family learns superfluity: the luxury of doing things, the delight in pure feeling. Drop your attitude, relax your gestures, the infant insists with a giggle. What power in a tiny creature—all this because the newborn infant can create its own parents, like the ancient Egyptian god, out of laughter.

Over the centuries, this utterly intimate connection with infants has created women who speak and breathe differently, who tell stories differently, from men. The debate goes on whether one can distinguish a man's prose line from a woman's. At times I think the difference sparkles on the

*The Child, the Family, and the Outside World* (Menlo Park, Calif.: Addison Wesley), makes this startling claim: "Everyone who feels himself to be a person in the world, and for whom the world means something, every happy person, is in infinite debt to a woman. At a time in earliest infancy when there was no perception of dependence, we were absolutely dependent" (p. 10).

page. There is no question, for me, about women's talk. Listen to Hélène Cixous. Though the passage is long, it recreates in its own sentences what I have been trying to describe about women's unique, rhythmic connection to language. Notice in this passage how woman's breath becomes enfleshed:

> Listen to a woman speak at a public gathering (if she hasn't painfully lost her wind). She doesn't "speak," she throws her trembling body forward; she lets go of herself, she flies; all of her passes into her voice, and it's with her body that she vitally supports the "logic" of her speech. Her flesh speaks true. She lays herself bare. In fact, she physically materializes what she's thinking; she signifies it with her body. In a certain way she *inscribes* what she's saying, because she doesn't deny her drives the intractable and impassioned part they have in speaking. Her speech, even when "theoretical" or political, is never simple or linear or "objectified," generalized: she draws her story into history.
>
> In women's speech, as in their writing, that element which never stops resonating, which, once we've been permeated by it, profoundly and imperceptibly touched by it, retains the power of moving us—that element is the song: first music from the first voice of love which is alive in every woman. Why this privileged relationship with the voice? Because no woman stockpiles as many defenses for countering the drives as does man. You don't build walls around yourself, you don't forgo pleasures as "wisely" as he. Even if phallic mystification has generally contaminated good relationships, a woman is never far from "mother" (I mean outside her role functions: the "mother" as nonname and as source of goods). There is always within her at least a little of that good mother's milk. She writes in white ink.*

While the baby laughs its own mother silly—into a state of "innocence"—the parents train the baby to be continent, to hold in check all of its bodily functions. Gradually—not fast enough, perhaps, for modern parents—the infant moves in fits and starts toward socialization, eating and sleeping and relieving itself at regularly scheduled times. But one small part of the infant's being remains stubbornly beyond parental grasp, shrewish

*Cixous, "The Laugh of the Medusa," p. 251.

enough to shrug off all gestures of domestication: The child might at any moment—unpredictably—break into uncontrollable giggling. Without warning, it just might fall to pieces over some passing trifle. Philosophical documents on laughter, religious statements and mandates forbidding laughter—all these provide instructions on how and when and how hard to laugh. They designate the proper attitude one should take toward laughter, because laughter is our last "sense" to capitulate to authority. No other bodily function requires such attention and close supervision. We may ask, "Is the baby potty trained?" but no one would dare wonder, "Does the baby have its laughter under control?" And yet, no other bodily function demands such controls, as if laughter dogged us as a vestige of some earlier, incontinent time—a more primitive period when we laughed and defecated and took our pleasure at will. Neatly tucked away, safely hidden from view, laughter threatens to blow our adult, civilized cover at every moment. Try to suppress your own giggles: They will out.

Imagine, then, being firmly seated in a position of authority and knowing that at any second the power to control and direct could be cut short by the lowliest peon—not with a Molotov cocktail or an Uzi automatic, but with riotous laughter. Jacques Derrida describes in *Of Grammatology* how Heidegger placed certain abstract words, like *Being, sous rature,* "under erasure," and canceled them as he wrote—because abstracts corresponded to no concrete reality. A medieval peasant embodied the same truth at a practical, more effective level. The peasant knew he could laugh at some stupid regulation and wipe the slate clean. He could deflate the word, by letting his own air out. From the point of view of the marginalized and the disenfranchised, if they cannot participate in the writing of history, they can at least try to erase it. To pull this off, however, one must realize that while a laugh can turn the subtleties of power inside out, making them suddenly visible, it can also turn power into pure brutality, for power, finally, has nothing to say to laughter—it remains dumb in the silent sense, dumbfounded in the weakest way. When it responds, it can only resort to mere physicality—torture, imprisonment, or even death. While the peasant uses his breath to resist, authorities use their pens to react—with verdicts, edicts, indictments, punishment through long-term sentences.

Western attitudes toward laughter have come down to us through one tradition only, the literate one—first through Greek and later through Learned Latin—that is, only the documents written by upper-class male writers, which told people what was funny and why, what they should laugh at and when, who could laugh and at what. The climax to this ludic history is the modern joke, a genre that began in that male-dominated, ancient rhetorical tradition, but took shape in writing, in the Middle Ages. No surprise, then, that the joke is alien to women. As I have argued, however, we should seriously question the usual conclusion: that men can just tell jokes better than women. Given the differences in socialization and education, men, rather than being able to tell jokes better than women, may have been literally ex-communicated—from the vibrancy and life of the vernacular, from the spirit of improvisation—and have had to depend on the structure of the formal joke to give their stories shape and direction. The structure of the joke provided the armature around which men could wrap witty, interesting stories that they dredged up from the vernacular.

How the modern joke actually came to take its present shape is a revolutionary episode in the history of literature. It is tantamount to the explosions deep inside a cyclotron, where two protons traveling at the speed of light collide head-on. The modern joke came into existence out of the collision of two highly charged worlds: the rhetorical, intellectual world (male, upper-class, literate) and the narrative, laughing world (female, peasant, oral). In other words, the modern joke fuses head and heart. While the light from this collision blinded his contemporaries, it enabled Chaucer to see the power of the punch line all the more clearly. His massive literary achievement has to stand as the punch line of this book. And his strategy of placing the joke in the mouth of a woman offers the reader the opportunity of seeing the Little Prince's fedora for what it is—an outsized boa constrictor.

## V

Chaucer did not fashion his female characters, the Carpenter's wife, Alisoun, for example, totally out of his fantasy, nor did he pluck the Wife of Bath, that other Alisoun, out of some dream.* He no doubt heard and overheard a great many women carrying on the routine of their daily lives—in castles, in houses, inns, towers, and in the marketplace—talking and gossiping, coaxing a word or two from their babies, then all of a sudden breaking out in a laugh. We need to see these two Alisouns, not so much as aberrations, but as representative medieval women, who listened to joking and appreciated it, and who, finally, given the chance by Chaucer, could get off a ribald tale of their own. The roots of literature, as I hope to demonstrate in the course of this book, lie buried not in hard work, revision, and serious description. That already smacks of high levels of literacy. Rather, like a sport, literature grew out of play and banter, joking and good times—out of humor and laughter, much of it, at least by the sixth century, the domain of women.**

Women stood in the frustrating position of fueling a good deal of literary activity while being prevented, themselves, from writing it down. They lived amid a burgeoning literacy but, like Gulag prisoners, were forced to compose everything inside their heads. Denied direct and immediate influence, they went unrecognized for what they were: universal donors, who provided lifeblood for all kinds of literature. Early writers like Chaucer, who could sniff out a good story, by necessity had to become eavesdroppers. Recognizing the power of the vernacular, Chaucer eventually hauled it out to

*The Wife confesses to great skill in financial matters, a skill that underscores her prowess as a storyteller. The most provocative discussion of the rules of money management and storytelling occurs in Freud's *Jokes and Their Relation to The Unconscious* (New York: W. W. Norton, 1963): "All these techniques [of humor] are dominated by a tendency to compression, or rather to saving. It all seems to be a question of economy. In Hamlet's words: 'Thrift, thrift, Horatio!'" (p. 42). A good story or joke must earn its keep—in holding our *interest*—since we have been asked to take time out of our busyness to listen to such frivolity.

**This argument merges with the claim of linguistic philosophers, from Wittgenstein on, that the true nature of language lies in puns and jokes—in what Condillac, the eighteenth-century philosopher, called "the frivolous." Literature *is* language; it thrives on play. It finds its own rules and recoils when they are imposed.

the bright light of day, and gave it shape in literacy, as the beginnings of fiction.*

Like ice fishers, writers had to slice through the frozen facade of courtly manners and decorum, and dive down deep to retrieve their style and subject matter. The life of literature lay outside the grammar schools—it was not to be found with spelling but with spells; it had less affinity with grammar and more with glamour. Chaucer thus includes virtually every social class on his pilgrimage, except for one—the nobility—and a glaring omission it is. Oddly enough, the lords, not the peasants, and certainly not the women, turn out to be the really silent ones on the pilgrimage. By leaving them out, Chaucer delivers aristocratic audiences a smart slap. He forces them to a rude conclusion: He doesn't trust them to tell an interesting story. They are just too highfalutin and rule-bound to say anything worth hearing. So instead, he silences them. Their voices would have been heard, eventually, in what was probably amused or possibly disgruntled response to his joke, as they sat in court, or as one miniature shows it, outside in the garden listening to his tales. Whatever the case, this sort of political joke allows us to see Chaucer's gentle genius and makes him all the more believable to a medieval audience. While they would have expected a full panoply of male storytellers, Chaucer surprises them with a number of memorable women, who, without needing alcohol to loosen their tongues, or jokes to shore up their stories, are able to connive, convince, gossip, trick, and generally amuse some thirty-three disparate pilgrims on the road to Canterbury with their marvelously intricate and extended monologues.

The two Alisouns are harbingers from the world of orality, forecasting what women would achieve once the Academy and writing were finally open to them. Again, Walter Ong:

> When they began to enter schools in some numbers during the seventeenth century, girls entered not the main-line Latin schools but the newer

*Every word we use to designate imaginative literature—fiction, story, fable—originated during Chaucer's time and connotes a playful and joking attitude toward language and reality. (The *OED* credits Chaucer with the first use of *tale*.) One medieval word, now obsolete, *jape*, means both a joking story and a lewder kind of ludic activity: sexual intercourse.

vernacular schools. These were practically oriented, for commerce and domestic affairs, whereas the older schools with Latin-based instruction were for those aspiring to be clergy, lawyers, physicians, diplomats, and other public servants. Women writers were no doubt influenced by works that they had read emanating from the Latin-based, academic, rhetorical tradition, but they themselves normally expressed themselves in a different, far less oratorical voice, which has a great deal to do with the rise of the novel.*

Walter Benjamin, the German social critic, says that "experience which is passed on from mouth to mouth is the source from which all storytellers have drawn."** A storyteller stands in the privileged position of being able, like a woman during pregnancy, to pass on that precious commodity called breath. As soon as Chaucer declared himself an author—the first Englishman to make such a bold claim—he had to make good by breaking radically with tradition and disavowing his reliance on other authors. Henceforth, he announced, he would tell his own stories, based on word-of-mouth experiences he had overheard on the road to Canterbury. Like a secular priest, he would pass on the breath of those thirty-two other pilgrims—a conspiratorial kiss shared with every member of his audience.† Of course, Chaucer's premise is a fiction—a semi-practical joke—but what he fabricates for the most part percolates up from the vernacular, joking world, as if his audience were overhearing common folk in the midst of noisy conversation. The word stars of that world shine most brightly in the lines of two women, the Miller's wifely creation and the Wife of Bath. And just so their audience won't forget what the medieval world was really like for women, they both, in typical medieval fashion, crouch behind an alias, the same alias, in a sisterhood of protection—Alisoun. So even here, when we have

*Ong, *Orality and Literacy*, p. 112.

**Walter Benjamin, *Illuminations*, trans. Harry Zohn (New York: Schocken Books, 1969), p. 84.

†Chaucer alleges to have heard all those stories on the road, to have remembered them exactly, and is prepared now to repeat every line and detail of all 132 of the projected tales. And he will tell them using the exact images, the precise rhymes, of the original tellers. Of course, he is a liar. But that's the only way he can get to the truth of fiction. By telling us a boldfaced lie, we know he must be making things up. That is, he must be an *author*, and in Umberto Eco's phrase, this "dishonest and healthy and liberating trick is called literature."

our own firsthand experience of two women playing a key role in the story of laughter, they try to hide from view. The two Alisouns embody the difficulties of gathering and sifting evidence for the history of laughter.

## VI

What I discovered in working on this book has surprised me. First, I have come to see that creative, imaginative literature in the West, as it made its way from its headwaters in the ancient world, has flowed through a deep, meandering bed dug by the history of laughter. My second surprise follows on the first. Some years ago, I published with a dear friend, Ivan Illich, a study of the ways literacy shaped the framework of the lay mind in the twelfth century in England, France, and Germany. This present work has now convinced me that reading and writing cannot be fully comprehended as ways of empowering human beings without first appreciating the connection between language and humor, between narration and joking. Play and language, jokes and literature—the connections may seem odd at first. But play is so basic to animals—humans and nonhumans alike—why shouldn't it inform language, the hieroglyph of life itself? Anyone who writes comes to know that truth. Sooner or later, every writer naturally embraces punning and joking. Language begs for it.

Starting with Saussure and Wittgenstein, philosophers have pointed to language's teasing, practical joke: It pretends to provide a reliable continuity between word and world. A lifetime spent investigating the nature of language convinced Wittgenstein otherwise; he came to see language as a stumbler—a cripple—and couldn't help but laugh at our hapless plight. Language, he was forced to conclude, better than any other function it performs, records the break between what we take pains to describe and what we know actually exists out there. At the end of the *Philosophical Investigations*, Wittgenstein could only advocate silence—a begrudging mysticism—as the linguistic state that best catches the essence of our humanity. The sensible part of ourselves, he declared, "keeps its peace." He ends the *Investigations* with a joke: "About which one cannot speak, one must remain silent."

For George Steiner, the break in our linguistic confidence marks the beginning of the modern period, a moment he places at the end of the nineteenth century: "Mallarmé breaks (*rupture* becomes a cardinal term) the covenant, the continuities between word and world. This move in turn generates the potential discontinuities between the word and previous or subsequent usages of the word as they are explored in the *Philosophical Investigations*. We are at sea, uncompassed."* This "uncompassing" that Mallarmé effected erupts in an artistic revolution of laughter, in surrealism and dada—poetic absurdities and visual punch lines. As more and more artists understood the joke at the very heart of language—in its DNA—laughter took over other art forms. Today, one has only to look at contemporary architects like Frank Gehry and Charles Gwathmy to see that jokes have been made concrete. In fact, joking may characterize best the *breaking* that postmodernists seem to relish so much.

The circle closes from Hobbes to Wittgenstein—from sudden glory to sudden silence—for both philosophers wound up in the same place, holding their sides and laughing. Hobbes saw the language of laughter in a cripple; Wittgenstein found laughter in a crippled language. Both caught a glimpse of reality "on the other side of language," as Wittgenstein puts it, and what they saw through that crack cracked them up. Cracking jokes allows us to break open reality for ourselves: Jokes upset expectations. They create their own realities. They rupture logic.

Like the two streams of air that animate us all, as Aristotle and others believed, if this book lives it is by virtue of two breaths: one that enlivens the body of facts—the corpus of documents and charters and manuscripts—and the other that draws risible air into its soul. Read the letter *and* the spirit

*George Steiner, *Real Presences* (Chicago: University of Chicago Press, 1989), p. 104.

of this text, the body *and* the soul. For sometimes meaning comes rushing in on us, not in the words themselves, but in the rhythm and jostle of sentences. What it means to "learn by heart" is to incorporate, to invite the beat and pulse of literature to indwell beneath our ribs, in our respiratory system. At moments of intimacy, we laugh with others about an event, and bring our breathing—our joy and excitement—into line with theirs. When we remember in that communal way, we recall through our bodies first, in the circulating "feel" of the experience. So alive is the recollected event for us we could swear we've been there before. It's as if we had it "by heart."

I have enjoyed the first laugh in writing this book. I hope the reader will have the last laugh. Everyone laughs in the future tense, for laughter reverberates with hope: It announces that the world is all right after all, and that it will continue, in its wobbly, quirky, unpredictable way. We know, at least, that things are not so serious that we cannot try to laugh them off.*

Even in his darkest moments, Nietzsche still held out the hope that "even if nothing else today has any future, our *laughter* may yet have a future."** Laughter echoes with a promise of hope of the highest order. We simply have to rest assured that tomorrow is an actuality. Once we know that, we can then undertake the task of trying to make it turn out better than yesterday. Surely the sound of laughter has always been heard as humankind's *Ursprache*, the Ur-expression of human beings unabashedly, unashamedly sounding themselves—as *persons*. Even grunts and groans require some pointing to convey meaning, but without a single word or gesture, laughter assures us that hopeful, playful—at times even mildly aggressive—human activity is taking place. It requires no training and little

*Laughing someone off is much more devastating, much more publicly humiliating, and much more final than telling someone off, and certainly more final than writing someone off. It's hard to recover from derision, as we shall see. It takes a collusion between the joker and the victim; it requires a deliberate act of forgiveness on both parts. Eating one's words, in an apology, or taking back one's words, can be distasteful, as well as unbelievable. A laugh permits an easier reconciliation: No words need to be spoken, and the possibility remains that the other person can laugh it off, too.

**Friedrich Nietzsche, *Beyond Good and Evil: Prelude to a Philosophy of the Future*, trans. Walter Kaufmann (New York: Vintage Books, 1989), p. 150.

experience to understand. It is the prelinguistic tag that we cannot shake, following us into adulthood and beyond. In its ability to make contact, it simply has no rivals. It trammels all barriers. Laughter loosens its transcendental meaning in a medieval Latin *hahahae*, or in a modern English *ha ha ha*, or in a Joycean *ha he hi ho hu*.

# 1

# The Hebrews: *"sacred discontent"*

*Most* of us, at one time or another, have experienced a laughter so joyous and spontaneous and so wonderfully heartfelt that tears began streaming down our cheeks. Think, for instance, of being reunited with a long-lost friend—embracing, laughing, and joking—and feeling so overwhelmed by emotion that we surprise ourselves by suddenly crying while laughing. Our surprise usually lasts but a second: There's nothing all that odd, after all, in a fit of laughing tears. If someone were to ask at that moment, "What's the matter? Why are you crying?" we could respond in all honesty, "Nothing's the matter. I'm just terribly happy." At that moment, laughter has revealed itself in its most fundamental form. Those occasions recall, I would argue, a much earlier state, a time before we began civilizing the emotions by arranging them into neat categories, when weeping and laughing had not yet separated from each other, a time so remote that infants did not have to wait until the fortieth or even the fourth day of their lives to laugh. They came into the world crying *and* laughing.

Linguistic evidence supports that claim. Some historians of language, like Robert Claiborne in his *Roots of English*, trace laughter back to the Indo-European root KLEG-, which means both "cry" and "sound," whence, he says, Germanic *lauch*, "a loud outcry." Likewise, according to Claiborne, the tears we *shed*, evolving from its root SKEI-, "to slice," means that they must be "cut" or "split," or "cut away" from some larger, more integrated whole, just as we indicate a rending of the emotions by saying we "break" into laughter. Notice, too, that the word *tear* presents an ambiguity on the page: a rip in a piece of cloth or a drop of liquid from the eye. In practice, laughing and crying are fraternal twins, born of one intense feeling; and that intensity dissolves artificial categories and distinctions in an emotional solution of simultaneous laughing and crying.*

Historically, happiness and sadness have not always been perceived as polar opposites. That great lover of paradox, Giordano Bruno, saw the confluence of these emotions as the most basic of human responses, and captured it in his personal motto: "In hilaritas tristis, in tristitia hilaris." According to Bruno, all laughter comes tinged with tears, and all weeping hides a bit of pleasure. Even at dire moments, when we cry over someone's death, let's say, we still allow ourselves a sigh of pleasurable relief at having been spared.**

Anthropologists have likened the relationship between laughing and crying in oral cultures to something resembling the ancient Chinese figure of the yin-yang. The yin-yang figure is familiar to us as two interlocking, black and white teardrops. The two teardrops—one appearing to fall to earth, the other rising heavenward—fit snugly together to form a circle,

*Leonardo da Vinci wrote a treatise on the human emotions for artists, the *Treatise on Painting*, first published in Paris in 1551. He observes that "between one who laughs and one who weeps there is no difference in the eyes, or mouth, or cheeks, but only in the rigidity of the eyebrows which are drawn together by him who weeps and are raised by him who laughs."

**Hildegard of Bingen, a twelfth-century mystic, describes how the intensity of an experience triggers physiological changes. Here is her account of her forty-third vision: "When joy *or* sadness touches our heart, small vessels of the brain, breast, and lungs become disturbed. On this account the small arteries of the breast and lungs send their humours up to the small arteries of the brain, which receive them and flood the eyes. And thus they give us tears" (emphasis mine).

which we can imagine either as parts turning around one another, or holding forever fast. In either case, the entire figure has no beginning or end.

In the world of primary orality, all events seem to be interrelated and unfold as part of an ongoing cycle. Nothing stands in direct opposition to anything else. True polar opposites develop only with literacy. Literate people have been socialized—alphabetized—into reserving their tears for sorrow and sadness. With literacy come discrete categories and precise definitions. Literacy does not tolerate much ambiguity. To return to Zen for an example, the ability to hold opposing notions in mind, of the sort demanded by a Zen koan, characterize the world of orality. The Zen master asks, What is the sound of one hand clapping? The student does not ponder the question on a piece of paper, returning to it again and again in close analysis in order to arrive at its meaning. Rather, the initiate moves off into isolation, trying to picture the solution, or simply finds contentment and ease in the heart of ambiguity. As a remnant of preliterate times, what appears to us as an insoluble emotional paradox—feeling both happy and sad at precisely the same instant—finds solution, liquidity, in the waters of our bittersweet tears.*

The phenomenon of "mixed pleasures," as Plato called it—the marriage of laughter and weeping, joy and sorrow—which to a modern consciousness seems as unnatural and unsettling as trying to rub your stomach with one hand and pat your head with the other, dominates the history of laughter. It begins well before the birth of Christ, and continues down through the jests of the ancient and medieval worlds, directly into modern, Freudian joke-telling. Most experiences naturally result in imprecise and mixed emotions, but probably none so dramatic (and none so common, either) as this merging of laughter and weeping. We moderns know them simply as two quite

*The first record of *bittersweet* to refer to the emotions appears in Chaucer; a sweet experience alloyed with a bitter aftertaste. The father of the modern joke, Chaucer should know that mixed feeling firsthand. Chaucer uses the term to refer to the experience of anticipating God's healing power for some pain we suffer. In the midst of sorrow we can anticipate solace. Prayer itself is a bittersweet thing.

distinct emotions. The march of history, too, has been fairly emphatic about these two categories, to the point of sealing their differences in two separate masks—a smiling one for comedy, and a frowning one for tragedy. And yet, even those two masks are cast out of one mold, or at least they hang side by side, one cheek touching the other's jowl.

For those historians like Francis Cornford who find the roots of drama in agrarian rituals, comedy and tragedy grow out of the same ritual, becoming distinct genres through emphasis either on the hero's death or on his resurrection and marriage. In *The Origin of Attic Comedy*, Cornford indicts Euripides for his preference of what Aristotle, like modern audiences, regarded as the proper ending for tragedy. He points out, for instance, that Aeschylus ends his trilogy, quite normally, with happy endings.

Laughter and weeping may be the most human admixture, one we experience every time we respond to one of those aggressive jokes that prompts derisive laughter toward a poor, hapless victim. We have all found ourselves laughing, almost against our wills, certainly against our better judgment, and certainly through our own sadness, at another person's misfortunes. But we also feel tremendous relief that it is not we who have received that nasty barb, or fallen on that slippery banana peel, or been afflicted with that crippling disability. And so there we stand, trapped inside our emotions, laughing and feeling sad at the same time. Oddly enough, then, it is not only joyous laughter, but derisive laughter as well, that can transport us back to that undifferentiated state before the circle of emotion—to continue the Zen figure—tore apart into separate tears. History provides a startling report of this earlier time of emotional integration.

A dramatically important set of clay tablets for the history of laughter, uncovered by archaeologists in the 1930s, provides evidence that simultaneous weeping and laughing once formed the ritualized emotional center of the lives of the earliest historical peoples. These tablets, inscribed sometime in the fourteenth century B.C., from the early Ugarit in northern Syria, have been named the Ras Shamra Texts, for the geographical area where they were found. The Danish scholar Flemming Friis Hvidberg, after laboriously examining their cuneiform script, has concluded that two inner texts, designated the *Myth of Ba'al-aliyn* and the *Death of Baal*, tell of an early Phoenician-Canaanite cult drama that celebrated the simultaneous death and rebirth of the vegetation deity Baal, god of rainfall and fertility, with tears of weeping and laughing. This cult migrated not only into the land of Canaan, but eventually worked its way from the Nile to the Euphrates, far north into Asia Minor, and much farther west. In all these places, people wept and wailed over the death of the gods as they buried them in the ground, and laughed and rejoiced at the very same time, in anticipation of their eventual resurrection and ultimate marriage to complementary goddesses. The goal of these ceremonies was union and harmony, the marriage of opposites, not so different from the marriage of light and dark, say, in one of Shakespeare's comedies. These texts provide some evidence for the theories of Cornford.

The sequence of action in the Ras Shamra tablets—along with analogous poems found in conjunction with the main text—strongly suggests that the poem was recited during an autumnal festival that welcomed the triumph of the wet season over the dry, and in which Baal presided as the god of fertility: The tribe buried him in the fall to ensure his rebirth after the rains in the springtime. As Baal moved into his underground home, witnesses to his burial wept and lamented his departure. But since the participants knew he would eventually return, they could periodically burst out in fits of laughter, a joyous counterpoint to their sadness.* The certainty of rebirth transformed and softened death. Furthermore, the tablets do not narrate linear time, but tell of a cycle of vegetative growth, of planting and harvesting: A circle obviously has no beginning or ending. The seasons maintain an eternal return; they generate change and so promote relief. Here is Hvidberg's summary of the Baal celebration: "We must visualize

*Aggressive joke-telling is an occasion for both weeping and laughing. An audience expresses sadness over the pain of the sacrificial victim, knowing, at the same time, that he or she will come back from "death."

that not only the gods, but the whole population participated in the autumn festival, first with—long-drawn wailing and whining—weeping, then with hilarity and erotically excited laughter."*

The pleasure and laughter at harvest festivities came larded with a heavy eroticism, as Hvidberg suggests, since only one vowel sound distinguishes the Hebrew root for "laughter" from "sexual intercourse." Through a pun, then, the text suggests something wilder and more erotic than pure laughter. But it fades quickly, for joy in the abundance of harvest was undercut by the knowledge that winter—another round of death—was fast approaching. Wailing would thus occasionally pierce the sounds of laughter. Hvidberg believes that the Semites lived so close to the continual turn of the seasons that they could easily ride the emotional wheel, rolling from sadness around to gaiety and back again.

Actually, the Ras Shamra tablets only serve as a starting point for Hvidberg's real concern, as the title of his work—*Weeping and Laughter in the Old Testament*—reveals. He believes that if he has read the Shamra tablets correctly, then remnants of cultic emotion from that earlier period should have survived into the early Judaic history of the Old Testament. (Though not his aim at all, Hvidberg is actually constructing a foundation for the history of the emotions.) He finds one vestige in the Book of Ezra 3:12, which describes the building of the Second Temple. Some of the priests and Levites, remembering the destruction of the older Temple, weep bitterly, while others rejoice in visualizing the new one. The Bible records the coalescence of sound, and this is the evidence Hvidberg is after: "The people could not distinguish the sound of joyful shouting from the sound of the people's weeping."

Traces of simultaneous weeping and laughing still characterize some Jewish holidays. The Jewish New Year, Rosh Hashanah, for example, has traditionally been celebrated during the time of harvest, a transitional period of joy and bundling in advance of a rapidly approaching, dead cold

*Fleming Friis Hvidberg, *Weeping and Laughing in the Old Testament: A Study of Canaanite-Israelite Religion* (Leiden: E. J. Brill, 1962), p. 56.

winter.* That Rosh Hashanah marks the Jewish calendar as a time of balance is underscored by the biblical image of the Lord holding in his hands the scales of justice: On the Day of Judgment, he will weigh the merits and faults in the hearts of the great and humble alike. The celebration of Rosh Hashanah is followed by ten days of atonement, culminating in the fast of Yom Kippur, when divine judgment is definitively sealed. The *hazan*, or cantor, announces this day of fasting by sounding the *shofar*—the ram's horn—which for some biblical commentators symbolizes the cry of the Jewish people, as the Sixty-First Psalm records: "Hear my cry, O Lord, listen to my prayers."** These commentators focus on breath, or *ruach*: The Lord is implored to hear and listen so the repentant one does not waste his breath. The *shofar* blower traditionally sounds two different kinds of notes. With one, a long shrill note, he intends to mimic a plaintive cry; with the other, a series of rapid, short notes, he intends to mimic a rapid release of laughter.†

Other biblical commentators focus on the ram's horn itself, as a symbol of the intercessory sacrifice of Isaac. Abraham's heroic willingness to sacrifice his only son combines powerful feelings of both sorrow and joy: Through divine intercession, Abraham is able to obey God's command by offering up his only begotten son and, at the same time, to keep him whole by having an angel substitute a ram for his son at the very last second.

As Abraham raises his sword high over his head, the world freezes for

*The secular New Year, of course, also wears the two-faced mask of Janus, symbolizing regret over mistakes committed in the old year, and jubilation over the prospect of a fresh start. Lingering problems can be overcome, the thought goes, with New Year's resolutions—turning over a "new leaf" in that crucial seasonal time. The meeting of these two emotions coalesces as the most poignant moment in the calendar—the final midnight stroke of the year, an instant that belongs neither to the old nor the new year, punctuated by much laughing and crying and, of course, the traditional kiss, a sometimes passionate and giddy reminder of the conspiracy of life that people enjoy with each other and with God.

**European carnivals—festivals that traditionally combine humor and seriousness (discussed later in this book)—are not only cyclical and annual, pagan and Christian, but also occur at times of liminality, for instance, at times of seasonal change.

†One early-fourteenth-century illustration from a German *mahzor* (prayer book) shows the *shofar* blower with his right foot on a three-legged stool, a gesture believed to defuse the power of the devil. The devil, meanwhile, tries to throttle the blower's soul and stifle the clear sound of the *shofar*. The *shofar* blower must concentrate on balancing the stool as he sounds each note clearly. Balance or centeredness, which requires a careful tempering of the emotions—to match the time, Rosh Hashanah—is the strongest defense against the assaults of the devil. Extreme outbursts tend to throw one off balance—to make one an easy target to knock over.

an instant. Abraham hangs suspended in that split second between the sorrow of losing his son and the joy of obeying his Lord. That moment exists in meditative, contemplative time: The world holds its collective breath in anticipation. Suddenly, Isaac sees the angel hove into view, and he breathes a sigh of relief. In the end, of course, Abraham does not have to cleave his son in two; his emotions, too, remain whole.* Even though all ends happily, Abraham lives out his days as an emotional border dweller, forever embodying the bittersweet. He comes back from the world of miracles into the world of humankind, but he breathes differently.

That is the lesson sounded with the *shofar's* blast at the end of the old year and the beginning of the new: the sound of breath renewed and redefined by divine intercession—through miracle—so that it finally expresses laughter and crying simultaneously. No sound can be heard, however, unless the *hazan* carefully and precisely shapes his lips, narrows and slows down his stream of air. The ram's horn virtually defies the *hazan*. But it cannot thwart the power of his controlled breath. The *shofar* resounds throughout the temple, signaling to the congregation triumph and reunification—of man with God's will, of the ultimate merging of joy and sorrow—of life itself. Air and sound, both of which live and die in the world of evanescence, so ephemeral and fleeting, symbolize not only the temporary nature of life, but the fact that the miracle of life, our breath, comes from the invisible world. We must control and shape it before we surrender our gift back to that invisible world. What we must pay attention to, what matters, the *shofar* indicates, lies in the most fundamental use of our breath—in crying and laughing.**

But apart from the passage in Ezra 3:12, and the larger example of Abraham's conjoined joy and sorrow, Hvidberg finds few examples of indissolu-

*The two meanings of *cleave* reveal once more the reluctance of things to separate: the word means both "stick to, adhere," and "break apart."

**Jewish marriages in the Middle Ages celebrated the duality of sorrow and joy: "The loose fur-lined cloak was worn as a sign of mourning [by the bride at weddings] for Jerusalem, its destroyed Temple, and the exile—painful thoughts which Jews always remembered at times of celebration" (Thérèse and Mendel Metzger, *Jewish Life in the Middle Ages* [New York: Alpine Fine Arts Collection, 1982]; p. 50).

ble weeping and laughing in the Old Testament. By the time the Bible gets written down, emotions have already passed through the sieve of civilization. Tears express one thing only—sorrow. Much more noticeable, laughter has pretty much lost its dual character, its capacity to express great liberating joy and to deliver demoralizing pain. In the period Hvidberg studies, virtually all the laughter in the Bible, even God's laughter, has been thoroughly drained of joy. The Bible concentrates on the terrifying power of derisive laughter, on God's ability to set human flesh aquiver. In fact, joyous laughter occurs only once in the Old Testament. But the event stands out as one of the text's key miracles, one that produces a living emblem of God's faithful dealings with the Hebrew people. For Christians, the event is made all the more remarkable by its foreshadowing of the Virgin Birth of the New Testament, itself another miraculous sign from God of his enduring faith in his people.

Annunciation in the Old Testament comes not from an emissary of God, an angel, but from God himself. Even so, and unlike Gabriel's visit to Mary, this annunciation is received with anything but awestruck acceptance. When God informs Abraham that his wife, Sarai, will bear him a son (Gen. 17:17), "Abraham fell upon his face and laughed." What else can Abraham do but laugh in disbelief? After all, he is one hundred years old. Sarai herself is in her nineties and has been infertile her entire life.

Later, in Genesis 18:10 and following, the Lord reassures Abraham that Sarai will indeed bear a child. Sarai listens to the news from inside her tent and, upon hearing it, laughs to herself, saying, "After I have grown old, and my husband is old, shall I have pleasure?" (Gen. 18:13). The Lord confronts Abraham about his wife's scornful laugh with a menacing line: "Is anything too hard for the Lord?" (Gen. 18:14). Frightened by the Lord's anger, Sarai denies that she ever laughed. But the Lord persists and reprimands her sternly: "You did laugh!" (Gen. 18:15). The Lord then leaves, telling the couple that they can expect his return in the spring.

That spring (recall the miracle of the risen god in the spring in the Ras

Shamra tablets), when Sarai miraculously gives birth to her son, her name is changed to Sarah, "the princess," so that everyone who utters the name elevates her by recalling the miracle of her life. In addition, God confers on the son of Abraham and Sarah his Hebrew name, Yitzchak, which means "he laughs." Sarah's announcement of the event stands out as the only instance in the Old Testament of joyous laughter: "And Sarah said, 'God hath made laughter for me; everyone who hears will laugh with me'" (Gen. 21:16). Thus Sarah establishes a covenant, one forged out of laughter, with everyone, including strangers, who hears the news of her miracle.

God has his own way of consecrating Sarah's pregnancy. While God blesses Ishmael, Abraham's son with an Egyptian slave, he saves his everlasting covenant for Abraham; and he seals that covenant through Isaac, Abraham's only "begotten" son with his wife Sarah, and the only rightful heir to the patriarchal lineage. Through Isaac, Sarah shall be the "mother of nations; kings of people shall come from her" (Gen. 17:17).

The Old Testament lists a number of different covenants, but the one between God and Abraham holds special status, usually interpreted as a sign of God's protective love for his people. Covenants, however, do not typically involve laughter. Just the opposite: A common Near Eastern covenant involved sacrificing animals by cutting them into pieces, a practice mentioned, in fact, in God's covenant with Abraham in Genesis 15:9–21. After animals were cut and the pieces placed opposite one another, participants walked between the rows, perhaps to symbolize that whoever broke the covenant might be sliced and severed from the community. The standard idiom in Hebrew for making a covenant is to "cut a covenant," which may derive from this custom. Circumcision, not laughter, is the ultimate cut, making every Jew a member of the community of the chosen and allowing each one to participate in public worship. The first reference to such ritual cutting in the Bible occurs when God commands Abraham to circumcise himself and all other males of his household (Gen. 17:10–14). The ritual cutting of circumcision tries to circumvent any physical or emotional cutting of an individual from the rest of the Jewish nation.

Patronymic stories play key roles in the Bible; they unravel the knottiness of the world in a single word. The birth of Isaac illuminates the basic Judaic attitude toward laughter. Laughter that wells out of joy, which in Hebrew is called *simcha*, cannot be initiated on earth by humankind. It can only be received, like breath itself, as a miraculous gift from God. Quite literally, this is what God shows Sarah through his miracle: Yitzchak is the embodiment of God's gift of laughter, and through this gift God converts Abraham and Sarah's scornful laughter of disbelief into one of potential joy—and transforms everyone else who becomes swept up in the joyful miracle of Isaac's birth. Isaac is truly God's son, but he is not the Word incarnate. Rather, he is Laughter incarnate—the second, more miraculous breath, the breath of Creation in the ancient Egyptian cosmogony, the breath that is prior to, and more universal than, language.

In the hierarchy of angels, Isaac is known as the "angel of light" because a supernatural brightness surrounded him at birth, an aura of preternatural delight, as if he had arrived in the world trailing his divine origins. Perhaps because he stands so emphatically as the embodiment of laughter, he also possesses a supernatural breath, one that cannot be easily extinguished. Forlang, in the *Encyclopedia of Religions*, says that "Jewish tradition makes Isaac an angel of light, created before the world, and afterwards incarnate as one of the sinless patriarchs over whom death had no power." God gives us a glimpse of Isaac's immortality early in the story of his life.

An important lesson for understanding the nature of laughter lies just below the surface of this story. Laughter is a gift that must be continually passed on. Jokes, witticisms spontaneously contrived, must be sacrificed for the welfare of the community. In fact, that is the only way we can ever hope to retain laughter's miraculous power. Moreover, and this speaks to laughter's origins, laughter calls forth a kind of divine intercession: The Isaac story seems to say that laughter can work miraculous things, so long as you stop believing that you own it, and so long as you stop hanging on to it for dear life.

The idea may not be as outlandish as it sounds. First, listen to the sociologist Erving Goffman, who can comment so intelligently on wit and laughter in ordinary conversation in just a couple of short sentences: "One of the heroes [of conversation] is the wit who can introduce references to wider, important matters in a way that is ineffably suited to the current moment of talk. Since the witticism will never again be as telling, a sacrifice has been offered up to the conversation, and respect paid to its unique reality by an act that shows how thoroughly the actor is alive to the interaction."* Second, the anthropologist Mary Douglas makes a similar point when she calls the joker a kind of "minor mystic," "one of those people who pass beyond the bounds of reason and society and give glimpses of a truth which escapes through the mesh of structured concepts."** Laughter has a penchant for breaking down normal categories, creating the possibility for the wildest things to happen. When laughter's on the scene, the normal state of affairs can only give way to surprise and wonder.

But the biblical story of Abraham and Sarah carries meaning much more important for the history of laughter. Women, it seems—Sarah in particular—have a divine connection to laughter. (Perhaps men—Moses in particular—have a divine connection with something very much different from laughter, namely law. Unlike stone tablets, laughter is extraordinarily light.) Isaac is not born out of union; Abraham did not inseminate his wife. God tapped Sarah, and in this Jewish version of Virgin Birth, what results is the birth of laughter. Isaac may embody laughter, but it is God, through woman, who ultimately gives laughter to the world. As a Jewish maxim puts it, "Man thinks, God laughs." What Sarah voices in her excitement—"Everyone who hears will laugh with me"—is the irresistible contagion of laughter. It is to her kind—the Ur-Sarahs throughout history—that we our-

*Erving Goffman, *The Presentation of Self in Everyday Life* (New York: Anchor Doubleday), p. 48. Notice that God and Sarah are engaged in something that does not occur very often in the Bible—divinely inspired social intercourse. In Hebrew, the words for *laughter* and *sexual intercourse* derive from the same root, and are so closely related that at times a reader has a hard time distinguishing *laughing* from *love-making*, a confusion that makes for some very interesting and at times very embarrassing sentences.

**Mary Douglas, *Implicit Meanings: Essays in Anthropology* (London: Routledge and Kegan Paul, 1975), p. 108.

selves must return in order to hear those early sounds of laughter. In the history of laughter, Isaac's conception stands out in the Bible as a key event, an important moment in the history of potency, made all the more crucial by the fact that it is the only moment of true belly laughter in the Bible. After the creation of the world and its first inhabitants, laughter must take its place as one of the principal miracles of conception, one of the most fertile and pregnant ideas in the first book of the Bible. In a very strategic sense, Sarah is the mother of invention.

Every other instance of laughter in the Old Testament is either scornful or derisive, ranging from the gentle mocking of Daniel to the most devastating examples, which emanate directly from God himself. Although he laughs only four times—in Psalms 2:4, 37:13, 59:8, and in Proverbs 1:26—each time, of course, he fills the cosmos with a horrible dread. Unlike the merry laughter of the Greek gods, the Lord's laughter reverberates with ultimate meaning; it points to the Alpha and Omega of laughter's power: If laughter can bring us into the world, it can also take us out. The Old Testament God can be angered easily, and he makes his feelings known. In every case, God's laughter, scornful and derisive, expresses absolute monarchy over those impious enough to reject him as God: The scornful must be made to feel that they count for nothing—they are mere ciphers—in relation to God's majesty. Their blasphemy only makes them look ridiculous, and thus they deserve to be derided—to be brought down a notch or two from their haughty superiority.

Whatever the explanation, God's laughter presents serious problems for theologians. For the ascetic monks, laughter gave the Lord too much anthropomorphism. Someone like Gregory the Great finds other, more knotty problems. In his *Moralia*, he goes to great lengths to place God's derisive laughter into a carefully constructed theological context. For example, in the Proverbs of Solomon (1:7, 26), where wisdom has it that "the fear of the Lord is the/beginning of knowledge," God warns that he will "laugh at the calamity" of the wicked, just so they can come to complete knowledge of his power. Thus, Gregory says that God laughs because he is unwilling to show the wicked any mercy, so they can finally come to him.

Gregory also cites a fifth place where God laughs, in Job 9:23, though biblical scholars disagree about the interpretation of the line: "When disaster brings sudden death,/he mocks the calamity of the innocent." Does he mock or truly laugh? Gregory insists that God laughs, not out of scorn this time, but because the innocent suffer pains out of their thwarted desire. They stand in the opposite position from the wicked, for they desire with their whole hearts to come to God. Listen clearly, Gregory argues: God laughs out of joy because the innocent will soon arrive at his bosom.

This holds even in Jewish eschatology, for example, in Psalms 126:1–2—"When the Lord restored the fortunes of Zion,/We were like those who dream,/Then our mouth was filled with laughter, and our tongue with shouts of joy." The Hebrew word in that passage for "laughter," *sachaq*, denotes the Israelites' superiority over their former opponents. Gregory calls this another example of God's laughter of joy over those who turn toward his love. (It is interesting to notice, however, that in Psalms 126:2, the Septuagint does not gloss *sachaq* as γελάω, "laughter," but χαρά, a "righteous joy," which has reference to God alone. The Greek translation constantly refers to joy (*simcha*) in the time of salvation, but not to laughter. On this point, Gerhard Kittel, the great biblical scholar, concludes that "Rabbinic ethics, with its thought of rewards, rejected laughter in regard to the coming aeon because this is something for God to give, not for man to give himself.")*

In the Old Testament, then, every instance of laughter but one reverberates as a cosmic warning: God laughs whenever he believes his people have rejected him. How foolhardy for humans to assert their autonomy! God can only laugh at such foolishness. Keep in mind that in the cult of Baal-Aliyn, laughter provided a direct, immediate, and sometimes frenetic way to merge with the divine. The Greeks experienced the divine through laughter, as well. Joyous laughter for the Jews, then, came to represent something alien

*Gerhard Kittel, *Theologisches Wörterbuch zum Neuen Testament*, trans. and ed. J. R. Coates (London: A. C. Black, 1949), p. 151.

and utterly pagan. Thus the advice of Rabbi Chanina Bar Papa (A.D. 300): "When you have an impulse toward frivolity (*lahastilka*), resist it with the words of the Torah." That is, if you feel yourself drifting from God and have the urge to laugh out loud, reading Torah will place you back in the proper somber and serious relation to the Lord. Religion—Judaism in particular—has little tolerance for the unsettling effects of laughter.

Realize that Bar Papa is calling for something far different from anything even remotely resembling casual reading, in which a person might grab a book off the shelf at random and turn page after page, in an easy chair, for enjoyment. Torah reading does not admit of free and easy browsing. The calendar absolutely circumscribes Torah reading: Judaic law permits the congregation to overhear only certain, prescribed portions of the Five Books of Moses, and only on certain days of the year. Open to any section of the Torah and the tone remains amazingly consistent—solemn and straightforward. The Torah instructs and educates; it teaches how to live a moral life. Compared to any other kind of reading—particularly modern, leisurely reading—Torah seems absolutely foreign. It belongs to another, more lofty, ritualized category.

But Bar Papa's warning carries more levels of meaning. He isn't merely telling Jews to avoid laughter; he is telling them *how* to avoid it. He does this because he understands so well the nature of laughter. I want to spend a bit of time here with the mechanics of reading Torah, so as to reveal one rabbi's representative view of laughter. To begin with, the Torah is a scroll that is wound tightly around two wooden staffs, in opposing directions, wrapped securely with a leather thong—so many turns in one direction, so many turns in the opposite direction—and tied with a special knot. A cloth cover fits over this double scroll, and the whole enterprise housed inside the ark. In the ancient Temple, the ark, which contained the stone tablets that Moses received on Sinai, could only be found in the most deeply recessed chamber called the Holy of Holies. The Bible tells us that the original consecration of Aaron and his son as *kohanim*—high priests, the only class lofty enough to be permitted to read the divine law—involved ritual immersion (*mikvah*, or "a cleansing, purifying bath") before they could enter the inner sanctum of this most holy of places where the received words of God were securely stored. A *shamas*, or "custodian," stands guard, like an angel, over the Torah itself. He makes certain the screen is closed in front of the ark so that no one can see the Torah, and that the doors of the synagogue are locked tight so that no one can tamper with it.

Reading in Hebrew—what a wonderful misnomer!—for the reader cannot merely pass his eyes over the text. Traditionally, to look at the Torah or to touch it also involves an elaborate ritual of unfolding and unpacking—both scroll and meaning. Prayers precede the opening of the ark. Then follows the slow uncovering, untying, and unrolling. One's hand must never desecrate the scroll by touching it; the reader—one solitary reader, who recites out loud for the rest of the congregation—uses a *yad*, a sterling silver finger, to trace the lines of the text. Finally, there comes the recitation, again radically different from, say, reading in English.

For one thing, Hebrew consists solely of consonants; the Hebrew alphabet—or better yet, *aleph-bet*—contains no symbols for vowels. The reader must add *vowels*—quite literally "voice"—by sounding each written character out loud, by adding his own breath bringing each character to life. But the reader's own character is vital, too, for the words come more or less alive depending on the strength of the reader's soul. Reading this way recapitulates God's dramatic act of breathing air into the dry bones of Adam and miraculously creating life. The reader thus sings or chants the text into existence. He knows what the words sound like because he has heard them read aloud before. Reading Hebrew promotes a close, conspiratorial relationship between literacy and orality, between permanence and evanescence, between reader and congregation. Silent reading is anathema to ancient Hebrew meaning, for the words only take on meaning, only come to life, when sounded. Silent reading falls far short of creating a textual community. Translation is an impossibility. The day when Hebrew ceases to be read precisely this way, the Kabbala warns, the words will fall like dry stones from the mouths of the Jews.

One of the oddest aspects of Hebrew reading, perhaps, is the fact that the language contains no words, only roots—comprised, usually, of three or four characters—that become words only when voiced aloud, when *inspired.* But since Hebrew does not even indicate vowels,* the reader must act like a musician, sight reading the row of characters, gathering every three or four into its correct root by voicing them out loud, while at the same time interpreting so the correct vowel can be added to each character to make proper sense of the sentence. The reader interprets and reads simultaneously. In the process of reading for meaning, nonsense gets knocked out. If the opportunity for a nonsense reading arises, such as "sexual intercourse" for "laughter," the reader must immediately eliminate the mistake, reject the nonsense. High seriousness is built into the act of reading Hebrew. But readers of the same sentence may reach different interpretations. Thus, multilevels of meaning abound; unending interpretation and explanation make up a kind of Jewish scholasticism. George Steiner explains the peculiar nature of this kind of reading:

> The *midrashic* method of reading is that of the argumentative, qualifying, revisionary gloss and marginalia on the holy text and on previous readings. Hermeneutical investigation bears on every level of possible meaning: semantic, grammatical, lexical. Formidably schooled memorization and philological virtuosity perform a dance of the spirit in front of the partially closed but radiant Ark of the letter.
>
> This reading without end represents the foremost guarantee of Jewish identity. Unwaveringly minute study of the Torah is enjoined before any other rite or obligation. Dialogue with the ultimately, but only ultimately, unfathomable text is the breath of Jewish history and being. It has proved to be the instrument of improbable survival.**

Now recall Bar Papa's warning: When you feel yourself tending toward frivolity, go read the Torah. How stifling his admonition should now

*Vowel points, as aids for beginning readers, are sometimes used in textbooks. They work like color keys for beginning piano students. Sophisticated reading relies on the reader knowing every permutation of every root. Hebrew literacy requires readers to contextualize rapidly and to read seriously.

**Steiner, *Real Presences*, p. 41.

feel, for when frivolity pokes us in the ribs, we feel the urge to laugh out loud at that exact moment. By the time a person has gone through all of the steps—and has waited for the right calendric moment—and finally has gotten to hear Torah read aloud, the impulse to laugh would obviously have long since passed. That's Bar Papa's aim. His instruction is ironic. He wants laughter left far behind, for the powerful breath of laughter seeks out meaning and subverts it. It blows roots apart. It craves nonsense. In the solemn, ritualistic event called reading, laughter arrives on the scene as an unwelcome, anarchic intruder. Reading the Torah in a spirit of frivolity would be like working on the Ford assembly line under the influence of LSD. Not only is it wrong and illegal, but it obviously destroys smooth operation—and endangers the lives of others. Laughter loves to hear bindings snap and barriers go down; it ranges wherever it pleases, reverberating in private and public places alike. It seeps into secret chambers. Laughter is nothing if not unruly and sloppy.

If a Jew craved laughter, then, he—for traditionally only men were permitted on the bimah to *daven*, chant aloud, from the Torah—had to reach for it subversively, mainly through irony. Women in fact sat in a separate section of the synagogue, so Bar Papa's interdict does not refer to women. Barred from Torah, women were also denied the particular training that reading afforded in irony and satire. Even Sarah's momentary outburst of scornful laughter God manages to mature and ripen into joy. The Hebrew male dedicates himself to finding meaning; he excavates each line for every possible nuance and subtlety. He knows that what lies beneath each sentence can be uncovered through deliberation and discussion; but rest assured another layer of meaning always waits to scuttle one's interpretation, to shake one's confidence in the finality of meaning.

So the Jew became adept at irony—at subverting meaning himself, at getting back, at making a point through indirect humor. When the Jew makes jokes, he does it within his literary tradition by paying particular attention to the word, to levels of meaning, to a playful acknowledgment of context, and if at all possible, to an interpretation that will evoke a laugh—

in appreciation for his keen wit. He turns himself into a rabbi with a sharp tongue; he becomes an authority and a final interpretation unto himself. Riding on the edge of biting and witty sarcasm, the Jewish joker works through stealth, avoiding direct punch lines or obvious quips and puns. How could a Jew not develop a wry sense of humor, when the Hebrew language itself continually plays the trickster? One might conclude that he does it in self-defense.

Jews found their perfect weapons in irony and satire, for the rabbis simply would not tolerate out-and-out laughter. In Hebraic tradition, raucous laughter implies a complete abandonment to the senses. Only that one small vowel point, as I have indicated, separates *sachaq* and *sechoq*, "laughter" and "sexual intercourse."* The Ras Shamra tablets use the same Hebrew roots, but there the context demands them to be read as "joyous laughter."** In the Old Testament, these words carry only unpleasant connotations of derision and scorn. All play—all foreplay, in fact—has been eliminated. Life is serious. The Old Testament God, so dark and cloudy, so removed from any trace of joyous laughter, demands comment. Why is he so radically different from the Canaanite gods? The answer will reveal something important about the history of the Hebrew people themselves.

For Hvidberg and many other Old Testament scholars, Yahweh did not originally express this characteristic divine displeasure. The Israelites quite deliberately assigned that attitude to him in Canaan because they needed to keep their desert God uncontaminated by the fertile vegetation deity whose commanding presence they found in that new land. The Hebrews, people of the Book, sharpen their intellects on reading and writing and, most of all, on a close and disciplined textual analysis that coaxes and cajoles a seemingly

*This connection between laughter and sexual intercourse also occurs in Middle English in a word like *jape*, "joke." Modern English keeps these strange bedfellows very carefully separated. But Hemingway, in *The Sun Also Rises*, cozies them up again by having Lady Brett Ashley and Jake Barnes play with the word *joking* for "screwing."

**The Bible even uses two other words, *tsechoq*, and infrequently, *la'ag*, to convey the idea of scoffing or scornful laughter. A fairly ample vocabulary exists in Hebrew for capturing the nuances of derisive laughter.

endless range of meanings out of each and every sentence. As I have tried to show, one slip of the breath can radically alter the meaning of a sentence. This distance between reader and text—between the knower and the known—breeds one of the most sophisticated of literate devices: irony. An ironic stance places a great distance not only between the Hebrew people and their texts, but between themselves and the embedded indigenous culture. Only the most sophisticated readers catch the nuances of irony, and of course every reader wants to be thought of as sophisticated. Such training develops an outlook so hypercritical it stands ready and eager to express dissatisfaction with virtually everything around. The mind is primed for making caustic comments. And the step from irony to sardonic humor is a short, short one.

This "sacred discontent," as one literary historian calls it, turned the Hebrews into highly critical observers, who could stand back and evaluate the scene, rather than fully participate in it. That distance enabled them to adopt a critical perspective and to assess every event—both large and small. The Hebrews' seminomadic way of life opened an even greater distance from the city-dwelling, sedentary Canaanites. Given their intense commitment to literacy, the Hebrews could thus begin to record their observations, an interpretive, permanent record of past events—in short, they began writing history. Again, different from the mythologizing Canaanites, the Hebrews turned to history, for that was where Yahweh revealed himself:

> A strange bond between Yahwism and science is suggested by the Hebrew habit of looking to history, or experience, for validation of the prophetic message. Apparently alone among ancient peoples, the Hebrews developed an exaggerated respect for "truth" as we commonly define it now—empirical verification—instead of respecting the "truths" of the mythological world. The latter, useful and valid for millennia of human development, were inadequate to the Hebrews' strange conception of Yahweh's role in history. The Exodus tradition in particular held that Yahweh erupted unpredictably into events, making himself known by "mighty signs and wonders" which cut across and set at defiance regular human experience.*

*Herbert N. Schneidau, *Sacred Discontent: The Bible and Western Tradition* (Berkeley: University of California Press, 1976), p. 25.

Effective irony exploits a keen, biting wit in order to keep "the other" at bay. But therein lies the danger, for while the ironist may aim at reform, his biting wit inevitably transforms him into "the other" as well, ensuring at best a marginal survival. The ironist lives as a stranger in his strange land, but without the hope or desire of ever becoming fully integrated. He lurks around the edges, on the periphery of the action, as a pariah whose tongue is feared by everyone, even when it speaks the truth—or rather, especially when it speaks the truth.

Ironic lines—derisive and scornful—do not normally evoke belly laughs: They hit with too much force and inflict too much pain. Besides, irony aims high; it hits well above the belt. Irony forces the victim to think, hard, about what just happened. A witty, ironic line makes us stop and figure out its meaning, but once we get it we only get angry. There's not much pleasure in catching on to our own slowness or stupidity. Indeed, it can prove embarrassing. No wonder, then, that in the world of the Old Testament, joyous laughter stands so clearly divorced from every other kind. No wonder, too, that it is a woman who gives birth to joyous laughter; sardonic humor belongs to the domain of man. In the Hebrew world, then, joy stands at a radically opposite pole from sorrow. Tears are reserved for crying only, not laughing. The Bible may even offer an account of this separation of emotions into discrete "humors." This separation takes place early in the history of the cosmos, on the second day of Creation.

The second day in the story of Creation records the most arduous and most remarkable episode in God's week-long labors, marked as it is by overwhelming sadness and weeping. After every other day, God registers his satisfaction by announcing, "And it was good." But, incredibly, not on the second day. The *midrashim aggadah*—homiletic interpretations of the Torah—report that the second day involved a struggle of cosmic proportions, even for God himself. It is hard to imagine God in a close contest with anybody or anything. For that reason, one feels compelled to read this divine struggle as a story of the highest significance. Indeed, the symbolic nature of this second day spills over into virtually every other biblical episode and suggests that separation is necessary before creation of any kind can take place.

On the second day of Creation, God first commanded the angel Rahab to separate the waters above from the waters below, but Rahab knew only too well that that spelled the beginning of the end of the status quo. And so he risked it all and refused God's request, which so infuriated the Lord that he put an immediate end to Rahab. In order for God to begin his creation of the firmament, the waters had to be separated. But how can water be separated? That is like trying to pick up mercury with the fingers. Who could do such a thing? No one. And so God eventually performed the task himself. The Midrash describes the ordeal: "He said let a vault rise amid the waters, to keep these waters from those; a vault by which he would separate the waters beneath it from the waters above. And so it was done. This vault he called the sky. So evening came and morning and a second day passed."*

But God's work was not entirely successful, for the waters so desperately desired to be together that they rebelled against being separated. The waters destined for on high embraced more tightly the waters below. Even the Chaos—which itself tends toward the humorous, toward the liquid—refused to make space for Creation. (*Chaos* remains one of the few nouns in English not susceptible to division; English has no plural for it.) Seeing the waters weeping on account of their separation, God could not say, "And it was good." For he, too, felt sad. Some sources say God used a shard to hold the waters apart; others say it was such a Herculean task that he had to spread his own mantle between the waters. Whatever the method, he finally sealed the "firmament" with the most evanescent and powerful thing imag-

*The author of Ecclesiastes records the aftermath of the second day in temporal terms, and in so doing recognizes it as a day ripe with potential for a civilized life: "For everything there is a season, and a time for every matter under heaven . . . a time to weep, and a time to laugh." Time requires separation—one season from the next, one hour from the next, and ultimately one emotion from another—"A time to weep, and a time to laugh." The author quickly adds that sorrow is better than laughter and even dismisses laughter as madness. No time is appropriate for simultaneous weeping and laughing, for the tears of intense happiness and joy. In Eternity, we might assume, there is no chronograph: Everything happens at once. Everything is timely. Separation does not exist.

inable—his own breath—by uttering his own ineffable name, and then ensured the integrity of the sky by appointing an angel to act as *shamas*, a perpetual guardian of the sky.* The separation of the waters represents the most crucial moment in Creation, for only after the waters had been parted could God set out to create the earth and its inhabitants. The rest of Creation depended on the outcome of that day's events. Curiously enough, God's work is not all that secure. For whenever a Jew curses, he or she causes a tear in God's mantle, thus threatening to flood all of Creation. When that happens, the guardian angel stands ready to repair it. Thank God.**

The end of the story obviously warns against cursing and returning all of Creation back to its humorous state. In broader terms, the story is a warning to keep our emotions in check, not to fall into excess. It speaks of obedience and, in particular, of slippery things knowing their place and holding fast to it. When we take these lessons to heart and view ourselves as a microcosm of Creation, then in moments of intensity we experience the waters undivided. The Second Day holds the secret to our civilized selves (dams and definitions) and the secret to our wilder side (damns and downpours).

*Given the root meaning of *shed*, SKEI-, we might more accurately say the waters above were shed from the waters below, that is, "cut away." Compare the German *Wasserscheide*, "watershed," in use since the fourteenth century to designate the line where a body of water divides into two streams.

**The male waters reside above, the female waters below. Periodically, rain falls, the waters embrace once again, the earth becomes impregnated, and a harvest follows. To damn God causes the dam that holds the waters apart to burst, a biblical reminder that the two words, *damn* and *dam*, are etymologically related, both born from the Teutonic *dampne*, "to punish, to stop, to prevent."

Hasidic Jews immerse themselves in a ritual bath, called the *mikvah*, for purification. The water for that bath must come from rainwater, because traditionally all water on earth emanates from the primordial river in Eden. Rainwater most nearly approaches the undivided waters because it is collected and mixed in heaven. Similarly, amniotic fluid is undivided: The baby in its mother's womb rests in absolutely pure liquid.

# The Ancient World:

## *divine origins of laughter*

*At* first glance, laughter in the ancient world does not look much different from laughter in the Bible. In both worlds, joyous laughter descends as a divine gift from the gods. Like the Old Testament God, the Greek gods also express profound displeasure through powerful and searing laughter. But there the similarity ends. For instance, in connection with laughter of any sort, joyous or caustic, women no longer play the prominent role. One quickly realizes that in Genesis Sarah may only be a vestige, a hint of a gendered reality that perhaps once characterized laughter in the Hebrew world. Whatever the case, by the time we reach ancient Greece, woman's presence has been entirely transformed. No longer does she deliver laughter to humankind; that is, she no longer acts as a mediator between God and mortals. She has been reduced to a punch line, at best, in the story of Prometheus and laughter, the kicker to a practical joke in the form of Pandora—woman as victim or victimizer. Laughter has been taken over by men—analyzed, shaped, directed, and regulated, like some precious commodity, and handed back to society as a set of rhetorical rules. Learn to use laughter as a weapon, the rhetoricians argue, and in so doing behave like gods. But this advice applies to men only—and only to those who live in the upper reaches of society. Peasants and women must find a more subversive route to godlike power.

Historically, that's what happens. Carnival, festival, charivari—folk celebrations of all kinds—have to be seen as the underground reaction set into motion in early modern Europe by centuries of domination by an aristocratic, highly literate class; they have to be felt as an entire peasant population trying to tunnel up from underground, like the great wooly mammoth I mentioned in the Introduction, to breathe fresh air, trying to assert their essential humanity by flipping the world of power and domination topsy-turvy through laughter. This particular phase of ludic history presents us with an obvious lesson: Laughter simply will not be suppressed. Try to push it down, restrain it, and it will follow the laws of hydraulics—contained in one spot, laughter will force itself up even more violently in three other, weaker spots. The result: a Keystone Kops scene of confusion and pandemonium, the world running loosely out of order.

For several reasons, these eruptions occur most dramatically when the leaders of folk celebrations turn out to be women. Women already so victimized that they stand ready to upset the social order in the name of justice, women who seem to sense that their risible birthright has been snatched from them, wait expectantly for a shot at subversion that only carnival offers them. By the fifteenth century, women were participating in a huge number of topsy-turvy festivals. The historian Natalie Zemon Davis offers a brief description of some of them in her essay entitled "Women on Top":

> Some May customs that were still current in early modern Europe, however, point back to a rowdier role for women. In rural Franche-Comté during May, wives could take revenge on their husbands for beating them by ducking the men or making them ride on an ass; wives could dance, jump, and banquet freely without permission from their husbands; and women's courts issued mock decrees. (In nearby Dijon by the sixteenth century, interestingly enough, Mère Folle and her Infanterie had usurped

this revenge from women; May was the one month of the year when the Misrule Abbey would charivari a man who had beaten his wife.) Generally, May—Flora's month in Roman times—was thought to be a period in which women were powerful, their desires at their most immoderate. As the old saying went, a May bride would keep her husband in yoke all year round. And in fact marriages were not frequent in May.*

I spend some time here on peasants and particularly on women because they offer us important clues for reading history. They argue for reading at the edges of the historical evidence, for reading as if something had gone mightily wrong, for sniffing around as if something did not smell right. As readers of history, we usually get to hear one voice only, the one in control. To hear the rumblings of peasants and women as they attempt to become somebodies, readers must begin to press their ears firmly to the page. Like cream, power rises, quite dramatically, to the top. And that's the level at which we most often read. But those in power know they must constantly look over their shoulders, for the underclass might just take it in their heads to rise, too, not by flexing political muscle, but through sheer exuberance and exhilaration—by dint of their own laughter. If the state is to be run effectively and efficiently, however, the folk must know their place. Otherwise, when the body politic finds something funny, great groundswells of raucous laughter wash everything clean. The ancient world made the first serious, well-articulated attempt at controlling laughter.

Aristotle invented the idea of the body.** He implies that the body is a consortium of different parts that organizes itself only through laughter, the earliest and most wholesome instance, surely, of an act of incorporation. How could anything be more important, this breath that makes us whole? While the ancients agree on the importance of the laugh, they differ on just

*Natalie Zemon Davis, "Women on Top," in *Society and Culture in Early Modern France* (Palo Alto: Stanford University Press, 1975), p. 141.

**Bruno Snell, in *The Discovery of the Mind: The Greek Origin of European Thought* (Oxford: Blackwell, 1953), discusses the absence of any contemporary notion of body in Homer. Homer merely uses words for various limbs that attach themselves to a central stalk, not unlike a kid's stick figure. Any history of the body must take Aristotle's *De partibus animalium* and the *Historia animalium* as a starting point for the description of the body's mazy interior.

when the newborn utters its first one. For Hippocrates, that incarnating laugh occurred as the infant dropped off into its first sleep; others believed the infant laughed as it awakened from that same, initial slumber. Pliny the Elder settled on the fourth day of life for the inspiration of laughter. But Aristotle's dating became standard.

Aristotle tells us, in the *De partibus animalium*, that the newborn does not laugh while awake until the fortieth day of its life, a moment that sounds like the biblical description of the second day of Creation, with its notion of upper and lower regions separated by a thin shard, and a divine breath heaving the whole enterprise into being. In Aristotle's biology, the *diazoma* or *phrenes*, a kind of membrane, separates the upper area (lungs and heart) from the lower (kidneys and spleen). The sensory soul lies cradled in the upper area. Whenever heated air reaches the crucial upper region, it affects the intelligence and sensation of the sensory soul with a "recognizable disturbance," causing what we today would call an "awareness." Warm air most quickly and easily reaches the soul through laughter, producing a "movement in the intelligence which is recognizable."

Only laughter possesses this singular ability to animate the soul, and it separates human beings so conclusively from the rest of the animals that Aristotle chose to refer to us creatures as *animal ridens*, "the beast who laughs." (Belief in an *animal ridens* is also supported by Galen and Porphyry.) Thus, for Aristotle, the infant miraculously and resoundingly becomes human only on the fortieth day. From that quaking instant on, we have a frame on which to hang the entire course of the history of the body.*

Whether we laugh on the fourth or the fortieth day, during sleep or upon waking from it, for Choricus and other ancient poets one thing remains certain: Laughter has been bestowed on humans as a divine activity, an animating fire that did not have to be stolen through some Promethean sleight

*The idea of the body will reach its first, major stage of enfleshment in Chaucer's invention of the modern joke, where body bulk—comprising both exterior surface and interior space—assumes new and important status.

of hand. The gods gave it freely and liberally. The Greek gods laughed more easily and frequently than the Hebrew God; indeed, hearty laughter at birth signified an infant's divine character. Pliny the Elder notes that Zoroaster laughed out loud at birth, a precocious self-annunciation that he had been born a god. The intensity of his laughter caused his brain to throb so violently that anyone placing a hand on his head would have it immediately bounced off—thus foretelling in risible deed Zoroaster's destiny as one of the elect.

Since laughter marked animals as human and the gods as divine, each time a person laughed he or she reforged that connection: strong incentive to be gay and jolly. Unlike the Hebrews, the Greeks did not have to wait for God's grace to bless them with the gift of joyous laughter. The Greek gods handed down laughter democratically to everyone, which created a bridge, built out of laughter, to shuttle mortals back and forth between earth and Mount Olympus. Several Greeks even made their idiosyncratic natures known simply by refusing to laugh. Pliny gives their "blasphemous" obstinacy a name, *agelastus*, "without laughter," and cites a well-known, contemporary example of absolute sobriety: Crassus, grandfather of the Crassus slain in the war against the Parthians. *Agelastes* all wear a forbiddingly sad face, and at times allow their souls to fill with such despair they can only be described as melancholics.* Leaden, cold, and damp, melancholics lack invigorating and integrating fire. They fall far short of becoming human beings.

*Agelastes* continue into the modern period. The Czech writer Milan Kundera, casting Aristotle into a more modern idiom, argues that those who cannot laugh can never reach individuation. The *agelaste* does not know that life is too important to take seriously; he or she has lost *tact* and so remains out of gentle and playful *touch* with reality: "No peace is possi-

*Austerity is quite different from *agelastus*. For Aristotle and Aquinas, austerity is a positive virtue that marks the foundation of friendship. In the *Summa Theologica*, in the 186th question, article 5, Thomas indicates that austerity excludes all enjoyments that distract from or destroy personal relations. For Thomas, austerity is a complementary virtue to true friendship or joyfulness. This joyfulness in personal relations Aquinas calls *eutrapelia*, "graceful playfulness."

ble between the novelist and the *agelaste*. Never having heard God's laughter, the *agelastes* are convinced that the truth is obvious, that all men necessarily think the same thing. . . . But it is precisely in losing the certainty of truth and unanimous consent of others that man becomes an individual."*

Greek gods love to love and frolic and quarrel, and so they of course laugh. They laugh at each other, and they laugh heartily at the foibles of the mortals. While the Hebrews sought love and election from their God, the Greeks desired something more personal—abundance and joyful friendship. They could ensure the first by communing with the spirit of the gods through sacrificial rites. They could also join them through friendship marked by *eutrapelia*, by spirited but tempered laughter.

From the time of Homer, the Greeks used two words for "true and joyous laughter," *gelao* and *gelos*.** While it is a prime characteristic of the heavenly deity, *gelao* does not confine itself to Olympus, but spreads throughout the rest of the world, infecting every person. So, for example, Gerhard Kittel glosses the reference to *gelao* at the coronation of Hadrian to mean that the new king had ushered in an age of joy. While joyous laughter is associated with light and air, caustic laughter, which will receive most of the attention in the history of laughter as shaped and disseminated in literacy, is associated with fire. Homer even reserves a special adjective for derisive laughter, *asbestos*, "unquenchable," for it behaves like the highest of the four elements, fire, burning with such intensity that nothing can extinguish it—a most powerful weapon! While joyous laughter is described with adjectives like "hearty" or "raucous," vaguely recalling origin or sound, caustic laughter remains firmly attached to tempers, temperature, and heat—attacks that sear with the heat of hell. In one of its earliest senses, *caustic* refers to anything hot enough to burn human tissues.

Since flames keep ascending skyward until they pass out of view, fire

*Nan Robertson, "Milan Kundera Accepts the Jerusalem Prize," *New York Times*, May 10, 1985, p. 24.

**Unlike English, Greek has the capacity to indicate hearty laughter in one word, *kaiagelao*.

provides a compelling image in many cultures of the connection between earthly existence and the heavens. (The Greek gods originally owned fire, so the opposite connection can be made—from heaven down to earth and back up to heaven again.) Fire also helps to illuminate the nature of laughter. Like water, fire can both destroy and purify—sometimes, purification arising, like a phoenix, *only* out of the ashes of destruction. But even when it does destroy, it always illuminates. The figures of Prometheus and Hephaistos, both of whom have fallen from heaven, have probably the strongest affinities with fire in all of classical mythology; not coincidentally, they are also crucial characters in the history of laughter. Hephaistos and Prometheus possess complicated natures. Both of them are thieves and tricksters, as well as artisans who can delight by fabricating and transforming—both materials *and* themselves—characters well suited to bringing laughter into play, particularly since the Greek philosophers themselves stole laughter and made it serve their own purposes. The histories of these two characters are told in two separate stories, one by Homer and the other by Hesiod. I want to look first at the tale of Hephaistos, as narrated by Homer.

The first laugh recorded in Western literature occurs, under fairly odd circumstances, in book 1 of the *Iliad*. Hephaistos, the god of fire and the crafts, fabricates a set of beautiful serving cups and fills each one to the brim with wine. Balancing them delicately on a serving tray, which he has also hammered out of a sheet of metal, he offers the entire gift with great pride to the assembled gods. But Hephaistos walks with an ungainly gait.* Tossed out of the heavens, he had injured his leg when he landed on the island of Lemnos—and so he ambles along awkwardly, spilling wine all over himself with each painful step he manages. At the sight of that ludicrous creature, the gods break out in "unquenchable laughter," turning Hephaistos into such an object of ridicule that he skulks off and hides, too embarrassed to show his face:

*In simple terms, Hephaistos is lame. Initially, lameness referred to any infirmity, but particularly to weak-wittedness; a *lummel* meant someone slow-witted, a "blockhead" (compare "lummox"). It also referred to a halting meter in poetry. When we say today that a joke sounds lame, we refer both to its lack of wit and to its miscues in rhythm.

—and the goddess, white-armed Hera,
smiling took the winecup from his hand.
Then, dipping from the winebowl, round he went
from left to right, serving the other gods
nectar of sweet delight.
And quenchless laughter
broke out among the blissful gods
to see Hephaistos wheezing down the hall.
So all day long until the sun went down
they spent in feasting, and the measured feast
matched well their hearts' desire.
So did the flawless harp held by Apollo
and heavenly songs in choiring antiphon
that all the Muses sang.* (ll. 590–603)

Homer sets Hephaistos' clumsy missteps into bold relief by referring to the gods' "measured feast," to Apollo's "flawless harp," and to the "songs" and "choiring antiphon" sung by the Muses. This incident closes book I, the end to the poet's breath for the moment, a pause in the cosmic guffawing—but not without a compliment of sorts to Hephaistos:

And when the shining
sun of day sank in the west, they turned
homeward each one to rest, each to that home
the bandy-legged wondrous artisan
Hephaistos fashioned for them with his craft.
The lord of storm and lightning, Zeus, retired
and shut his eyes where sweet sleep ever came to him,
and at his side lay Hera, Goddess of the Golden Chair. (ll. 604–11)

The musical references suggest that Hephaistos is more than physically lame: He stands incomplete, incapable of harmonious joy. Barred from heaven, he can no longer work passionately and creatively with heavenly fire; he cannot hammer rhythmically. Instead, he must labor painstakingly

*The *OED* confers on this episode its highest honor by placing it in its own category, "Homeric laughter" (The same holds true for the *Odyssey* 20.346). Notice that the translator, Robert Fitzgerald, has Hephaistos "wheezing" his way down the hall, connecting a shortness of leg with a shortness of breath. In nineteenth-century theater slang, a *wheeze* was a joke or comic *gag*, as the *OED* defines it, "a catch phrase constantly repeated."

at the earthly forge like other artisans. His life encapsulates the history of laughter. Joyous laughter has been snatched away from him—from the man who knows fire so intimately—shaped into a caustic weapon by the gods, and thrown back into his face as ridicule. Since Hephaistos cannot keep his balance anyway, the gods have an easy time with him (in that musical sense of measured time), knocking him down. If only Hephaistos could see that the gods have presented him with a test: He can never be regarded as healthy unless he can withstand the ridicule, by joining with the gods in their raucous laughter. In short, he must laugh the attack off. He must allow the caustic laughter to cauterize his wounds. Then the gods might choose to see him as hearty and healthy, that is, as a whole person. Hephaistos does not know it now, but the gods have a trick or two up their sleeves for him.

The gods turn to craft in their desire to reshape Hephaistos, and they do it by co-opting his own element, fire—the fire of their laughter. At the moment, however, he can neither physically nor metaphorically stand up to their abuse. They have him way off balance, his lameness handicapping him in the most profound, spiritual way. But the gods hold out hope.*

In the *Works and Days*, Hesiod tells his story of sardonic laughter. Prometheus, a descendant of the original Titans, stole fire from the gods through a trick and gave it to mortals; Zeus then stole it back, hatching an even more diabolical trick to get even with him. When the gods drag Prometheus away to face his punishment, his stupid brother, Epimetheus, takes his place as representative of all humankind.** In his thoughtlessness (and naiveté), he accepts a gift as an apology from the gods—Pandora and her jar, in which resides the entirety of humanity's miseries. Hesiod explains that Zeus, who could foresee the long list of woes that this gift would ultimately generate,

*Hephaistos' birth, like Isaac's in the Hebrew tradition, belongs in a special category: Hera, the wife of Zeus, grows angry with Zeus and conceives Hephaistos without the aid of her husband—a kind of virgin birth.

**According to Carl Kerényi, *The Religion of the Greeks and Romans* (New York: E. P. Dutton, 1962), Hesiod presents Prometheus and Epimetheus as brothers because the two aspects of their personalities were once contained in one person.

laughed out loud in satisfaction at a practical joke brilliantly conceived and beautifully hatched.

We might be expected to believe, out of common sense, or just plain intuition, that the first laugh recorded in the West would spring from feelings of joy. But as I have indicated, it is not born of rejoicing with the gods or from sheer pleasure in life. It reverberates throughout classical Greece as a loud laugh of derision and ridicule. Even though the first laugh in English does emanate from joy, it is all too short-lived. That laugh occurs in the seventh-century epic *Beowulf*. A group of warriors, celebrating a recent victory over their enemy, fills the great Hall of Heorot with their rowdy, bold-spirited laughter. The noise drifts slowly out across the open fields where Grendel, the evil monster, hears every bit of the commotion. Envious of those happy humans, Grendel rushes the hall, snatches the best, most courageous warriors, and carries them off to his underwater home, where he devours the lot of them. Joy immediately turns to sorrow: Heorot fills with sounds of keening—deep, dispirited wailing—and weeping.*

The laughter in *Beowulf*, while not scornful, certainly hits the reader with all its irony. One must always be on guard. One's happiness can always be quickly snatched away. Even in Anglo-Saxon England, laughter tempts fate, and one must be prepared to pay the price. God always has the final laugh. Godlike superiority gives laughter its strongest, most characteristic feature, for the majority of all recorded laughter has been filled with a scorn that sears. Almost all of it arises out of envy, as we will see, out of the desire of one person—or one monster—to get even, ironically, by rising above the rest of the crowd.

Scornful laughter holds much more potential for dramatic action than joyous laughter, primarily because it wells up out of a deep-seated

*The first mention of the word *laughter* in English occurs in King Alfred's ninth-century translation of Pope Gregory the Great's *Pastoral Care*, which Gregory wrote shortly after becoming pope, probably in 591. Gregory meant the book, which deals with the "cure of souls," as a guide for his bishops, and through them for priests in general. Alfred used it, too, to educate and instruct—a handbook for moral behavior. The line about laughter derives its wisdom from Ecclesiastes—laughing now only brings tears later—"Wa eow ðe nu hliehað forðan ȝe sculon wepan." That sentiment, in its ultimate effect, gets played out in *Beowulf*.

*agon*—a contest of wills—and creates the right conditions for pain and thus the possibility of change. It has to, for people react strongly to scorn and criticism. No one can remain neutral in the face of derision, for scornful laughter always conveys an arrogance of the heart, an announcement that the laugher thinks he or she stands much higher than anyone else on the social scale. The scornful laughter plays the ultimate role—God. Meanwhile, those victimized by scornful laughter fight like hell to get even, and the war is on! How will the battle resolve itself? An audience gathers around just dying to find out, for there are emotional lives hanging in the balance. Ego pits itself against ego. So while joyous laughter does not simply drop out of the history of laughter, it must struggle mightily against the overwhelming authority of derision to stay alive. Derisive laughter clearly dominates. In the history of laughter, Abraham constantly offers Isaac up for sacrifice. Sarah waits expectantly in the background.

Throughout time, laughter never shakes its dual character; it is always associated with both the devilish and the angelic, with both the positive and the negative. The critical separation of the Second Day never touches laughter. Laughter can produce tears and smiles at the same time. Even in the contemporary period, the novelist who probably knows more about laughter and who plays with it more than any other writer, Milan Kundera, dramatizes laughter's inherent ambiguity. Kundera, however, cannot resist playing himself, and so he inverts laughter's origins, laying it in the lap of the devil:

> Things deprived of their putative meaning, the place assigned to them in the ostensible order of things . . . make us laugh. Initially, therefore, laughter is the province of the Devil. . . . The first time an angel heard the Devil's laughter, he was horrified. It was in the middle of a feast with a lot of people around, and one after the other they joined in the Devil's laughter. It was terribly contagious. The angel was all too aware the laughter was aimed against God and the wonder of His works. He knew he had to act fast, but felt weak and defenseless. And unable to fabricate anything of his own, he simply turned his enemy's tactics against him. He opened his mouth and let out a wobbly, breathy sound in the upper reaches of his vocal register . . . and endowed it with the opposite meaning.

Whereas the Devil's laughter pointed up the meaninglessness of things, the angel's shout rejoiced in how rationally organized, well conceived, beautiful, good, and sensible everything on earth was.*

In a sentence, Kundera says it all—the angel "simply turned his enemy's tactics against him." And the battle continues.

Tremendous power resides in a single scornful laugh. Who in his or her right mind has not at one time or another fired off a well-aimed derisive shot at an unsuspecting target, and not experienced great joy in slowly squeezing the trigger? One gets to be the judge and jury, meting out punishment to every offender. The history of laughter is in part the history of those in various positions of authority—philosophers, writers, politicians—trying to harness and shape that power, just as technicians succeeded in harnessing the cosmic forces of wind and water. Those who desire control will try to grab hold of power wherever they can find it—even in something as elusive as laughter. But laughter proves difficult if not impossible to corral, for it behaves in such an unruly fashion. Slowly, though, the possibilities present themselves, and by the late Middle Ages derisive humor has been shaped into what we know as the aggressive joke, complete with "punch" line. By the time of the Renaissance, scornful laughter is put to practical use by the royal court in public forms of humiliating punishment.

From the beginning, the church stood in firm opposition to laughter. After all, lowly peasants just might learn to fear a scoffing laugh as much as the divine Word. Or worse yet, they might organize and launch their own scoffing attacks—and feel as powerful as God. Scornful laughter could turn every peasant into a self-styled vigilante—no horse to buy, no gun to own, no armor to wear—Everyman with a license to kill! Not even the most marginalized peasant would willingly give up such a shot at power. But that gets ahead of the story. We first need to complete the ancient history, and then

*Milan Kundera, *The Book of Laughter and Forgetting* (New York: Alfred A. Knopf, 1981), pp. 61–62.

focus on the Greek philosophers as their ideas pass into the hands of the Roman rhetoricians. Then we can look at the church's reaction and the whole range of insubordinate responses that well out of the spirit of revolt.

To return to the stories of Hephaistos and Prometheus, the two vignettes have much in common. Both stories of course use fire as their controlling figure: Hephaistos manipulated it as a smithy at the forge; Prometheus stole it from the gods. Each longs to master this elusive element that behaves so much like quicksilver. But Hephaistos and Prometheus find themselves victimized in a struggle that involves fire: Both play with fire and eventually get burned by it. Hephaistos is temporarily banished from working with heavenly fire, and Prometheus has fire snatched out of his hand by the chief god of the heavenly pantheon, Zeus. Both characters end up being derided for their handicaps—in one case, the handicap takes a physical form, and in the other is revealed in a brutal foolishness, a mental imbalance. If we think here of the poetics or mythology of fire, these two figures spark or ignite excitement because they both belong to the family of craftsmen or tricksters—supposedly clever and skillful, but not skillful enough. The result is their own undoing—lameness and stupidity—reducing them to objects of pity and derision.

Finally, and what is crucial for the history of laughter, both Prometheus and Hephaistos act like Titans. A Titan's basic nature tends toward quarrelsomeness, preferring the complicated and baroque solution, the knotty and convoluted, to the simple and direct. The object of Titanic intelligence, as Kerényi points out, is always invention, "even if only an artful lie, a deception which the gods themselves admire and are enticed by."* A Titan will pull you out of time, or out of line, through wit and playfulness. Prometheus is a Titan by birth. Hephaistos, an Olympian, has fallen into the character of a Titan; his lameness results from leaping into a quarrel and siding with his mother in a domestic argument high on Olympus. He shows

*Kerényi, *The Religion of the Greeks and Romans*, p. 89.

his Titanic nature through his wondrous ability to forge: As a metalsmith, he makes cups and trays—articles of pleasure.* He knows how to turn something solid into a substance malleable enough to shape through hammering, and then how to harden it once more; he knows how to make something out of nothing, how to give it a beautiful form and a proper temper. His work is a thing of beauty, as well as a lesson for anyone who watches. But he has not internalized the process: He cannot take the heat. Thus, he lacks definite shape and wants for flexibility. To get there, he must learn to apply his craft in a much more reflexive, and a much more social, way.

Having laughed at Hephaistos earlier, Zeus makes amends by teaching him how to forge the perfect practical joke. True to his craft, Hephaistos uses the forge to weave an indestructible metal net, like a mighty spider, to ensnare his wife, Aphrodite, and her lover, Ares, exposing them in *flagrante delicto*, to the great delight of the eavesdropping gods.** Having had fire used against him, he has at least learned one lesson well: He won't get burned again! Hephaistos catches on to this lesson so quickly because he thinks like a plotting, crafty Titan. But his biographers never picture him as laughing out loud in joy, only as acting in a clever manner, a side he displays best by playing the vengeful practical joker. Indeed, he puts his education to practical use, proving that sardonic laughter—ridicule—can serve as a tough but effective teacher. Hephaistos turns the tables on the gods and makes them laugh out loud:

> [Ares'] shouts brought the gods trooping to the house with the bronze floor. Up came Poseidon the Earthshaker; Hermes, the bringer of luck; and the archer king, Apollo; but the goddesses, constrained by feminine modesty, all stayed at home. There they stood, then, in front of the doors,

*Daedalus, too, works as a metalsmith. James Joyce uses him as a model of the writer, the divine dissembler, or as Joyce says, "the artificer." When we tell stories or jokes, we "forge" a new reality.

**In some African cultures, and in some American Indian tribes, the symbol for the trickster is the spider. The name for trickster among the Oglala Dakota tribe, in fact, means "spider." Tricksters not only spin out practical jokes to trap their victims, they weave intricate plots to capture the imagination in amusing, clever stories. The spider weaves the warp and woof of its enticing yarns in the form of a sticky net. One must proceed with caution, for the web remains largely invisible to the inattentive eye.

the immortals who are the source of all our blessings; and when they caught sight of Hephaistos' clever device a fit of uncontrollable laughter seized these happy gods. (Book VIII, ll. 321–27)*

In this incipient stage, caustic laughter, like its partner joyful laughter, is also a heavenly quality. Fire stands as its appropriate symbol, for fire marks the difference, to use Levi-Strauss's dichotomy, between the raw and the cooked. That is, it creates cuisine and thus symbolizes humankind's urge toward civilization. A caustic sentence "cooks" a person, forcing that unsuspecting victim into maturity and ripeness. Getting hot under the collar often prepares the way for important insights. To find ways of getting out of hot water can have a salutary effect. A person can make serious choices, can discover, in effect, how to turn irritation into victory. So many cultures treat fire as a precious commodity, and do not pass it around easily or willingly. To possess it demands a quick wit and fast feet. It must either be stolen in a fennel stalk by a trickster like Prometheus, or imprisoned in a forge by a crafty metalsmith like Hephaistos.** One has to wonder, at this point, just what Prometheus has stolen: Is it fire solely, or fiery laughter?

As Hesiod and Homer both demonstrate, caustic laughter grows out of heat and conflict and struggle, which makes it an ideal motivating force for those battles of the soul that take place between the covers of fiction. Joyful laughter might permeate an entire story, or even an entire novel, it might even inform a saintly life like that of Saint Francis, but it cannot provide the fuel for high drama. High-flying, joyful humor signals conversion; it announces that the battle has been won, that victory is in hand. This is fine stuff, but as we've seen it simply does not make for the most interesting stories.

The first laugh in Western literature, then, had to be one of derision,

*Homer, *The Odyssey*, trans. E. V. Rieu (New York: Penguin Books, 1946). This episode, so filled with charm and guile, inspired paintings by Titian and Tintoretto, as well as an Iris Murdoch novel, appropriately titled *Under the Net*.

**". . . fire is the material basis of civilization. According to varying ancient versions, Prometheus stole it by applying a torch to the Sun's wheel, or by robbing the forge of Hephaistos. The giant fennel in which he carried the flame is a stalk about five feet high filled with a dry white pith like a wick, which is still used in parts of Greece to transport fire" (Michael Grant, *Myths of the Greeks and Romans* [New York: New American Library, 1962], p. 108).

since it so decidedly plunges characters into lamentable situations, preventing them, as the word *de-rision* implies, from rising above problems, forcing them, like Stephen Daedalus, to forge their lives in the "smithy of the soul." The smith, a lifelong intimate of fire, is accustomed to resistance and, by learning to apply the right degree of heat, is able to bend things to his or her will. Out of that struggle, as if mirroring divine creation, the smith manages to create something beautiful and useful, knowing that, in order for objects to hold their beauty forever, they must be infused with an even temper—merging intense heat with extreme cold, joining opposites. Like a fiction writer, whose subject is untruth—the believable, seamless lie—the smith is a crafty artist.*

The stories told by Hesiod and Homer resound with meaning. Like fire, the gods' sardonic laughter attempts to consume or purify Titanic seriousness and self-importance and to set petty quarrels into proper perspective. One question will remain a central concern for the Greeks: How to leaven high seriousness with just the right amount of laughter? The right recipe—just how much heat to apply—is what they aim for. But more important, the Greeks struggle with limiting the power of *asbestos* laughter, for it has the character of a *pharmakon*, a drug, which, like all drugs, has the capacity both for healing and for destroying. And, as with every potent drug, dosage is extremely critical. At this point, the rhetoricians have not yet taken laughter over—that is, brought it down from its heavenly heights—and so, for the moment, Zeus still occupies the all-powerful position, legislating through his supremely arch, sardonic laughter. He reigns as the supreme embodiment of Greek laughter.

But Zeus' sardonic laughter is radically different from the Hebrew God's. While it may seem destructive, as Kerényi observes, "nobody dies *of it*." Zeus laughs but he is concerned solely with destroying Titanic self-importance, so whatever wounds he inflicts result in a restorative, meta-

*In Middle English, *craeft* means "strength, skill, power." Likewise, *cunning* derives from Old English *cunnan*, "to know (how)." *Wit*, too, from Old English *witan*, means "to know (how)."

phoric death. He aims to purify. Before the angry Jehovah, however, all of humankind, in Abraham's words, will find themselves reduced to "dirt and ashes" (Deut. 4:24: "For the Lord thy God is a consuming fire"). When the Lord unleashed his vengeful fire, recall, he decimated all of Sodom in a flash. "Before Zeus, the laughing onlooker," Kerényi concludes, "the eternal human race plays its eternal human comedy."* Act too highfalutin and feel the purifying sting of Zeus' fiery tongue. But act out in front of the Hebrew God and you are liable to find yourself a human inferno. The choice seems rather clear: humiliation or immolation.

Zeus breathes fire; Prometheus steals it; Hephaistos manipulates it. All three know intimately the power and importance of hot stuff. But Hephaistos, in particular, knows that special art of imparting flexibility and strength through tempering (even though he himself may not have taken that lesson to heart). Hephaistos has lived in heaven and on earth; he knows the gods and mortals alike. He has visited both sides of Creation. Moreover, he provides laughter's key link with ancient medicine, for early Greek medicine exploited the connection between fire and caustic laughter and tried in the healing process to bring people back to an even temper. Miletus, for example, a fourth-century A.D. doctor, makes the correspondence quite specific in his *On Human Nature*: "Laughter is called *gelos* by the Greeks, and *gelos* comes from *hele*, which means health. For those who are hot are considered to be very inclined to laugh. And . . . *haema* (which signifies *blood*) is said to be from *aetho* which means 'I am burning.' For it is the hottest of all the humours made in our body; and those in whom blood abounds, their mind is more joyous."** Likewise, Hippocrates explains the four elements,

*Kerényi, *The Religion of the Greeks and Romans*, p. 195. Kerényi argues that Zeus' malicious laughter at the end of his quarrel with Prometheus, recounted in the *Works and Days*, is not a classical response from the god.

**Whether or not Chaucer knew Greek medical theories, he exploits the connection between fire and laughter, utilizing it for comic effect in "The Miller's Tale." That laughter sprang from fire permitted the church to doubly condemn a hearty laugh, for fire was also home to the devil. Chaucer hints at these devilish connections as well in "The Miller's Tale," a subject I take up later in this book.

in his *De humoribus*, by drawing correspondences with the four humors. Blood corresponds with purifying fire, and purified blood, he indicates, produces great laughers, easily spotted by their ruddy complexions.

While blood engendered laughter, the later Greeks generally considered laughter's invigorating source to be located within the spleen. The idea increased in popularity in Roman antiquity: "Splen ridere facit, cogit amare re cur" (Laughter is made by the spleen, and love in the liver). The Greeks believed that those who have their spleens removed find it impossible to laugh. Pliny attributes playfulness to the size of the spleen, for the spleen feeds on thick, black blood, he maintains, the kind of blood that usually engenders the disease of *melancholia*. In this period of Greek medicine, which became quite mechanical, the spleen acted as the great filtering engine of the body. It rendered the blackest, nastiest blood pure enough to bubble once more with laughter. Early medieval encyclopedists, such as Isidore of Seville and Bartholomew of Anglicus, also point to the spleen as the organ that sponsors laughter. Bartholomew, in book 7 of his *De proprietatibus rerum*, divides the inner organs into four physiological functions: "Some men ween, that the milt is cause of laughing. For by the spleen we are moved to laugh, by the gall we are wroth, by the heart we are wise, and by the liver we love." Medieval poets, far removed from medicine, such as John Gower and John of Trevisa, saw the spleen "as the cause of laughing."*

To judge by a Doctor William Stukely, who wrote a medical history entitled *Of the Spleen: Its Description and History*, in 1720, the idea that the spleen could cleanse the body of melancholia kept its hold on the imagination of medical science well into the eighteenth century: "As the vein was to draw or convey this melancholy to the spleen, the artery by fresh streams of blood coming to it in so plentiful a manner was by degrees to concoct and clarifie it therein till at length it was fit to be admitted into the mass again.... As the *atra bilis* created anger and melancholy, so the spleen

*We cannot know for certain whether medieval thinkers were referring to what the Greeks called the spleen, but we can still watch as the organ gets socially constructed over time.

which was to purge it off render'd us cheerful and alert."* By the middle of the eighteenth century, however, novelists had begun sabotaging the smooth-working machine called the spleen. If they could make it fail, they knew they could create interesting characters. These characters, unbalanced by an excess of thick blood—and so truly "humorous," even "ill-humored"—populate literature as the first eccentric literary creations. In writers as disparate as Swift and Dickens, these characters emphasized a new kind of humor, more biting and aggravated than the old melancholic form, so obviously controlled by the inner workings of the human body that it was given a new name in the eighteenth century: *splenetic*.**

While Greek medicine offered a mechanical explanation for the production of caustic laughter, the Greek rhetoricians knew that the effect of the spleen could be artfully recreated, cultivated, and learned through a careful exercise of the wit. Through crafty artifice and training, a person could assume the power of Zeus himself. We must understand this as a significant moment. It means that without holding high public office a person could assume and exercise power, with the simplest tool at hand—the human voice. More pointedly, at this point in history, humor reveals itself as one of the swiftest routes to power. By sharpening one's wit at the whetstone of rhetoric, a person could take command over his or her immediate world.

This new creature, fabricated out of laughter, would soon dominate the stage as well as the page. The Greeks called him the jester (although there were exceptions, as we will see, most fools were men). The name

*Shakespeare treats the spleen as if it were the most human of the organs: "Angels, who with our spleens, would all themselves laugh mortal" (*Measure for Measure*, 2.2.123).

**According to the *OED*, the word *caustic*, as an adjective to describe wit, enters English around this time, roughly 1717, in Tobias Smollet's *Humphrey Clinker*. A *clinker*, a brick exposed to such intense heat in the oven it vitrifies out of shape, recalls the fiery origins of derisive laughter. Humphrey Clinker takes on his quirky character through a corrosive wit and because of it faces the world rock solid. While not in common use until the eighteenth century, the word *splenetic* first appears in the work of an English writer, Gabriel Harvey, sometime tutor to Edmund Spenser: "I was never so splenetique as when I was most dumpish but I could smile at a prize jest." A person down in the dumps, as Harvey claims he was, has actually derided himself. He must try to climb out of his "depression." To that end, a jest can be uplifting.

should not mislead us: The jester may have played the fool, but he fell far short of being a fool. Moving center stage, he spoke with authority and, more important, with frightening outbursts of power. He is the forefather of the court jester who begins to appear in the Renaissance. The sayings of Cleobolis, one of the so-called Seven Wise Men, who wrote before the Pre-Socratics, warned of the jester's penetrating wit: "Do not laugh at the jester, for you will be hated by those who are ridiculed." For the jester can retaliate as effectively as a flamethrower, not just by venting his anger, but by carefully aiming it, perhaps at the most vulnerable, or the most handy, target, namely, the person who has stumbled, or worse yet, the one who stands precariously off balance. The jester attempts to educate and purify with his fiery tongue. He does not set out simply to punish. For that reason, Chilon, another of the Seven Wise Men, would have only the most gentle, good-natured of people resort to jesting: "If you are by nature harsh," he advises, "endeavor to be gentle, that men may feel shame before you rather than fear." Harsh natures—due to weak spleens—produce particularly nasty jesters. Over the years, the Greeks sharply distinguish between this brand of nasty jesting, which they condemn and call illiberal, and a more proper, dignified, and cultivated form, which they call liberal jesting, available only to those who can take advantage of the teachings of the rhetoricians. And so the jester becomes a force to be reckoned with in the ancient world—a teacher and a judge—and the way he metes out justice can be seen as an articulation, however pale, of ancient Greek religion. Indeed, the philosophers single out liberal jesting as a goal of the ideal life.

Very early in Greece's philosophical traditions, the justification for engaging in jesting of any sort was seen to reside in the achievement of the central goal of the ideal life, the Mean—the balance point between two extremes, or between two emotions. In this case, jesting helped to prevent seriousness from becoming too grave and heavy. Rhetoric kept the pans balanced by obliterating any sharp division between the jest and an earnest statement by teaching a crucial lesson: that serious truth may be delivered through witty, barbed lines. Here was an attempt to urge the emotions back to that prior, integrated state we looked at in regard to the most ancient religions. When things get too serious, laughter can also provide a break, enabling even more prolonged periods of seriousness. The younger Pliny's remarks, which he enumerated in a series of letters, gave the doctrine of comic relief its authority, as the seriocomic inevitably passed into the Middle Ages. As Pliny urges his friend, Fuscus, "Unbend your mind with poetry; I do not mean of the long and sustained order (for that can only be achieved by men of leisure), but those witty little pieces (*iocor*) which serve as proper reliefs to every degree of care and occupation."

*Iocor* was not merely employed as some abstract literary practice. Like Chilon and others, Pliny views this kind of jesting as the essential informing philosophy of the ideal life. Only through laughing—even by ridiculing others—can people maintain their even temper, Pliny argues, and prevent themselves from falling off the edge into that dreaded illness, despairing *melancholia*. Pliny even implies that laughter that has been shaped by rhetoric can help the spleen to operate properly or, even more therapeutically, that laughter can actually take over the function of the spleen entirely. At any rate, laughter provides the best opportunity to travel the middle of the road, the path of the Mean: "Nothing in my opinion gives a more amiable and becoming grace to our studies, as well as our manners, than to temper gravity with gaiety, lest the former should degenerate into austereness, and the latter run up into levity. Upon this maxim, it is, that I diversify my more serious works with light and playful (*iocesque*) effusions." This leavening of laughter stood as a panegyrical topos all the way through the sixteenth century, winding up in the courtly instruction books, where it found expression in an Italian term called *sprezzatura,* a playful, modest gracefulness in writing, swordsmanship, and in the highest of all the arts, in love.

The idea of the seriocomic can be traced back as far as the Cynics and Stoics, who evolved a rhetorical style that combined the humorous and the serious. The early Stoics sought to retrieve the time when laughter and weeping were conjoined, or at least to recognize the absurdity of separating the emotions into contrived, discrete categories. For them all laughter remained deeply embedded in tears. So whenever the Greeks mention laughter, they attempt to shape it, to hold it in check, by quickly discussing how laughter might be best used to underscore seriousness, as if unbridled derisive laughter might destroy a person, or joyous laughter prove to be a frivolous pastime, a sweet nothing. Throughout the ancient world, then, laughter became useful because of its ability to carry one beyond the moment—painful or pleasant—to a more enduring, serious point. Theories of laughter fight against dividing the emotions into those things that make us feel happy and those that make us feel melancholic.

The fight turns out to be a tough one. As early as the fifth century B.C., just when the Greek alphabet begins taking hold, we find signs of the clear division of the emotions. By this time, Heraclitus, a member of the Ionian school, had already become known as the Weeping Philosopher, and Democritus of Abdena, the Laughing Philosopher. According to Hippolytus, Democritus laughed at everything. In fact, he laughed so much that the people of Abdena believed he had gone insane and called Hippocrates to heal him. But when Democritus explained to him through a long series of examples that he was laughing at the folly of humankind, Hippocrates could only conclude that Democritus was truly a wise and serious man, and that he was laughing to make a serious point.

Though he has at times been misread, Democritus counseled a laughter of good-natured tolerance rather than sarcasm, a laughter free of indignation. In his *Testamonia*, he advises against laughing derisively at the misfortunes of others and urges pity instead. Mary Grant, to whose invaluable study, *The Ancient Rhetorical Theories of the Laughable*, I am deeply indebted, summarizes the nature of the laughing philosopher: "His general attitude toward the faults of mankind is not that of a serious reformer, but of one who ridicules them good-naturedly while remaining somewhat aloof."* Notice that even in Grant's assessment of the situation, derisive laughter

*Mary Grant, *The Ancient Rhetorical Theories of the Laughable: The Greek Rhetoricians and Cicero* (Madison: University of Wisconsin Press, 1924), p. 15.

needs to be administered wisely and judiciously; it must be delivered with its heavenly source in mind, and that means remaining "somewhat aloof." The one who ridicules must regulate his or her own power by intending only goodwill and gentle criticism. The truly serious reforming must ultimately be left in the hands of someone higher—in this case, Zeus. Laughter's caveat: Try to be gentle; try to learn. The French still say, "Le ridicule tue" (Ridicule kills).

The point should be well taken, particularly at this early stage in laughter's history, for certain things stand out. First, and most startling, joyous laughter is short-lived; it makes a brief appearance and then vanishes from discussion. Yes, this laughter is divine, and, sure, it marks people out as human, but it simply does not carry the force—or interest—of aggressive laughter. People simply take joyous laughter too much for granted. No one in authority can capitalize on it. But derisive laughter is akin to nuclear power: Philosophers will reveal its moral secrets; rhetoricians will explain how to harness its explosive potential; politicians will legislate its use for peaceful, regulatory purposes.

Very quickly, then, derisive laughter, scorn, and sarcastic barbs dominate the literature. The architecture of laughter clearly reflects its inherent concern with power relationships: The gods strike from on high, aiming for the lame or lazy, the rebellious or rude—those mortals who seem too unsound or too cocksure. But the gods are not merely jealous creatures who need to drive the essential godlike quality out of every poor, unsuspecting mortal. They aim to teach a lesson—straighten up, get on with it, behave. They also provide an ancillary lesson: Hanging on to one's divine strength—joyous laughter—takes work. A few shocks may teach one to appreciate it more. Some hard knocks might even shore it up.

In Hephaistos' case—and we are entitled to read his story like any other mythological portrait that illuminates the world, except in this case the light shines on laughter—he was too caught up in his own work, too close to it, to take its lessons immediately to heart. More than anyone, he should have understood laughter's nature. His profession predisposed him to it. But in the end, with a little help from Zeus, he manages to evoke laughter himself—and from no less an audience than the gods themselves. He promotes a communal joy, sprung from the trap of a practical joke. A person who has been burned learns best to treat fire with respect. And Hephaistos, after his own humiliation, knows more than any other the power of laughter. With all his faults, Hephaistos presents us with a model of Everymortal: We all need reason and patience. Hephaistos reacts without stepping back and thinking; he quickly loses his temper. And that does him in for a time. Only through the graciousness of Zeus does Hephaistos learn to taste the sweetness of revenge—a revenge through what stung him in the first place: the laughter of public ridicule. Through hatching his own practical joke, Hephaistos regains his balance. His story takes the Greek audience from the *Iliad* to the *Odyssey*, the bridge between the two stories constructed out of laughter.

So, finally, Hephaistos and Prometheus tell of survival, what we colloquially call "baptism by fire." We must be able to take it, but sometimes we must also be able to dish it out. Finally, however, we need to rise above petty feuds and quarrels and, like Zeus, laugh the whole thing off. Strength of character will ultimately make all the difference. For the Greeks, in their lofty way, laughter can take one there. But what a great chunk of the population they leave out!

# 3

## The Greek Philosophers: *ridicule kills*

*The* Greeks really launch the history of modern laughter. Aristotle points out its heavenly source; his contemporaries characterize its joyfully liberating nature. But the Greeks are nothing if not political creatures. They seem to explore every possible configuration of power in the *polis*. Homer shows laughter—that joyous gift from the gods—as something that mediates between the gods and the mortals, a metaphoric bridge connecting the two worlds, just as he uses laughter to carry Hephaistos from his one great epic to the next. Homer seems to say that philosophical talk about laughter is fine, but look what happens to laughter in practice, look at the enormous power in that flamethrower called laughter.

So the Greeks begin to ask the most perplexing, most modern-sounding questions: Why do we laugh at others? What happens when we do? They begin to analyze, that is, the most invisible, most evanescent of things, human breath, and what is even more astounding, they begin to develop a scheme to master it. One might suppose that only speech can civilize human breath, by giving it shape and order. But what about the second breath, the one we supposedly catch on the fortieth day? To control that one, the Greeks have to go the alphabet one better. A well-wrought sentence may take one's breath away, but a good joke renews that breath. Learn to utter sentences, they propose, not ones that raise an eyebrow, but those that raise a laugh. For the Greeks, then, the proper kind of jesting constitutes the ultimate in civility.

The Hebrews deliberately separate themselves from the laughing god of Canaan. The rabbis, as we've seen, seldom discuss laughter, as if it does not exist, or in hopes of seeing it quietly fade from the scene. When they do mention laughter, it is only to warn against its use. In contrast, the Greeks love to exploit laughter. They look at laughter head on and expose it to the analytical light of day, revealing all its modes—satire, scorn, derision, irony, as well as good old belly laughs. But the essential nature of laughter for the Greeks lies in the sense of the bittersweet: weeping and crying. What better place for the Greeks to find the true nature of laughter than in those historical vegetation rituals of simultaneous weeping and laughing? That's really what Homer dramatizes in book 1 of the *Iliad*, except he brings the action indoors and Hellenizes it. Zeus laughs while Hephaistos weeps. And joke telling: Doesn't the same dance of the emotions characterize that social interaction? The joker laughs while the victim weeps. The specter of the dying and resurrected deity hovers in the background; his figure informs every modern session of joke telling.

We think of the Jews as having a monopoly on the joke. After all, the stand-up Jewish comic was a nightclub cliché from the twenties through the sixties. But in fact the jest—the precursor of the joke—is a Greek formulation handed down to the medieval West, and shaped during that period into the modern joke. The jester, in fact, as a Greek creation, stands before an audience as a demigod, a Zeus manqué. The gods have allowed him to steal fire. The early Christians would have considered such a figure an iconoclast, representing a bold and aggressive challenge to God's power; for the ancient Jews, he would have been a blasphemer, a challenge to God's supreme authority. The Greeks develop a philosophy of laughter in cooperation with the gods and formulate rules for its most provocative social uses, by working out a new frame for its conceptualization: Laughter employed as a measure of reform—meting out justice with a laugh, the jester does the work of the gods.

We take this kind of laughter so much for granted that we can easily miss the remarkable achievement buried here. We tell aggressively nasty jokes and pointed, witty stories as if they have always existed, when in fact they have a fairly recent history. This ludic history had to begin in joy—that's the raw material of laughter—laughter in its most amorphous, unbounded, and enfleshed state. But for the Greeks, as soon as laughter gets situated politically, it touches sore spots and produces pain and sorrow. But don't we feel powerful when we fire off a well-aimed joke, as powerful and as righteous as a little god? This is the gift the Greeks bequeath to us, the gift of laughter with its full range of power, able to raise people out of the doldrums and to plunge them into the depths of despair. In the Old Testament, recall, scorn and derision remained the special reserve of God. Now the Greeks seem to say, Pay attention and we will show you how to pull it off yourself. But be careful, this is dangerous stuff. You might get burned!

Laughter so preoccupies the Greek imagination that virtually every philosopher, beginning with the Pre-Socratics, feels impelled to say something about it. While the Pre-Socratics do not formulate any penetrating philosophy of the laughable, they lay much of the foundation on which later theories will solidly rest. That foundation turns out to be a curious one, one that smacks of a Protestant, even a Calvinist spirit: Laughter is fine, so long as it allows people to produce more work.

Starting out gently, the Pre-Socratics insist that even the most benign laughter should be employed toward a practical end—namely, relaxation—so that citizens may more easily take up serious pursuits. But the Pre-Socratics escalate swiftly. They see no future in joyous laughter, nothing of substance out of which to grind a grand theory. Borrowing their model from the gods, they hold that even powerful, aggressive laughter can be used practically—to effect reform—but only so long as the reformer himself remains free of faults. Zealous reformers always risk going too far—the temptation of poor mortals who play very ineptly the role of demigods. Given a taste of power, people seem to want more and more, a temptation they can best guard against by refusing to laugh excessively, or by refusing to correct the faults of all of humankind.

Instead, say the Pre-Socratics, the reformer can achieve better results by setting his or her sights on a single target. The real importance of the Pre-Socratics lies here, in their articulation of the major, unspoken rule that makes joking such a frightening experience, especially in the modern period: A jester displays his or her wit most sharply when it is directed at some unsuspecting victim, preferably in full view of an assembled audience. The Pre-Socratics cleverly recognize that the jester's task is made easier, and wit revealed most effectively, when the victims are manipulated into exposing their own vulnerabilities themselves. The skillful jester goads hapless souls into anger by hitting them where they live with a joke, and then exposes them even further when they begin fuming and protesting their innocence. The audience meanwhile sends up a nervous giggle as this victim or that "flies off the handle."

The joker thus recreates the heavenly battle between the Olympians and the Titans by staging a battle of controlled wit against those who cannot hold their temper in check—against the temperamental.* Hephaistos and Prometheus serve as models here. The jester can cripple opponents by rendering them objects of ridicule like a Hephaistos, or by laying bare their stupidity like Prometheus' other self—Epimetheus. Quite often, the skillful jester can pull off both results from a single jest. When the fighting settles

*Imagery associated with this battle of wits usually describes a collision of hot and cold (or in terms of the four elements, fire versus earth): staying cool, or turning a cold shoulder, as opposed to getting heated, or hot under the collar, and so on. The same dramatic meeting of extremes, as we have seen, occurs in tempering metals. (*Mettle*, as in one's "disposition," is only a variant spelling, circa seventeenth century, of *metal*.) Perhaps Hephaistos should be installed as the god of temper.

down, the triumphant jester has earned a lofty position, like Zeus, too high and too dangerous ever to be the object of revenge. Only a fool would take that challenge on.

As for the nature of the jest, we must turn to a fifth-century Sicilian philosopher named Gorgias. We do not have his statements firsthand; he must be read through Aristotle. Gorgias (483–375 B.C.) brought rhetoric into Greece at the same time that the alphabet arrived, and was the first to capitalize on wit's explosive nature, urging its use as the most effective weapon in the orator's arsenal. The alphabet itself, literacy, is the grindstone on which the jester's lethal sword is sharpened. The alphabet makes critical analysis possible; when it meets the power of laughter, the explosion can be deadly. Gorgias advises: "Kill your opponent's earnestness with jesting and his jesting with earnestness." While we tend to think that Freud owns this key psychological insight, even at this incipient stage of rhetoric, jesting generates imagery suggestive of varying degrees of maiming or outright murder.

As for the victim, a subject of great concern during this period, Socrates provides the most interesting example by adopting a carefully calculated stance of self-ignorance—a clever practical joke that enables him to play the role both of jester and victim. Another way of describing Socrates' character is to say that he turns his wit back on his own personality, crafting himself into the very thing he hopes to cure in others; that is, he turns himself into a dummy. (Think of Woody Allen in this tradition.) As Falstaff says of Mistress Quickly, one simply does not know where to have him. He is so shrewd and tricky, so slippery, we must read his every statement with care. Classicists believe this clever chimera is a fairly accurate portrait of Socrates, but we can rely, unfortunately, only on fragments of his writings. Joannes Stobaeus, a Macedonian who lived in the fifth century A.D., and who compiled extracts from many Greek writers, preserved several of Socrates' fragments. Of those few scraps, one concerns laughter: "One should use laughter as one uses salt, sparingly." The line stands out in the history of laughter because it reverberates with so much meaning. First, it implies that excessive laughter—even of the most gentle sort—can easily turn into derision and scorn. So use it sparingly; it's exotic stuff and it doesn't come cheaply. But Socrates' line also contains a very subtle warning against inflicting pain, for while salt spices up food, we also know how it smarts on open wounds. Use even a pinch too much, and it stings like hell.

In choosing salt, Socrates settled on an image that would carry many layers of meaning—or grains of truth. Salt had already become a standard sign of hospitality in Greece, but a hospitality restricted to the highborn and well-situated. Salt marked clear social divisions at table between those people who sat "above the salt" and those who sat "below the salt." Salt symbolized status. (We still say a person is worth his or her salt.) It remained expensive well into the Renaissance, a commodity precious enough to be used as salary (*sal*). In Attic Greece, a carefully honed wit was called *sal atticum*. A properly seasoned wit is a matter of decorum and bearing—one must not overdo it and risk becoming salty—unpalatable and so disgusting. True wit commands respect; it situates a person high on the social ladder. With it, however, comes responsibility; one must exercise restraint. Given what we know of his rhetorical style, Socrates intends, I think, to pour from his one fragment all these possible meanings—quite a load from one line. In fact, the line provides readers with a perfect example of wit itself, where an entire story comes rushing out of one clever line. Whatever else Socrates has to say about laughter, though, must be inferred through reading Plato.*

We read Plato on an enormous variety of theoretical topics—truth, justice, reason, and so on. We don't think of Plato as the father of laughter. But in fact he devotes an awful lot of attention to laughter. He comes to the sub-

*Plato's dialogues may have a connection to the acrobatic tricks of the mimes. George Steiner describes something of this dancing quality of Plato's intellect: "The formidable gaiety of the Platonic dialogues, the use of the dialectic as a method of intellectual chase, stems from the discovery that words, stringently tested, allowed to clash as in combat or manoevre as in a dance, will produce new shapes of understanding. Who was the first man to tell a joke, to strike laughter out of speech?" (*After Babel* [London: Oxford University Press, 1977], p. 22).

ject, not out of veneration for its origins, or out of appreciation for its beauty, but out of respect for its power. He respects its ability to subvert so effectively the status quo, its Herculean strength to twist the taut lines of power into mere haywire. He, too, smells something wrong: He knows that laughter can dig in its heels as a most awesome foe to authority, and he recognizes that with a single laugh each and every citizen, regardless of rank, carries an incipient power to blow things apart. Moreover, derisive laughter takes over the role of a court of law, meting out its own brand of justice immediately and decisively. Indeed, it rewrites laws on the spot. The Republic cannot tolerate such a threat to its authority. People do not need to be governed so much as they need their passions controlled. So, as a leader—a philosopher in the grandest sense—Plato must make certain that laughter does not run wild. Through his dialogues, Plato plots the nonviolent overthrow of the people by modulating their breath. He accomplishes this goal in the most professional and businesslike manner, with an arresting and quiet elegance.

Plato writes about laughter, removed and distanced from it, as if he were the president of a large production company, where smooth running and efficiency guarantee success. Boisterous laughter on the part of the workers is tantamount to anarchy or, worse yet, sabotaged production. The chief executive officer, like the respectable politician, must exhibit appropriate, serious behavior, for the public equates seriousness with sincerity, honesty, and perhaps most important, with competency. Plato outlines his general concerns about laughter, appropriately, in his broadest work about the ideal society, the *Republic*, where he declares flatly that the danger of laughter lies in excess. But he never defines how much constitutes excess. He does tell us, however, that excess of any kind leads to a loss of control, and that excessive laughter is particularly heinous because the reaction it generates always culminates in violence. Even before the situation reaches that violent state, however, effusive laughter turns the average citizen into one of the most unattractive characters in the state, the βωμολόχος, or "buffoon." The buffoon exhibits the worst sort of behavior, for his actions wind up splitting community feelings apart. In an instant, he lets fly his intemperate laughter and is reviled for it; tempers flare, and violence breaks out—all in all, behavior unbefitting citizens of the Republic. The warning against excess turns out to be an admonition against being too plebian—against acting out on the streets like a commoner. The guardians of the Republic must stand above all the riffraff. Notice that Plato does not condemn laughter here because it challenges the gods in any way; he condemns it because of what it does to the person, because of public appearances.

The citizens of virtue and the guardians of the Republic are curators of dignity, and since laughter can so easily entice people into pursuing excesses of all kinds—primarily through its promise of pleasure—Plato forbids his leaders from taking an active interest in it. He even finds the representation of excessive laughter loathsome: In the *Republic*, he condemns those who show the gods or people of worth losing good judgment to laughter and so quite understandably deplores Homer's portrayal of the gods laughing derisively at Hephaistos. Quite clearly, then, Plato seems intent on erecting strong barriers between the elite and all others, based on an elevated attitude toward excessive laughter and frivolity.

Plato's overriding concern always sacrifices the individual to the greater good of the state. The individual projects his own decorum and dignity onto the decorum of the state. Whenever Plato sees even the possibility of threat to the welfare of the state, he demands that it be protected. Drawing on the Pre-Socratic notion that laughter can effect reform, Plato sometimes suspends his injunctions against laughter to permit the jester to act as a kind of vigilante, a satiric, stand-up journalist. For instance, in the *Republic* (5.4520) ridicule, even motivated by vengeance, may be used effectively against wrongheaded or disruptive new ideas, "so we must not fear the jests of wit which will be directed against this sort of innovation." Elsewhere, and this sounds most unusual for Plato, he maintains that even his *bête noire*, the comic poet, may serve a useful purpose if his conscious intent is not retaliation for private wrongs, but reform for the good of the state.

Plato turns these general prohibitions against laughter into duties and obligations in the *Laws*. It is one thing to poke fun at institutions, and quite another to direct jibes at other citizens. As a general notion, citizens of the ideal state must respect one another and refrain from abusing each other physically or emotionally; thus Plato hopes to eradicate anger like a cancer that has invaded the body politic. In book 11 of the *Laws* (934–36), Plato utters his harshest prohibition against angry laughter: Injury to another person through angry words or deeds must be severely punished, for "there is no man who is in the habit of laughing at another who does not miss virtue and earnestness altogether, or lose the better half of greatness." And he concludes by drawing hard, fast, and clear lines about the few times when jests may be delivered *ad hominem*, but even then allowing them only when the jester acts from goodwill and has received official sanction: "A comic poet, or maker of iambic or satirical verse, shall not be permitted to ridicule any of the citizens, either by word or image, either in anger or without anger. And if anyone is disobedient, the judges shall either at once expel him from the place, or he shall pay a fine of three *minae* . . . those only who have already received permission shall be allowed to write verses at one another without anger and in jest, but in anger and in serious earnestness they shall not be allowed." Plato's abiding concern here, as elsewhere, is with propriety, decorum, and the correct appearance of things—let us all act as if we harbored not a jot of anger toward each other—so that the state can run smoothly and efficiently. But notice, even to jest one needs to obtain permission, official sanction, for Plato aims at *control*, at regulation, at making certain that authority remains centralized.

Plato knows how literacy reorganizes society. As the first real man of letters in the West, he understands that literacy immediately centralizes authority, since only those people in positions of power, and only a few at that, dare call themselves literate. Those few promulgate all the laws, all the regulations and contracts—in *writing*. Laughter works just the opposite effect, decentralizing power by situating it in each individual, even more effectively than speech, for every person who laughs does so with the greatest articulation and eloquence. Laughter requires no training, no rules. For speaking one's mind, one needs a forum, but one can always laugh in the face of authority—even when that face appears at some remote distance. One of the earliest political philosophers, Plato acknowledges how laughter can stand in the way of the efficient governance of the state. One can begin to understand Plato's concern at this early date: Justice and punishment belong in the hands of the law, in the control of the state, not in the mouths of jesters—and certainly not in the mouths of common citizens, those village folk who make fast judgments with snappy lines, cut-ups who try to cut each other down in the streets.*

Finally, Plato begrudgingly allows for humor as a way of educating his citizens; in great part, he uses Socrates as the embodiment of this idea. So in the *Laws* (7.910E and 8.838G), he invokes the Pre-Socratic attitude toward laughter—that it may be used to make a serious point more acceptable. (Aristotle will also use this argument for his ethical justification of laughter.) But Plato does not refer to the Cynics and Stoics, even though they have already made this mixed style—the *diatribe*—so popular that Horace will later satirize it. Instead, Plato introduces the concept as his own and gives it a new name, σπονδογέλοιν, which translates as "speaking truth under cover of a jest." In medical terms, the jest allows a bitter pill to be swallowed with a bit of sugar coating.**

Having made that concession to laughter, Plato raises the ethical considerations of the laughable both in the *Republic* and in the *Laws*, by asking the familiar question: How should one use humor for serious matters? Rather than arguing the merits of the seriocomic, he demonstrates what he means, incarnates his idea, through an actor, Socrates—a personification of

*Think about the number of places today where we know it is generally inappropriate to laugh and act giddy: libraries, funerals, classrooms, hospitals, offices, during lovemaking and business meetings. The list goes on and on. This assigns to laughter a tremendous reserve of disruptive power. To have an absolutely serious, secure state, laughter would have to be excised from each soul. And in a certain way that is what Plato would like, or at least he would like to place a governor on the machine that makes us laugh.

**One Hebrew scholar, Max Kadushin, places the *aggadah*, the nonlegal material in the Talmud, in the same tradition. The blurring of final meaning involves, he says, "serious play" (*The Rabbinic Mind* [New York: Bloch, 1952], p. 108).

the Ironic Word, the Logos Askance. How better to show the effects of humor than to create someone who can tell serious stories with a wry sense of humor? Socrates is a gullible, innocent, and somewhat ignorant character, who always manages to ask precisely the right disingenuous questions, prompting pages and pages of penetrating insight. Most of the time he weaves his brilliant arguments in partnership with an unsuspecting respondent. Socrates engages others as a kind of disarming and ancient Israelite, whom we suspect of knowing much more than he speaks.

Plato terms this stance εἰρωνεία, "a pretended self-deprecation or affected ignorance," and thus invents the trope of *irony.* Socrates he calls the *eiron.** By becoming a poseur, Socrates manages to deflect criticism while moving his intricate arguments forward in small increments, quietly turning his critics into students without scaring them off. No one feels the need to best him, for he seemingly offers no challenge and thus no threat. Through his own practical joke, he rids himself of the aura of authority. In addition, so that others will remain open to his argument, Socrates disarms them by feigning his own ignorance. And thus Plato can make dramatic his own ideas about the nature of laughter and win arguments with virtually no opposition. No dummy, Plato has the last laugh.

But Socrates never laughs out loud. In the dialogues, social intercourse is always carefully choreographed, permitting a kind of laughter that remains politely quiet—private and internalized. It pleases but never aggressively disrupts. Socrates never takes center stage to make a display of his wit. He presents at all times a model of decorum and refinement. He shows the way. But he's also a trickster, speaking out of both sides of his mouth. Irony is the best rhetorical trope for saying two things at once, with one tone of voice—the satire insinuating its meaning by pushing hard on the serious, threatening always to bend it radically out of shape, for instance, by sending

*The technique of combining the serious and the comic was developed and dramatized by the mime and pantomime after the collapse of Greek and Roman comedy at the beginning of the Roman Imperial Age. It survived well into the later Middle Ages, particularly in sermons. Quite obviously, every effective joke-teller, from Socrates to Sam Kinnison, understands this strategy, but we can find its most dramatic representation in what comics call the "deadpan" expression.

it into the burlesque. With astonishing economy, irony satisfied the Greek concern for melding the humorous with the serious.

Irony is a trick, not an overtly aggressive one, but a trick nonetheless—both playful and deadly serious. In this regard, Socrates really appears as a transitional figure: He embodies a trope—irony—that will find its most challenging home in literacy. Indeed, the ability to uncover an ironic statement constitutes the ultimate test of a reader's literacy. (No wonder Swift's "A Modest Proposal," the greatest sustained piece of irony in English literature, surfaces in England during a time of rising literacy.) Irony separates the casual scanner from the analytical reader. One can spot irony in a speaker fairly easily by watching facial expressions and noticing gestures, but readers do not enjoy the luxury of such clues. Irony takes work. When readers finally catch on, they feel smart, but only fleetingly, for at that same moment they also understand that they have been hoodwinked. In that instant of insight, readers see into the text and into themselves, realizing how naive they have been.

An encounter with irony, then, affords simultaneous pleasure and pain—joy and sadness. The ironist has set a trap from which readers can of course escape but only by figuring out the author's sense—preferably in a hurry. Otherwise, they will forever feel lame—as lame as Hephaistos. But even after readers let themselves in on the joke, they can never feel as smart as the author/creator, who remains all the more firmly ensconced in a position of authority, and who laughs secretly and silently at the ease with which the poor, benighted readers have been manipulated.

After a bout with irony, the reader will always move across the page with a decided limp. Questions nag: Can my reading ever be trusted? Have I lost my edge? Do I really understand? Thus the *eiron*, Socrates himself, enjoys the pleasure of that pernicious imp, the last laugh—the great echoing laugh of superiority. The victim has no choice but to go on, a bit more cautious, a bit more critical, a bit wiser, and a bit more unsettled. By drawing on Socrates, Plato moves laughter a giant step closer toward its culmination in literature with the modern joke. At the same time, he moves it many steps away from the great bulk of laughers—the nonliterates whose laughter erupted not from their brains but from their bellies, those marginal folk who were considered too dumb in their illiteracy even to bother with.

The trope of irony, with its capacity for saying two opposing things at once, suits a man like Plato, who holds mixed feelings about laughter. He both condemns excessive laughter and yet recognizes—and enjoys—its power. We all have this dual reaction to laughter, he insists, particularly to sardonic laughter. Even spectators at a tragedy, he points out, find themselves "smiling through their tears." Ridicule, sarcasm, satire—these elicit from us the same kind of "mixed pleasures." And yet civilized, cultured responses demand clarity and precision, a single emotional response. (Literacy encourages us to see in such discrete categories, in either/or configurations, not in gray and shady tones. That's why, when we read, irony trips us up—it thrives in orality where discrete categories break down.) This idea of the "mixed pleasure," the combining of sadness and joy, Plato sees as so rudimentary—a cultural hangover from those earlier, vegetative days—that he insists that we remain acutely aware of it in our lives.

Socrates explores this "mixed pleasure" in some detail with Protarchus in Plato's most important work for the study of laughter, the *Philebus*. That discussion remains, even today, the *locus classicus* for understanding why we take pleasure in another's misfortunes; it affords the most bracingly modern statement about laughter that we have from antiquity; and it explains how the emotions can subvert propriety and decorum, unless we continually analyze them with a scientist's curious eye, as a way of trying to understand them.

Realize the radical shape Plato's analysis takes here. To dissect life at its most fundamental level means analyzing one of its most complex and elusive areas: the emotions. The bedrock of those emotions, Plato seems to imply, the thing that provides a model for a wide range of other responses, is laughter. By understanding laughter, Plato intends to excavate the seriousness of living. We commonly believe that, in mapping the subconscious, Freud seized that territory for himself, thereby helping to usher in the age of modernity. But Plato preempts Freud.

Plato, in fact, pulls off something quite astonishing. He claims laughter, or the propensity to laugh, as the substratum of all the emotions. While he's not quite sure if laughter should be classed as an emotion, he finds no better place for it. Laughter fulfills such a basic, such an odd and controlling, function in people's lives that he feels somehow impelled to treat laughter as an emotion. How else to treat it? What else to call it? Even such a stately authority as the *Oxford English Dictionary* seems unable to classify laughter, reducing it to "an instinctive expression of mirth." But to call laughter instinctive leads nowhere, for what one group of people finds funny another group may find merely stupid and puerile. Everyone laughs, but at radically different things. And so, in the end, the dictionary definition tells us not very much at all.

Laughter certainly finds expression, like love or hate, through the body. But laughter produces terrifically powerful reactions to situations—powerful enough at times to send one into something close to convulsions. The most delicately nuanced pun, the most subtle wisecrack—the most finely etched emotional event—can set off that explosion of laughter. I can think of no better analogy than nuclear fission, where the unsettling of a single atom sets off a chain reaction of millions of rapid-fire explosions. To many minds, that may be one of the most frightening and most compelling images of modernity.

So the question remains: Where *should* one place laughter? If it is not quite an emotion, is it more intellectual, say, than anger or jealousy, more calculating than love or fear? That we choose to refer to a *sense* of humor is surely significant. Do we think of it as the sixth sense? The four humors, as Galen articulated them, refer to a set of inner senses, a way human beings have of organizing an experience once it has been internalized, a way of letting experience "touch" them. These inner senses may be akin to what we today call "common sense," in two ways. First, we all share the senses in common. And second, the inner senses provide a natural way of responding to the world.

The senses numbered five and went under the name "external" or "outward" senses, and so closely were they connected to the intellect that a person could be described as insane with the phrase, "not in his or her right senses." Characters in Shakespeare, driven by blind passion, thus stand in opposition to reason and nobility. As Lear loses his reason, for instance, he must first come back to his senses, quite literally, by learning to *feel*, before his sanity can be restored. As the four humors faded as an idea, sometime near the end of the Middle Ages, reasoning and logic—the intellect in general—came to serve as the standard, civilized guide to the emotions. However, I would argue that one pesky inner sense, the principal "humor," remained throughout history—our sense of humor. This sense remained because it best helped to integrate, or more accurately, organize, all the other senses. The term "sense of humor" I can find no earlier than the late eighteenth century, just as the term "wit" comes into popular use. The two terms fight against each other in a battle of intellect against emotion. Wit refers to a keenness of intellect and finds expression in clever wordplay of all kinds, and in interesting, sometimes even outlandish, ideas or situations. A humorous person, during that same period, behaves loosely and idiosyncratically—unpredictably.

I have moved ahead of the story, but it is important to see what Plato faces. He simply does not know where to place that renegade called laughter. In the *Philebus*, he tries for the impossible. He hopes to explain why people feel the way they do, and then to tell them how they *should* feel. He uses an outer sense (perception) to explain an inner sense (humor). In the end, Plato aims at only one thing—the refinement of the emotions.

Those of rank feel differently from hoi polloi, Plato points out, and they express feeling using different gestures and manners from those lower down on the social ladder. By making those distinctions, Plato opens a wide chasm, an alienating distance that he measures by something as basic as differences in laughter. Sure, we can spot differences in class—through dress, style, sometimes even through living arrangements. But in the presence of noisy laughter even a blind person can tell, Plato would argue, when he or she faces someone from the lower class. Those who dwell down below, for instance, bellow their laughter like boors and slobs. They cannot be trusted with their emotions; they will not hesitate to laugh at funerals or to turn giddy in church. They giggle in bed and in the bushes. Plato intends to elevate laughter from its heartfelt, soulful home, to something intellectual. He has Socrates serve as our guide.

Plato's most important discussion of laughter comes immediately after Socrates has been discussing the emotion of envy, in the *Philebus*, with Protarchus. And although Socrates does not connect the two—envy and laughter—their juxtaposition in the dialogue suggests a connectedness. It also sounds intuitively correct, so much so that I will argue later that envy motivates even the most seemingly pointless joke in our own time. At any rate, in pointed, sometimes baffling questions for Protarchus, Socrates tries to elicit from him the various ways people can appear ridiculous, all of which, it turns out, emanate from an attitude that might be called "Know *not* thyself"—in contradistinction to the Delphic oracle's famous dictum. Such ignorance stems not from a rhetorical strategy like irony, but from out-and-out delusion. Through self-ignorance, people delude themselves into thinking they are richer than they are (a fault of property); taller than they are (a fault of physicality); and finally, the most common and ultimately the most damaging, people can blindly believe they are smarter than they actually are (a fault of the mind). Socrates keeps leading Protarchus down a philosophical path, until he gets him to see that ignorance, in whatever form, constitutes a grave misfortune. And yet, Socrates asks, don't we all laugh at the unfortunate? Protarchus agrees. Socrates then wants to know how this inconsistency can be resolved and thus understood:

SOCRATES: And do we feel pain or pleasure in laughing at them?
PROTARCHUS: Clearly, we feel pleasure.

SOCRATES: And was not envy the source of this pleasure which we feel at the misfortunes of our friends?

PROTARCHUS: Certainly.

SOCRATES: Then the argument shows that when we laugh at the folly of our friends, pleasure, in mingling with envy, mingles with pain, and laughter is pleasant, and we envy and laugh at the same time.

PROTARCHUS: True.

SOCRATES: And the argument implies that this combination of pleasure and pain exists not only in lamentations, or in tragedy and comedy, but in the entire drama of human life, and in ten thousand ways.

Self-ignorance in our friends, then, makes them appear ridiculous, and we take great pleasure in laughing at them. But ignorance is an evil; thus, we are wrong, finally, to laugh at the evil our friends so painfully suffer. But even when we know the truth, we keep on laughing anyway, for in our hearts we take a secret delight in seeing them fall, especially those we think society holds in higher esteem than us: It raises us above them in social status, or in respect. Envy (*phthonos*) is the real source of our pleasure, but envy weighs down the soul like lead and causes a wicked mental pain. The only way out, Socrates counsels, is not to take delight in misfortune. Take pity instead. Have compassion for the ignorant.

People cannot rid themselves of envy very easily, for unlike anger or even jealousy, no one confesses to it without being coerced to do so. Envy works in a most passive way: We hope and pray that some event will come along to cast down our rivals, wipe out their fortunes. But we would never take such a bold action ourselves. The envious simply hate their rivals and at the same time politely smile in their faces. The envious refuse to confess what they harbor in their hearts, for envy is such a belittling emotion. That's why envious people move through society as secret pariahs, the toughest culprits to spot. How can we deal with people who pretend to love us but in their hearts would love to see our demise?* Those who envy dissemble and

*The Fourth Lateran Council, in 1244, required yearly confession because the church saw that envy was quickly becoming a social problem and knew how difficult it was to confess such a

deceive; they wear the mask of duplicity. How wonderful when those we envy become butts of jokes, objects of ridicule, when they stand exposed in public for what we think they truly are—jerks and frauds.

The problem can grow even more complicated. In social organizations, rife with competition and struggle, ridicule is subtly fostered. Where the rewards are limited, with lots of people scrambling and grabbing for the smallest token, competition becomes especially keen. Great rivalries develop between the haves and the have-nots, the latter secretly wishing for the thundering and swift downfall of the former. When authorities momentarily suspend the laws and regulations, let's say during times of carnival or charivari, and all restraint falls temporarily away, dark secrets are broadcast and the oppressors exposed. The world turns topsy-turvy. Aristocrats become butts of jokes. For those who sit in lofty positions of power, the time carries with it a certain amount of danger: What if the carnival cannot be called off, or if the rules of the game become blurred and are taken for real? What if things get out of hand? Plato recoils at even the suggestion of such a possibility, and this fear may have prompted the laws regulating the production of comedies in his ideal state (*Laws* 7.816–17).

The concept of mixed pleasure is the fuel that keeps the history of the laughable steaming forward, from our first evidence of it in the Ras Shamra Text, down to the popularity of modern jokes. As society gets more and more complicated and competitive, people seem to respond by telling more and more jokes designed to ridicule. At least, the trajectory of laughter arches toward the aggressive, often cruel, joke. Over the centuries, however, the idea that the joker might be inflicting pain on his victim recedes into the background, practically gone from discussions of humor by the time of Cicero. By Chaucer's day, people enjoy telling barbed jokes, taking great delight, not just in getting off a good joke, but in getting a rival. This marks a new stage in the history of laughter. One can see this startlingly new emotional matrix developing in Chaucer, specifically in "The Miller's Tale," in

feeling. By the fourteenth century, in a growing market economy—at a time, that is, when personal wealth could alter social status—envy (*invidia*) had replaced pride (*hubris*) as the most heinous of the seven cardinal sins.

which, out of sheer, witty exuberance and delight in their own power, characters blind themselves to the pain they inflict on others.

At times, it is almost impossible to believe any of Plato's critical remarks on laughter, since he ends up using laughter to such advantage in the person of Socrates. This simply attests to the difficulty anyone encounters in trying to understand fully a phenomenon so complex and contradictory as laughter, or when anyone tries to promulgate rules so abstract and so entirely divorced from the people who live cheek by jowl and who actually do the laughing. But as the first man of letters in the West, Plato has the opportunity to take a critical stance toward laughter. Perhaps not coincidentally, he is also the first writer to take laughter seriously. Laughter is one of the few bodily functions he discusses in his works, because for him it is one of the most mysterious.

Plato forces laughter to give up its convoluted identity by asking: Why would anyone laugh at someone else's misfortunes? He concludes that our reaction stems from a "mixed emotion" of sadness and joy, and that we should try by all means to purge ourselves of that contradictory feeling. Obviously, he knows that people laugh, but he also firmly believes that the impulse must be carefully controlled and judiciously exercised. Although he would prefer to ban it altogether, Plato compromises to allow laughter a place in his Republic—a very tenuous place, and only under certain conditions, the privilege granted solely to the most refined. But even then he sets a careful political agenda: At times a victim—the butt of a joke—might have to be sacrificed for the good of the state.

Plato analyzes the root cause of what has been called "Homeric laughter"—the contemplation of the physically ugly or the defective—and cautions us to be on guard against it. Aristotle wants to refine that urge out of us altogether. He appears to be much more protective of laughter than Plato. But then he ought to be. After all, it is supposedly he who has singled out laughter as the vital sign of humanity. But the story is actually slightly complicated. Aristotle has made his claim about laughter as an offhand comment, oddly enough, on tickling: "That man alone is affected by tickling is due firstly to the delicacy of the skin, and secondly to his being the only animal that laughs. For to be tickled is to be set in laughter, the laughter being produced by such a motion as mentioned of the region of the armpit" (*De partibus animalium* 3.10).

Christian philosophers after the eleventh century learned what Aristotle said about the human capacity for laughter primarily through the writings of Notker Labeo, an instructor at Saint Gall, who translated Aristotle and Boethius into High German. In his *De partibus logicae*, Notker passed on to the entire Middle Ages, not Aristotle's attitude to laughter, but Boethius'. Boethius took it on himself to install the capacity for laughter as a property (*proprium*) of humankind, one of the five *praedicabilia* from the ancient world used to categorize all the objects in the universe, the others called *genus, species, differentia*, and *accidens*.

I linger here for a moment, for Notker really sent laughter into the Middle Ages with a blessing far beyond what Aristotle had intended. While Aristotle discusses the *praedicabilia* in his *Categories* and *Topics*, he does not mention laughter there. But philosophers who followed Aristotle certainly did, like Lucian of Samosata (*Sale of Creeds*), as well as Quintilian (*Instituto oratorio*), Julius Pollux (*Onomasticon*), and Porphyry (*Introduction to Aristotle's Categories*). From them, the idea passed onto Marcianus Capella in *De nuptiis philologiae et mercurii* ("homo est animal risibile"), and to Alcuin, teacher of Charlemagne, who says, "Homo est substantia animata, rationalis, mortalis, risus capax." Boethius, then, fostered the idea that laughter constituted a "property" of the human race. That idea so appealed to the medieval mind that it permeated medieval philosophy. Thus laughter came to occupy a special place.

As the animating force for all human beings, by definition laughter must possess enormous power and potential. So this thing called laughter hits Aristotle as a paradox: While laughter converts all us animals into human beings, it can also turn on us and turn us all into boors and villains. Furthermore, the road to our happiness and even to our humanity, for Aristotle, lies with this quixotic thing called laughter. The road would be a smoother one if all that nastiness were simply gone.

So while he follows Plato in grounding laughter in the contemplation of the ridiculous, Aristotle wants to restrict the practice to laughing at mistakes and deformities that are neither painful nor destructive to the individual.* Thus, he forbids laughing at physical or mental handicaps in public. And he believes that he can disabuse people of the habit once they find some safe outlet for their desire. He finds that solution in drama. Notice the masks of tragedy, he says, which look both ugly and distorted but in the end cause no pain. And while, like Plato, Aristotle sees laughter as an emotional response, he frees it from the taint of envy. This means that laughter can never be connected with evil—either through a jester's possessing an evil character or through the jester's evil behavior. Aristotle seems to have been heard: Envy disappears from analyses of joke-telling, but envy itself does not obviously fade away. Indeed, it grows stronger and stronger over time.

Aristotle elaborates on the intrinsic value of laughter in his principal book about correct behavior, the *Nicomachean Ethics*. At first glance, it might seem odd that laughter should be discussed as an ethical consideration. But notice that Plato has already established the ground rules: Laughter involves questions of decorum; one must laugh only at certain times and only in certain situations. That Aristotle discusses laughter in a work titled the *Nicomachean Ethics* only points to laughter's essentially rascally nature. Laughter nips at our heels, a tireless pup, and if we expect to move through life with anything approximating happiness, Aristotle believes we had better learn to domesticate that frisky little creature.

The *summum bonum* of human nature is happiness, arrived at through pursuing serious things in a virtuous manner. Everything we choose, Aristotle argues, we choose for the sake of something else—except happiness. Happiness represents an end in itself. To exert oneself and suffer

*The ridiculous is so important to the Greeks because it provides the bedrock for both tragedy and comedy: When it occurs in the powerful, it is detestable and tragic; in the weak, comic and laughable.

all one's life merely to find a tiny reward in amusement, however, would be sheer childishness; but "to amuse oneself in order that one may exert oneself, as Anarchasis puts it, seems right; for amusement is a sort of relaxation, and we need relaxation because we cannot work continuously. Relaxation, then, is not a end; if it is taken for the sake of activity" (*Nicomachean Ethics* X, 1176b., 27). Most critics conclude from this passage that Aristotle values seriousness above levity, but in fact Aristotle implies that the former cannot exist without the latter.* They complement each other. They function as two sides of one experience: the Good Life.

For Aristotle believes that people need to see models of the emotions in their elevated, carefully shaped and controlled state, and to that end he turns away from Socrates' "drama of life"—the comedy of life—to comedy on the stage. He hopes to divert our pleasure away from envying wealthy or beautiful neighbors (which, finally, results in pain for everyone) to delighting in faithful, dramatic representations of their follies—our degree of pleasure directly proportional to the accuracy of the imitation. By so doing, we might purge ourselves of the need to ridicule the person next door. One can only wonder at the profusion today of both stand-up comics on stage and domestic sitcoms on TV—nothing more, really, than stylized ridicule: Do we all have an enormous need to get even with our associates, and do comedy clubs and TV networks serve the function of the classical stage, helping to purge us of our nasty feelings so that we can return, cleansed, to the factory or the office? Judging from the sheer number of comics and sitcoms, our need seems insatiable. Or perhaps we have moved beyond the possibility of reaching catharsis and purgation, our envy just too deeply seated, too powerful, to eradicate.

That's Aristotle's point: Real-life emotions are too powerful and unpredictable to leave unattended. Who knows when we might get bowled over by a laugh? Let the stage be transformed into a gymnasium, a place of

*This misreading has had far-reaching implications. The classicist Paul Lejay claims that out of this confusion arises the idea of the hierarchy of the genres, by which types of literature are ranked according to their degree of seriousness.

education, where the audience can be instructed on the subjects of restraint and decorum. Unlike real life, the dramatic stage serves as a place where behavior can be directed; order assumes the throne there, even in the midst of chaos. Even when the original objects repulse or frighten, people still take delight in faithful, artistic representations of them. Subsuming ethics under aesthetics, Aristotle hopes through the actions of theatrical performers to rid society of its need for humiliation through derisive laughter. People generally learn through imitation, Aristotle argues, and "learning something is the greatest of pleasures" (*Poetics* 144b 8–15). So laughing at actors can in Aristotle's scheme purge society's need to deride rivals.

In book 4 of the *Nicomachean Ethics*, Aristotle dramatically elevates wit by including it, after friendliness and truthfulness, as one of the three social virtues. Wit comes from the intellect; it is brainy and easily bridled. Wit also acts as a catalyst: By telling the truth playfully, one can create close friendships. Wit sits behind the jest the way a director hovers behind a play, necessary but invisible, giving shape and providing direction to the action; and so in social situations it is wit that really breathes life into laughter. If laughter has made us all human, then surely, in significant ways, laughter can be utilized to guide our lives.

In our own day, we believe that a person is born with a sense of humor: He or she has a finely tuned one or not. But everyone has the capacity to laugh. In Aristotle's day, wit could be acquired through education and diligence—in a very real way, a sense of humor became an object of study, something to be learned and mastered. Aristotle thus treats wit as an aspect of rhetoric, for its principal tasteful expression, the jest, is a trope that develops out of *learned* discourse. For us, a sense of humor cuts across class distinctions. But for Aristotle, since wit requires education and refinement—practical exercises in rhetorical skills—the illiterati lead lives doomed to boorishness and can never rise to the ranks of the witty. For those who do qualify, however—the already-risen—Aristotle lays out rules for sharpening the wit.

The first rule, the ultimate guide for every aspect of human behavior,

Aristotle calls the Mean, the *via media*, which one achieves by avoiding extremes—both of excess and deficiency. Laughter in particular thrives on excess, but excessive wit quickly turns one into a vulgar buffoon and destroys friendliness. A deficiency of wit creates an unpolished boor and is likewise isolating. These types are easy to spot, since they insinuate themselves awkwardly into social intercourse. The boorish person takes offense at everything and so contributes nothing to useful conversation. At the other extreme, buffoons disrupt the social scene by ridiculing everyone. They will have their jokes at everyone's expense "and are more concerned to raise a laugh than to keep within the bounds of decorum and avoid giving pain to the object of their raillery" (*Nicomachean Ethics* VIII, 1128b., 14). Truthfulness, friendliness, and wit—in the ancient world these are characteristics to be cultivated and refined, goals to be attained. Bear in mind, these are lofty, aristocratic ideals. No artisan, no worker or peasant, could ever conceive of such a life. He or she would work and play, and exchange bits of daily news, without thought of categories like "education" or "wit."

Aristotle respects those who, jesting with good taste, take care not to offend or harm, and he classifies them as ready-witted, tactful, and versatile. These types will naturally refrain from excessive jesting and will avoid inflicting pain by shunning offensive or personal subjects. But more important, they will say and allow to be said only those things suited to the language of the gentle person. Some subjects, that is, remain off limits to the jester—for instance, jokes about the law: "A jest is a sort of abuse, and there are things that law-givers forbid us to abuse and they should, perhaps, have forbidden us even to make jest of such" (*Nicomachean Ethics* IV, 1128a., 30). Truly witty persons, respecting such proprieties, indulge only in jests they themselves can stand to hear and avoid certain jests altogether; gentle wits become models of the law and show others the proper way through their controlled actions. In this way, jests exert a strong moral force. And here Aristotle makes an astounding claim: While the buffoon is turned into a slave of laughter, the true wit stands solidly as a free person and from that position can legislate against others! Of all things, laughter can liberate and lift a person into a new category—the democratic, free soul. Thus situated, one can face the world as a free-spirited leader who commands respect from others—all because of one's correct attitude toward laughter. This is a most important contribution to the history of the laughable, for Aristotle's distinction between the liberal and the illiberal jest will be used to rationalize joking into the Roman period, and well beyond into Cicero's time. Echoes of it can be heard in Freud's theories of *Witz, Humor*, and the *Komik*.

But having found a secure home for the jest within rhetoric, Aristotle must contend with one of its more painful modes: the ironic. Irony inflicts pain as it separates the quick and insightful, as we have seen, from the sluggish and dull. As it sorts, it creates hierarchies and makes value judgments about people. In the *Rhetoric*, building on the attitude adopted by Socrates, Aristotle, too, makes irony a mark of aristocratic intelligence: "Irony better benefits a gentleman than buffoonery; the ironical man jokes to amuse himself, the buffoon to amuse other people." Irony here sounds much like Plato's definition—self-deprecation with humor—and like Plato, Aristotle finds he has mixed feelings about it. So much so that he sounds a warning about its subversive powers as a rhetorical device: "Irony is disdainful," he says, "and we become angry with those who treat our seriousness with irony" (2.2.24, 1380).

But even here, Aristotle, like his teacher Plato, finds a way out of this arms control treaty. Sometimes barbed jests, sharpened by irony, become absolutely necessary rhetorical weapons, for the courageous citizen—an ideal type for Aristotle, and a key aspect of the free soul—must never allow defeat. Citing for his authority Gorgias' line about rhetoric's potential for "killing" an opponent, Aristotle thus permits angry rhetorical attacks when all else fails. While he certainly presents his analysis of jesting in terms less modern and less psychological than Freud's, Aristotle nevertheless perceives that jesting can assume the form of an out-and-out violent attack, that it makes possible the annihilation of another person. And because he understands the power of laughter so well, he must find a socially acceptable place for it, and the safest place is in outright attacks confined to the area of rhetoric. For Aristotle, then, these stylized attacks are like stage productions—carefully scripted playlets. Once they step outside that arena, however, beware jesters armed with rhetoric. They can kill with ridicule!

Aristotle's institutionalized solution to excessive, hurtful laughter—consigning it to theater productions—perpetuates the problem he hopes to solve. Unwittingly, he has constructed a theater driven by envy and frustration rather than one, as in the Old Comedy, driven by a sense of participation. Aristotle makes the theater sound neat and tidy, purged of its Dionysian revelry. Indeed, he is like the politician struggling to reform the theater, for descriptions of the Old Comedy seem much wilder than anything he contemplates. Aristophanes' plays, for instance, were characterized by licentiousness and a grossness of allusion that appealed to the general populace. As one historian observes of Aristophanes: "The wildest flights of extravagance were permitted to him. Nothing bound him to a dangerous emphasis or a wearisome insistence. He could deal the keenest thrust, or make the most earnest appeal, and at the next moment—if his instinct told him that it was time to change the subject—vary the serious strain by burlesque. He had, in short, an incomparable scope for trenchant satire directed by pure tact."* The critical term, of course, is "tact." Tact transforms meanness into the Mean.

But no matter, for in Aristotle's conception of the theater, only the select—the well-educated, the rhetorically trained—could take center stage as jesters; the rest had to stand back as observers, watchers, auditors. They might desire to make that step *up*, but for most that would never happen. They were presented with a world they could never enter, their frustration symbolized by a stage elevated high above their seats in the pit.

Aristotle's attitude has discrete hierarchical inequities built into it. His theater could only inspire more frustration and envy. He's a philosopher, not a playwright. He follows Apollo, not Dionysus. He holds in his hand the

*Francis Macdonald Cornford, *The Origin of Attic Comedy*, ed. Theodore H. Gaster (Anchor Books, New York, 1961), p. 158.

staff of authority, not the phallus (*phallika*) of comedy.* Aristotle gives us a picture of the state absolutely calm and orderly; Aristophanes turns the world topsy-turvy. The former caught the attention of other theorists and philosophers of laughter. The latter caught the fancy of the folk. It is in the riotous spirit inspired by Aristophanes that carnival took hold.**

Finally, Aristotle allows one last form of angry jesting, one that flies in the face of the Mean. Since the Mean reflects maturity, young people sometimes have difficulty adhering to it. So Aristotle permits the jests that young people crack, "not in order that anything may happen to yourself, or because anything has happened to yourself, but simply for the pleasure involved" (*Nicomachean Ethics* 1378b., 25). He calls these derisive jibes examples of "educated insolence," which youth tell so that through their wit they can feel superior to others. This idea of superiority through wit has prompted more than one historian to connect Aristotle with Hobbes, who, recall, defined the passion for laughter as a "sudden glory arising from a sudden conception of some eminency in ourselves by comparison with the inferiority of others, or with our own formerly."

Aristotle recognized both cognitive and bodily aspects in emotional responses. His much-discussed theory of purgation in tragedy through pity and fear answered Plato, who demanded that dramatic poetry result in positive benefits for humankind. This led Aristotle to restrict the kinds of plots suitable for tragedy. At the same time, he rejects the Platonic notion that dramatic poetry appeals simply to unintelligent feelings divorced from reason. Thus, he argues for the benefits of comic presentations of the ridiculous and restricts the categories of appropriate laughter: It must come neither from envy, nor from invective, but from the observation of faults and mistakes that do not cause great pain.

*The erotic, as a domain reserved for comedy and the ludic in general, persisted into the Middle Ages and beyond, infecting Renaissance and Restoration drama.

**The comedians, especially Aristophanes, commonly employed a long line. They emphasized the importance of breath in their plays, particularly through the anapestic rhythm of dialogue, delivered at high speed. Perhaps such attention to air recalls comedy's alleged origins in song, or even more basic, in the breath of laughter.

But while Aristotle literally sets the stage for a theory of purgation through comedy, he never fully elaborates such a theory. This is what the anonymous author of a document on the laughable, titled the *Tractatus Coislinianus*, tried to correct. The tractate, appended to one of Aristophanes' plays, which dates it, roughly, no later than 385 B.C., states at the outset that pleasure and laughter purge the emotions that most typically prompt joking and laughter. From historical evidence, those emotions, as we have seen, are probably a combination of anger and envy. Following Aristotle very closely, the *Coislinian Tract* makes precisely the same substantive distinctions of propriety between the illiberal and liberal jest, which becomes the focus of laughter as jesting and laughter move, in their elevated, philosophical forms, from Greece into Rome. We will follow the other, dramatic, thread from Aristophanes, when we take up the subject of peasant laughter, in a discussion of folk festival and carnival.

We have evidence from Diogenes Laertius that Theophrastus wrote a treatise on laughter, which has unfortunately not been preserved. The loss is considerable, for it would have provided the necessary connection between Aristotle and later Roman writers on laughter, namely, Cicero. The connecting subject surely would have been the jest, that expression of a finely tuned, carefully educated wit. Theophrastus' own ideas were carried forward, at least, by two writers on laughter: the first, Demetrius Phaedrus (first century A.D.), in some sketchy fragments; and the second, Plutarch, who quotes from Theophrastus in discussing the suitable jest, in his *Quaestiones conviviales*.

Plutarch borrows from Xenophon, a contemporary of Plato's, who, like Plato, followed Socrates. In his *Cyropaedia*, Xenophon tells of a banquet given by Cyrus, during which Aglaitades, one of Cyrus' serious captains, finds fault with two humorous stories told during dinner. Plutarch retells the story as a way of defending the agreeable jest. Cyrus' own defense incidentally touches on the nature of fiction, laughter's Siamese twin: Aglaitades claims that the narrators told their stories merely to raise a laugh and were unconcerned with the truth of what they were saying. Cyrus strongly disagrees, arguing that his storytellers never hold any damaging self-delusions; for instance, they never claim to be richer, or more courageous, or more capable, than they are for the sake of their own gain. And "those who invent stories to amuse their companions and not for their own gain nor at the expense of their hearers and not to the injury of any one, why are these men not called 'witty' and 'entertaining,' rather than 'humbugs'?" In other words, why can't wit be elevated to the same respectable level as seriousness? And why must we always be so concerned with standards of truth? These are, of course, important questions for the future of fiction: Verisimilitude rather than truth must become the standard for stories—what literary historians have dubbed *untruth*. But even jests—incredibly short, witty stories—must adhere to a high degree of verisimilitude to be truly funny. If they appear distorted and outrageous in their respect for the truth, they sound merely silly.

In this context of the liberal jest in Xenophon, Plutarch emphasizes that, above all, jesting must give pleasure, evidence for which is again provided by Cyrus, who comments on the social customs of the Pharisees: "They asked one another such questions as people are more pleased to be asked than not, that they indulged in such banter as is more agreeable to hear than not; he observed how far their jests were removed from insult, how far they were from doing anything unbecoming, and how far from offending one another." From this, Plutarch concludes that, as an art, jesting can be cultivated, studied, and learned; if that is true, then rules can be established and the genre perfected. Jests must appear, as an initial rule, to spring naturally from conversation. Other people will automatically treat ill-timed and irrelevant jests with insolence: If one cannot jest with good nature, one should not jest at all, for jests can cause great pain, more pain in fact than is possible through insult. Plutarch even approves of the Spartan custom of stopping a jest midsentence if it tends toward bitterness.

The overarching rule is that jesting must provide some degree of pleasure to the listener. And this is best accomplished by learning the proper subjects for a jest. One can impute faults to a victim, but *only* if the jester knows that the person is in fact free from those very faults.* Certain physical irregularities can be ridiculed, others not. People with hooked or snub noses can be safely laughed at, but not people with foul breath. Baldness yes, blindness no. The quixotic moods of lovers make for pleasant jokes. Finally and perhaps most difficult, jesting is always taken more kindly and graciously when jesters laugh at themselves.

We might ask, If there is a more plebeian, less elevated form of the jest, what would it be? It would obviously have nothing to do with rhetoric. Most likely, it would lack linguistic finesse. The answer, I think, is that the jest would be embedded in everyday life. It would be the practical joke, with an emphasis on *praxis*. It would aim, not necessarily at other people, but at institutions or offices. That's what a jest would look like if it were being played out, rather than remaining in a play. What a dazzling display if Aristotle's wit had met Aristophanes' grotesqueries. What would we get? Perhaps a day, or even a week, when every peasant dedicated himself or herself to overturning traditional roles, when each person would walk out of the theater and take to the streets. This is the punch line I am asking the reader to listen for, as the underground humor builds more force and finally collides with these ancient theories of wit and demeanor. To restate the case, we can anticipate a dramatic collision between meanness and the Mean. The explosion will be heard around the world and felt in every small village and town.

*The modern, aggressive joker, filled with envy, on the other hand, plays on a knowledge of a victim's faults to provoke laughter—and always in full public view.

# The Rhetoricians *and the beginnings of fiction*

*The* ancients recognized an astonishing fact about warfare: A single, sardonic laugh can devastate even the most powerful human being, landing its death blow at a person's vulnerability with such deftness that it leaves behind no visible scar, but a wound that may take a lifetime to heal. While the victim may feel sickened, even thoroughly wiped out, in the end he or she feels compelled, as we shall see, to take a public stance and to laugh the attack off. Such awesome power caught the attention of the philosophers in antiquity. Eradicate derision totally, they advised, or at least learn to harness its power by shaping and containing it for the greater good of the community. Left unchecked, sardonic laughter would only tear the fabric of society into tiny shreds. How could anyone, even the mightiest of governors, be expected to rule with every citizen—even the lowliest slave—armed to the teeth?*

*According to the *OED*, the adjective *sardonic* comes from *Sardinia*, specifically from the *Sardonia herba*, a plant probably similar in its effect to marijuana or loco weed, which according to the sixteenth-century physician Ambroise Pere, "renders man insane so that the sick person seems to laugh." So, too, the wounded and the humiliated must resort to seeming insanity and pretend, at least, to laugh at their assassins.

On the other hand, how could anyone hope to give shape to something so evanescent and ethereal—to something that worked its wickedness with such incredible stealth—as laughter?* One would first have to find answers to two questions, the second more knotty than the first: What do people typically laugh at? And why? And then would come the toughest task of all—trying to elicit laughter out of some unsuspecting, sober person, with the use of nothing more than a string of interesting sentences. The inevitable solution for all this, we moderns know, the surest, most elegant, and most socially acceptable way to evoke laughter from another person, lies in the joke—short, witty stories that get the "drop" on their victims through clever punch lines. And that is what we witness with the early rhetoricians, a slow and steady movement toward the modern joke.

To describe the atomic bomb's unique ferocity, people resorted in the nineteen-fifties to such heroic phrases as "Science has harnessed the power of the sun itself." For their part, the rhetoricians experimented with harnessing what they considered the most powerful of human potentialities. In an image I used earlier, one might even equate cracking a joke with splitting the atom. But before that explosion could take place, the scientists of humor, the rhetoricians, first had to formulate rules and theorems.

Obviously, the joke could be utilized as an effective weapon in rhetorical battles. But what about its more peaceful uses? How could the joke be used, for instance, as part of daily social intercourse? The ancient world tried to answer such questions by corralling laughter within the rules of ethics and decorum. When is it appropriate to crack a nasty joke? And against whom? Plato offers an immediate answer: Jokes should never be used whenever a citizen perceives that the excesses of others stand in immediate need of reform. Avoiding such direct attacks, the joker helps ensure the welfare of the entire Republic. The Stoics and Cynics give another response. They too attempt to correct the excesses of others, but for them excess grows out of high seriousness. The Stoics aim to snap people out of taking themselves

*The poet Baudelaire seems to have recognized the staggering power of a joke: "The wise man never laughs but that he trembles."

too seriously. To that end, they recommend a style that mixes the humorous and the serious, using laughter to free people from their serious endeavors, or more accurately, as a way of allowing them to enter a more balanced way back into the serious. As Ernst Curtius observes, "jesting here, as in the Christian preaching of the late Middle Ages, serves the purposes of *ridendo dicere verum*, [Speaking the truth, laughingly]."* The strategy is actually a simple one: People can generally accept serious news more readily and easily when it is presented to them in a humorous manner.

But whenever one lets fly with a joke, under whatever conditions, the joker must observe the rules of decorum. An anonymous book on rhetorical practice, the *Rhetorica ad Herrenium*, a book that medieval English writers relied on for instructions on correct rhetorical strategies, allowed that "*iocatio* [joking] can on the basis of some circumstances, elicit a laugh which is modest and refined." The anonymous author never discloses the exact nature of those "circumstances," a silence that in itself may force the reader to contemplate the appropriate moments to crack a joke. Quintilian, too, permits jesting, but the *vir bonus*, "the good man," must never sacrifice his dignified bearing to a witty line. Dignity is a trope of public speaking—the panegyric—and so public speaking is framed principally around one's ability to master the urge toward outbursts of laughter. Pliny the Younger urges "the orator to relax occasionally by composing witty poems." For Pliny, the seriocomic constitutes not only a rhetorical ideal, but an ideal way of life. The ultimate responsibility for formulating rules for joking, and the making of what today we call politically correct jokes, the rhetoricians take as their own. They act as the new scientists in antiquity; they hold the key to the most powerful weapon. They can unlock its secrets, but finally it will be up to the *polis* to exploit laughter with intelligence and restraint.

But the rhetoricians effectively remove the general population from all discussions of laughter. Their laughter is refined stuff—when done correctly—suitable as we have seen only for aristocrats. The rhetoricians dis-

*Ernst Robert Curtius, *European Literature and the Latin Middle Ages*, trans. Willard Trask (Princeton: Princeton University Press, 1953), p. 417.

cuss laughter at so theoretical a level that it speaks only to a scant few. A wide gap exists between rhetorical theory and peasant concerns. On the street, the peasants swill their ale, and plot and joke and laugh. Cicero, particularly, lays out such elaborate rules for jesting and funny storytelling that spontaneous outbursts, gossip, nonsense, and practical joking seem all the more repugnant, lowly, and dirty. The rhetoricians have no use for such unruly folk activity. Through refining the art of laughter, the rhetoricians turn every peasant into a kind of outlaw, and in the process, cause the whole world of peasants and artisans, male and female, to turn to more and more rowdy brands of humor.

Plutarch's precise rules for jesting fed nicely into a new school of rhetoric under the Stoics in Pergamum, the city famous for giving the West one of the crucial tools of literacy—parchment. The new school combined the earlier, practical rhetoric of the Peripatetics with a new way of presenting material called the Plain Style, which raised oratory to a higher plane—to the level of art. This is a dramatic and radical moment in the history of rhetoric: The discipline of rhetoric, still being taught in universities today, got its inspiration not from the serious pursuit of a scholarly subject, but from a playful abandon to the possibilities of humor. The ironic humor of Socrates coupled with theories of the liberal jest of Aristotle and Plutarch gave rhetoric its distinctively comic bite. Coming to Rome after they had conquered Greece, many of these Stoic teachers, like Diogenes of Babylon and Papatius of Rhodes, introduced the Plain Style and its humor into the Scipionic Circle, where it was ultimately adopted by the person who most vigorously incorporated the art of jesting into oratory, and who in turn heavily influenced medieval theories of rhetoric—Cicero.

When we come to Cicero, it is as if he has beckoned us to the edge of some lofty cliff and invited us to enjoy the commanding, breathtaking view. He presents a vista that opens our eyes to all the wonderful possibilities that jesting and laughter can provide. And he points especially to the highest art of the rhetorician, the delight in merely telling funny stories. Through it all, he bears the welfare of the state in mind, arguing that if a good belly laugh can keep a body healthy, it should also invigorate the body politic.

As an orator, he received a good deal of criticism for his jokes, and even Quintilian regrets that he made so many in his speeches. Cicero could never resist the temptation to make a pun. It must be remembered, however, that the age considered him the great wit. Caesar continually relied on a collection of Cicero's *bons mots*. Ready to defend himself—of course, through humor—Cicero claims that people attribute to him every joke ever told during his time, including those made by the very sorriest of jesters.

In Cicero, wittiness and jesting occupy a more solidly respectable place in the art of rhetoric: Wit no longer is a weapon, as it had been with the early rhetoricians, used to defeat one's enemies, and no longer a virtue in the service of some Aristotelean Mean. Instead, drawing on laughter's divine source—the gods' generous gift to us mortals—Cicero claims that wit, properly employed, can reveal the charitable and cultural nature, the very essence, *quidditas*, of the speaker. True invective—*iocans petulans*—springs from anger, and the malicious character of the speaker. The "petulant joker" can never be considered brave, only belittling and spiteful. But observing rules of propriety—in subject, language, spirit, time, and place—the refined speaker engages wholeheartedly in good-natured humor, using invective only rarely, and bearing the welfare of the state constantly in mind.

As the supreme social critic, Cicero refines Aristotle's liberal jest by dividing it into smaller constituent parts. With one step, he makes it possible for someone like Chaucer to perceive the possibilities in joke-telling by dividing socially acceptable wit (*sales*, "salt") into two main kinds:* the *dicacitas* and the more important *facetiae*. Since these two categories will eventually culminate in the modern, literate joke, they deserve our attention

*Recall Socrates' image of salt used sparingly.

at this moment. Here is Cicero's preliminary distinction between the two kinds of wit, from his principal work on rhetoric, *De oratore* (2.80): "Etenium cum duo general sint facetiarum alterum aequabiliter in omni sermone fusum, alternum oercatutum et breve, illa a veteribus superior cavallatio, haec altera dicacitas nominata est" (For, there being two sorts of wit, one running with an even flow all through a speech, while the other, though incisive, is intermittent; the ancients called the former "irony" [*facetiae*] and the other "raillery" [*dicacitas*]).

In practice, *dicacitas* consist in barbed one-liners whose clearly self-conscious aim it is to elicit admiration and awe from innocent bystanders—particularly from those who have been spared the direct hits of the joker. *Dicacitas* live momentarily, illuminating for the instant with a bright flash and glare. They do not have a life that carries them over large spans of time. Because of the gentility of their wit, *facetiae*, on the other hand, tend to draw laughter out of every member of the audience. These *facetiae* always come off as gay and light-spirited little stories, characterized by the ancients with such words as *hilaritas* (general jesting and sport); *iocus* (jocularity, or modern joking); and most revealing of all, *festivitas*, from Latin *festus*, the word for both "festivity" and "feast," for game and the eating of game.*

Eating sumptuous meals and telling witty stories come together in the history of laughter. They share many characteristics. Witty stories wither during Lent; they feed on the expansiveness of a full menu: A good storyteller must always be an omnivore. Dietary restrictions cramp his or her style. There can be no sacred cows: Everything is fair "game." The storyteller has to take in all of experience, digest it, and then comment on it. Like a joyous cook, the storyteller concocts a temporal delicacy that will be swallowed by his or her guests. And if the cook makes a mistake, there's always the next meal—there's always a next time—to correct things. If the meal seems too

*While the *OED* can provide no source for the phrase "a game leg" (a crippled leg), the phrase might just recall Hephaistos, who certainly had a "game leg," a lame leg that the gods seized on for their own sport and game. The gods make Hephaistos their prey, their game, in the hunt for a good sardonic laugh. A loose association between game and leg is reinforced by the slang term "gam" for leg, from *jambon*, a shank of ham, and the heraldic term *gamb*, for leg. The crippled gam comes from somewhere else, perhaps from Hephaistos.

bland, the chef can always spice it up on another try, and of course, every good chef, every good storyteller, adds a few personal ingredients.*

We might, then, call Cicero the first chef of humor, for he points out, indirectly, that the recipe for humor begins in a very real way in the kitchen, where the fire can be carefully regulated and directed—in a sense, domesticated. He understands also that we quite literally have to have an appetite for humor; in particular, we have to have the "stomach" for aggressive joke-telling. (These days, protracted sessions of joke-telling at some other person's expense—typically good-natured and well-intentioned sessions that ridicule well-known public figures—are called "roasts" and "toasts": Celebrities are cooked over slow-simmering fires, rather than cremated in gigantic, red-hot blazes. Hephaistos knew a different kind of fire, hotter and wilder than the kitchen variety: He didn't make temporal dishes, he fabricated permanent utensils and vessels.)

*Dicacitas* are not associated with anything so nurturing as food and eating. On the contrary, they are associated with death and weaponry. Cicero characterizes them by words that circulate around the general adjective *aculei*, "arrowlike"—an appropriate image for witty attacks against targets of opportunity. Cicero shifts Homer's image of "winged words," a reference to the feathery part of the arrow, all the way down the shaft to the other end—to the arrow's head, emphasizing its ability to penetrate a victim's skin, to wound, and perhaps even to kill.

In a further division, Cicero divides the jest made *in verbo*, about words, from jests made *de re*, about facts. *In verbo* jests are best suited to *dicacitas*, and *de re* to *facetiae*. Jesting *in verbo* produces laughter that is "awakened by something pointed in a phrase or reflection" (*De oratore*

*Athenaeus, a late-second-century A.D. writer who claims authority on comedy, having read, he brags, more than eight hundred plays from the Middle Period of Comedy, tells of a great cook (in his *Deipnosophistai*) who proudly places himself on the same high level of the best, jesting comedians: "I have earned in my profession as much as any comedian has ever earned in his own; my art is a smoke-blackened empire."

So much medieval slapstick is cooked up in the kitchen that Ernst Curtius even gives it a name: "kitchen humor."

2.244), and this most naturally belongs with *dicacitas*, from *dicto*, "words." Any form of *paranomasia*, plays on words such as puns or double-entendres, also belong here. Some people, Cicero believes, can play with language this way innately. But still, Cicero leaves no room for spontaneity and improvisation, since nothing in a display of rhetorical wit should be left to chance. Ragtag play, horsing around, and slapstick characterize a lower class of uneducated, untutored boors. The jester, on the other hand, can be trained for success. The jester always remains carefully in control, like a military officer dominating the battlefield. The jester knows when to pile on details, when to back off, or digress, when to marshall forces and rush in for the kill.

*Facetiae*, in particular, benefit from study and practice—from what the age calls *doctrina*. *Facetiae* belong to an art that can be more easily mastered, and thus Cicero finds them superior to the *dicacitas*. Here, we arrive at Cicero's monumental contribution to the history of literature and, not incidentally, to the history of laughter. By focusing his attention on *facetiae* told *de re*, he fuses the idea of fiction to laughter itself. Anyone who has ever been bored by a story knows how important humor can be in keeping interest alive, or in sharpening the point of a narrative.

*Facetiae* told *de re* behave just like fictional characterizations—*te ipso tota narratio*—and Cicero's conclusion about them places them solidly in that category: "Now the beauty of such jesting is, that you state your incidents in such a way, that the character, the manner of speaking, all the facial expressions of the hero of your tale, are so presented that those incidents seem to your audience to take place and to be transacted concurrently with your description of them" (*De oratore* 2.240). *Facetiae* handed the mimes a whole narrative core for their dramatic performances. In a straight line from Xenophon, Cicero not only sees the necessity for verisimilitude in funny stories, but he establishes fiction, in the West at least, as the proper context for humor. That seemingly offhand juxtaposition that Cicero effected is as exciting and as important as any scientist's radical discovery that can be imagined.

The success of the *facetiae* lies in bringing to life the accurate nuance, the subtle *facts*, of a person's character. In fiction, as in oratory, it means capturing a vulgarized but accentuated imitation, what Cicero calls *depravata imitatione:* caricaturing in order to emphasize a point. Exaggeration produces a good deal of the humor. I leave the summary of Cicero's *facetiae* to Quintilian, who writes about the laughable shortly after Cicero: "In narrando autem Cicero consistere facetus putat, dicacitatem in iociendo" (Cicero believes that narrative is revealed through wit [*facetiae*] and joking through smart attacks [*dicacitas*]).

*Facetiae* developed into such a powerful and popular force in storytelling that various well-known writers even prepared collections of them, beginning with Petrarch and continuing well into the sixteenth century, influencing in turn scores and scores of other writers, including early writers of fiction like Chaucer. In writing fiction, the author has to weave a well-constructed, beautiful lie—a metaphoric reality—so that the tale will be taken seriously, for the author intends to perpetrate the story on a reading or listening audience; he or she hopes to hoodwink them into accepting the fabrication as real. The successful author must be serious with his or her audience and, at the same time, delight in playing a practical joke on it. This is as true for that trickster Mark Twain as it is for Chaucer, who instructs us not to take his brilliant Canterbury *narratio* seriously. He is, he says, merely playing a game, and since the word *game* by Chaucer's day already means "cripple," we should assume he employs it deliberately. Indeed, he lets fly a few jokes that cripple the other pilgrims. Since both author and joker must enjoy being playful, it makes sense that Thoth, the god of writing, is also the inventor of play, the one who, as Jacques Derrida has pointed out, "puts play into play."* Small wonder, then, that so many authors, from Boccaccio to Bellow, delight not only in telling stories, but in telling stories that are funny.

*I am aware that literary playfulness finds expression in something termed a *work* of art. I see no contradiction: On close examination, play often reveals a good deal of solid, mostly gritty, preparatory work—whether one is exercising the body *or* the judgment. Besides, as best as I can gather, *work* was first used in reference to God's works, his creation. A "work of art" carried theological implications and smacked of the highest form of imitation. It did not necessarily mean backbreaking labor, or working by the sweat of the brow.

This symbiotic relationship between joking and fiction, as we have seen, begins in the ancient world. The relationship is made even tighter by the distinctions between comedy and tragedy in that period. Classical tragedy is said to be about *mythos*, "plot" or "history," while comedy concerns itself with *logos* or *hypothesis*, "argument" or "supposition." As Francis Cornford puts it: The distinction between tragedy and comedy resembles "history as opposed to fiction . . . [since] the story element in comedy was a free invention."* In tragedy, destiny wove itself into the very fabric of the plot. Face to face with fate, characters were nothing; plot overwhelmed the loftiest, most strong-willed political figures. Comic characters, on the other hand, roamed freely, raveling their stories, like spiders, as they meandered on their merry ways.

Cicero sees that comedy's mazy narration can greatly benefit the orator, and so he makes it the heart of his new kind of jest, the *iocare in re*: a story about the "truth of a person [brought off by] fabricating every detail." For Cicero, the orator closely resembles the stand-up comic, dazzling an audience with wit and imagination, shaped into little "shticks," and causing every member of the audience to wonder what is true and what is not.** Magically, the orator throws the Muses back at the audience, so that they sit "bemused" and "amused": struck dumb by art and humor.

All of this carries enormous implications for literature, for this kind of jesting permits that remarkable move called original creation, elaborate detailed tapestries from a single thread of truth—what we would be tempted to call, in other contexts, a lie, or a fabrication out of "whole cloth"—the wool, spun and knitted by the author, who so very deftly pulls it over the reader's bewildered eyes. The crucial concern here is believability: Can the author convince the listener or reader, who sits in judgment examining

*Francis Macdonald Cornford, *The Origin of Attic Comedy*, ed. Theodore H. Gasler (New York: Anchor Books, 1961), p. 138.

**Listen to the pattern of present-day, stand-up comics. They constantly surround their stories with phrases like, No seriously, this really happened. Such phrases increase as the laughter increases—both audience and comic playing their game together.

the alibi for leaks, or for holes where the breath may have seeped out?* In a court of law, the jury expects the truth to arrive with a straight face. Laughter has little place where sentencing is at issue. In the court of kings, however, sentences might require smiles, or myriad other facial gestures to present a convincing case. The ancient world spawned an entire class of professionals who were adept at gesturing stories. These actors were called mimes.

In the prologue to the *Wasps*, Aristophanes uses the phrase, "like a laugh from Megara," which refers to crude jokes and vulgar comedy, popularized by mimes in Megara in central Greece, beginning around 600 B.C. Athanaeus calls these mimes *autokabdoloi*, "unprepared" or "improvised," suggesting that much of their work in theaters was authorless and improvised. They nearly always forced poets to take a secondary place, fusing into one person the roles of actor and author. Athanaeus also refers to one of those Megarian performers, Eudiccus, as a *gelatopoios*, "one who arouses to laughter," which he seems to have done not just by gesturing and acting out funny stories, but also through juggling and tumbling. Acrobatics demonstrate the truth of joke-telling and laughter in a spectacular way: the adept joker must be able to keep several narrative balls aloft while, at the same time, negotiating leaps of the imagination.

In Megara, then, a type of nonchoral play developed, absolutely distinct from Attic comedy, which not only influenced Athenian theater but prepared the way for further development of the mime. These farcical plays introduced grotesquely clad stock figures, most of them wearing the phallus, who presented scenes of real life alongside burlesques of mythological subjects. They performed with improvised dialogue, and according to Allardyce Nicoll, a historian of drama, became professionalized by the fifth century B.C.**

*The initial meaning of *auditor* carries an accounting sense: listening out loud to bills of lading for errors of addition and exclusion.

**Allardyce Nicoll, *Masks, Mimes, and Miracles: Studies in the Popular Theatre* (London: George G. Harrap, 1931), p. 106. (I take up the subject of phallic laughter later in this book, in a discussion of the Russian critic Mikhail Bahktin.)

In Rome, the genre took hold and flourished after 300 B.C. as Atellan farce (*fabula Atellana*), named for the town of Atella in Campania, not far from Naples, where the playlets originated. Chaucer's Miller, the fat boor, may ultimately owe his life to one of the stock characters from Atellan farce—big-jawed creatures with hooked noses and wide nostrils (the Miller has "nosethirles blak and wide"). This character is sometimes called Mandacus ("jaws") or Maccus (*maccan* means "stupid"). A forerunner of the Pulcinello character in Italian *commedia dell'arte*, Maccus grinds between his mighty jaws both great amounts of food and gossip. By 55 B.C., Cicero declared the Atellae defunct; mimes had surpassed them. The mimes exerted such power that, according to Nicoll, they gradually drove out not merely the *fabulae Atellanae*, but standard forms of comedy and tragedy as well: "Mimes became masters of the playhouse and ascended to the stage."* The popularity of the mimes can be explained in great part by the breadth of subject matter they embraced. Hermann Reich, who has traced the history of the mime in great detail, says that if tragedy is about imitation, and if comedy is also about imitation, then mimes spring from something much more real, from *bios*—life itself—and in its burlesque of every aspect of daily living, may reveal the essence of literary inspiration.**

Mimes, who we normally conceive as silent actors presenting their dumb shows, actually enable "fiction" to find its initial voice in the Middle Ages. After the collapse of Greek and Roman comedy at the beginning of the imperial age, mimes take on a new life. Ernst Curtius summarizes the history of those players:

> The pantomime, that is, the mimic dance with musical accompaniment, usually without words, was already popular among the Greeks even in the classic period. The mime—first a realistic representation of a single scene from popular life, later also developed to a dramatically constructed farce—had its florescence in the Hellenistic Age and could be either in monologue or dialogue. In Rome both genres were popular from the time

*Ibid.

**Hermann Reich, *Der Mimus* (Berlin: 1903), p. 37.

> of Augustus. Despite numerous attacks on the part of philosophers, and later of the Church, they held their own until the end of Antiquity, and indeed longer. For the mimes for which we have such manifold evidence in the Middle Ages are . . . the successors of the antique mimes. In late Roman Antiquity mime and pantomime become species of entertainment which belong on the same program with musical and acrobatic performances.*

These mimes organize themselves, rather loosely, into troops of itinerant storytellers, translating the jest from the classical world into the Middle Ages and, like troubadours of humor, spreading it as *facetiae* in England, as *Schwanke* in Germany, and as *gestes* in France. As they moved into England and Europe, their underground laughter had an effect on various forms of folk festivals.

Mimes are the missing element connecting jokes and storytelling: The mime, adept at telling a story, will centuries later evolve into the modern author. While we follow these storytellers on their march, we need to know what they were walking into. In some ways, it is like watching Custer ride off to Little Big Horn: The medieval church had set a trap for them. We need to look at the attitudes the church fathers adopted toward the laughable, and what they chose to seize upon and make gospel in the New Testament. "Truly it is not for us," announced Saint John Chrysostom, the most famous of the Greek fathers, in his *On Priesthood* (c. 390 A.D.), "to pass our time in laughter."

*Curtius, *European Literature*, p. 417.

# Medieval Life *and* *laughter*

*Medieval* cosmology divides the world into three parts—heaven, hell, and middle-earth. The two extremes, heaven and hell, can be characterized in terms of their two opposing emotional responses—laughing and weeping. Christian hell, spatially imagined as "below," exists as a place of punishment (*poena*) where the unrepentant suffer the pain (*poena*) of God's absence (*poena damni*) and the tortures of fire and sundry other physical torments (*poena sensus*). Satan and his band of fallen angels preside over those accursed creatures whose souls have grown so heavily freighted with sins committed and sins conceived that their bodies fall downward. Eternally damned, they can do no more than bewail their fate, their tears powerless to extinguish the flames of hell.

Medieval prayers took sinners on the road toward repentance, so they could know the eternal bliss of heaven, a place situated somewhere "above." The soul's natural home, its *patria*, heaven reverberates with mirth and laughter. At the moment of death, the soul sheds its fleshy prison, and thus loses all *gravitas*, its weight and seriousness. Once free of such worldly longing, according to early writers on the subject, like Aristotle, the soul acquires *levitas*, lightness, ascending easily and gracefully heavenward. In a religious sense, the soul defies gravity—indeed, it frees itself of the constraints of gravity. Once in heaven, the soul exists practically as pure *pneuma*, air, free to express its true, Aristotelean nature—laughter. Several major medieval writers, including Chaucer, describe the soul's flight to heaven. That cosmic journey is such a common one that it created its own genre, known as apotheosis poetry, that is, the poetry that elevates one to the level of the gods.

From the vantage point of heaven, the disembodied soul can finally see all worldly longing for what it truly is—vanity. This recognition finds expression in a traditional plaint called the *contemptus mundi*—for example, in Lucan's *Pharsalia*, in Dante's *Divine Comedy*, and in Boccaccio's *Teseida*—through laughter. It's most apparent in Chaucer's world-weary character, Troilus, who, in his own personal apotheosis, "logh right at the wo/of hem that wepen for his deth so faste" (*Troilus and Criseyde*, ll. 1820–21). In its ascendancy, the soul always enjoys the last and wisest laugh.

The medievals of course spent their mortal lives dwelling between those two extremes of heaven and hell, in middle-earth, where laughing and weeping swirled around each other, competing for supremacy. On the earthly plane, the church held sway, and it argued for supreme seriousness, for the mighty tears of sorrow. Any other reaction was mere flippancy or stupidity, or outright pride. Early Christian writers took a dim view of laughter. The Cappadocian father Basil, for all intents and purposes, outlaws laughter of any kind. As he admonishes in *On the Perfection of the Life of Solitaries* (Epistle 22), "The Christian ought in all things to become superior to the righteousness existing under the law, and neither swear nor lie. He ought not to speak evil, to do violence, to fight. . . . He ought not to indulge in jesting; he ought not to laugh nor even to suffer laugh-makers." Hugh of Saint Victor, arguably one of the most influential of twelfth-century writers, in his *Ecclesiastien homilae*, calls laughter nothing but outright evil: "Notandum quod gaudium tantum arguitur, risus vero omnino reporbatur, quia risus omnimodo malus est; gaudium non semper malum est, nisi quando de malo est" (Joy may be good or evil, depending on its source, but laughter is in every respect evil). For Saint Ambrose, laughter betokens pride, while tears represent an outward sign of the true penitential spirit.

Ecclesiastes 7:4 encapsulates the Church's attitude toward laughter: "The heart of the wise is in the house of mourning; but the heart of fools is in the house of mirth." Commenting on this passage, a fifteenth-century sermon in Mirk's *Festial* teaches that "the world's mirth makes a man forget his God and himself also." Hildegard of Bingen, a Rhineland mystic of the twelfth century and certainly one of the most interesting and eclectic women in the Middle Ages, comments frequently on laughter. She is a poet and a scientist, a painter and a musician, abbess, playwright, prophet, preacher, social critic, and an outspoken healer. She argues that laughter gives dramatic proof of our depraved state, that in a prelapsarian world we would all experience an inner joy—something akin to bliss, I imagine—and would have no need of anything so crude and deliberate as bodily laughter. Laughter offers an anodyne to labor; and labor, recall, God delivered as punishment for disobedience in the Garden of Eden. Laughter is a quid pro quo; involuntary outbursts necessary only because humanity's souls have been darkened by sin. Washed of our sins, we would have no need of laughter. We would know only true joy.

As if that were not basic enough, the church found even more fault with laughter. A common church view held that, in a world circumscribed by seriousness and sobriety, laughter makes a mockery of heaven. Laughter suggests that Heaven can be lived in the here and now. Everywhere in the New Testament, one finds a laughter very different from that of the Greeks. The Greeks do not hide the truth about laughter. On the contrary, they write almost incessantly about the power of laughter, not least, of its ability to reform and reorganize society. They seem to realize that people will of course laugh, and thus the Greeks try to domesticate and tame laughter—to corral it and use it to advantage. But the medieval church moves beyond anything resembling detente, or even peaceful coexistence, by trying to eliminate laughter altogether, by returning to the sobering spirit of the Old Testament. Luke 6:21 instructs Christians on the inherent wisdom of postponing the time for laughter. God rewards the hard and diligent work of living on earth with joyful laughter in heaven: "Blessed are you that weep now, for you shall laugh." Five verses later, Luke warns, "Woe to you that laugh now, for you shall mourn and weep." Even Adam embodies the lesson of straitened sobriety. After 900 wearisome years of life, the medieval poem the *Cursor mundi* tells us, Adam learns that at last he can die. On hearing the good news, Adam laughs for the very first time: "Quhen he herd he suld live namare, / than he logh, bot nevere are" (ll. 1399–1402).

Present-tense laughter announces a break with God—it suggests a worldliness obtained through getting and spending.* Even in heaven, Pope Gregory comments in his *Moralia*, the laughter of the elect will assume special status, radiating from the heart and not from the body. It will be heartfelt and not belly-sounded. The Carolingian reformer Benedict of Aniane takes laughter out of the idea of temporality altogether: "Since the Lord condemns those who laugh now, it is clear that there is never a time for laughter for the faithful soul." Once again, as Hugh of Saint Victor allows, joy, depending on its source, can be good or evil, but laughter is always evil.

Into that somber shadow of life, as we know, traveling bands of jugglers and acrobats brought their lighthearted jests and jokes. How could the medieval attitude toward laughter be anything but mixed? Both influences, the heavenly and the hellish, meet in every laugh. This is precisely the nature of laughter. We might indeed consider the Middle Ages—the Latin Middle Ages in particular—as laughter's most compatible home: Laughter, with its clearly contrary nature, seems designed for such an age.

*James 4:9 underscores the theme. To those who would be pure of heart James says, "Let your laughter be turned to mourning and your joy to dejection. Humble yourselves before the Lord and he will exalt you." Laughter does not lead to humility. Indeed, it fills one with the most inflated sort of hubris.

While practically every other literary critic could find in the Middle Ages only the sober and serious, Beatrice White made this observation more than forty years ago, in an essay shockingly titled, "Medieval Mirth":

> It was in Latin that the medieval intellectual found generous possibilities for laughter from verbal play to parody, burlesque, and satire, which the vernacular literature lacked. . . . Latin writers like the English Walter Map, Giraldus Cambrensis, Geoffrey of Monmouth, Alexander Neckham, and Nigel Wireker could incite medieval laughs which were by modern standards sophisticated—"smiles which from reason flow, to brutes denied." In their well-developed conceits and plentiful puns lies a world of wit for those who can discover it. The songs of the Goliards, from the ninth-century anonymous author of *Andecavis Abbas* to the Archpoet are the most rewarding quarry for this reasoned laughter, which has no limits in time and only one country, "terra ridentium."*

Latin was the language of school, the university, estate management, legal proceedings, and, of course, the church. Latin religious literature exerts such a strong influence that by the later Middle Ages laughter's more divine nature—that part associated with heaven—comes boldly forward. A writer like Chaucer even perceives the great religious potential in something so crassly secular as a joke. But in order to make that conversion public, Chaucer has to do something outlandish and shocking: He has to take on God, and he has to play a very significant joke on his audience. That story will come shortly.

Remember, Chaucer comes from a place called "merry old England." That phrase, now proverbial, can be traced to a twelfth-century English historian named Henry of Huntingdon, who termed his precious island *anglia plena iocis*—more than merry, actually, and much closer to "jesting" or even "joking."** A century later, Friar Bartholomew, another historian, borrowed the phrase and added a few bits of detail: "England is full of mirth

*Beatrice White, "Medieval Mirth," *Anglia* 78, no. 3 (1960): 288–89.

**The eighth and ninth centuries abound in warnings against laughter: Alcuin writes an invective against mimes in 791, and around the same time Saint John of Damascus describes people at *spectacula*, "watching from morn till night." In 813, the Synod of Tours announced the "clergy should flee from obscene jesting." In the tenth century, church councils fulminated against mimes. By the twelfth century, England had grown quite merry.

and of game, and men oft-times able to mirth and game; free men of heart and tongue, but the hand is more better and more free than the tongue."*

Everything, including hell itself, could serve as grist for the medieval laughter mill. Jongleurs gambled with Saint Peter for souls in the hottest regions of the netherworld. Dante consigns the sullen to the hottest region, the lowest circle in hell, because they had remained so doggedly sad in the face of God's sweet air. But make no mistake: Life on earth in the Middle Ages required great effort. While there may have been occasion for laughter in the ancient world, where the gods sat on Mount Olympus high above the winds of tragedy and death, in the Middle Ages life on earth remained bound to the most stringent restraints on pleasure. Ecclesiastes 2:2 asks the sobering, rhetorical question: "I said of laughter it is mad, and of mirth what good doeth it?"

Tragedy and death marked the Middle Ages; each day brought new sorrows. No death loomed with such staggering significance, however, as Christ's. The Crucifixion brought the sobriety of salvation to bear against laughter, as a saying of Saint John Chrysostom makes succinctly clear: "Christ is crucified and does thou laugh?" Longer life for a medieval Christian only meant prolonged tribulation. A dictum as old as the fourth century—"Ridere non devant habentes oculum ad judicium ultimum" (He cannot laugh who sees the Divine Judgment)—reminded every Christian of the ultimate seriousness of life on earth, and it remained popular well into the fifteenth century. The solemnity of the Final Moment could stifle the heartiest attempts at laughing out loud. A well-known compendium of sermon *exempla*, the *Alphabet of Tales*, contains the following vignette, which aimed to dramatize the sobriety inherent in the Final Moment: "We read in the *Vitis patrum* [Lives of the fathers] how one time an old man saw a young man laugh, and he said to him: 'Son, how may you find it in your heart to laugh? Must not you and me and we all before heaven and earth give a reck-

*G. G. Coulton, *Medieval Panorama: The English Scene from Conquest to Reformation* (New York: World Publishing Company, 1955), p. 65.

oning of our entire life? And therefore I marvel at how you can find it in your heart to laugh.' " Judgment braces; it raises the most decisive question: Will I be saved? Laughter, as I have said earlier, always posits a future. But the Day of Judgment—Death—may be the only thing that cannot be laughed off. The question lingers longer than any laugh: What will my future—my eternal future—look like? No matter how spirited the medieval's time on earth, no matter how one struggles, Destiny always snatches that last and most satisfying laugh from one's lips.

*Jacob's Well*, a fifteenth-century collection of sermons, contains an even more vivid story about the injudiciousness of laughing in the face of the Awful Truth. It is much more insistent in its depiction of laughter as a totally loathsome and inappropriate companion to life on earth. The account overwhelms the reader with its narrative detail:

> The story is told of a King who never laughed. Even with a great feast prepared before him he still would never laugh. A friend reproved him for his sullen behavior, and asked him why he never laughed, even when faced with the prospect of a lavish banquet. The King answered: "I will show you and thus tell you why I do not laugh." So the King ordered a chair suspended over a burning hot fire by a thin thread, which was continually threatened to be cut down by a sharp sword. Around the chair he placed thirty-five men with drawn swords, ready to pierce the heart of anyone who might chance to sit in the chair. Then the King ordered this death chair to be surrounded by sumptuous delicacies. After which he asked: "Could you be merry under these conditions?" [The King explains that he has constructed a vision of his life for all to see:] "A great feast before me; behind me the bitterness of my sins. In the future I see uncertainty, and on my left hand I see vexations of present adversities, while on my right I see only troubles that come after prosperity. And through all this I see as the thirty-five sharp swords the sentences of the Almighty God. Above me I see death clutching on to the thin string, never knowing when or at what hour death will break the cord, and underneath me I see nothing but the prospect of the fiery pit of Hell, into which I am afraid to fall. Within me I can see only my own frailty. And this is the feeble chair in which I am asked to sit. Therefore, it should not be a marvel at all that I do not find it in my heart to laugh."

Recall that the ancients had a name for such highminded sobriety, *agelastus*, and saw it as a perverse aberration. By the time of the late Middle Ages, such high seriousness has come to characterize virtuous wisdom.*

Medieval Christian life was dominated by one overarching realization: The world would end, and it would end at a precise, predetermined time. It was a moment to strive for, to work toward, for in Eternity one could anticipate the possibility of laughing forever. But it was also a moment to be feared—nothing to be laughed at. Ephraim the Syrian, a saint who lived in Mesopotamia in the early fourth century, defended orthodoxy by opposing laughter in all forms and at all times. Quite possibly the most influential of all Syrian writers, his orthodoxy spread throughout monastic Christianity. Saints Basil and Cassianus adopted his severe stance against levity. "The Christian monk will enjoy laughter only in the future," says I. M. Resnick, a historian of medieval monastic life, "when he has finally escaped the snares of the devil and entered into the heavenly Jerusalem."** Only the devil laughs in the present and only, as the early German writer Rupert of Deutz points out, when he dupes the faithful.

One of the principal rulebooks for monks, the *Regula magistri*, from the sixth century, lists laughter as a despicable vice that wounds the soul, and that must be rooted out of monastic life. The *Regula* gives precise instructions for stifling laughter: If a brother begins to laugh, tell him "to do what you do with seriousness, because the time of our monastic life is not a time of joy for laughing, but a time of penance." A sixth-century monastic rulebook, the *Regula Pauli et Stephani*, cautions that laughter leads only to arguments; therefore excessive laughter (*supra modum*) tempts the devil. The anonymous, fifth-century *Regula Patrium Serapionis* orders that any monk overcome by laughter ought to be punished by two weeks of something called "the scourge of humility" (*flagello humilitatis*). The great ency-

*Not all sermons mined a vein of seriousness. The Italian poets Boccaccio and Dante both allude to the use of jokes in sermons. In England, preachers added little stories, called *exempla*, to enliven their sermons, many of them funny, and many of them racily funny. The technique, called *ioca seriis miscere*, developed over the course of the Middle Ages into common practice.

**I. M. Resnick, "'Risus Monasticus': Laughter and Medieval Monastic Culture," *Revue Benedictine* 97 (1987): 99.

clopedist Isidore of Seville even recommends a punishment of "three days of excommunication" for monks who laugh during performances of the canonical hours. Saint Columban's *Regula coenobialis* commands: "He who because of coughing in the beginning of the psalm does not sing out well is commanded to make amends by six strokes. . . . And he who smiles in the service . . . six strokes; if he breaks out into the noise of laughter, a special fast unless it has happened pardonably."*

Saint Benedict, drawing on Ecclesiastes 21:23, promulgated what would finally turn out to be the monastic norm concerning laughter: That is, some moderate laughter, under certain circumstances, could be tolerated. But the way there was tricky and required a linguistic loophole. In the *Regula* for delimiting the behavior of his monks, Saint Benedict seems to outlaw all laughter. Rule 53: "Verba vana aut risui apta non loqui" (Do not speak idle words, or such as to move to laughter). But then, in the very next rule, Benedict seems to recant a bit, as if in recognition of the futility of calling for such an impossibility as absolute abstinence from laughter. Rule 54: "Risum multum aut excessum non amare" (Do not love great or excessive laughter). But the monastic rule may leave an out, for it is silent on the question of moderate laughter; some might even suggest that, by focusing on excessive laughter, the church fathers even condone its moderate forms. This interpretation gains support from Athanasius, a fourth-century bishop of Alexandria and saint, who points out that Anthony's speeches were "spiced with Godly wit"; and even Paul, in his Letter to the Colossians centuries earlier, urges them to "make their speeches gracious, seasoned with wit [*in gratia sale*]."**

The model of Chrisitian life, of course, is Christ. Even the simplest of his acts and deeds and thoughts carry the most momentous implications. As the Middle Ages perceives him, he is the Son of the Hebrew God—serious, sol-

*The important connection between fasting and sobriety will be taken up later. Some Jewish texts also reveal an ascetic attitude toward laughter. Witness the *Manual of Discipline* from Qumram: "Whoever laughs foolishly with audible voice shall be fined for thirty days" (See Resnick, "'Risus Monasticus,'" p. 96).

**Quoted in Ernst Robert Curtius, *European Literature and the Latin Middle Ages*, trans. Willard Trask (Princeton: Princeton University Press, 1953), p. 421.

emn, devoid of any trace of joyous laughter. Publius Cornelius Lentulus, president of Judea in the reign of Tiberius Caesar, wrote a letter to his monarch that purports to contain an eyewitness account of Christ. The letter offers a remarkably detailed description of Christ, including his skin color and blemishes, and the range and nuance of his emotions. Lentulus points out quite decisively that, while Christ smiles and frequently weeps, "no man has seen him laugh." Thus a Wycliffite sermon announces: "Of Cristis laughing we reden never in Holy Writt, but of His myche penaunse, teris, and shedynge of blod." A note of Benedict of Aniane's *Concordia regularium* mentions that one Salvian of Marseille, a fifth-century Latin writer, translated the sober Christ to the Latin church.*

Ferroleus draws on the fact of the dour Christ in his sixth-century *Regula ad monachos* (Rulebook for monks) to turn monks away from levity. Benedict of Aniane, Peter the Chanter, and Saint Anselm of Canterbury all refer to Christ's somber demeanor, as do John Chrysostom and John of Salisbury in his *Polycraticus* (1154): "No man has seen him laugh, but he has frequently wept in the presence of men." The *Cursor mundi* gives a more precise rendering of the facts: "That thrice he wep we find i-nogh / Bot we find never quar he logh."

Christ's sobriety raises an important theological issue. Christ walks the earth as a fully enfleshed human being. His humanity has been depicted in the most bizarre iconography. Leo Steinberg, a Renaissance art historian, has, for instance, collected fifteenth-century images of the resurrected Christ that show him, as unbelievable as it sounds, with an enormous erection. Steinberg says that artists used this detail to convince the viewer—especially the doubting viewer—that Christ, after his death, could still partake of everything fleshly. Christ returns, not as some ethereal ghost, but as flesh and blood *capable* of consummating even a sexual relationship.

*The Victoria and Albert Museum owns a sculpture by Antonio Rosselino (c. 1465–75) that one art critic, John Pope-Hennessy, has called "The Virgin with the Laughing Child"—the only depiction I can find of Christ laughing. Pope-Hennessy attributes Christ's happy demeanor to the "unreflecting temper of childhood" (John Pope-Hennessy, "The Virgin with the Laughing Child," in *Essays on Italian Sculpture* [London: Thames and Hudson, 1968], pp. 72–77).

Shouldn't we expect from this living body a laugh or two? Church fathers and the early commentators on theology seemed reluctant to concede the point. Perhaps for them laughter was far more dangerous than sex. At any rate, they fudged the issue by arguing the notion of capability. Peter the Chanter, for example, advised Christians to adopt a cheerful disposition (*mentis hilaritatem*), basing his case on the example of Christ: For Peter, Christ retains the *capacity* for laughter, for *risibilitas*, he says, constitutes a *proprium* of all human beings.* So Christ chooses to remain sober and serious; he elects not to laugh. But the idea of a nonlaughing Christ bothers some people. A group of twentieth-century biblical scholars have accepted the idea that Christ never laughed, but have attributed to him nevertheless a sense of humor, examples of which they find scattered throughout the Gospels. They have produced their arguments in seriously reasoned books that carry such titles as *Humor in the Bible*, *The Humor of Our Lord*, *The Humor of Christ*, and *The Comic Vision of the Christian Faith*.

A sober Christ does not merely bother someone like Nietzsche, it enrages him. Nietzsche wishes that Christ "had remained in the wilderness, and far from the good and just! Perhaps he would have learned to live and to love the earth—and laughter too."** Christ's problem, for Nietzsche, comes from his contact, not just with civilization, but with the rule-bound, righteous side of civilization. In its ability to break rules and bend behavior, laughter creates its own wilderness; and according to Nietzsche, Christ could have used the training to advantage.

But capacity won't fully explain why Christ gets depicted as an *agelaste*. Why doesn't he laugh? Or, rephrased to focus light on the history of laughter, how would a laughing Christ differ radically from a sober one? The easy and perhaps obvious response is to say that people would have a

*In addition to Christ, many saints also refused to laugh—Eugendus, Saint Anthony, and Saint Martin of Tours. Among pagans, church officials argued, sobriety was not a virtue, but, as the *Concordia regularum* notes, a defect "born of an excess of bile or other defects of nature." Only the Christian, aware of the impending Day of Judgment, knows why he or she should not laugh now. Only the devil risks everything by laughing now.

**Friedrich Nietzsche, *Beyond Good and Evil: Prelude to a Philosophy of the Future*, trans. Walter Kaufman (New York: Random House, 1966), p. 223.

hard time taking a laughing Christ seriously. He could laugh off our imprecations; he might forget us entirely, or worse yet, he might dismiss us. At any rate, he probably would not take our plight to heart. With a Savior not only capable of laughing, but one who has been known to laugh out loud, our prayers might wind up lost amid those heavenly, funhouse sounds.

Christ's sober demeanor, however, runs much deeper. In her work on taboo, *Purity and Danger*, the anthropologist Mary Douglas discusses notions of hygiene and the sacred. "Primitives," Douglas says, "make little difference between sacredness and uncleanness." But that does not hold for religions like Christianity: "For us sacred things and places are to be protected from defilement. Holiness and impurity are at opposite poles."* In the context of the Christian Middle Ages, a laugh is always a "dirty laugh," humor always "earthy humor." Every joke is "off color," a color that runs to varying shades of humus and earth and shit. A laughing Christ is not only a frivolous Christ, he is something worse: a dirty, defiled one. And a defiled Christ has no power, no efficacy. Christ must remain *white*, in the purest sense of that word. Folk laughter at carnivals, festivals, and feasts is groundling, even underground, humor. It is earthy in the sense that Nietzsche wanted Christ to "love the earth." Folk laughter is at best a soiled, off-white humor; at worst, a black humor.

Whiteness and purity are states achieved not just by ritual cleansing—through washing and ablutions—but through strict observance of rules and restrictions. White is not only a color, that is, but a condition, a state of the soul's being. By definition, laughter breaks all rules; and in its tendency toward chaos, laughter also inclines toward defilement and desacralization.

We might wonder if the Father is like the Son: Does the Christian God laugh? Radically different from the Hebrew God, the Christian God not only laughs, but gets exonerated for his scornful laughter. Charlemagne's teacher, Alcuin, remarks that when God laughs with scorn at the nonbe-

*Mary Douglas, *Purity and Danger: An Analysis of the Concepts of Pollution and Taboo* (London: Routledge and Kegan Paul, 1966), pp. 7 ff.

liever he is actually doing something good. Alcuin doesn't explain why. Pope Gregory the Great continues the same theme, and explains that when God laughs at the wicked, in Proverbs 1:26, his laugh indicates an unwillingness to extend his mercy to them. Gregory even has a name for this: "A Just Laughter." God also laughs in Job 9:23, at the tribulations of the innocent. Here, Gregory exonerates God by saying that he does not really laugh scornfully. God does not laugh at the pains of the innocent, for the innocent are actually suffering the pains of desire: They desire to know God. In effect, God is laughing for joy, rejoicing over the fact that the innocent will eventually work their way toward him. The innocent can enjoy a laugh, then, because it stems ultimately from the beneficence of God. Thus Bildad says to Job that if he is really blameless "[God] will yet fill your lips with laughter, and your mouth with shouts of joy" (Job 8:21).

Christ himself encounters a version of this laughter of disbelief in his own ministry. In the most vivid story of his healing miracles, a ruler came to Christ begging him to restore his dead daughter to life. When Christ informed him that his daughter was not dead but only asleep, a crowd gathered around the daughter and "laughed at him" (Matt. 9:24). They laughed again in Luke 8:53, "knowing that she was dead," and laughed once more in Mark 5:40 for the very same reason.

Christ also knows the exhilarating power of laughter, but he allows it only after the Day of Reckoning. Thus, Jesus promises laughter, in Luke 6:21, to those who wait for heaven: "Blessed are you that weep now, for you shall laugh." As Gregory the Great maintains, true, joyous laughter can only be enjoyed in heaven, but that heavenly joy never turns to raucous laughter.

Although Christ may not have laughed, it is possible to read at least one of his acts as a joke. And jokes—original, playful ones—may be easier for medievals to read into Christ's life than outright laughter, particularly joyful laughter, for the hope of reform usually guides the actions of the practical joker. The silliest of practical jokes can finally prove to be quite moral. A common metaphor for the Incarnation, for example, is the mousetrap. Augustine, a person who loved puns and wordplay of all sorts, uses this image in at least three separate sermons to explain Christ's Incarnation as a divine trick played on Satan.* Here is Sermon 263, for example: "Exsultavit diabolus quando mortuus est Christus, et ipsa morte Christi est diabolus victus, tanquam in muscipula escam accepit. Gaudebat ad mortem, quasi preaepositus mortis. Ad quod gaudebat, inde illi tensum est. Muscipula diaboli, crux Domini: esca qua caperetur, mors Domini" (The Devil exulted when Christ died, but by this very death of Christ the Devil is vanquished, as if he had swallowed the bait in the mousetrap. He rejoiced in Christ's death, like a bailiff of death. What he rejoiced in was then his own undoing. The cross of the Lord was the Devil's mousetrap; the bait by which he was caught was the Lord's death).**

Augustine and others also commonly describe Christ's body as the bait on a divine fishhook, which again lures Satan to his own demise. As one critic observes: "God thus plays a trick, a joke, on the demon, but it is a joke with the most serious, far-reaching consequences. . . . The Deceiver is deceived, and God's control of history, this cosmic game, is proved supreme."† Christ is a fisherman, by some accounts an angler, another word for someone who does not deal in a straightforward manner, but who likes to play the "angles," hoping to hook the big one. In the extremes of behavior, we say this person is crooked. Not to say that Christ is dishonest, but he hardly ever speaks straightforwardly, preferring to describe the outlines of truth in parables (parabolically).‡ Sir Izaak Walton's *Compleat Angler* uses fishing as a metaphor for achieving accurate perception—for being able to see the truth in lies. To that end, Walton instructs his readers how to calculate the exact

*Peter Brown, in his remarkable biography of Saint Augustine, attributes the love of linguistic play not merely to Augustine's quirky character, but to Africans in general.

**"De Ascensione Domini," in J. P. Migne, ed., *Patrologia Latina*, vol. 38, col. 1210 (1844–64).

†Carolyn Dinshaw, "Dice Games and Other Games in Le Jeu de Saint Nicholas," *PMLA* 95, no. 5 (October 1980): 810.

‡It is important that Christ knows how to play the angles, for the devil is believed to travel in a straight line only; he cannot negotiate zigzags or curves. Mazes are religious configurations in the early Middle Ages, training grounds for learning how to evade the devil.

Christ's power turns out to be his own undoing. Roman soldiers crucify him on four right angles—on a cross. The Crucifixion has been iconographically presented, at times, as an anchor, an etymological play on angle. (Note: In Old English, *angle* is spelled and pronounced *angel.*)

location of the fish as the water distorts its position to the untrained eye, and how to fool the fish into taking the bait. In its own way, the *Compleat Angler* is an analysis of duplicity and parabolic vision. It is also an extended metaphor for handling the devil, who never deals with humankind directly, and who certainly does not speak directly, but rather out of the side of his mouth (again, parabolically), and who seems always to sound off on one tangent or another. People can easily miscalculate his ideas and actions as he works his wiles through the distorting medium of evil. To steal human souls, however, is no easy task, forcing him to use every trick in and out of the book.

To return to Christ's laughter: His great joke involves water. In the Middle East many fakirs still demonstrate their extraordinary powers by walking across hot coals, a tradition that dates from before the time of Christ. But to show the enormity of *his* great power, Christ goes one better. Anyone can walk on heat, he seems to imply, even intense heat. So try this one: Try walking on cold. Try strolling on a body of water. Now there's a true miracle!

The Latin church railed so forcefully against laughter because obviously people love to laugh, and laughter can be terribly upsetting—socially, politically, and religiously. With every other controversial subject—from adultery to indulgences—the church held conflicting views. The church left open all possibilities, all interpretations—on a wide range of topics. But with laughter, the church did not equivocate. It announced strongly and flatly: Do not laugh! To prevent people from laughing seems on its face an impossibly absurd task. How could the church enforce such a policy?

It chose to convince people of the evils of laughter through a discussion of language. For one thing, language is a far less abstract topic than laughter. It is also more immediate and more common than laughter. And besides, the church already held a theory of language: After all, Christianity started with the Word. Christians had to be on guard whenever they spoke, for English was itself a language fallen from the purity of ancient languages like Hebrew or Greek.

Church fathers, as early as Clement of Alexandria (Clemens Alexandrinus), who was born around 150 A.D., initiated this linguistic drive against laughter. In his *Paedagogue*, Clement adopts Plato's tough moral line: "Men who imitate laughable or ridiculous behavior are to be excluded from our city. All exterior words have their source in the temperament and in the character; therefore, no foolish words can be spoken without betraying a foolish temperament."

Clement calls human speech, even in its imperfect state, our "most respectable possession"; it would be wrong to abuse language further by turning it into a joke. Clement's argument against laughter, like Hildegard's, finds people's need for frivolity and laughter to emanate from their fall from grace. In Paradise, words and deeds merge, and thus illusion and fantasy make no sense there. The serpent, who tempts Eve, is an intruder. He knows duplicity. His words are like laughter; something else, some meaning, lurks just beneath the surface of everything he says and does. Laughter marks a separation of humanity from God's spoken Word. Only outside the Garden can we see something silly or hear something ridiculous—that is, see or hear something that does not perfectly match up with our expectations—that makes us laugh. Jacques Ellul, in a curious book about the religious character of language titled *The Humiliation of the Word*, points out that the Fall is guaranteed the moment "sight is considered independently of the word":

> In Genesis 3 we read that "the woman *saw* that the tree was good for food, and that it was a delight to the *eyes*, and that the tree was to be desired to make one wise" (Gen. 3:6). This is the first time sight is a separate issue. This sight refers to the tree of the knowledge *of good and evil*; that is to say, the tree of discernment of the truth. She sees; she no longer hears a word to know what is good, bad, or true. She sees—reality. She sees the *reality* of this tree. What she sees has no relationship with the word—neither with the serpent's word nor later with her own word, and finally not with Adam's word when he speaks to God.*

*Jacques Ellul, *The Humiliation of the Word*, trans. Joyce Main Hanks (Grand Rapids, Mich.: William B. Eerdmans, 1985), p. 96.

Eve sees a way of taking charge of reality herself; she gains that very modern notion of sight turned inward: *insight*. At that moment, she hears God's Word differently because it is placed in doubt. The possibility that Christ could laugh would mean, given the way Clement frames the argument, that we hold in our hearts the conception of Christ as one of us—fallen into a murky, doubtful, and earthy state, where all words mean little, all things look silly, and all jokes sound dirty. But according to the patristic linguistic theory, Christ, as the Word, could never laugh. For someone like Clement, laughter makes the Fall an event that takes one into the so-called liberating world of secularity, where the restraints of religion have been dropped. Laughter is a signal of delight at being free of the confines of Paradise; it sounds the call of blasphemy more loudly than any other utterance ever could.

But then Clement, too, must deal with reality: People laugh, and so he allows laughter, but only in moderation. Unrestrained laughter, he concedes, is a sure sign of lack of self-control and discipline: "We need to take away from man any of the things that are normal to him, but only set a limit and due proportion to them. It is true that man is an animal who can laugh; but it is not true that he therefore should laugh at everything." An English courtesy book designed to teach Christian children proper manners and correct social behavior, the *Ratis Raving*, which dates from the fifteenth century, claims the same benefits for following moderation in laughter, except in rare instances of exceptionally clever joking: "Nocht loud of lauchtyr amang men, / Thar smylyng scantly may men ken. / Bot syk a bourd may quhilum fall, / That al men lauch, baith gret and smal" (Among men, do not laugh loud, / where a scant smile may suffice. / But sometimes people may hear a joke / so that all men, both great and small, laugh).

Tertullian and Saints Cyprian and John Chrysostom all wrote against the idolatry of ancient spectacles, particularly the distortions of the mimes in wearing masks and women's dresses to produce laughter. Spectacles and deception: They combine the two concerns of independent sight and angling duplicity. According to Saint John Chrysostom, bishop of Constantinople in the fifth century, only the devil bestows jests and laughter; God grants seriousness. The devil therefore is the unspoken producer of those spectacles. Tertullian, in a powerful image, contrasts the pagan spectacle with the only true spectacle—the Second Coming of the Lord: "Then will the tragic actors be worth hearing, more vocal in their own catastrophe; then the comic actors will be worth watching, much lither of limb in the fire." He concludes by citing Corinthians 2:9: "But what are those things which 'eye has not seen nor ear heard and which have not entered into the heart of man'? Things of greater delight, I believe, than circus, both kinds of theater, and any stadium."*

Seriousness and moderation, as we have seen, are ancient ideals of dignity, of the *vir bonus*; these became incorporated into medieval asceticism as a way of dealing with jocularity and laughter in the religious. In his *Life of Anthony*, Athanasius says that the saint was neither overly morose nor overly frivolous nor excessive in his laughter. Curtius quotes Sulpicius Severus on Saint Martin: "Nemo unquam vidit iratum, nemo commotum, nemo maerentem, nemo ridentem"—that "none should fly into a rage, or into excitability, or fall into sorrow, or into laughter." He adds that the Syrian Ephraim (d. 373) composed a parenesis against laughter by monks; Saints Basil and Cassianus did the same.** Moderation, the middle road, the Aristotelean Mean—these offered the safest, most sound conditions for enjoying an occasional round of laughter.

It is an interesting development, one of those curious and powerful times in the history of ideas, that the Aristotelean Mean—the average, if you will—transforms into meanness, nastiness. Laughter, or more accurately, the need for laughter, helps effect that transformation. To escape from the narrowness of asceticism (the Mean), sardonic laughter, or what might be

*Chrysostom begrudgingly allows that sometimes laughter can lift the hearts of the desperately sad; and sometimes laughter merely wells out of us on seeing, say, a long-lost friend.

**Curtius, *European Literature*, p. 420.

construed as humiliating laughter (meanness), helps to make life bearable. It offers a "break." The classical Greek image of someone under "stress"—an image that persisted well into the Middle Ages—likens them to an arrow held fast under maximum tension by a bowstring pulled taut. (Today, we might say such people feel "held back," "under pressure," "uptight," and so on.) Pulled too far, the string may break, and the arrow drop feebly to the ground. But once the archer pulls the bow to precisely the right spot and then releases it, the person, to continue the metaphor, takes off in a trajectory of liberation. The flight, heading briefly and exhilaratingly toward heaven, symbolizes the need for mirth and laughter in people's lives.

Compare this description of the life of Saint Anthony, in the medieval poem *An Alphabet of Tales*, in which the saint, using the image of a bow and arrow, argues for mirth and sport to ease an otherwise drawn-out and taut life:

> Then Saynt Anton sayd unto hym agayn, "loo! son, thus it is in the werke of allmyghtie God; ffor and we draw it oute of measure, we may sone breke itt; that is to say, and we halde our brothir so strayte in everything that they come to no murth nor no sporte, we may lightlie cause them to breke their order. And therefor us muste some tyme lowse our pithe, and suffre them hafe some recreacion and disporte emang all their other chagis, as Caton says, Interpone tuis interdum gaudia curis."*

Middle-earth could be a confusing place for any clear-thinking medieval. Tears and laughter, as we have seen, competed for the soul of every man, woman, and child. In sermon after sermon, priests preached against the evils of bodily pleasures, to which people inevitably gave in. Nowhere was the contradiction more immediately felt, I suggest, than with laughter, which, unlike sex, could be enjoyed in public, and at the drop of a hat. We have already seen that the church castigated those who continually and excessively laughed, and consigned their souls to an eternity in hell. By the late Middle Ages, the church characterized laughter as an addiction, one to be

*This is an odd bit of advice from Saint Anthony, since he, along with Eugendus, and Saint Martin of Tours, as I have said earlier, had a reputation for never succumbing to laughter.

worked on and "kicked." Reginald Pecock even offered a crude version of a twelve-step program to get the monkey of laughter off the backs of Christians. His *Rule of Christian Religion* (1460) insists that laughter, like dicing or drinking, can be easily given up: "Also every day in ech houre of the day we mowe forbeare certeyn usis if oure outward wittis, as is of sight, of speche, of taast, of thought, of laughing, of joking and of gambling; though not al, then some; though not always, yet at certeyn times."

The church took a hard line against laughter as a way of protecting itself, for it recognized laughter as the nexus, the weak point, which connected all authority with the general population. In fact, one might argue that the church viewed authority, not seriousness or sobriety, as the antonym of laughter. If trouble developed, it would most likely occur at that juncture, with fluidity as the connector—humor. The church got it right. The rabbis, too. If organized religion hoped to remain organized, only seriousness would keep it solidly together. The zany, the foolish, the joking clown only brought distractions and chaos. Authority achieves focus by fasting ("fastening" one's attention); joking distracts and diffuses with its insistence on feasting. Joking draws us off guard and relaxes us. And in the Middle Ages, laughter slips away from authority and into the masses. Jokes constantly threaten to break out and overwhelm those who would control them. In such a volatile political atmosphere, the church could not afford many such slips.

It took a sociologist, not a literary critic or historian, to perceive the ludic potential that lay under the surface of daily medieval life. Johan Huizinga, the first scholar to look with fresh eyes into the Middle Ages—indeed, *under* the obvious facts of the period—wrote a brilliant book that he entitled, significantly, *Homo Ludens: A Study of the Play Element in Culture*. In it, he characterizes medieval culture, *sub specie ludi*: "The influence of the play-spirit was extraordinarily great in the Middle Ages, not on the inward structure of its institutions, which was largely classical in origin, but on the ceremonial with which that structure was expressed and embellished."* Huizinga describes medieval society as one marked by the informing spirit of games and play in virtually every aspect of life, and he documents the way writing, fighting, and loving found expression in incredibly ritualized, circumscribed behavior. Huizinga finds a society dying to put its playfulness into practice, but held in check by rules and regulations. He describes a period of incipient laughter, of a joke just waiting to be told.

And jokes did get told. Many medieval authors, including priests themselves, drew on the ancient strategy of using humor to instruct. Medieval writers like John Arderne, harking back to Hippocrates, advise leeches "to have a stock of good tales and honest that may make the patients laugh [or] induce a light heart in the patient or sick man" (*Treatise of Fistula*). Priests used the device of beneficent humor to such effect that the *Summa predicantum* files a complaint against their overuse: "If anyone tells some open folly in the pulpit, they retain it in the memory well enough; not so the useful things . . . those folks hearken with the greater zest for vain, quaint and laughable matter in the sermon, which may provoke them to mirth . . . the good things they fail to bring away. The remarks that were out of place, they are all too ready to seize upon, to repeat them again and again with glee."

The most detailed defense of joking and laughter comes in the form of an extended dialogue between two characters, Dives and Pauper.** In this dialogue, Pauper convinces Dives that God desires his creatures to find mirth and joy on earth, and particularly on the Sabbath. I quote at length here:†

PAUPER: Miracle plays and dances that are done honestly and principally for devotion, with some mirth, and for no ribaldry,

*Johan Huizinga, *Homo Ludens: A Study of the Play Element in Culture* (Boston: Beacon Press, 1955), p. 180.

***Dives* derives from the Latin for "rich man" and occurs in the Vulgate, in Luke 16, and according to the *OED* is first used in English, by Chaucer, to mean "rich man" in the *Canterbury Tales*. Pauper is of course the poor man. The dialogue between these two characters represents a kind of mini-carnival, in which abundance confronts abstinence.

†The text was written around 1405, but it has not been printed since 1536 and remains obscure. I owe this transcription to the medievalist V. A. Kolve.

are lawful, so long as they do not lead people from God's service, nor from hearing God's word, and that there be no error mixed in with such plays against the faith of Holy Church. All other plays should be prevented on Holidays and workdays.

DIVES: Then it seems by your words that at Holidays man may lawfully make mirth.

PAUPER: God forbid else, for as I said holidays are ordained for rest and relief both of body and soul. And therefore in natural law, in written law, and in the law of grace, from the beginning of the world, holidays and Sundays are a time of worship of God whose day it is. Therefore the prophet says: This is the day God made; make we now merry and be glad.

DIVES: Saint Augustine says that it is less wicked to go at the plough and at the cart and card and spin on Sundays then to lewd dances.

PAUPER: Saint Augustine speaks of such dances and plays as were performed in his time when Christian people were much intermingled with heathen people, and by old custom and example of those heathen people engaged in unhonest dances and plays that stirred folks to lechery and to other sins. And if dancing and plays now stir men and women on holidays to pride and lechery and gluttony and sloth, and to idleship on work days, as it is clear some of them do today, then those plays are unlawful on holidays and on the work days. Saint Augustine condemned such plays, but he did not condemn honest plays and dances.

DIVES: We find that in holy writ God bade his people to torment their souls on holidays and to move toward sorrow and mourning.

PAUPER: Solomon says, the hope, the desire, and the longing that is delayed torments the soul. For the more that man or woman long after a thing the more it is a disease, until that time he has his disease and his longing. But it is so that the mirth, the ease, and the welfare that God has ordained on the holidays is a token of endless rest and joy and mirth and welfare in heaven's bliss that we hope to have without end. For there men shall respite without end from all manner of travail, thought and care. And therefore as I said first God wills it that we think on holidays of the rest and joy and bliss that the holidays betoken,

> and that we keep that idea of what is to come in our minds always, and not to show great heaviness and to do bodily penance on any great holiday.

The dialogue drips with moral suasion, as the poor man—the peasant—shows that he knows and, more important, respects the limits to pleasure. But obviously mirth and joking and even hilarity worked their way through medieval life; they could never be turned aside. And periodically, as in the dialogue between Dives and Pauper, one sees the struggle made public. But notice, Pauper argues for limits, emblematic, really, of pleasure within bounds. Even certain saints sometimes showed a greater side of their humanity by running counter to the sober spirit of Christ and other saints, displaying the virtue they called *hilaritas*, their capacity to laugh like other human beings. Indeed, a theological strategy developed of conversion through *risibilitas*. Around these saints gathered a collection of jokes called the *ioca sanctorum*, short, witty stories by which the saints show themselves as amused and cheerful beings, as willing sometimes to laugh and play until they feel that their companions are prepared to hear more serious things. The historian Benedicta Ward, in her *Miracles and the Medieval Mind*, points out that in these *iocae* "miracles were not mocked, though false claims were ridiculed. . . . Odo of Cluny . . . was said to have made his companions 'laugh till they cried, and were unable to speak to one another.' . . . Aldhelm of Malmesbury entertained the local people by songs and jokes until they were prepared to listen to his more serious remarks."*

The two major collections of *iocae* circulated around the trickster powers of Saint Faith and around the twelfth-century shrine of Saint Thomas of Canterbury. Numerous jokes—miracles of laughter—grew up around the healing water that Saint Thomas dispensed at his shrine. (It is no coincidence that Chaucer's pilgrims decide to tell stories, many of them decidedly humorous, on the way to their destination, the shrine of Saint Thomas; or that the Miller's story revolves around water.)

*Benedicta Ward, *Miracles and the Medieval Mind* (Philadelphia: University of Pennsylvania Press, 1982), p. 211.

The second part of this chapter records the great swelling tide of laughter that buoyed the spirits of medieval peasants, what Mikhail Bakhtin calls in a brilliant phrase, "the second revelation of the world in play and laughter." Their church showed them one miracle, in the eschatological life of Christ. But laughter revealed quite another, a highly secularized miracle that used parody and jokes as its essential tools and revealed to the great numbers of lay citizens the tremendous power they could exercise outside institutions and organizations. As modern readers, we easily forget that medieval seriousness as it is articulated by Holy Church achieved its efficacy through the great threat of perdition and pain, of suffering and sorrow. Life threatens the Christian at every moment in the Middle Ages. Laughter knows no such tamping. Medieval laughter continually promises liberation because it forever frees itself of sanction. Given the history of laughter, this should come as no surprise. And indeed, sometimes laughter in the Middle Ages signals holiness. A famous story is recounted in the *Knight of Tour-Landry*, in which Saint Martin and his godson, Brice, are saying Mass one day:

> And whanne the masse was done, seint Martin asked [Brice] whi he laughed, and he ansuered, that he saw the fende write all the laughinges that were betwene the women atte the masse, and it happd that the parchemyn that he wrote in was shorte, and he plucked harde to haue made it lengger with his tethe, and it scaped oute of hys mouthe, and hys hede had a gret stroke ayenst the wall, and that made me laugh. And whan seint Martin herde hym, he knewe that seint Brice was an holy man.

If God "inspires" each cathedral with his holy breath, then every peasant lives in his or her own fleshy cathedral of holy laughter. And what a weapon each of those peasants possesses. A medieval peasant knows life, in great part, as a ludic performance.

V. A. Kolve extends Huizinga's play theory to a ludic version of medieval history itself, in which the Redemption—the Crucifixion and the Harrowing of Hell—is transacted as a tournament, or a game, between Christ and Satan, on the stage. This image of the jousting Christ becomes especially popular in the twelfth century when religious emphasis shifts from

Christ's redeeming power over the devil to Christ's redeeming love of the human race. In his new role, he arrives on the scene as the chivalric, courtly knight of love. This ritualized, courtly behavior—gamelike in its fastidious observation of rules—is set into special focus in drama, in "plays." For instance, in a play like the *Coliphizacio*, in anticipation of the Crucifixion, Christ's "tortores" buffet and slap him in playful and deadly imitation of the children's game of blindman's bluff.* "Christ dies [in the Corpus Christi plays]," Kolve points out, "in a chaos of noise, violence, jests, and laughter, in a series of spontaneous, improvised games. Though we know the essential action of the play, we never know precisely what the tortores will do next: game blends into game in an endlessly changing series."** A new string of ludic words during this period also tumble into the action, putting an even finer point on the festivities: *jape*, *bourde*, and *layke*. All sorts of games lurk just below the surface of the story in medieval drama, ready to erupt in rowdy, uncontrolled sport. They well forth in the spirit of what Natalie Zemon Davis calls "festive life," popular recreation among urban folk aimed at the conscious pursuit of fun and the freedom that comes with hilarity, perhaps along with the side benefit of unsettling the reigning political order.

These festivals—*Ventilsitten*, as the Germans call them—allow people to "let off some steam." That German designation raises a continuing, perplexing question about festive life: Do these celebrations allow governments to exert control more easily, to rule with a heavier hand, because peasants have been permitted, in a sense, regularized times when they can act crazy and wild? In this scenario, life becomes increasingly more unbearable for the marginalized and the underclasses. But in a more optimistic reading, carnival teaches revolution by providing a heady taste of freedom. How can peasants, the argument goes, ever be governed the same again after they experience the world turned topsy-turvy?

*See Barry Sanders, "Who's Afraid of Jesus Christ: Games in the *Coliphizacio*," *Comparative Drama* 2, no. 2 (Summer 1968): 94–100.

**V. A. Kolve, *The Play Called Corpus Christi* (Palo Alto, Calif.: Stanford University Press, 1966), p. 200. The reader should see especially the chapter titled "Religious Laughter."

Mikhail Bakhtin opts for a lukewarm acceptance of the second scenario, a compromise really between the two choices: Festivals tend to make life more tolerable, he says, providing people "with an actual experience of life without hierarchy as against the fixed categories of 'official' medieval culture."* But he falls short of seeing incipient revolution in carnival life. I embrace Natalie Davis's analysis of these carnival acts, which offers a more radical assessment of their political efficacy. Festivals can perpetuate certain values, but they can also criticize the political order, helping to "decipher king and state." Davis maintains that

> before the existence of classes and the state, the comic realm was equal to the serious; with slave and feudal societies, including that of the sixteenth century, the carnival becomes a second life, a second reality for the people, separated from power and the state, but still public and perennial; in bourgeois society (and alas, one feels, in . . . socialist society as well) it is reduced to the home and the holiday. The carnival does not, however, reinforce the serious institutions and rhythms of society as in the other functional theories just mentioned; it helps change them.**

This carnivalization of everyday affairs through tricks and laughter characterizes life in virtually every town and village in England and Europe from the time of the late Middle Ages through the sixteenth century. Carnival took place on various occasions, as Davis and others point out, timed to the "calendar of religion and season (the twelve days of Christmas, the days before Lent, early May, Pentecost, the feast of Saint Jean Baptiste in June, the Feast of Assumption in mid-August, All Saints) and timed also to do-

*Mikhail M. Bakhtin, *Rabelais and His World*, trans. Helene Iswolsky (Bloomington: University of Indiana Press, 1984), p. 84. Carnival is a phenomenon that has lasted into contemporary times, and consequently "carnivalesque" can make sense to us all as a general term meaning merriment, a festivity that sometimes gets drunkenly out of hand. The term *carnival* carries a fairly precise meaning as it's applied to medieval recreative festivals; I discuss some of those forms in this book. Bakhtin comments on the importance of understanding that *carnival* can never be a precise term: "The word combined in a single concept a number of local feasts of different origins and scheduled at different dates but bearing the common traits of popular merriment. This process of unification in a single concept corresponded to the development of life itself; the forms of folk merriment that were dying or degenerating transmitted some of their traits to the carnival celebrations: rituals, paraphernalia, images, masques" (p. 218).

**Natalie Zemon Davis, "The Reasons of Misrule: Youth Groups and Charivaris in Sixteenth-Century France," *Past and Present* 50 (1971): 49.

mestic events, marriages, and other family affairs."* In short, good times broke out whenever people felt the urge for fun, revelry, for political disport and solid parody of the seriousness of life as it found expression in celebrations large and small.

In the waning years of the fifteenth century, urban festivities were sponsored loosely by groups of friends, or more professionally, by guilds, what E. K. Chambers, the historian of medieval drama, calls *sociétés joyeuses*, in France, or "fool-societies" and "playacting societies" in other places, and which Davis more accurately calls "Abbeys of Misrule," since these lay groups parodied the clergy in many respects.** By the beginning of the sixteenth century, one finds lay leaders of revelry with such revealing titles as the Abbot of Misrule, the Abbot of Gaiety, the Prince of Pleasure, and the Prince of Fools. Davis refers to even more colorful names in the city of Rouen, which boasted a Cardinal of Bad Measure, Bishop Flat-Purse, Duke Kickass, and the Grand Patriarch of Syphilitics.

The abbots of misrule functioned as street politicians, organizers of disorder through the spirit of carnival, giving enormous scope, to quote Davis, to those great levelers, "mockery and derision." They took it on themselves to exercise jurisdiction over the most private aspects of village life—a rule of order imposed through misrule—particularly over the behavior of married couples, singling out for public humiliation newly married women who failed their first year to conceive a child, henpecked husbands, adulterers, and their favorite target, old men who married young women. They concocted strange punishments: a dunking in a nearby stream, a ride backward through the village on an ass, or a public reprimand through one of the most rowdy and rough ceremonies, the charivari. The charivari points out what can happen when the populace takes the law into their own hands: the out-

*Natalie Zemon Davis, *Society and Culture in Early Modern France* (Palo Alto, Calif.: Stanford University Press, 1975), see especially "The Reasons of Misrule," p. 98.

**The "abbots of misrule" were elected from the ranks of raw youth, which means these groups were infused with great sexual vitality.

come may prove more conservative than what governments themselves have legislated.

Take the case of an old man who has taken a wife many years his junior. The charivari would recruit a group of young, masked boys to gather outside the house of the couple, beating pots and pans and drums, playing horns and ringing bells, making as much noise as possible—"rough music"—sometimes for a week at a time without stop. Some historians of drama see these noisy celebrations as recreations of primitive and magical customs, the meanings of which have been long forgotten, but whose original intent may have been to drive the devil away.

Natalie Davis gives a practical interpretation for them. With life expectancy fairly short in the Middle Ages, remarriages were common. An old man who married a young girl broke no written law, but he removed an eligible female from the pool, a fact that the young men resented. Banging on pots and pans was not just loud noisemaking, but a commotion, a disruption, a raucous laugh at the *vieille carcasse, folle d'amour*, the "old carcass, the fool for love." The charivari announced to the entire village—broadcast the news of social impropriety in the most direct, vernacular way. Without uttering a single word or passing a single judgment, the boys posited a model of proper behavior to everyone within earshot. These self-styled abbots—who might today be taken as a gang of unruly youths—in effect took the law into their own hands and announced their selfish interests by condemning aberrant behavior, that is, the aberrant behavior of others. In their commitment to disorder, they agitated for strict norms of behavior. The result was custom more conservative than the law of church or state.

Anthropologists and historians describe other times of festive, more anarchic behavior as opportunities for peasants to turn the world upsidedown, or to reverse the general order of society. These celebrations have been grouped under the name *carnival*. Richard G. Parker, an anthropologist who has done extensive fieldwork on carnival in Brazil, offers one of the most informative definitions of that specific folk festival:

It has been interpreted, through its essential opposition to the world of daily life, as a kind of ritual of reversal or rebellion in which social life is turned on its head and time played back to front. It has been seen as a world of laughter, of madness and play, in which the established order of daily life dissolves in the face of an almost utopian anarchy, in which all hierarchical structures are overturned and the fundamental equality of all human beings is proclaimed. Above all else, it has been understood as a celebration of the flesh in which the repressions and prohibitions of normal life cease to exist and every form of pleasure is suddenly possible. Indeed, even the name of the festival itself has been interpreted as meaning "a farewell to flesh" (from the Latin *carnis* or "flesh" and *vale* or "farewell")—a kind of final triumph of sensuality before Lent. And although there has been at least some awareness of the specific manifestations of this celebration of sensuality across both time and space, of the concrete symbolisms that are present in different historical periods and different cultural contexts, the basic formal unity of this carnivalesque tradition has been an underlying assumption of almost all of the significant work that has been carried out.*

Bakhtin has probably done the most interesting and provocative work on carnival. He points out that these festivals have been influenced greatly by local pagan rites, that their gaiety and sadness derive from the change of seasons, and particularly from the death and renewal of certain vegetation deities: the simultaneous crying and laughing that accompany the burying of seeds in the ground. Such moments recall the weeping and laughing recorded in the ancient Ras Shamra Texts. These seasonal changes represent times of liminality, transitional moments when structures are most fluid, when even the light appears so changeable that ordinary objects can no longer be easily discerned. In those zones of twilight—moments when normal definitions begin to fall away—the most farfetched ideas sound plausible. Systems and organizations and institutions take on a curious vulnerability. When categories shift, the world reveals itself in a flash, free of its usual strictures and props. Peasants can become kings. Think about New Year's Eve, and the resolutions that flow like champagne at the midnight hour. People weep over the year past

*Richard G. Parker, *Bodies, Pleasures, and Passions: Sexual Culture in Contemporary Brazil* (Boston: Beacon Press, 1991), p. 141. It makes more sense that *carnis* be read as "meat" instead of "flesh," since Lent is a time first of dietary deprivation in church ritual.

and rejoice over the new chance that the new year brings. New Year is Janus-faced; it is a time of heightened liminality.

In imitation of such events, carnival offers societies—all societies, any time—the chance for a renewal that springs from destruction, a renewal borne on the back of that intensive laughter that moves to tears. One can imagine a time when the carnivalesque was not confined to a separate, isolatable event, but rather a spirit that ran throughout the society helping to keep seriousness at bay. In Christianity, the church fathers kicked laughter out of their organization. Government did the same, reserving for itself a spirit of high seriousness.*

Anthropologists have demonstrated the cross-cultural similarities among carnival festivals, most notably in their inversions of real-world order, in their travesties—men dressed as women or as animals, or women dressed as men—as well as in their promotion of sexual license. Reversals of gender or sexual promiscuity, however, do not get at the real liberation inherent in carnival. Inversions and perversions merely establish the theme for, allow the unfolding of, the disordered world. Inversions and reversals set the clocks running backward; they signal that anything goes. It is that individual confrontation with freedom that actually constitutes carnival's spirit of true liberation. In their own way, jokes represent small carnival celebrations. They, too, signal revolutionary acts through their creations of bizarre worlds, pitting their fantasies against the dreary, disabling, and deadening routines of the world. Carnival combat results in the most far-reaching, democratizing pattern—the creation of a community of laughers.

So completely does carnival level status and hierarchy into a commons of laughter that the writer Terrence Des Pres even believes the idea of the carnivalesque informed the Jewish experience in that most absolute of horrors, the Holocaust. He explains himself in a shocking essay titled "Holocaust Laughter":

*The spirit of Saturnalia, the world topsy-turvy, engendered a vast amount of comic vernacular literature in medieval Europe, among the most famous, the *Order of Fair Ease* and the *Land of Cockayne*.

> I do *not* mean to say that the Holocaust becomes a carnival, but rather that in a world of death the spectacle of life defending itself is open to unusual perspectives. In Bakhtin's view, carnival laughter draws its authority from the utopian hunger of humankind in general. Such laughter is in revolt against everything fixed; it is hostile to rules, regulations, hierarchies, anything closing down life. It celebrates the regenerative powers of human community as such, life and plenitude of life, at the expense of particular forms. Against internal as well as external threats to communal well-being, this kind of laughter is ruthless. It pulls everything down to earth, officialdom and worldly power especially.*

Des Pres notes that in Holocaust studies the general public insists on total seriousness, for the comic, it feels, "belittles or cheapens or denies the moral severity of the subject itself." But Des Pres argues for the benefits in a comic approach to the Holocaust, for "it's not fear and sorrow we need more of, but undaunted vision. The paradox of the comic approach is that by setting things at a distance it permits us a tougher, more *active* response. We are not wholly, as in the high seriousness of tragedy, forced to a standstill by the matter we behold."** Even with something so desperately depraved as the Holocaust, then, jokes and a joking attitude can be restorative and an aid in human survival. Des Pres points to Emmanuel Ringelbaum's *Notes from the Warsaw Ghetto* to confirm the value of jokes in the face of even the most terrible evil. Ringelbaum documents the jokes that concentration camp inmates told in order to keep their sanity. Most of Ringelbaum's jokes, Des Pres maintains, reappear in Leslie Epstein's *King of the Jews*, a comic novel about the Holocaust. Jokes and the carnivalesque constituted one of the only ways concentration camp inmates could maintain even the fiction of a future. These inmates could only prepare for the end, to borrow from Nietzsche, in the form of

> a carnival in the grand style, for the laughter and high spirits of the most spiritual revelry, for the transcendental heights of the highest nonsense and Aristophanean derision of the world. Perhaps this is where we shall still

*Terrence Des Pres, *Writing into the World: Essays, 1973–1987* (New York: Viking Penguin, 1991), p. 282.

**Ibid., p. 286.

discover the realm of our *invention*, that realm in which we, too, can still be original, say, as parodists of world history and God's buffoons—perhaps, even if nothing else today has any future, our *laughter* may yet have a future.*

In the temporal inversions of carnival, the immense possibilities of the future replace the awful constrictions of the present, the numbing mistakes of the past. One of the most noteworthy inversions, in which jesters seized positions of authority, took place in a carnival controlled not by lay people but by clerics, and known until the end of the fourteenth century in England (and even longer in parts of France) as the *festum asinana*, *festum stultorum*, or *regis stultorum*, the Feast of Asses, Feast of Fools, or the Court of Fools. These examples of student revelry, performed at Christmastime, remained in force an amazingly long time: The earliest prohibitions date from the first half of the seventh century, proclaimed by the Council of Toledo; the last from the Parliament of Dijon in 1552. In these inversions, a choirboy in a cathedral or a member of the lower clergy in a university would assume the position of bishop, while other boys would parody the Mass by leading a group of asses around the cathedral. "Such excesses as clerks dressed as women dancing in the choir, playing dice in church, censing the church with the smoke of burning shoes, riding through the town singing ribald songs—the evidence for all these activities comes typically from the observation of outraged opponents."**

Joannes Belethus, rector of theology at Paris, indicates in his *Rationale divinorum officium* (1182–90) that the Feast of Fools arises from the festival of the archdeacons, which was held either on Circumcision or on Epiphany or on the Octave of the Epiphany—"festum hypodiacorum, quod vocamus stultorum." Epiphany (a "shining forth") constitutes one of the classic moments of liminality; indeed, what shines forth is a light so joyously democratic that it will eliminate all class distinctions. Christ will prompt the

*Nietzsche, *Beyond Good and Evil*, p. 150.

**John M. Ganim, "Carnival Voices and the Envoy to the *Clerk's Tale*," *Chaucer Review* 22, no. 2 (1987): 126.

truly devout to become "Fools for God."* In that context, the Feast of Fools begins.

Joannes Belethus can only hint, of course, at the medieval sources of something like the Feast of Asses. True beginnings—Ur-origins—most often elude historians. We can, however, take notice that at the earliest stages of the Roman state, official occasions like triumphal processions and funerals were derided and mocked. But as the state matured and class structure solidified, "all the comic forms were transferred, some earlier and others later, to a nonofficial level. There they acquired a new meaning, were deepened and rendered more complex, until they became the expression of folk consciousness, of folk culture. Such were the carnival festivities of the ancient world, especially the Roman Saturnalias, and such were the medieval carnivals."**

Asses figured prominently in these Saturnalias, in western Europe, particularly in France. Iconographically, Saturn is shown as leaden, dull, and slow, an appropriate symbol for the tired end of the year. In these festivals, the Christmas Fool, weary and wearing an ass-eared cap, dies at the hands of the spirit of the New Year—the child Horus (an Egyptian deity usually represented with a falcon or eagle), or sometimes the infant Zeus, in a winter version of the Lenten combat.

Athenians celebrated the seasonal transformations of the Spirit of the Year in "the *Lenaea* festival and corresponding performances throughout the ancient world, including northwestern Europe. The initiate identified himself with the god, and seems to have undergone twelve emblematic transformations . . . as he passed through the successive Houses of the Zodiac before undergoing his ritual death and rebirth."† These "transformations" have come down to us neatly rendered in a novel of sorts, *The Trans-*

*Francis of Assisi, arguably the greatest of the medieval saints, called himself "Joculator Dei," a "Joker for God," an "Acrobat for God." Francis always stood ready to be surprised by joy, ready to laugh with a spontaneous cheer born of his intimate experience of God. Johan Huizinga points out that, because of their attempt to become intimate and friendly, some saints fell into buffoonery. Thus in spite of all the reverence paid to him, Saint Joseph became "Joseph le Rassoté" (Joseph the Fool) in art and literature, a clown dressed in particolored rags. See Johan Huizinga, *The Waning of the Middle Ages* (New York: St. Martin's Press, 1949), p. 170.

**Bakhtin, *Rabelais*, p. 6.

†Robert Graves, ed., *The Golden Ass* (New York: Farrar, Straus and Giroux, 1951), p. xv.

*formation of Lucius; Otherwise Known as the Golden Ass*, by Lucius Apuleius, from the second century A.D. Most interesting for the history of laughter, in his fourth chapter Lucius attends a "Festival of Laughter" in the town of Hypata, where the citizens "hold a solemn festival in honour of Laughter, the best of all gods, which must always be celebrated with some new practical joke." Suddenly blessed by Laughter, Lucius is told, "Laughter will now lovingly accompany you wherever you go and never allow you to be glum, daubing your forehead with the cheerful colours that mark you as his own."* An ironic and satiric blessing, certainly; but nonetheless Lucius must understand laughter, must celebrate its power and ingest it as his own, before he can do the hard work of the rest of the year. For that work will require strength of character. After all, the world turns cold and icy; only an inner strength can pull him through—an inner strength that can only come from laughter.

Thus, transformation plays a central part in these festivals, even in their medieval incarnations; and the fool, having presumably undergone the entire year-long cycle of transformation, can speak from experience and with authority. But one should not be fooled by appearances—the seeming innocence that enables most practical jokes to spring their traps—for the fool also speaks with worldly wisdom.

How *ass* comes to mean "posterior" may arise from the carnivalizing use of the animal in medieval festivals. The ass inside the church smacks of the substratum, animal vibrancy that Bakhtin touted as the vital force of peasant laughter. The transformation of *ass* also may have been helped along by another word, *arse*, "the posterior," in use since around the year 1000, which sounds very much like it. And finally, Shakespeare has his clownish, naive character Bottom, transformed into an ass, so that in a sense he becomes all bottom. Dumbstruck by love, Bottom wakes up in the forest one day with an ass's head, in one of Shakespeare's most festive come-

*Ibid., pp. 60–61. Graves writes in his introduction that "there really was such a festival at Hypata" (p. xvii).

dies, *A Midsummer Night's Dream.** The play dates from around 1594–95, just the time when *ass* leaves polite conversation as a crude anatomical reference.

However we become asses or asinine, festival and comedy fuel that transformation. Enid Welsford, who has written the most detailed social history of the fool, describes the utter religious reversal that the Feast of Fools or Feast of Asses called into being and celebrated: "The transformation began with the singing of the Magnificat at Vespers, when the words 'He hath put down the mighty from their seat and hath exalted the humble and meek' were repeated again and again, while the *baculus* or staff of office was delivered into the hands of one of the despised subdeacons who as 'Bishop or Pope or King of Fools' led his fellows into the stalls of the higher clergy, to remain there and usurp their functions for the duration of the feast."** Then the Mass was burlesqued, censing done with pudding and sausages. Once the asses had assembled inside the church, the celebrant, instead of saying *Ite missa est*, brayed three times (*ter hinhannabit*). The congregation responded with similar braying and howling until the church sounded like a stable.

By the middle of the fifteenth century, the feast not only held on strongly in France, but indeed by contemporary accounts grew even wilder. E. K. Chambers reprints part of a letter, dated March 12, 1445, sent by the dean of theology, University of Paris, to the bishops of France. Its preamble, in an initial attempt to condemn such feasts, points out that the sole surviving remnant of the pagan Kalends can be found in the *festum fatuorum*. The dean, Eustace de Mesnil, then describes its current version:

Priests and clerks may be seen wearing masks and monstrous visages at the hours of the office. They dance in the choir dressed as women, panders or

*Shakespeare uses a new verb in the play, *gleek*—"Nay I can gleeke upon occasion" (3. 1.150)—adding yet another level of finesse to the fine art of jesting. The *OED* defines the term—both noun and verb—"to make a jest at another's expense," "to mock," "to play a trick on someone."

**Enid Welsford, *The Fool: His Social and Literary History* (Gloucester, Mass.: Peter Smith, 1966), p. 200.

minstrels. They sing wanton songs. They eat black puddings at the horn of the altar while the celebrant is saying mass. They play at dice there. They cense with stinking smoke from the soles of old shoes. They run and leap through the church, without a blush at their own shame. Finally, they drive about the town and its theaters in shabby traps and carts; and rouse the laughter of their fellows and the bystanders in infamous performances, with indecent gestures and verses scurrilous and unchaste.*

Every carnival celebration gains its strength from juxtaposing contrary images. The lesson of the Magnificat is relevant here, as it argues a time of serious political reversal, a time when the mighty shall be humbled and the meek elevated. Hierarchy and status crumble before Christ's power. Parishioners recite the Magnificat at a key transitional time, at vespers, the sixth canonical hour in the divine office, which marks the end of the day and the beginning of evening. The major opposition in carnival takes place at the most crucial moment in the Christian calendar, the transition to Lent. This movement is shown as an opposition that takes place between two figures, Carnival and Lent, between what the French call *jours gras* and *jours maigres*, generally personified by a fat man in combat against a thin, old woman.

Carnival stands for an expansiveness gained through an omnivorous appetite, a mighty appetite that demands more than satisfaction—Carnival loves to feel absolutely stuffed. Carnival abhors dietary restrictions of any kind and taboos of all sorts. On the other hand, Lent loves to impose the rigors of abstinence, enforcing a specific time to refrain not just from meat and eggs, but also from sex, play-going, and all other forms of recreation. Iconographically, Lent is represented as an emaciated creature (Lent means "lean time"). Carnival, in contrast, looks young, cheerful, fat, sexy, a prodigious eater and drinker, a tireless and potent sexual giant—truly a Gargantuan and Falstaffian figure. Carnival is Oliver Hardy, Bud Abbot, Sancho Panza; Lent is Stan Laurel, Lou Costello—straight men in comedy teams, who never really get the jokes, who in fact stand in their way, and so act more as checks on humor: "strait" men.

*E. K. Chambers, *The Mediaeval Stage* (Oxford: Oxford University Press, 1903), p. 153.

These two opposing impulses—expansiveness and constriction, freedom and rule—characterize a good deal of our experience. Our natural, ebullient impulses need tempering by the demands of living in society and thus recognizing the rights of others. Language itself follows these two general courses: Orality—storytelling—seems to roam in subject and sentence without regard to restraints of any kind. Literacy, on the other hand, must obey myriad rules and revisions—in grammar and syntax and sense. The combat between Carnival and Lent (*carnaval et carême*) is a dialogue, really, a joking but serious contest in which there can be no victor, because the combat itself is of crucial importance. That combat produces a space that illuminates for an instant the true nature of institutions—a kind of consciousness. The anthropologist Victor Turner calls the opening of the space a "metalanguage of reflexivity": "We human beings are all and always sophisticated, conscious, capable of laughter at our own institutions, inventing our lives collectively as we go on, playing games, performing our own being."* Thus Navajo clowns, called Koshari or Mudheads, occupy one half of the Navajo pueblo—or moiety—and mock the serious celebrations taking place in the other half of the pueblo.** In these parodic, carnivalesque ways, societies, and particularly preliterate societies (or, better, nonliterate societies) are able to talk about themselves.

Two final ideas about carnival: First, like jokes, carnival always posits a future, a future that insists conditions can be better, and more fun. Carnivalesque freedom allows folks to breathe in a world released from all obligation and restriction. For the brief time that the celebration continues, it offers the reality of that dreamy desire of a golden age:

> Popular-festive forms look into the future. They present the victory of this future, of the golden age, over the past. This is the victory of all the people's material abundance, freedom, equality, brotherhood. The victory of the future is ensured by the people's immortality. The birth of the new,

*Quoted in Kathleen M. Ashley, ed., *Victor Turner and the Construction of Cultural Criticism: Between Literature and Anthropology* (Bloomington: Indiana University Press, 1990), p. xix.

**The Koshari dress in particolors, or more typically, wear women's clothes, quite likely turning the celebration into a *travesty* by acting as *transvestites*.

of the greater and the better, is as indispensable and as inevitable as the death of the old. The one is transferred to the other, the better turns the worse into ridicule and kills it. In the whole of the world and of the people there is no room for fear. For fear can only enter a part that has been separated from the whole, the dying link torn from the link that is born. The whole of the people and of the world is triumphantly gay and fearless. This whole speaks in all carnival images; it reigns in the very atmosphere of this feast, making everyone participate in this awareness.*

The dream of the golden age ends, of course, with the arrival of Lent. The piper asks for his payment. But having participated in carnival, the idea of an easy liberty remains in everyone's head and heart, in much the way that the character Pauper hoped it would. Every peasant and pauper can savor on his or her tongue that lingering taste of freedom. Yes, Lent may have arrived, but the carnival spirit can erupt again at any moment; the laughing peasants know that in an instant the world can be turned topsy-turvy. And they know that laughter is the most potent weapon for putting an end to human time, for creating, as Augustine put it, "the Sabbath of the world." Indeed, Augustine argued in the *City of God* that to play for God is a way to please him.

The second idea is connected to the first: Like a joke, carnival plays the murderer. The new world, that is, always holds a gun to the head of the old world. Those elements that surface in the battle between Carnival and Lent—the fat and the lean, the killer and the victim, the bully and the weakling, along with a renewed sense of the future, and a freeing of society from all class distinctions—all come together in the later Middle Ages with Chaucer and the first written joke in English. Chaucer reaches down into the highly ritualized dialectic of folk festivals and places the characters and their actions into literature. He carnivalizes fiction.

*Bakhtin, *Rabelais*, p. 256.

# 6

# Chaucer Punches *the first joke home*

*Menin:* Homer intended the opening word of the *Iliad* to sound a two-syllable alarm. That noun, the exact meaning of which has been lost in antiquity, some classicists have translated as an emotion close to "rage" or "wrath"; buried in it, the idea of revenge and the frenzied hope of getting even at any cost. Homer assigns the word to Achilles, to convey the ferocity of his anger at the gods and to make apparent his hubris—to think he might possibly settle a score with the gods. Achilles' desire carries the poem's audience to the very heart of danger; it brings them face to face with that frightening concept called "divine retribution."*

Achilles' explosion prompts a feud with the gods that takes up a good deal of the *Iliad*. The fallout from Achilles' anger drifts like so much soot over ancient literature. It begins to settle during the later years of the Middle Ages, giving power and shape to Chaucer's *Canterbury Tales*, at a time

*The *Iliad*, the poem that as we have seen records the first laugh in the West, also gives its audience the first extended discussion of revenge. While I would not argue that laughter and revenge always appear together, I will argue that they are absolutely inseparable in aggressive joke-telling.

when unconditional love—*caritas*, Christian forgiveness—no longer seems capable of neutralizing such uncivilizing notions as revenge. If literature provides any record of social change, then forgiveness is scarce by the late Middle Ages. Chaucer shows us that.

The driving force behind the *Canterbury Tales* can best be described as that ancient passion of *menin* transformed into something much more socially acceptable—a storytelling competition between some thirty-three pilgrims as they wend their way from London to the holy city of Canterbury, and back home again. Chaucer takes the edge off the idea of revenge by describing all the literary activity in his poem as a game: He sees competition at the heart of healthy play and sport. In Chaucer's formalized ritual of revenge, no one is supposed to get hurt—at least not physically.*

But he begins in the most serious way. The Knight tells the first tale, a story of high seriousness that explores the deadly consequences of competition. That is, it explores the idea of competition removed from any spirit of play and sport, and drained of all mirth and high spirits. No one but the gods laugh in the story, and even they can manage only a smirk, a sardonic twitch that reveals the tale's literary connections to the classical world. At the conclusion to the Knight's tale, the Miller interrupts the order of the telling to say that he will seek revenge on the Knight. He challenges the Knight's storytelling ability: "I will *requite* [pay back] the Knight's tale," he announces. The Miller's interruption, a frank declaration of his desire to display his storytelling prowess, stands out in the history of laughter as a key moment for several reasons.

First, the Miller wrings as much meaning out of the idea of revenge as possible. His tale itself is about revenge: wife against husband, lover against rival, student against landlord, woman against man, city dweller against country bumpkin, and so on. But in telling his tale, the Miller seeks very specific and deliberate revenge on one of the pilgrim characters, the Reeve.

* *Revenge* is not recorded in English until the fourteenth century. *Retaliation*—paying back in kind—does not arrive until centuries later. The English in the Middle Ages prefer a word that they borrow from the literature of love, *requite*, "to match someone's advances."

Without ever speaking the words, the Miller reveals his envy over some aspect of the Reeve's life—most probably the Reeve's young and beautiful wife.* Finally, and most important, the Miller does indeed take "The Knight's Tale" and converts it into a perfect gem of humor: He requites the Knight's seriousness with a carefully constructed and witty little story that can be called the first *joke* in the English language.

To get there took a stroke of literary brilliance: Chaucer noticed that the physicality of the practical joke could be converted into a verbal punch line, thus making the victim more vulnerable—emotionally and psychically—not to a physical blow, but to some key word or clever sentence. Chaucer also created an iconography of joking: Punch lines come across with much more force when they are delivered by a large person. Conversely, a skinny person falls over much more easily than a solidly established one.

In "The Miller's Tale," Chaucer has drawn aside the curtain and offered his fourteenth-century audience a glimpse into the literate future. He has taken those witty oral forms that Cicero first mentioned—the *dicacitas* and *facetiae*—and given them new shape in literacy. While the Miller tells a story that revolves around several practical jokes—a fake flood, a misdirected kiss, a perfectly aimed fart, a singed ass—his tale itself constitutes a colossal, nasty joke about gullibility and cuckoldry, fired at the Miller's archrival, the Reeve.

This is more than a dramatization of one pilgrim venting anger against another, or a case of wild and unformed feelings of retaliation dredged up from some dark place in the Miller's being. The rivalry between Miller and Reeve has roots that reach deep into the folk soul of the English people. This rivalry reflects the very spirit of comedy, the movement of the calendar, and the regeneration of nature. What's at stake here is medieval life itself. The poem cannot continue without the emotional interplay of

*Recall Plato's discussion with Protarchus in the *Philebus* that people take pleasure in their neighbors' misfortunes out of feelings of envy. Envy results from perceived differences in status: The envious person feels that another occupies a higher position in life, and desires to "get even."

these two characters. Their relationship is so basic and archetypal that it provides the emotional momentum to keep the action moving forward. The Miller, fat and bullyish, is Carnival incarnated, while the stingy and parsimonious Reeve walks through the tale as the enfleshment of Lent.

It was Chaucer's genius to see the comic potential for literature in these two fleshy characters from folk festivals, the Miller and the Reeve. The Fat Man loves to try to knock over the Skinny Man. The punch line, originally a slap thrown by Punch to knock his rival Judy flat on her back, Chaucer alphabetizes into a verbal right hook. Telling playful jokes, or plotting practical ones, posits an opponent—someone who hovers in the background just begging to be knocked over and defeated. In aggressive joke-telling, the identity of the opponent comes to the forefront: The joker always faces a recognizable rival, whom he hopes—actually longs—to defeat. And in that liberating instant of laughter, another, more powerful and ubiquitous enemy falls—just for an instant—by the way. That enemy goes under various names—the Day of Judgment, the Day of Reckoning, and as most often personified, Death. For a split second—in no more time than it takes to utter a laugh—the burden of life is lifted.

Undaunted by mandates from Ecclesiastes, dicta from the church fathers, the urgings of priests and writers not to laugh, medievals still laughed. For no other moment in the life of a medieval peasant, not even times of confession or absolution, could provide a taste of liberation so piquant. At the conclusion of "The Miller's Tale," the second in the *Canterbury Tales*, the pilgrims have reached a ludic version of Canterbury. On the road to the shrine of Saint Thomas, before they actually pass through the gates of Canterbury, the pilgrims find the lightness of liberation through laughter.

In a quite remarkable way, a way that Bakhtin would notice many centuries later, the carnivalesque invigorates fiction with a power all its own. The carnivalesque embodies the heart of the fictive experience, for the combat between Fat and Skinny is the deepseated *agon* that keeps the story wheel turning. In Bakhtin's terms, the seriousness of the novel—in Chaucer's case, the seriousness of fictive creation in general—continually runs the risk of being undercut: Seriousness can be banged up, beaten down, knocked over, and even humiliated, by comedy's trick-bag of perverse jokes and travesties.

In the end, in a dynamic of storytelling that Bakhtin calls the dialogic, in which opposing voices compete with each other in the novel, seriousness and playfulness grapple for control, and out of that struggle of emotion, meaning is generated. Such a dramatic polyphony of voices—heteroglossia—can undermine any sense of authorial command, thus providing for readers, like a hearty laugh, an aesthetic distance that enables them to step far enough back from experience to evaluate it and to criticize it freely: "Languages do not *exclude* each other, but rather intersect with each other in many different ways. . . . It might even seem that the very word 'language' loses all meaning in this process—for apparently there is no single plane on which all these 'languages' might be juxtaposed to one another." The linguistic conclusion to Bakhtin's theory of heteroglossia is language dissolving into the ultimate polyphony—into the meaningful sound understood by everyone everywhere, regardless of age or gender, and that of course is laughter.

To place Bakhtin's argument squarely in the context of laughter: Fictional discourse reaches meaning through the inherent joking nature of language itself, through its inclination to undercut itself. Meaning is a hard-fought battle, a give-and-take negotiated out of the spirit of the carnivalesque as the proliferating meanings of each sentence fight against the restraints of syntax and grammar. The narrative shape of the novel—the overarching grammar that keeps meaning from bursting at the "seems"—

*Mikhail M. Bakhtin, *The Dialogic Imagination: Four Essays*, ed. Michael Holquist, trans. Caryl Emerson and Michael Holquist (Austin: University of Texas Press, 1981), p. 291. In the introduction to this collection, which is unsigned, an interesting comment appears: "Bakhtin comes very close to naming Socrates as the first novelist, since the gadfly role he played, and which he played out in the drama of precisely the dialogue, is more or less what the role of the novel always has been" (p. xxxii). That is, Socrates himself, as an *eiron*, speaks with two voices: He is playing, by playing a role. This is the very nature of language itself. If fiction is rooted in language, then it must be rooted in play as well. For Bakhtin, the novel especially thrives on jokes; the novel is the "laughing genre."

the comic spirit continually threatens to deform. Ebullience, Bakhtin would argue, is the basic impulse, the natural state. Whatever civilizes us tries to restrain those impulses, tries to hold them "strait." This interplay between tension and release describes the very rhythm of living, from the most basic bodily functions (sneezing and orgasm) to the most contrived cultural events (weekend blasts and summer vacations). Poets have even described the journey into death as a welcomed release from a lifetime of tension. Laughter also fits the pattern: The clever joker creates a tension in the telling, only to release it all in the punch line, that moment of anticipated pleasure. Frivolity and pleasure struggle continuously to shake the restraints of social order.

The pattern informs the move from hunger to satiety; it can be felt in suppressing a sneeze or in finishing the spinach in order to indulge in a rich dessert. To give in to our "fatty impulses" is to indulge our mischievous, even outlaw sides. As Bakhtin puts it: "The healthy 'natural' functions of human nature are fulfilled, so to speak, only in ways that are contraband and savage, because the reigning ideology will not sanction them."*

Carnival spirit focuses this human desire for ebullience to break the constrictive hold of rule and regulation. The rounded belly of the Fat Man can never be filled, however, because the Skinny Man finally puts a stop to the seemingly unending supply of food and wine. Fat Man knows this, which makes his play all the more desperate and urgent. That's a dangerous model to present to a medieval Christian, who lives life in the shadow of a final Lenten time—in the dark shadow of the Day of Judgment. Why shouldn't the peasant dance and play, then, why shouldn't the peasant seize the moment, in the face of such a sobering fact of life? The church worked hard against that taking place, of course, through a suffocating number of ascetic rules. But carnival offered a powerful political and pleasureful option. The underground possibility that life could be lived as one grand joke lent a certain irony to daily experience. In a macabre way, it predisposed the medievals toward laughter.

*Mikhail M. Bakhtin, *Rabelais and His World*, trans. Helene Iswolsky (Bloomington: Indiana University Press, 1984), p. 214.

Carnival spirit is thus a commanding one, as it grabs hold of a whole array of medieval rules, regulations, and even church rituals, and threatens to shake them into tiny pieces. But in Chaucer's hands, carnival does something much more interesting with rules at a metalevel. Carnival—the Miller, that is—breaks the rules of traditional storytelling. He crosses the line of fiction and tells a story about the private life of the pilgrim Reeve, which exposes his weakest moments to all the other pilgrims standing around.* To be exact, the Miller announces that he will tell a story about a carpenter—the Reeve just happens to be a carpenter—whose wife has turned him into a cuckold. The Reeve, feeling uneasy, cries foul. He rallies the crowd by reminding them that this is supposed to be a storytelling session: Of course, that's what Lent's responsibility has to be—to remind everyone of the rules, to reel behavior back in from the edge of excess. But the Miller, demonstrably drunk, merely offers a feeble apology calculated, in good carnival fashion, to infuriate the Reeve even more. Carnival craves more and more chaos. I'm just telling a story, the Miller says, so if the story fits, then you've put it on yourself. I didn't tell you to wear it.

Chaucer has converted *menin*, the ancient thirst for revenge, into something that, in the mature years of the Middle Ages, becomes more socially situated. *Menin* provides motivation for the more than fifteen thousand lines of the *Iliad*. Some two thousand years later, an updated version of that emotion provides the stimulus for the first joke in English, in "The Miller's Tale." But in order for the Miller to be free to tell that joke, Chaucer first has to play out his own revenge. If he hopes to become an author—of original stories, of jokes—he has to take on God, for the Middle Ages knows only one supreme author and authority, and that is God.** The three

*One of the keys to David Letterman's success lies in his uncanny ability to play with the traditional boundaries of television. Often Letterman takes the "program" out of programming by taking his cameras onto New York's streets and transforming private citizens into public figures—if only for a few minutes. Letterman can more easily pull off his electronic gags because of the late hour of the show. Carnival begins on television only after the late news—the Lenten truth—a reversal, perhaps, of the ordering in folk festivals. I take up the subject of contemporary laughter in chapter 8.

**The *OED* credits Chaucer as the first English writer to use the word *author* in its secular meaning; to use the word *tale* in its literary sense; and to use both the words *audience* and *auditor* without their legal implications.

pursuits, then—laughing, joking, and storytelling—reveal their interlocking connections right before our eyes, in Chaucer's extraordinary poetry. The Miller's joke, a medieval short story—or as close as medieval narrative can get to it—derives its fictive originality and uniqueness from its life as a *joke*. I want to spend some time with Chaucer, then, not just because he brings his audience to that powerful moment when the first joke gets fired into the stratosphere. More than that, Chaucer helps us moderns see that the threads connecting storytelling and joking were woven together very early on and cannot be easily disentangled.

The Great Mother of Invention gave birth to fraternal twins—storytelling and joking. She nourished them both on a special formula, which literary critics have called *untruth*. Like metaphor, storytelling and joking assume that the essence of life emerges in the line separating truth and lies, in that space where neither and both exert their power. The vocabulary of narration reveals this delicate balance: fiction, fable, story, tale—each claims to be true and, at the same time, false. Jokes, too, oscillate between lying and the most subtle form of truth-telling. While they start out as lies, innocent and benign, jokes often hit with the accuracy of truth, although the sting may sometimes be slow in coming.

Even Saint Augustine, who, as we have seen, loved puns and witty *bons mots*, had difficulty defining their slippery nature: "Jokes should not be accounted lies, seeing they bear with them in the tone of the voice, and in the very mood of the joker a most evident indication that he means no deceit, although the thing he utters be not true. . . . A person should not be thought to lie, who lieth not" (*De mendacio* 5). The ambiguity that jokes and stories share allows both joker and author to get away with murder. The joker pleads, "I'm only kidding. It was only a joke." The author wriggles off the hook by saying, "Come on, it's only a story."

In writing fiction, the author weaves an intricately beautiful lie—a metaphoric interlacing of narrative threads—so that his or her reality will be taken seriously. The author plots in order to perpetrate a story on the audience, to hoodwink it into accepting the fabrication as real. To be successful, the author must take storytelling seriously and, at the same time, take delight in playing a practical joke on the audience. Thus Chaucer instructs us, in his Prologue to "The Miller's Tale," not to take his Canterbury *narratio* seriously. After all, he announces, "I'm only playing a game," a tongue-in-cheek bit of instruction, surely, for Chaucer sets the stakes in some of his games fairly high.

The connection between joking and narration begins early in history. The ancients, for instance, simply recognize little if any difference between stories and funny stories. Ancient mimes seem to have embraced festive folk life and to have represented it professionally on stage: "We shall no doubt be close to the truth . . . if we imagine the earliest professional entertainers as a motley group of jugglers and acrobats, gradually enlarging and enriching their repertory by taking over whatever elements in folk festival seemed to them likely to appeal to the populace, becoming figures of importance until there was but little distinction among the varied cithera-players and chorus-singers, mimes and rope-dancers."*

The Latin word for "story," *geste*, produces the modern English *jest*, a kinship that the English recognize as early as the time of King Alefric. They use the word *racu* in some places to translate the Latin *historia*, and in other places to translate *commoedia*. Thus, Anglo-Saxon glossaries define the word *racu* as both "narration" and "laughter." Anglo-Saxons refer to their poets as *hleahtorsmi* (laughtersmiths) and *gleemen*. The Anglo-Saxons—those dark souls of the Dark Ages—seem totally taken with laughter and recognize a gradation of nuance in their outbursts, utilizing more than a half dozen words to characterize laughter: *hlaehhan*, *cancettan*, *cancetung*, *ceahhetan*, *heleahtor*, *ceahhetung*, *cincung*, most of which perform double duty by denoting both "gladness" and "contempt." (Anglo-Saxons even have a word, *hlagol*, to mean "inclined to laugh.") But as Beatrice

*Allardyce Nicoll, *Masks, Mimes, and Miracles: Studies in the Popular Theatre* (London: George G. Harrap, 1931), p. 36. Agathocles, according to Diodorus, was both a *gelatopoios* and a mime (pp. 35ff.).

White points out, "it is always a masculine joyfulness that is referred to, *hleahtor wera*, the 'roaring laughter' of men, and the sound of it is suggested by the ghastly grinding of icebergs in collision."* At least, that is the laughter we hear in the warrior-filled epic poetry. But what a falling away! All that derisive meanness and the refinement of various kinds of laughter and mirth have long ago disappeared.**

A great distance separates funny stories, or even laughtersmiths and gleemen, from what we moderns recognize as actual joking. And it's that elusive creature, the joke, I want to track down. The nature of fiction—the way it renders experience palpable—makes it inevitable that the joke and a rudimentary form of the short story should emerge at the same moment; and that moment in the history of English literature occurs, albeit in embryonic form, in the tale delivered by Chaucer's Miller.

Since "The Miller's Tale" may not be fresh in the reader's mind, I take a few moments here to outline its action. By retracing the events of the tale, I also hope to show how the form of the well-made, old-fashioned short story follows the form of Chaucer's early joke. The plot moves quickly. The Miller announces that he will tell a tale about cuckoldry. No sooner do the words leave his mouth than his pilgrim rival, the Reeve, protests: Tell something more wholesome, less offensive. The Reeve protests too much, of course, revealing himself to be a cuckold of the first order and, at the same time, laying his insecurities wide open for everyone to examine.

Every joker begins by asking a version of the same question: "Have you heard the one about the . . . ?" or "Stop me if you've heard this one," for laughter thrives on surprise. An old joke only evokes a yawn. True, the Reeve has not heard this one—and he doesn't want to—but he clearly knows the substance of what's coming, and that's his problem: He cannot

*Beatrice White, "Medieval Mirth," *Anglia* 78, no. 3 (1960): 286.

**The Irish love the absurd more than the English seem to. For instance, when Cuchulinn lies in the midst of his own blood and entrails, a raven flies down and trips on Cuchulinn's intestines. Cuchulinn bursts out laughing, and as the poet says, "and that was the last laugh that Cuchulinn had" (quoted in ibid., p. 288).

stop the boorish Miller. Carnival consumes with a voraciousness that cannot easily be halted.

Chaucer underscores the rivalry between the two pilgrims graphically: The Miller, bully that he is, outweighs the skinny, choleric Reeve by several hundred pounds—when he punches, it hurts. Miller and Reeve face off in the now-familiar tradition of fat and lean comic partners, a tradition, as I have mentioned, that has come down to us in figures like Abbot and Costello, Laurel and Hardy, Mutt and Jeff, and Ralph Cramden and Ed Norton. As the Miller unfolds his story, it is clear that he intends to throw his weight around, and the Reeve will undoubtedly get hurt. The Miller goes directly for the bull's eye—the Reeve's jugular—with his opening shot: An old, wealthy man, who like the Reeve just happens to be a carpenter, marries a young, beautiful girl, Alisoun, and because he feels deeply jealous, he keeps her under tight restrictions. But unfortunately, he's also cheap and not real swift. So to make some extra money, the old carpenter, John, rents out a room in the attic of his house to a handsome, young university student, Nicholas. And thus we have the "happy incident," an unstable opening event that promises to produce a story filled with fun, surprise, and a bawdy moment or two.

The young couple, Alisoun and Nicholas, meet in the field one spring afternoon and Nicholas immediately catches Alisoun by the "queynte" and begs for her love. After a few lines of protestation, Alisoun gives in, and Nicholas begins, as Chaucer says, "stroking her about the loins." They can now do nothing but conspire to keep John at a safe distance so they can continue to "rage and pleye."

Alisoun hatches the plan; Nicholas carries it out. In a tiny story within the story, Nicholas warns John about a fast-approaching flood, so horrendous, he tells him, it will make Noah's flood seem like a summer shower. To escape certain death by drowning, Nicholas counsels, John must hammer together three little tubs and secure them to the roof of the house, high above the waterline. John complies, and with the gullible old man safely tied to the roof and curled up inside his tub and fast asleep, Alisoun and Nicholas descend to the ground floor to spend the evening in the marriage bed. At this point, the tale has moved, in a certain sense, back to its beginning, except that Chaucer has switched the partners. It doesn't stay there long, for the story also moves back again to a position of dynamic instability: Just as Alisoun and Nicholas have settled themselves into bed, Chaucer ruins their fun by throwing a new complication their way—an additional thread that he will use to knit up the climax of the story—another angle added to the lovers' triangle. Absalom, a parish priest, who has also had his eye on Alisoun, comes to her bedroom window, in true courtly fashion, to serenade his lady and charm a kiss out of her. After a few minutes of off-key singing, Absalom pops the question and asks for his kiss. Alisoun consents, but now she is so enamored of practical jokes that she hatches yet one more. Pucker up, she coyly says, as she eases her naked behind out the window. Blinded by the excitement of getting his kiss at long last, Absalom unwittingly kisses her keester, as Chaucer describes, "ful savourly," evoking from Alisoun one of the giddiest iambic lines in literature, as well as the first human laugh recorded in English: "Teehee! quod she, and clapte the window to."

Practical jokes invite immediate escalation, just as stories inspire competition. "Can you top this?" is implied in every joke and story. As Absalom slowly understands what he has done, he resolves to get even, which in practical terms means he must raise the ante. He returns to Alisoun's bedroom window and begs for another kiss, just as wonderful as the one he got before; and Alisoun is only too willing to comply. But Nicholas interrupts. He now decides that he wants to get his fair share of the fun; this parish fool should kiss his behind, too. So Nicholas, after taking his evening "pisse," closes in on his evening "kisse." He slides his naked bottom out the window "over the buttok, to the haunche-bon," and because the night has fallen fast, Absalom asks his little turtledove to let him know where she is: "Spek, swete bryd," he croons, "I noot not where thou art." Absalom's request prompts a rhyme that Chaucer's devilish mind simply cannot resist: "This Nicholas leet fle a fart."* But Absalom stands ready this time. Taking careful aim, he brands Nicholas smack in the ass with a red-hot poker.

Nicholas has fired off no ordinary fart.** Cosmic in its proportions, Chaucer declares it "as greet as it had been a thonder-dent." The noise fills the night air. The tale lacks only one element to make it complete—rain. Without knowing it, Nicholas becomes the weatherman. Writhing in pain, clutching his smoking behind, he manages a pathetic cry: "Help. Water. Water." That's all John needs to hear. In his dopey sleep, he concludes that Noah's flood has actually arrived and dutifully cuts the rope holding him fast. The tale falls apart in nursery rhyme simplicity: "Downe gooth alle." John falls three stories headlong into the street, bringing all the neighbors running out of their houses alarmed by all the great commotion.† Nicholas and Alisoun also dash outside, adding to the confusion. All three characters wind up on the street, leveled, finally, by the action of the tale.

When the Miller finishes, the pilgrims all howl with laughter—all but the Reeve, who curses and swears at the Miller; he's angry, disgusted, and what's worse, humiliated. Thanks to the Miller, thirty-odd pilgrims now know the awful truth of his life, and in embarrassingly graphic detail. The Miller has stepped outside the boundaries of fiction, violating the rules of storytelling by revealing secrets of the Reeve's personal life. He has backed the Reeve into one of society's most feared corners, forcing him to play the butt of a joke.

Ultimately, Chaucer has thrown every character out of his little house of fiction. Indeed, "The Miller's Tale" follows a carefully planned architectural blueprint. In the beginning of the tale, the characters play their parts

*The *OED* confers on Chaucer the dubious distinction of being the first author in English to use the word *fart* with its modern spelling, and the first to use the phrase "to let flee a fart."

**As Bakhtin points out, "the inappropriate word"—inappropriate because of its cynical frankness, or because it profanely unmasks a holy thing, or because it crudely violates etiquette"—enables fiction to generate its particular kind of truth by colliding with and breaking asunder authorized discourse (*Problems of Dostoevsky's Poetics*, trans. Caryl Emerson [Minneapolis: University of Minnesota Press, 1984], p. 118).

†Notice "The Miller's Tale" contains three stories: the flood, the cuckolding, and the jilted rival. John "falls" through all three of the stories.

on three separate stories—from attic to ground floor. As the action rises, all three characters climb outside the confines of the house—outside the frame of the story, if you will—and perch precariously together up on the roof. (One could argue that this occurs just at the "pitch" of one emotional movement in the story.) When the action begins to run down, so do the principal characters—Alisoun and Nicholas climb down from the roof and reenter the house at the first story, at the scene of the original sin, the bedroom. The punch line—the climax of the story—comes in the form of a single word, "water," which in good storytelling fashion connects the inside of the house to the outside, and the tale to the jokes, both practical and verbal. The punch line makes dramatically apparent the Reeve's remarkable stupidity and gullibility. The story's denouement entails a literal undoing of the narrative threads that hold all its elements together, a cutting done by the Reeve himself as he comes to groggy consciousness. In the unkindest and most ironic cut of all, the Reeve "undoes" himself. The architectural pattern that holds "The Miller's Tale" together prefigures a template used to describe the shape of the well-made short story in the nineteenth century, which literary critics have named the Freytag triangle.

And so, after keeping all those narrative elements so brilliantly aloft, when Chaucer finally decides to bring them down again—all at once—he makes them land in a brand-new category, in something that comes to be called the *joke*. It's an incredibly difficult genre to grasp, the joke, one that not even Freud, the master analyst himself, seems able to define with any precision or clarity. The *OED* doesn't admit *joke* until 1670, and then only with the vaguest of definitions: "Something said or done to excite laughter or amusement." Freud merely lists a series of characteristics for the joke, culling them from other experts, and then concludes by summarily dismissing them all as fairly worthless to a true understanding:

> The criteria and characteristics of jokes brought up by these authors and collected above—activity, relation to the content of our thoughts, the characteristic of playful judgement, the coupling of dissimilar things, contrasting ideas, "sense in nonsense," the succession of bewilderment and

enlightenment, the bringing forward of what is hidden, and the peculiar brevity of wit—all this, it is true, seems to us at first sight so very much to the point and so easily confirmed by instances that we cannot be in any danger of underrating such views. But they are *disjecta membra*, which we would like to see combined in an organic whole. When all is said and done, they contribute to our knowledge of jokes no more than would a series of anecdotes to the description of some personality of whom we have the right to ask for a biography.*

The most often cited recent definition comes from the anthropologist Jan Brunvand: "The term 'joke' refers to an episode or story that is laughable, obviously fictional, based on one event, and which ends abruptly, usually with a 'punch line.'"** A help, certainly, but not much more.

As for the punch line, the *OED* does not even mention it. (*Punch line* comes from Punchinello, a fat clown who bullies his way through the *commedia dell'arte* of the sixteenth century. He evolves into Punch, the puppet who takes such delight in pummeling his Judy.) We know the punch line as a functional instrument—the way it ties the narrative together, concludes fictive matters with economy, and most important of all, the way it releases the charge of laughter in the story. The punch line, of course, reveals the teller's true wit. In Chaucer, the tale must continue a bit beyond the punch line, by necessity, a capitulation to the medieval tradition of ending stories with a moral.

As we have seen, while we play practical jokes for a wide variety of reasons—to establish our power, to exercise control, or maybe for just plain fun—we tell aggressive jokes at our neighbors' expense out of envy. Usually, we envy that other person's better social situation, and thus we maneuver to keep our distance from them. Envy plays a crucial role—probably the most crucial role—in shaping the history of laughter. Laughter muscles its way into the heart of competitive society with the tough and formidable envy clearing the way.

*Sigmund Freud, *Jokes and Their Relation to the Unconscious*, trans. James Strachey (New York: W. W. Norton, 1963), p. 14.

**Jan Harold Brunvand, "The Study of Contemporary Folklore: Jokes," *Fabula* 13 (1972): 10.

Unlike the other medieval sins, envy has left behind a difficult history to trace, sometimes in and sometimes excluded from the traditional inventories of sins. Because the earliest compilations of sins—the one drafted by John Cassian in the early fifth century, for instance—develop within a spirit of asceticism, envy is absent.* But even when Pope Gregory added it back to his seven cardinal sins—a list that became standard—envy refused to take root, cropping up only infrequently in paintings and in literature, from the twelfth well into the fourteenth century. In fact, it disappeared for so long that, in 1213, a popular writer like Thomas Chobham could state flatly that people could have no idea what envy possibly means. Even as late as the first decade of the fourteenth century, some writers mistakingly derived *invidia* from *invisu*, "invisible," instead of from *invidere*, "to look askance," or "to look badly."

When envy finally reappears, it comes back into action because something powerful attracts it: money. In a gift or barter economy, people share their excess, and social status automatically levels out. Envy has no place. But in market economies based on the assumption of scarcity, envy flourishes. Without it, the machinery of commerce sputters and stalls. Competition and expansion lose steam. No wonder, then, that as the Middle Ages became less agrarian and more mercantile, more commercialized and prosperous, envy did not merely return but, like a long-awaited guest, rushed back in to inform social relationships. Just one short century after its reappearance, the poet Eustache Duschamps was announcing the rapidly approaching end of the world, due in great part, he complained, to the pernicious enemy eating away at the spiritual center of medieval life—envy.

Besides its stuttering history, appearing and disappearing and then appearing again, envy differs from the other sins in a much more crucial way: No one seems to know exactly how to define its baffling and elusive nature. Helmut Schoeck, who has written the most comprehensive work on

*Joannes Eeremtia Cassianus in a treatise on monastic life, *De institutione coenabiorum*, describes the eight spiritual dangers of monastic life in the East: gluttony, unchastity, avarice, anger, gloom, apathy, vanity, and pride.

the history of envy, says, quite shockingly, that "there is, strictly speaking, no such thing as envy. . . . It is impossible to experience envy as an emotion or as a mood in the same way that we can feel anxiety or sadness. Envy is more compatible with 'being afraid'; we envy something or someone in the same way that we are afraid of something or someone. Envy is a directed emotion: Without a target, without a victim, it cannot occur."*

Schoeck notices how envy refuses to behave quite like any other emotion—not in the same way, certainly, as, let's say, love. Unlike a person in love, the envier does not expect—indeed, does not want—any reciprocation in feeling. On the contrary, he or she fears a response in kind, for unlike passions or feelings, envy takes up only a tentative and uncomfortable residence in the heart and usually ends in a violence that ranges far beyond the expectations of normal behavior. Envious people always perceive inequalities; they see through a distorting eye: Their rivals enjoy a higher social status, in their eyes, or command more respect or earn more money, and they demand rectification—an immediate return to balance and equality. But since the envious also believe that the normal checks and balances have gone awry, they take the law into their own hands and, egged on by the hope of getting even, play both jury and judge. With such vigilante action, anything can happen—the results can be devastating, infecting scores and scores of innocent bystanders. The Arabs with keen insight, then, identified envy as a disease and, as with most diseases, prescribed a cure: a flight of the soul up through the heavens returning the affliction back to the body that had initially handed it out—in this case, the moon.

The moon appropriately exercises jurisdiction over envy because it moves through phases; tradition knows it, quite understandably, as the planet of change. More than two-faced, the moon comes up with a different face each night. Envy, too, plays the shape-shifter, hiding behind various disguises. Most of the cardinal sins are easily spotted: Sloth, gluttony, and avarice are nearly always recognizable—sometimes, to our embarrassment,

*Helmut Schoeck, *Envy: A Theory of Social Behavior* (New York: Harcourt, Brace and World, 1966), p. 7.

far too recognizable. The Middle Ages knew them as sins of the flesh. But medievals knew envy as something more odious—a disease of the soul—and perhaps more distressing, they knew it is a difficult one to confess. No envious person ever says, "Look, I'm envious, let's work this out." The envier shows only a smiling face, at times even offering a compliment or two to the enemy—all the while detesting such associations or wishing the other dead. True to his envious nature, the Miller never lets on to the Reeve that he would like to see him fall—at least he never tells him the truth flat out. He works by indirection.

Iconographic representations of envy usually reveal this duplicity or changefulness through some kind of image of doubling. In the Arab illness, for example, the afflicted person turns pale and yellow in both sets of cheeks—facial and derrière. Giotto's famous fresco of the Last Judgment, on the wall of the Church of S. Maria dell' Arena at Padua, depicts envy as a woman with two horns, to indicate, beyond immediate connections with devilish activity, that envy often arises out of sexual competition. But more important, Giotto's woman unfurls a snakelike tongue that doubles back on her own forehead, graphically illustrating that the envious person ultimately risks filling with the poison of his (or her) own sting. He or she grows increasingly frustrated while hoping for the destruction of the rival, or the rival's loved ones or property, preferably by natural disaster, or some horrible accident. The envious person never takes decisive action, never dirties his or her hands, for more than most culprits, he or she loathes being exposed or fingered as a pitiful envier, frets under cover, plots in secret, with ragged, devious ideas neatly hidden away in the imagination. The envious one needs others to see him or her as a nice person, and so the public face always wears a gracious smile. Finally, and perhaps most significant, Giotto's envious creature totes a bag of money. Money—buying power and, ultimately, status—moves the envious person to suffer in silence.

But if that "age of ambition," as the fourteenth century has been called, was to prosper, then recalcitrant, unpredictable envy would have to be institutionalized or tamed—made to serve society. Otherwise, envy threatens to put a cap on economic growth, for no one suffers a neighbor's evil eye with pleasure. And so, under the pressure of feeling envied, one learns to limit the acquisitive drive, turns away from the desire for making money. Jokes provide a way for a society to discharge envy's negativity. They allow the envious person a way to release frustration, as well as a clever way to confess his or her soul. Jokes force a merger between the anger and the smile. They capitalize on envy's most surprising peculiarity: Unlike the other cardinal sins, envy—the most pernicious of the Terrible Seven—has the amazing potential for triggering its own corrective, for realigning social situations so that they can settle into equanimity. Jokes act as a guide for disembedding from envy its most promising and beneficent image of doubling: the twin pans of justice. Chaucer does more than develop the first joke, a feat remarkable in itself. He plays the double role of cultural critic and social scientist: He analyzes fourteenth-century society and discovers that envy itself might be the catalyst for change and progress.

All through the *Canterbury Tales*, one can sense envy bubbling, deep underground, like some fiery, primordial tar; one can feel its heat rising to the surface in the Wife of Bath's anger over her husband's social rank, in the Prioress's desire for court respectability, in the Pardoner's choice of subject matter, and on and on. When the pilgrims begin telling their own tales, they tap into the lopsided social relationships that underlie their various friendships. Envy circulates from the simplest level (who can tell the best story) to the most complicated (who possesses enough worth to arrive first at the Sunday altar). Finally, on reaching their destination, the Parson sermonizes the Canterbury congregation: "Envye is the worste synne that is. For soothly, alle othere synnes been somtyme oonly agayns o special vertu, / but certes Envye is agayns alle vertues and agayns alle goodnesses."

The Parson says, "Love thy neighbor," but that is only an admonition, a commandment, a phrase that counsels how to act decently. In biblical reckoning, the ninth and tenth commandments also address themselves to envy, by setting limits on work: "Six days shall ye work" and "The seventh day is the Sabbath of the Lord." But Chaucer knows he cannot exclude envy from fourteenth-century society. By exploiting the power of jokes, he pushes envy in a new direction, he cultivates it. Chaucer provides a way to plough it into the soil of daily existence, thereby enriching social interactions. He enables people to play out their feelings of envious hostility through aggressive, hostile joke-telling.

While Chaucer had no way of knowing Plato's discussion of envy in the *Philebus*, he certainly did know the early medieval representations that depicted the vices and virtues in fierce combat. In that *psychomachia*, "the fight for the soul," the virtues always triumph. *Caritas*, Christian love, consistently trounces *invidia*. But Chaucer does much more than contextualize this static, abstract struggle: Through laughter, he does something much more socially dynamic. He converts *invidia* into *caritas*. Chaucer points the way to loving thy neighbor. He enfleshes the struggle for the soul in a rivalry between the two polar characters, Miller and Reeve. In the action of those two characters lies Chaucer's great insight. He senses that, even if no one ever stumbled or fell, never slipped or got butted, we would still try to knock them over—either physically (with well-laid practical jokes) or verbally (with well-aimed punch lines).

The Miller and the Reeve have been rivals for some time, it appears, probably long before the pilgrimage started: The Miller rides at the head of the pilgrimage, the Reeve at the hind end. The Miller slowly reveals that he envies the circumstances of the Reeve's marriage—quite specifically the Reeve's young and pretty wife. He can rectify this sexual outrage either by raising himself or by lowering the Reeve. Jokes accomplish both movements simultaneously. The joke teller elevates him- or herself by displaying, to everyone's delight, a keen wit, and lowers the other by exposing that person before an assembly of peers as a dunce. Try as he or she may, the victim rarely ever second-guesses, and thus is hardly ever able to defuse, the punch line. But that's the only way to put a stop to the ludic onslaught. Having been placed so diligently on guard, of course, the victim is rendered even more unstable and precarious, a wobbly target just begging to be knocked over.

And so the Miller can in an instant "get even" by humiliating the Reeve (literally, turning him into *humus*, "dirt," "earth," or even "shit"). While jokers necessarily satisfy their needs at their victims' expense, victims can retain at least some of their self-esteem by rising out of and, finally, above their humiliation. If they fall into anger or leave in a rage, they lower themselves even further, bury themselves, by prompting the audience to laugh *at* them. "How small," the audience mocks, "So-and-so can't even take a little joke," or "So-and-so can't play the game; what a poor sport"—pointing to the fact that joke-telling, as Chaucer has already told us, is at one level nothing more than a well-articulated *game*.

The victim can of course retaliate, return the fire, by telling a joke back on the aggressor. But it had better be a clever one, more clever than the one the joker told, not like the Reeve's feeble retort, in which he tells a tale about not one but two students who cuckold a Miller and seduce his daughter as well. Victims cannot retaliate through an escalation of numbers, but only through an escalation of skill. They have to exercise more wit, more control, more rhetorical skill, than their opponents. That's a difficult if not impossible task, for having gotten there first, the joker always has the upper hand. Think about paying back someone like Don Rickles. One can try, but the risks are great. A misfired joke from the victim can only send him or her further down in the eyes of the audience. The Reeve's vain attempt shows him as a frustrated loser.

The Reeve as victim can survive socially in one way only, by standing his ground and, even against his own better judgment, laughing the joke off, pretending that he forgives his oppressor, the Miller. In that way, the Reeve demonstrates that he knows how to play the game like a good sport—that he can, like a cat climbing out of its litter box, shake it off. The audience reinforces his magnanimity by laughing along *with* him, applauding his effort at being a "big" man (as big as the Miller). By acknowledging a victim's willingness to accept the person who has humiliated him or her, the audience allows the victim to stand even taller. A new community develops, one in which joker, victim, and every member of the audience come together as equals;

this newly formed community is forged out of the power of joke-telling and laughter. Thus, jokes become powerful weapons in rectifying inequities that run throughout the social system. The court of last resort, jokes momentarily set the pans of justice level again. But that only describes half their power.

Recall that our stars, Miller and Reeve, come from the world of folk festival, and specifically from Lenten carnival, where the world turns topsy-turvy. Top is down; up is below. Heaven is no longer the place from which divine grace emanates: The underworld provides the sufficiency of life-affirming powers. Indeed, in the medieval world of correspondences, in which the macrocosm finds its reflection in the microcosm, universal truths can be read in the human body. But there, too, carnival inverts the geography of flesh. The head, like heaven, no longer reigns supreme. People walk on their hands. The lower half of the body takes over as the seat of reason, with the ass assuming the place of the face, the anus the mouth, and a fart a terse sentence. "The Miller's Tale" emphasizes the genitals, the ass, farting, pissing, and screwing, for good reason: Carnival venerates the bawdy body. It drives straight, clean talk right out of earshot; only joking, and in particular dirty joking, makes sense.*

Only out of humiliation—earth and humus and shit—out of the very bowels of the earth, that is, the underground, can rebirth occur. In the medieval body politic, peasants, and women of every class, constitute the underbelly. This is one of Bakhtin's major insights about carnival: "Things are tested and reevaluated in the dimensions of laughter, which has defeated fear and all gloomy seriousness. This is why the material bodily lower stratum is needed, for it gaily and simultaneously materializes and unburdens. It liberates objects from the snares of false seriousness, from illusions and

*Some curses, in their desire to invoke the subversive force of carnival, turn the world around. One such curse, still popular today, "kiss my ass," flips the human anatomy. But that curse is only offensive during times of noncarnival, when the ass functions as a private, not a public part of the body. There again lies the spirit of carnival—its political power: In revolution, the private must turn public; there can be no secrets. The laughter in the Miller's performance rests, in great part, on exposing the dark secrets of the Reeve's life. Besides everything else, the Miller's joke is corrective; the Reeve knows he has done something socially unacceptable by marrying a woman much younger than he. And so the Miller excoriates him publicly. The Miller's tale can be viewed as a linguistically sophisticated form of the charivari.

sublimations inspired by fear."* The victim of a well-aimed joke dies. He or she cracks up, keels over, splits his or her sides, gets slayed or murdered. Whatever the exact phrase one selects for this peculiar kind of ludic death, a truth remains: The victim experiences a death. But he or she dies in preparation for being reborn more vigorous, more sound, more powerful, than in former life. The punch line, then, the symbolic fall of the victim, signals the hope of a heroic rebirth. That rebirth takes place in the embrace of the audience, in Chaucer's case, in the safety of the surrounding thirty-odd pilgrims.

In the spirit of carnival, where compass points swap places, John's resurrection begins with his fall from the roof. Nicholas's fart—the "unspoken word"—really sets the chain of events in motion. The anus is the lowest (highest) stratum of the body. The fart, an expulsion of air from the anus, makes a travesty of inspiration—God's blessed gift of life, or more to our point, the divine air of laughter.

All of this should remind us of the combined weeping and laughing that characterized those ancient texts, the Ras Shamra tablets, in which the dying god moves underground so that he can be harvested several months later. The pilgrim audience feels sympathy for the dying Reeve, but they will also feel joy the moment he decides to embrace the Miller in that grand renewal of friendship, for he embraces the Miller, not only for himself, but for every pilgrim who stands around. The joke pushes the victim in that one direction only—toward forgiveness. The more aggressive the joke, the more clever the teller, the greater the push toward forgiveness.

The collection of fifteenth-century sermons titled *Jacob's Well* explains that only mercy can rid our hearts of envy, and the sermons instruct good Christians to remove the "ooze of envy" from their souls. For a moment, by bringing the pans of justice into balance, the joker has rid him- or herself of envy and thus gained some satisfaction. And while it may not yet be heartfelt, both teller and victim must at least *act* as if they have dropped their grudges

*Bakhtin, *Rabelais*, p. 374.

and inch their way toward forgiveness. They must at least *play* at being merciful. By being forced to act with mercy, and getting reinforcement and reward for it, both aggressor and victim are able to move toward true forgiveness. The practical result of aggressive joke-telling turns out to be a lesson in *caritas*, in that most powerful of all Christian impulses, unconditional love, which requires both joker and victim to drop all judgments—at least to behave as if they have dropped all judgments.

This spirit washes the audience clean, too. As Chaucer says about the pilgrim audience, after they hear the Miller's *jape*: "For the moore part they laughe and pleyde"—laughter promotes true feelings of community. The experience of joke-telling begins to sound like a religious one, perhaps a more efficacious one in fact than religion can offer. In this spirit of *communitas* generated by *levitas*, each person embraces the other as an equal. The temporary effect of joking, then, is to create a feeling that things are even-Stephen, or more accurately—to use the Clown's phrase, the master of laughter in that most sober of plays, *Hamlet*—that all is "even-Cristen," a state in which everyone under God's gaze stands as an equal. Mary Douglas speaks to this point: "Whatever the joke, however remote its subject, the telling of it is potentially subversive. Since its form consists of a victorious tilting of uncontrol against control, it is an image of the levelling of hierarchy, the triumph of intimacy over formality, of unofficial values over official ones."*

Jokes may thus spread the Good News faster than religion. They communicate such delight that as soon as we get a joke—and the more clever the joke, the more deeply we are apt to "get" it—we immediately feel the urge to pass this gift of pleasure on, to collar the nearest person, embellish and retell the funny little story, increasing its value by adding our own interest to it. Gift-giving was particularly refreshing during the fourteenth century, when wage labor was on the rise. It startled by breaking the cash nexus. It can still startle. We are rarely presented with the opportunity today of passing on a gift just because we like it so much.

*Mary Douglas, *Implicit Meanings: Essays in Anthropology* (London: Routledge and Kegan Paul, 1975), p. 98. The chapter Douglas entitles "Jokes" has importance for a discussion of laughter cross-culturally. See also her "Do Dogs Laugh?" in the same volume.

Hermes, the patron trickster for the early Greeks, gets nudged aside in the early Middle Ages by Merlin, the patron saint of letters. This shape-shifter leaves his epigrams on swords and on tombstones, and circulates his letters between lovers and between enemies, between Arthur and his barons. More than prolific, he is capable of performing the wildest feats of magic, as well as of seeing into the future. Legend knows him best of all as a trickster, a riddler—revealing the truth in apparent lies—and a profound practical joker. In the second *Life of Saint Kentigern*, Merlin serves as a clairvoyant fool in King Rederich's court and with his "foolish words and gestures . . . excites to jokes and loud laughter the lords themselves and their servants." For Merlin, writing results, above all else, in laughing matter.

If Merlin serves as the patron saint of playful writing, Chaucer is its incarnation. He is attracted to joking, not because of his keen sense of humor, but because he is in the very marrow of his bones a writer: He knows that the punch line cannot hit its mark unless victims present themselves as fully fleshed characters, their vulnerability made palpable. The Miller must be close enough to the Reeve to know, as we say, where he "lives." A joke misfires unless it finds a personality rife with consciousness and sensibility. Idiots, dolts—*stupidus* of all stripes—will simply miss the point, or the point will miss them, fly by without so much as a glancing blow, or pass over their heads. Corraling the joke into a literate context forced Chaucer into becoming a mature writer, into dropping flat stereotypes in favor of more rounded characters. At this early stage of storytelling, characters come to life, oddly enough, so they can be murdered, metaphorically speaking, by other characters. This paradox radically affects the storyteller as well, for in writing jokes Chaucer moved to another level of seriousness: In medieval terms, he became an author.

Chaucer delights in what Ezra Pound calls *logopoeia*, "the dance of the intellect among words." To acknowledge Chaucer's wedding of joking and storytelling is to recognize that joking is first cousin to medieval *narratio*, fiction, a genre that culminates in the modern novel. Indeed, the first great European novelist, Rabelais, confesses that he was inspired by a cosmic punch line, and immediately after hearing God's laughter began writing his own lengthy, brilliantly conceived joke, *Gargantua and Pantagruel.*

Play and language, jokes and literature—the connections may seem odd at first. But play is so basic to animals—humans and nonhumans alike—why shouldn't it inform the very foundations of communication itself? Laughter eventually takes over the heart and soul of anyone who writes for any length of time. Sooner or later, every writer turns to punning and joking. Language begs for it. Starting with Saussure and Wittgenstein, philosophers have exploited language's elusive nature. The so-called natural language philosophers have focused on the implied connection between word and world, uncovering that nexus as nothing more than a substantial fault line.* The modern world can no longer claim that words hold any necessary or natural correspondence to objective reality; to use them as exact descriptions of sensory experience is to make of language a lie. Every word, then, functions as a tiny joke—on the speaker, on the listener—a practical joke that reality continually plays on the observer. "Language," as the novelist Iris Murdoch has written, "is a comic form, and makes jokes in its sleep."** Language may hammer away all it wants, but reality will simply not give up its essence. Language can only coax and cajole, and try to tease meaning out of events and objects. At the heart of language, playfulness finds its most happy home.

The joke explodes with the most profound linguistic truth. It creates an often wild fictive reality and, with a single line, or sometimes with a single word, pricks our hermetically sealed, tightly structured linguistic world and reveals—presto!—that nothing's really there. Nothing but air. Nothing but pleasure. The same truth is mirrored in the laughter of anyone who overhears the joke: Nothing remains but air and pleasure. Every joke reveals the same embarrassing truth about the Emperor. He wears not a stitch of cloth-

*One medievalist notes that parody precedes "straight" fiction because the language of fiction in the Middle Ages can be nothing more than a parody of scriptural language (Peter Haidu, "Repetition: Modern Reflections on Medieval Aesthetics," *Modern Language Notes* 92 (1977): 875–87).

**Iris Murdoch, *The Black Prince* (London: Chatto and Windus, 1973), p. 55.

ing—that much we already know. But the joke confers on every person a most singular power, the startling insight that we can clothe the Emperor however we please, with whatever fancy dress or ragtag suit we choose. But more than that, we can also strip him naked, for the Emperor only rules with rules. He only exerts control through the tightening grip of language, which means that he needs each and every one of us to play the game like good sports. And that's terrific news for jokers, for if they find themselves feeling even slightly rebellious, they can overwhelm the Emperor and turn his authoritarian world upside down. The joker aims at the heart of reality—at its rules.* And if he's not careful, the Emperor just might glance in the mirror and discover, for himself and on his own, that he's wearing nothing but a tired and tattered clown's costume.

Some secret knowledge, then, gets revealed in every laugh; insiders receive their initiation at the hands of the clever joker. But how early does this training begin? If Aristotle has us laughing on the fortieth day, what's his point? Might it not be that laughter offers the first step in stepping back, into the distancing that consciousness requires? Harold Bloom, in one of his many moments of insight, declares: "The introspective consciousness, free to contemplate itself, remains the most elitist of all Western images."** He has Shakespearean characters, particularly Falstaff and Hamlet, in mind. But beyond characters, Bloom has self-awareness in mind. It may just be possible that the remarkable moment in human evolution, when the individual steps outside himself or herself and observes from some remove, starts with a laugh. Inclining toward laughter requires a certain attitude—even the slightest attitude of removal will do.

In the context of jokes and laughter, Falstaff and Hamlet have more in common than might seem apparent at first blush. Both love to play and sport; both love the cracking sound of jokes. Falstaff plays his practical jokes

*The diminutive of Latin *rex*, "king," is *regulus*, a "kinglet" or petty king (notice the king shrinks as he extends his power), to feminine *regula*, "a measuring bar," hence a "ruler," and figuratively a "pattern of conduct," a "discipline." Everything that is *right* and *correct* emanates from *rex*: What a powerful root!

**Quoted in "Harold Bloom: Colossus among Critics," by Adam Begley, *New York Times Magazine*, September 25, 1994, p. 34.

with Prince Hal; Hamlet lays his on Gertrude, his mother, and on the usurping king. Falstaff's the court fool, in a sense, speaking wisdom through the fog of dry sack; and Hamlet, too, plays the court fool, speaking wisdom while feigning madness. For each of them, play is the thing. Laughter educates.

Traditional schooling and teaching miss the essential lessons that only laughter can provide. Traditional education relies on norms and structures; it extends over a semester, or a year, or even four years. Laughter, however, educates suddenly and with abrupt intensity. It is as if, when we utter a simple laugh, we suck into our lungs a super charge of empowerment, and in the process reach new heights of joy—and, perhaps, of sadness. But comedy triumphs over tragedy: Joy prevails. That feeling buoys us and carries us over time.

I would argue that comedy should be viewed as a "higher" form than tragedy, because the movement of comedy subsumes tragedy in it. Comedy more realistically resembles life, where tragedies both great and small are encompassed in its grander, wider sweep. Even in the face of serious illness, or someone's death, we know the advice: Life must go on. In a certain sense, we all at some point in our lives must shrug off pain, laugh off adversity, and reach for community and union—for the impulse and trajectory of comedy.

I end this chapter by quoting the contemporary surrealist philosopher Georges Bataille, on the subject that prompted this entire discussion, the knotty surprise we call language:

> We perceive that finally, for all the exercise of knowledge, the world still lies wholly outside its reach, and that not only the world, but the being that one is lies out of reach. Within us and in the world, something is revealed that was not given in knowledge, and whose site is definable only as unattainable by knowledge. It is, I believe, at this that we laugh. And, it must at once be said, in theorizing laughter, that this is what ultimately illuminates us; this is what fills us with joy.*

*Georges Bataille, "Un-Knowing: Laughter and Tears," *October* 36 (Spring 1986): 91.

# 7

## Let No Air Escape; *or, the renaissance has the last hahahae!*

*The* church in the English Middle Ages exercised control over its congregants by assuming responsibility for their inner lives, which it did, initially, in the most benign and gentle way—by providing pastoral care for their souls. By the end of the Middle Ages, church policy had reached beyond matters of the soul, however, in an attempt to exert influence over a person's physiology as well. In one of the most invasive moves imaginable, the church, in the sixteenth century, began to exercise a peculiarly powerful kind of authority by attempting to regulate the respiratory system of its congregants. Naturally, air always constitutes the crucial ingredient for maintaining life: To own the air is to hold the key to life—both physical and spiritual. Medieval theology had already transformed breathing—that most ordinary of all activities—into a religious event of extraordinary import. Suddenly, in the expanding world of early Renaissance political power, the church went after that most evanescent, most invisible of all things: air.

So all-encompassing was this newly constituted authority over breathing, in fact, that it included the very buildings in which people prayed—with attention paid both to the outside of religious buildings as well as to their interior. Spires atop medieval churches and cathedrals enabled those buildings to be sanctified by being filled—"inspired"—with God's breath. Inside, priests acted as spiritual conduits or filters between God and the congregation—between architecture and flesh—by passing that consecrated breath along, during Mass. Christians reinvigorated their breath during each church service, and particularly during the celebration of every Mass in an act of spiritual intimacy. As mentioned in the Introduction, at a particular moment in the Eucharist, priests would typically blow a little puff of that divinely inspired airy stuff into the mouths of each congregant, in what medieval liturgical practice termed the Conspiratorial Kiss (*osculum conspiratio*). Priests then conspired, "breathed in harmony,"—with every member of their congregation. As congregants received their kisses, they in turn became consecrated vessels, living structures for housing God's breath. In a sense, they mimicked the architectural importance of their church or cathedral, so that, by the late sixteenth century, anyone who strived toward lofty goals of any sort was said to "aspire." A person's outward beauty spoke of an inner beauty that radiated forth from the person's soul.

The idea of outside and inside gradually became specific and distinct phenomenological categories in the sixteenth century. This vision in turn paved the way for related revolutionary notions during the same period, such as the idea of a closed circulating system that described the boundaries of the inside of a person as separate and distinct from his or her external being. I cannot call such a dramatic order of change anything less than the social reconstruction of the human body. Laughter itself gets repositioned in that new ordering of the body—as a substance, not unlike blood, that should be housed safely and permanently inside each person.

By 1616, William Harvey, in front of the London College of Physicians, could even provide a scientific picture of his new, hermetic model of the human being, identifying blood as the dynamic force that took its meandering course inside the body. Harvey shocked his medical audience by describing blood flow in a way unimagined to that point. Blood moved throughout the body, he announced, through the aid of a system of filters and conduits, and through hundreds of veins and arteries, in what he termed "circulation." For Harvey, skin color and complexion provided accurate indicators of internal blood-flow conditions, a more precise measure of inner health than the rough picture afforded by the earlier theory of internal fluids, the four humors.* Traditional contemporary views of blood movement make Harvey's claim sound all the more revolutionary. I quote here from Henry Sigerist, a historian of medical science:

> The starting point of all physiology was the elementary observation that there are substances in nature such as food and air that are necessary for life. Without food an organism starves to death and without air it suffocates. But it was also found that there is a substance in the human body that must be necessary for life because it occurs throughout the organism, namely, blood that escapes from every wound. Physiology began with speculations about the relationship between these substances.
>
> The theory that dominated physiology before Harvey derived from Galen, who had taught that blood was digested in the stomach, moved to the intestines, when it passed through the veins into the liver. In the liver food was turned into blood and was impregnated with the natural spirit, a principle that was believed to regulate what we now call the vegetative functions of the body. Part of this dark liver blood streamed into the entire organism, while one part went through the vena cava into the right ventricle of the heart where a further division took place. One portion of the blood went into the lungs, where it unloaded waste materials of the body.**

*The Renaissance even used laughter to classify people's temperaments: *hi*, *hi*, *hi* signaled melancholics; *he*, *he*, *he* signaled phlegmatics; *ho*, *ho*, *ho* signaled sanguinity.

**Henry E. Sigerist, *Civilization and Disease* (Ithaca: Cornell University Press, 1945), p. 167. Notice that before Harvey, medical theory held that the three essential substances for human life—food, air, and blood—all began with one element, food, which by some miraculous process got transformed into blood and air. Harvey's theory caught on fast because of other, more mundane ideas of circulation. Ivan Illich points out that "by the end of the eighteenth century Harvey's theory was generally accepted in medicine. The conception of personal health based in the brisk circulation of blood fitted the mercantilist model of wealth—just before Adam Smith—based on the intensity of money circulation" (*In the Mirror of the Past* [London: Marion Boyars, 1992], p. 147). In the ancient world, recall, Hippocrates equated a swift movement of the blood in the body with vibrant health, and he stated emphatically that laughter was necessary to keep the blood hot

The idea of a circulating system that made its way through the body and back to its original starting point was unknown before Harvey.

The church had already developed a model similar to Harvey's. In the church's scheme, a laugh would be tantamount to a wound—a sudden and unexplained release of vitality—in this case a loss of air. Thus, while the medieval church infused the respiratory cycle with the loftiest of religious significance, it also deviated from the ancient attitude in the way it treated the holy stuff. The church quickly realized that, if it were to maintain tight control, it would have to make certain that breathing—inhalation and exhalation—took place without breaks in the system. So, beginning in the sixteenth century, church policy construed any unexpected release of air as an act of blasphemy. To ensure that air remained coursing safely and silently *inside* the body, for example, Puritans forbade, wherever and whenever they could, what they considered the most disruptive breaks in the smooth circulation of air—not just through laughter, noisy and disruptive as that might be, but also through another unwelcomed break, namely, farting.

To secure this goal, Puritan sensibility put a stop to raucous performances of medieval miracle plays in church, and as we've seen, to the injection of funny *exempla* into sermons. Dante, in the *Divine Comedy*, had complained that "nowadays men preach with jokes and japes." The practice went unheeded for centuries. Francis Bacon said "Enough," and argued that "certain things ought to be privileged from jest, namely religion, matters of state, great persons, any man's present business of importance, and any case that deserveth pity" (*Essay on Discourse*). It was in fact Bacon's belief that people had begun turning away from religion because "of a profane scoffing in holy matters."

Medieval mirth could no longer provide a theme for any aspect of religion or religious life—from the grotesque displays of gargoyles that adorned the sides of cathedrals to the devilish illuminations that brightened the mar-

and fluid, which ultimately guaranteed a patient's return to good health. Healthy blood produced hearty laughs. Medical writers like John of Arderne carried that belief through the Middle Ages. By the time of Harvey, the humorial solution of laughter has begun to be subsumed to the solvency of Adam Smith's cash flow and liquid assets. A new term, "financial well-being," came to characterize a person (and the inner life).

gins of manuscripts. Once more, the Puritans demanded a clear and discrete separation between categories, this time between jesting and earnestness. That distinction, as the historian Keith Thomas maintains,

> is reflected in the silent disappearance of the grotesque from church decoration; in the suppression of the mystery plays; and in the successful closing of church and churchyard to pipers, rushbearers and morris-dancers. As for religious burlesque, that was now thought intolerable; the Elizabethan secretary, Henry Barrow, was horrified by the former episcopal practice of keeping "counterfeit and natural fools openly in their house at the time of their solemn idolatrous feasts to make a sermon of ribaldry or folly in the most high despite God."*

Elizabethan bishops warned the laity against "unseemly scoffs, jests and ribaldry." Government joined the church to make the illegality of laughter an issue of public concern. A statute enacted in 1547 outlawed offensive jokes about the Eucharist, and royal injunctions promulgated in 1559 prohibited jokes against the clergy in general. A 1606 statute forbade jocular references to God on stage. High seriousness became synonymous with a deep religiosity. Laughter, on the other hand, meant frivolity, looseness, an attitude of devil-may-care. It meant everything but the solemnity associated with a Puritan religion.

A certain hush fell over the sixteenth century in England. Indeed, the Puritans choked off breath with such certainty and efficiency that their policies effected change in the most basic way—at the level of language itself. The letter *h* functions as an aspirant, a slight release of air. Sounding its early Latin name, *ha*, one recreates its breathy function. A whole series of words in Old and Middle English begin with the combination *hw*, the initial *h* requiring speakers to emit a puff of air before sounding the rest of the word. By the sixteenth century, every *h*, the principal aspirant, has been silenced by being tucked away somewhere in the interior of the word, or by being dropped altogether. Breathy words like *hwaet*, *hwuch*, and *hwa*, for in-

*I am indebted to Keith Thomas's "The Place of Laughter in Tudor and Stuart England," *Times Literary Supplement*, January 21, 1977, for some of the historical information in this chapter.

stance, refigured themselves into less airy ones like *what*, *which*, and *who*. This change takes place most dramatically with the word *laughter* itself, which in Old English is spelled with an almost impossible to pronounce whirlwind of air: *hlehhan*. Against such legal, ecclesiastical, and linguistic assaults on breath, laughter had to struggle mightily to survive.*

But survive it did. In the Preface to this book I argue for a new kind of listening, one that requires the reader to press his or her ear firmly to the page, attuned to a laughter that runs, like an underground river, just below the topography of the main historical events. I call this the telluric laughter of the peasant. The stronger, the more adamant the insistence to avoid laughing, the more we can detect it roiling underground, and the more we can hear it reverberate with that character of a bad boy or a bad girl who has gotten away with murder. Puritans hoped to have their admonitions get under the skin of every peasant and in that way to control people's lives. But they could not succeed. It cannot be coincidental, for example, that the most ribald novel in the Renaissance appeared in the midst of the most tightlaced and thoroughgoing political and spiritual oppression. Rabelais's *Gargantua and Pantagruel* stands as a historical tribute to the indomitable peasant spirit capable, at any given moment, of turning the world on its head. That novel prompted Mikhail Bakhtin to cheer its author's keen understanding of laughter: "The four-hundred-year history of the understanding, influence, and interpretation of Rabelais is closely linked with the history of laughter itself."** Bakhtin goes on to say that not only was the novel embraced by aristocrats at court, and by the educated in humanist circles, but that it was especially loved by the people themselves—a manifesto for the revolution of the high-soaring comedic spirit of humanity everywhere.

*Gargantua and Pantagruel* bears witness to an important intellectual movement. By pushing laughter underground, the Puritans also pushed it

*The two principal poems in Old and Middle English, *Beowulf* and the *Canterbury Tales*, both begin with the letter *h* in their opening words, *hwaet* and *hwaen*, respectively. The hero of these orally-delivered poems, it could be argued, is air. Each poem opens by celebrating the miracle that makes the poem possible in the first place—human breath itself.

**Mikhail M. Bakhtin, *Rabelais and His World*, trans. Helene Iswolsky (Bloomington: Indiana University Press, 1984), p. 59.

underbelly. Laughter became substratum in all senses, gargantuan by becoming Gargantua-like. That is, laughter came to be expressed bodily—in its urgency to get heard. It moved from mind to matter, from wit to shit. A fat stomach like Falstaff's, round as the world itself, rises from the subplots of Shakespeare's political plays ready to explode its great quantity of air, upsetting the balance of power in the plays' main plots. Carnival laughter always forces attention on the belly, buttocks, and bladder. Substratum laughter, or as Bakhtin prefers to call it, "grotesque realism," always "degrades," in the sense of decomposing, of turning into compost and being reborn underground, prompting Bakhtin's catchphrase, "laughter degrades and materializes."* To materialize means to enflesh again, to reestablish the body as solid reality, and thus to return the person to wholeness and substantiality.

But more is at stake here than just one individual: The joking victim undergoes a humiliating experience only to be reborn, not merely for him- or herself, but for all humankind. He or she offers the possibility of hope by offering the possibility of future generations: "Not the biological body, which merely repeats itself in the new generation, but precisely the historic, progressing body of mankind stands at the center of this system of images."** Shakespeare dispenses with Falstaff, the blood and guts of *Henry IV, Part 1*, but the king—the idea of kingship—lives on in the main action forever, reinvigorated by subplotted, substratum festivities and carnival activity.

Let me quote Bakhtin further on this theme of degradation and renewal—on death and rebirth—through humiliation. It is a theme that runs all the way through the history of laughter, one that we have seen as far back as the Ras Shamra Texts, as the dying god is buried in anticipation of his ultimate resurrection:

> Degradation here means coming down to earth, the contact with earth as an element that swallows up and gives birth at the same time. To degrade is to bury, to sow, and to kill simultaneously, in order to bring forth

*Ibid. Remember that the victim in hostile joke-telling always feels humiliated, as in *humus*—dirt or shit—but moves through that decayed state in his or her passage toward rebirth and, as we have seen in Chaucer, into the welcoming arms of forgiveness.

**Ibid., p. 367.

> something more and better. To degrade also means to concern oneself with the lower stratum of the body, the life of the belly and the reproductive organs; it therefore relates to acts of defecation and copulation, conception, pregnancy and birth. Degradation digs a bodily grave for a new birth; it has not only a destructive, negative aspect, but also a regenerating one. To degrade an object does not imply merely hurling it into the void of nonexistence, into absolute destruction, but to hurl it down to the reproductive lower stratum, the zone in which conception and a new birth take place. Grotesque realism knows no other lower level; it is the fruitful earth and the womb. It is always conceiving.*

The Renaissance church particularly detested this brand of laughter known as substratum. For one thing, substratum laughter reversed all official church orientations, where up led to God, and down to hell and the devil. Hell offered no possibility of rebirth, signifying only eternal damnation. As far as the church was concerned, substratum rebirth from the earth—from under the earth—might happen with plant life, or with pagan vegetation deities, but not with humankind. Only Christ was resurrected from the tomb, from under the earth. Carnival laughter could not get any more sacrilegious or secular, but it also destroyed the inside/outside boundaries that the church so diligently tried to maintain as discrete. In substratum, carnivalizing laughter, the inside of the body continually threatens—through farts, belches, vomit, and especially through defecation—to show up in all its gross and blatant display on the outside of the body.

Shit represents carnival gaiety—neither life nor fully degraded matter, a liminal substance just like the festival of which it was such a vital part. Carnival replaced earth with shit as the halfway point between heaven and hell: halfway between the living and the decaying body. In carnival terms, feces represents a fertile, life-affirming force, and a substance, of course, that violated the church's sense of purity and cleanliness.

And so the church took one more step toward regulation by taking

*Ibid., p. 21.

control of another of its congregants' internal systems, the digestive system, through a range of dietary laws. Church ritual demanded the most radical alterations in diet just at that moment in the Christian calendar when larded bellies might be expected to explode in laughter, just as the burgeoning of spring gave way to the constrictions of Lent. By restricting diet, the church could aim at containing those other essential substances—blood, air, and now farting and shitting. Restrict one's diet, the logic runs, and reduce the process of elimination.* The combat between Carnival and Lent is not only a fight between abundance and deficiency, but also between ingestion and elimination, the elimination in particular of what decomposes the most and with the most odor—meat. The purest food for a Christian, of course, is the Body and Blood of Christ, the wafer and the wine, which, presumably, do not translate into waste matter, but into Christ himself, who surpasses decay.

In demanding a leaner, more restricted diet, the church signaled that boisterous, carnival-spirited, peasant belly-laughs had severe limits, that the carnival could not only be expected to end, but to end in a most glorious display of spiritual rebirth, in the Resurrection of Christ. Even the lowliest peasant came to experience that renewal by revivifying his or her own respiratory system, forty days after the deprivations of Lent, with a brand-new religious air—through the infusion of the Holy Spirit. The highest Mass took place at Easter, the Flesh and the Blood of Christ most religiously charged on that day. The Renaissance termed this renewal through the Holy Ghost an act of Spiration. The repentant Lenten Christian, through the Resurrection, made his or her own successful journey back from the dead, from degradation—symbolized by a mark of ashes on the forehead—by

**Diet* is a curious medieval term, meaning both the customary course of food, as well as a restricted quantity or kind of food—a regimen. But it also refers to the ordinary course of one's life, to the "space of a day"—probably from association with Latin *dies*, "day,"—and by extension to "the ordinary course of the church," or to an "assembly of church officials" that controls church business. The word reverberates with ambiguity. Initially, at least, *diet* functions both as a secular and a religious term and suggests both a sufficiency and a paucity. At Lent, *diet* in its initial sense turns into *diet* in its secondary sense.

catching this most holy "second wind." The ultimate triumph over degradation, of course, is Christ himself, who returns from death to complete materialization.

This attitude toward the two circulatory systems—alimentary and respiratory—carries such profound religious meaning that it was one of the ways Judaism distinguished itself from Christianity. In Deuteronomy, the Lord recalls the miraculous way he sustained the Israelites during their entire time in the wilderness with *manna*, "bread from heaven," until they had entered the land of Canaan, "a land of wheat and barley, of vines and fig trees and pomegranates, a land of olive trees and honey, a land in which you will eat bread without scarcity, in which you will lack nothing, a land whose stones are iron, and out of whose hills you can dig copper. And you shall eat and be full, and you shall bless the Lord your God for the good land he has given you" (8:8–10).

Since God created everything, it would make sense that food—all food—should be holy. But the Lord complicates matters. Everything in the universe emanates from God's mouth. "Let there be light" begins it all. What else proceeds from the mouth of the Lord, however, are commandments. The Israelites must learn, not merely to stand in awe of God's bounteous production, but to stand in fear of his commandments—they must learn to obey by "walking in his ways and by fearing him." They must learn to ingest his word along with his food: The body cannot be nourished without the soul. That's the key lesson in the wilderness, and the only way God provided for his people: "And you shall remember all the way which the Lord your God has led you these forty years in the wilderness, that he might humble you, testing you to know what was in your heart, whether you would keep his commandments, or not. And he humbled you and let you hunger and fed you with manna, which you did not know, nor did your fathers know that he might make you know that man does not live by bread alone, but that man lives by everything that proceeds out of the mouth of the Lord."

Most people recognize the first part of the phrase, "man does not live by bread alone," but few know the second part, that the Hebrew people actually live by food, and commandments affect that food. In the merging of food and commandments, proper eating is a religious experience, offering a way to honor the Lord. God urges that certain food be consumed and commands that others be avoided. The Hebrew people must learn to pay strict attention to dietary laws, observing them not only during the many festivals throughout the year, but also during routine food preparation, in an elaborate process known as "koshering," whereby some food gets socially reconstructed as clean and is thus consecrated for consumption. So potent were those taboos against pollution that just by touching certain animals a Jew ran the risk of becoming immediately impure.

A Jew must thus learn by heart a complicated hierarchy of noningestibles, which the rabbis call "the abominations of Leviticus." Leviticus 11 and Deuteronomy 14:3–20 specify animals that by nature are unclean and so can never be purified, even through koshering. Things that can never be eaten constitute a varied list, including those animals that do not both chew their cud and walk on cloven hooves, those that walk on all fours without arching their feet, all "birds of abomination," creatures of the sea without fins or scales, swarming creatures, those that crawl on their bellies, or those with many feet. In addition, the Bible commands in several places—and so we may take it as a firm admonition—that a kid should not be seethed in its mother's milk.* Kosher slaughtering requires slitting the carotid artery of the animal as the creature hangs upside down. All blood must be drained out of the animal in order for a Jew to consume its flesh. Thus, no animal can be eaten that has died of natural causes, been rent apart by beasts, or that for whatever reason, still contains blood.

While the Hebrews devote a great deal of attention to deciphering the food chain, they have less of a need to regulate breath, because for them breath always remains sacred. Hebrews know two words for breathing:

*For an interesting analysis of these food categories, see Mary Douglas, *Purity and Danger: An Analysis of the Concepts of Pollution and Taboo* (London: Routledge and Kegan Paul, 1966).

*nesama*, which refers to the physical act of taking in air; and *ruach*, which means "spirit," "wind," and sometimes even "disposition." In this sense, the Hebrews, like the ancient Greeks, could be considered to believe in two separate streams of breath. *Ruach hayim*, "the breath of life," translates more generally as "living creatures"—humankind described by its most salient and most sacred activity. The biblical account of the creation of Adam clearly reveals the sacredness of breath: God brings Adam to life by breathing his own *ruach* into a lump of formless clay.* As we've seen, Jews imitate God's action every time they read Torah out loud by infusing their own breath into dead characters on the parchment and, by so doing, bringing them to life.

The story of Adam and Eve's expulsion from the Garden of Eden can actually be read as a blueprint for religiously charged breathing and eating—for respiration and digestion. God's own breath animates Adam, who walks the earth as a living sanctuary. His expulsion from the Garden of Eden—along with Eve's—constitutes the initial breaking of Hebraic dietary laws. The serpent offers the fruit of the tree of knowledge of good and evil to Adam and Eve, which they know as an "unclean," taboo food, for they have heard all too well God's commandment: Thou shalt not eat of this tree! The creature that offers the fruit, the serpent, has its legs taken away as punishment, condemned forever to crawl the ground as the principal abomination of Leviticus, a horrifyingly unclean, permanently humiliated creature. Adam and Eve's punishment is to have the status of their own breath radically changed. After their expulsion from the Garden, *ruach* is only a gift, a loan that has to be returned to God. Eternal life—everlasting breath—God removes from them.

To summarize then: The church in the Middle Ages and in the Renaissance kept a close watch over breath, because it wanted to invest it with di-

***Adamah* in Hebrew means "earth" or "clay." Depending on context, *nesama* may sometimes mean, besides breath, the soul itself. Adam's life is a vibrant, carnivalesque rebirth, one that arises quite literally out of the earth. (His springing to life in the Old Testament prefigures Christ's coming back to life in the New Testament.) Notice that the serpent remains forever on the earth (Latin *serpens*, "creeping, crawling thing").

vine holiness and, further, to ensure that holiness. The Jews needed no such attention to breath because the Bible—and the rabbis—give to breath an immediate status of holiness that informs its entire history both inside the body and out. In matters of food, the two religions switch places. Christians pay less attention to food because the transformative power of food, the Blood and Body of Christ, describes the heart of the Christian experience called transubstantiation. Jews, on the other hand, need to maintain the construction of food as holy stuff and so devote a great deal of attention to making distinct categories of what can and what cannot be ingested. Each time Jews eat a meal properly, they can rest assured that they are eating their way to holiness.

Church officials persisted, throughout the Tudor and Stuart periods, in their determination to outlaw every trace of laughter. By that time, every writer seemed to recognize that all laughter could carnivalize, that all laughter was ultimately inversionary. The church had particular reason to fear such laughter, for all its rules and officiousness made it such a ripe target. "Anyone who peruses the records of the church courts in the century before the Civil War," Keith Thomas notes, "cannot fail to be struck by the frequency of ribald and irreligious humour."* According to a contemporary account, James I's courtiers once tried to cheer up the king by staging a mock christening with a courtier dressed up as a bishop, the marquis of Buckingham playing the godfather, and a pig standing in for the baby. That joke misfired, but a subsequent attempt by Buckingham's son to amuse Charles II by preaching a bawdy sermon on the "Song of Songs" proved more successful, perhaps because the "Song of Songs" is such a sensual poem.

Laughter of course resounded from the villagers, who staged parodies of virtually every sacred rite. Peasants engaged in mock baptisms of farm animals—pigs, cats, and calves—to destroy the pretensions of ecclesiastical ceremonies conducted by corrupt churchmen. Their satires included blas-

*Thomas, "The Place of Laughter," p. 78.

phemous catechisms, bawdy jokes about Holy Communion, and hymns set to popular tunes. For example, Samuel Puckering, a Lincolnshire churchwarden, sang a psalm to the tune of a popular ditty called "Cuddle me, cuddy." At Blatherwick, Northamptonshire, in 1637, the local lord of misrule donned a surplice, read a mock wedding service, and ended by escorting the couple to their wedding bed. At Beccles, in 1640, the soldiers conducted a mock ecclesiastical court and did "justice on a man and wench that were taken in their sin, along with merry mad pranks not fit to be written."* One can only imagine what sort of pranks could not find their way into print.

Burlesques of religious rituals made officials bear down all the harder. But the burlesque of rituals extended beyond the church. Outspoken fools and jesters ingratiated themselves less and less with conventional society. Colleges and the Inns of Court had long suffered their Christmas princes and lieutenants, chosen from among the most witty students, to ridicule authority in the same way that mayors and lords of misrule carried out their inversionary tactics in the countryside. These young M.A.s, known as Terrae Filius at Oxford and Prevaricators at Cambridge, were appointed annually to deliver speeches at the chief academic ceremony of the year. Their addresses consisted of bawdy jests and insults aimed at the private lives of the vice-chancellor, heads of houses, and other dignitaries. At Oxford, in particular, these speeches began to come under severe attack. It was one of "the grossest immoralities," reported a leading churchman, that young men should "boldly and openly reproach, villify, name and point at their superiors . . . and falsely accuse them to their very faces in the presence of persons of all nations, degrees and qualities; and all this in so bold and rustic a manner as is intelligible to every idle wench and country bumpkin." Throughout the Stuart period university officials contrived ways of silencing these licensed buffoons. They tried persuasion, threats, even bribery. One vice-chancellor pulled an orator down with his own hands, "the scholars standing amazed

*Ibid., p. 78.

to see his courage and resolution."* Another, in what must have been absolute frustration, called in the troops to stop the Terrae Filius.

At court, every famous king had his own fool, a licensed madman who gave the king both advice and entertainment, provided his remarks did not get too personal. The fool preserved the king's decorum by making jokes for him without His Majesty having to stoop to folly. Kings were beyond telling jokes and, for that purpose, professional comedians—buffoons—worked well. But something more interesting was at work here as well. Earlier I tried to show that air, in the form of the aspirant *h* had evaporated from certain key words—indeed, from *laughter* itself. As that happened, as laughter became more and more repressed and moved underground to the level of the villager and peasant, breath found a zany surrogate at the aristocratic level in the fool. Indeed, fools come from a tradition of airiness. The word *fool* derives from the Latin *follem*, literally "bellows." In late popular Latin, *follem* carried the sense of "windbag," what we would call "empty-headed," or more colloquially an "airhead." Thus, the fool has often been depicted as a ranter letting off his charges of hot air in the court. With a fool by his side, the king owned an official set of lungs.**

Henry VIII's jester, Will Summers, known to literary historians as one of the most accomplished of what the period called "artificial fools," continually cracked scatological jokes, at which Henry reportedly "laughed heartily." Summers knew enough to keep his jokes lighthearted and impersonal, never attacking the integrity of the king himself. When that in fact did happen, that is, when fools crossed the bounds of decorum, kings did not receive their remarks kindly. King James's jester, Archie Armstrong, according to one historian, became known as one of the wildest, most impulsive court jesters and would often "make mischief and interfere with pol-

*Ibid.

***Fool* evolves into a food term in the eighteenth century, a fruit puree mixed with cream. The dessert may have taken on its foolish sense because the cream gets beaten into the puree with a sufficiency of air. But maybe not: We have already seen the connections between joking and eating. The word *farce* is first a food term, "stuffing." Later, it came to refer to comic reliefs, interlarded between acts of a play.

itics." He figured prominently in state documents as a consequence, and a great many details of his life have been recovered. We know, for instance, that he was born a Scotsman, and became naturalized in 1612 when James ascended to the English throne. When Archbishop Laud imposed his prayerbook on the Scots, Armstrong pushed a bit too far, it appears, and asked the Canterbury prelate, "Who's the fool now?" for which "scandalous words" he was dismissed by the Privy Council. Charles II's fool, Tom Killigrew, tested the limits, too, when in 1666 he rebuked the king for spending more time with courtly affairs than with the affairs of the court.*

Most Elizabethans knew their fools, not as real characters, but as dramatic creations, and probably best of all through five flamboyant characters in Shakespeare: Touchstone, Feste, Lavatch, King Lear's fool, and a minor fool in *Timon of Athens*.** Tucked safely inside the plays, fools could speak truth boldly to power, not only under the protective cover of a feigned, foolish innocence, but through poetic license, through the contrivance of plot and the necessities of dramatic action. Shakespeare renders the fool for what he is, a seeming idiot or madman—a social grotesque who is willing to make an ass out of himself. Dressed in costumes of particolors or, what turned out to be much more outlandish and shocking, decked out in women's clothes, the fool utters invaluable truths in parabolic, sometimes highly metaphoric ways.† The eloquence of the fool often casts him in the role of court poet, as well. Indeed, in Old Irish *fili* means both "fool" (jester) and "poet." In stance and speech, the Renaissance fool resembles a dramatic

*Enid Welsford, *The Fool: His Social and Literary History* (Gloucester, Mass.: Peter Smith, 1966), p. 175.

**Shakespeare's fools are all men. A few examples of female fools, however, surfaced in France: A female fool named Mathurine, who flourished in the courts of Henri IV and Louis XIII, "was accustomed to walk the streets of Paris disguised as an Amazon and followed about by a crowd of jeering children. Her warlike dress may have been due to a certain pugnacity of disposition, for the fool had strong political and religious views" (ibid., p. 153).

†Natalie Davis claims that "only with the male fool or clown do we find literary examples of male transvestism serving to challenge order. In the seventeenth-century *commedia dell'arte*, a black-faced Harlequin dolls himself up as a ridiculous Diana, goddess of the chase, replete with crescent-moon ruff, fancy clothes, and a little bow. The result is so absurd that not only are boundaries between high and low effaced, but . . . reality itself seems to dissolve" ("Women on Top," in *Society and Culture in Early Modern France* [Palo Alto: Stanford University Press, 1975], p. 132).

refinement of those two key historical fools who spoke in haunting parables or who played the guileless innocent—Christ and Socrates.

Kings sometimes replaced fools with dwarves, who served the same purpose—to amuse and entertain. Wealthy men in the Roman Empire kept half-witted or deformed slaves, known as *mariones*, *stulti*, and *fatui*, for their pleasure and pastime—deformed henchmen of the laughable. Fools, too, bespoke a deformed kind of reason, and so appeared many times with physical deformities or as grotesques of one kind or another—with hunchbacks, pot bellies, or large noses. But we should remember the tradition from the ancient world, articulated most elegantly by Hobbes, of laughter arising from our own feelings of a "sudden glory" at seeing deformed, handicapped individuals. The Renaissance took that tradition of physical deformity and installed it as a principal source of official laughter. Like the mixed emotions that Plato pointed to in the *Philebus*, the Renaissance enjoyed its own love-hate relationship with the deformed: Aristocrats knew they should not laugh at them, but they also found themselves somehow attracted to them. Jokebooks, enormously popular during the period, encouraged poking fun at the disabled and the less fortunate, while books of manners urged people of proper breeding to avoid such scandalous humor.

For centuries, people had laughed at those less fortunate than themselves, and Renaissance deformity enfleshed that tradition. The owner of a demented fool or a misshapen dwarf was automatically elevated, placed on a higher level than the poor, besotted pet. If the fool or dolt could utter bits of wisdom, so much the better—a clever trick, a sport of nature, an *idiot savant*. Dwarves and fools moved through the Renaissance as versions, in a very real sense, of that first object of ridicule in literature: Hephaistos.

But just as Henry Barrow condemned the Elizabethan bishops' keeping of fools, so laughter dimmed in other places. Even the most strong-willed of writers, like Thomas More, whose own spirit King Henry, along with various cardinals, simply could not break, ultimately turned to more somber prose. More was a person who all his life loved to goad and tease, like a fool, with his incredibly sharp wit. But he had no license. He occupies an important place in the history of laughter if only for one linguistic feat: More was the first English writer to convert the word *geste*, "story," into the word *jest* in its modern, funny sense. After the second decade of the sixteenth century, however, More's prose turned dramatically serious. As Keith Thomas observes, "More had to defend his practice of mixing 'merry tales' with serious matters. . . . the witty anecdotes which enliven his writings, or those of Hugh Latimer became increasingly infrequent in religious literature."*

The "merry tales" to which Keith Thomas refers have a long history. They form part of a genre called "jokebooks," a genre More himself helped to cultivate in England. For More to abandon such merry tales required no small compromise on his part. But he moved, nonetheless, not unlike a repentant Christian heeding instructions in Ecclesiastes, from laughing to crying. In 1516, More had printed his version of Plato's *Republic*, which offered the possibility of the perfect commonwealth, and made its case through a prose style strongly charged with Socratic irony, jests, and even outright laughter. In that work, *Utopia*, More uses *jest* in a new, nuanced way: "He himself was oftener laughed at than his jests were."**

Less than twenty years later, in 1534, imprisoned in the Tower of London on charges of treason, More wrote a somber philosophical treatise entitled *Dialogue of Comfort Against Trybulacioun*. Perhaps because he faced the imminent certainty of his own death—the king beheaded him in 1535—More resuscitated a tradition we have seen in early Christian writings, the apocryphal eyewitness account of Christ's life, and used it in the *Dialogue* to convey his own drear view of the world: "And for to prove that this life is no laughing time, but rather the time of weeping, we find that our saviour himself wept twice or thrice, but never find we that he laughed so much as once. I will not swear that he never did, but at the last wise he left us no example of it. But, on the other side, he left us example of weeping."

*Thomas, "The Place of Laughter," p. 79.

**Ibid.

The *Dialogue* reflects an obvious shift in feeling in Thomas More, but it also reveals a more widespread shift in sensibility in England itself. More was an outspoken, independent wit. If the crown and church could gag or even get rid of him, they might also frighten all those other wits gathered around More—and there were scores of them—into stark sobriety.

Indeed, More had been so powerfully and originally connected to laughter that he inspired others to write their own encomia to the god of hilarity. For example, the Dutch humanist Desiderius Erasmus wrote several works dedicated to reforming the reformers themselves. And he chose to use the very weapon they feared the most—laughter. His first ludic work, a satire against theologians and church dignitaries, *The Praise of Folly* (1511), Erasmus claims to have written at More's insistence. Erasmus even explains, using a fanciful play on Thomas More's surname, how he came to praise such a bizarre thing as folly:

> The first thing was your surname of More, which comes so near the word *Moriae* (folly) as you are far from the thing. And that you are so, all the world will clear you. In the next place, I conceived this exercise of wit would not be least approved by you; inasmuch as you are wont to be delighted with such kind of mirth, that is to say, neither unlearned if I am not mistaken, nor altogether insipid, and in the whole course of your life have played the part of a Democritus.*

Assuming the personality of folly itself, Erasmus opens the book by insisting that everyone should praise folly, for every authority, both religious and secular, every mythical god and literary hero and heroine, seems to uphold folly as an ideal. To be foolish, Erasmus cleverly suggests, means to exercise the highest form of virtue and wisdom.

Erasmus takes great pleasure in playing the fool by speaking the fool's truths. He turns reason head over heels, pretending that every dumb law, every stupid act, has usurped reason's place. In another book attributed to More and his clique of wisecracking friends, *A Hundred Merye Talys*, the

*Desiderius Erasmus, *The Praise of Folly* (Ann Arbor: University of Michigan Press, 1958), pp. 1–2.

world turns less intellectual and sardonic and descends deeply into the scatological and derisive. Think of the deformities of the fool or the dwarf as inspired subjects for literature, and you have the jokebook called the *Hundred Talys*. Thus, while standards of good taste were being formed in the late sixteenth century forbidding aristocrats to laugh at gross deformities, jokebooks heeded no such warning. In the jokebook, Keith Thomas tells us, "every disability, from idiocy and insanity to diabetes and bad breath, was a welcome source of amusement. 'We jest at a man's body that is not well-proportioned,' said Thomas Wilson, 'and laugh at his countenance if . . . it be not comely by nature.' A typical Elizabethan joke-book contains 'merry jests of fools,' and 'merry jests of blind folks,' while some of the tricksters' pranks are brutal in the extreme."*

Jokebooks made duplicity possible. Aristocrats could take delight in reading in privacy about freaks and marginal characters, while maintaining a public stance free from such obvious bad taste. Literacy created a society of secret readers. And if pornography quickly came as a concomitant of printing—and it did—then so did the reading of semi-underground jokebooks about the deformed and the freakish.

Drawing on the distinction of jokes propounded by Cicero and somewhat by Quintilian, these Renaissance jokebooks gathered together funny one-liners (*dicacitas*) or witty stories (*facetiae*), clever puns and sayings. Hundreds of these collections appeared in Italy, Germany, and in Holland, but very few in England: The Puritans of course hated them. Mimes and other performers had carried Cicero's oral forms from the classical period into England and the Continent in the Middle Ages; but as more lay people became literate, the *facetiae* got more widely disseminated through the jokebooks, beginning in the late fourteenth century, with remnants of them hanging on all the way into the Victorian age.

Jokebooks gathered material from various classical and medieval sources: from satire attributed to the *scholastikos* of Hierocles of Alexander

*Thomas, "The Place of Laughter," p. 80.

in the fifth century, to *fabliaux* and sermon *exempla* of the High Middle Ages, to popular sayings of Italian humanists and German peasants. Most often writers of these books placed the jests or apothegms (*apothemata*) in the mouths of some real or imaginary trickster with names that Renaissance aristocrats quickly came to know: John Scoggan (Edward IV's court jester), Howlglass, Mother Bunch, Master Skelton (the poet John Skelton, considered something of a wit), Robin Goodfellow, Old Hobson, and even George Peale (author of *The Merrie Conceited Jests of George Peale*). To assign these *jests* to characters kept the experience close to *gestes*—actual stories. It was a way of saying, as jokers like to claim, This story is true. According to Keith Thomas, the genre reached its peak in 1739, with a collection of jokes "fathered ironically upon [a] deceased comedian, Joe Miller; in innumerable later versions, *Joe Miller's Jests* dominated the field until late Victorian times; though the older jokes still circulated in an underworld of chapbook literature."*

To Petrarch must go the credit for resurrecting Cicero's rhetorical theories of the *facetiae*, which had lain dormant since Macrobius last mentioned them in the fifth century. Petrarch declares that he has read Cicero's dialogue on joking in *De oratore*, but he doesn't say what particularly appealed to him. I suspect it was his deep interest in courtly love, a ritualized game that carries along with its tone of earthiness a playful jesting, in repartee between the two lovers.

Whatever the case, Petrarch presented the first collection of such jokes to the world in 1344, an arrangement of some 114 *facetiae*, which he admits to have borrowed from Macrobius' *Saturnalia* and Suetonius' *Lives*. Through these *facetiae*, he aims to expose the pretensions of the famous, from the ancient (Diogenes) to the contemporary (Pope John XXII). Like love, laughter has the power to pierce illusion and get to the heart of truth.

*Ibid. The real Joseph Miller was a seventeenth-century actor at Drury Lane who purportedly loved telling jokes. *Joe Miller's Jests* was actually written by John Motley. The 1836 edition of the jestbook dropped 49 of its 249 jokes, in deference "to the greater delicacy observed in modern society and conversation." Tastes had clearly changed by the Victorian period.

Among the most influential of Renaissance collections was Poggio Bracciolini's *Facetiae*, first published in 1470. Poggio delights in wordplay, puns in particular, but more than that he loves exaggerated stories about members of the clergy. Poggio is one of literature's great liars himself, letting his readers know—with a wink—that he has heard these *facetiae* in the *bugiale*, the anteroom where papal secretaries gather to tell stories (*bugia* in Italian means "a lie"). But while Poggio clearly takes great pleasure in laughter, he still finds it slightly dangerous stuff and advises reading his funny stories only because they provide some relief from the struggles and tedium of hard labor.

Two other collections, one by the well-known humanist and neo-Latin writer, Giovanni Pontano (*De sermone*, 1509), and the other by the equally well-known German humanist Heinrich Bebel (*Facetiae*, 1508–12), also enjoyed extraordinary popularity. Bebel sees laughter as a way out of the seriousness of contemporary life, and loves to satirize in his *facetiae dicta* the traditional butts of the sermon *exempla*: unfaithful wives, stupid peasants, and illiterate and immoral churchmen.

While Bebel may have had more imitators, Pontano is more important to our story, because he brings back into the Renaissance the Aristotelian virtue of *facetudo* (elegance), a mean between the extremes of *scurrilitas* (buffoonery) and *rusticitas* (rusticity). The way there, for Pontano, lies through *relaxatio animi*, the relief, as in Poggio, from labors that only a bracing laugh can provide. He also makes one of the first accommodations of laughter to the political world. The true prince, he argues, should pay attention to laughter as a balance to the highs and lows of courtly life.

Thomas More's old friend Erasmus, always on the lookout for a good laugh, also published a joke collection, *Convivium fabulosum*, as part of his *Colloquies* in 1524. One can easily imagine that he took as a model for his *Convivium* his visits with More, for his book contains ten jokes or stories told in a lively symposium by nine friends, all of whom have names suggestive of laughter (Gelasinus, Eutrapelia). Erasmus brings laughter unequivocably into the world of politics, going beyond Pontano in seeing *festivitas* as an essential attribute of the solid humanist and arguing for laughter as a controlling attribute of the prince. And finally, in a weird detail that would appeal to peasant sensibilities, Erasmus points to the buttocks as the most honorable part of the body, since people seem to use their hind ends more than their heads.

Erasmus probably influenced the writing of that anonymous English jokebook *A Hundred Merye Talys*. But the *Talys* betray their origins in Puritan England, containing only mildly salacious stories and jokes, the most disruptive being the tales of farting by various members of the aristocracy.* The *Talys* draw on no Continental or classical sources but appear native to England in origin and conservative in effect. In addition, only a few of the tales come across as fully developed, and only a few as delightfully obscene. And while they range through all the social classes, they take as favorite targets ignorant or lecherous churchmen and promiscuous women. In the end, they opt for the status quo, except, perhaps, for number 41, which has as its protagonist Master Skelton, who grows into a popular jester later in the period in the anecdotes of the poet John Skelton.

The jokebook really comes full circle, and laughter makes its most complete and astonishing accommodation to the entrenched political and social order, with the English translation in 1528 of Baldasar Castiglione's *Book of the Courtier*. Castiglione sets out to write an instruction manual on proper behavior and decorum for princes, which he models closely on Cicero's *De oratore*. As a result, the *Book of the Courtier* carries a lighthearted tone (the word *ridere* is one of the most frequently used in the book), and scores of copies came off the printing presses all over Europe.

Castiglione ends book 2 with a collection of what might at first seem odd for a book on princely behavior, a series of comic sayings, and something even odder, a list of practical jokes. Castiglione may sound like Erasmus, but he's absolutely serious, for a good prince, he insists, must know

*The seventeenth century produced numerous poems on the subject of farting, discussed in more detail later in this chapter.

how to rein in the most unruly of bodily habits, and that is laughter. Other books on princely behavior emphasized almost every aspect of self-control, from running in the streets, to picking one's nose, and of course to causing a nuisance through raucous and disruptive laughter. William III refused to have the earl of Manchester serve as ambassador because he "blew his nose in the napkins, spit in the middle of the room, and laughed so loud and like an ordinary body." William may have tolerated everything else, but the laughter was too much. Jacobean conduct books warned readers to avoid "those jests that are usually frequent in the mouths of common people, which commonly savour . . . of baseness and scurrility."*

Castiglione cleverly weaves the subject of jokes into his general philosophy of princely behavior, in which courtiers must train themselves to exhibit a graceful ease, *sprezaturra*, in all things—from swordsmanship to horseback riding to oratory—so that any subject learned looks to all the world like "second nature." The prince in all things must cultivate a studied nonchalance. In the case of oratory, to gain such Zen-like command of that rhetorical skill, the courtier must learn to master the art of *facezie*, "for the human being," as Castiglione says, "is an *animal risibile*," and etiquette demands the courtier to "bring delight and ease tedium." And indeed, Castiglione takes his joking seriously, providing techniques on how to arouse thirty-five different kinds of laughter, which he illustrates with jokes from Cicero.

But then Castiglione makes a more astonishing claim for laughter in the courtier's life. The courtier must recognize that it is not only essential to be well-versed, say, in swordsmanship, but to conceal such supreme skill until the appropriate moment. Appearance in sixteenth-century Italy is just as important as what one can actually do. The Greek historian Sallus said about Julius Caeser that he "preferred to be good, rather than to seem so." That is not the case in the Renaissance. Representation is all, and only laughter can provide the courtier with the one virtue that will en-

*Thomas, "The Place of Laughter," p. 80.

able him to succeed politically—superior cunning. The idea is to look untutored and unskilled, but to perform when called upon with deftness and precision.

Cultivating this benign duplicity means knowing how to represent oneself publicly, a "self-fashioning" that however polished and refined always remains vulnerable to that enemy laughter. With a joke, through ridicule, the prince can swiftly blast apart an opponent's act. One must therefore master the art of laughter. Tell a good joke, ridicule an opponent, and thoroughly destroy that conniving rival. Castiglione thus provides lists of practical jokes for the courtier to practice, of the sort Machiavelli might have offered in his own version of the courtier's manner book, *The Prince*, in how to dupe those who stand in one's way and, in perhaps his most extraordinary stroke, make them feel good about it to boot.

The true prince stands apart from the crowd by refusing to laugh at the misfortunes of the malformed, the enfeebled, or even the pretentious: That's too easy, too cruel. Besides, attitudes toward such derisive laughter were beginning to change. Puritan pamphleteers, like Edward Derling, railed against the grotesque kind of laughter found in jestbooks, disapproving of such lapses in good taste as the "witless devices of Gargantua, Howlglass . . . the fools of Gotham." The practice of holding idiots, like household pets, to get a few laughs, continued to draw attacks: "We are not to sport ourselves with the folly of the natural fool," advises one Puritan reformer named Perkins, allowing that "it hath been the use of great men to keep fools in their houses. . . . Nevertheless, to place . . . a recreation in the folly of such person, and to keep them only for this end, it is not laudable." Thomas Fuller, the late-seventeenth-century author, a preacher at the Savoy, and after the Reformation, a "chaplain in extraordinary" to the king, was criticized by a contemporary for his fondness for "puns and quibbles" and "trencher jests," but Fuller still knew the limits of good form by finding it "unnatural to laugh at a natural."*

*Ibid., p. 79.

This new sense of refinement that began to resettle English sensibility, a refinement in what might be called taste, would be reinforced by manner books and manuals of decorum later in the period, urging people even more to refrain from laughing at the deformed. By the late seventeenth century, human weakness no longer seemed a fit subject for laughter. Even the most well-known fools in literature got swept away in this new cleaning. So, for example, when the playwright Nahum Tate adapted *King Lear* at the end of the seventeenth century, he wrote the Fool completely out of the action so as not to offend his audience.

What we see taking place in the Tudor and Stuart periods involves a reshaping of what might be called inner sensibilities; a first step, if you will, toward the compassion that we associate with the romantics. That refinement can be traced best through a changing attitude toward laughter. The grotesque is thus one of the surest ways to understand laughter as the sixteenth century moves into the seventeenth. Refusing to laugh at the deformities or misfortunes of others became the principal way for Puritan aristocracy to separate itself from the general riffraff. When one group adopts a set of strict manners, it automatically creates another, outsider group of boors and slobs—and boisterous laughers. Only the unrefined laugh out loud.

John Bunyon, the late-seventeenth-century author of *Pilgrim's Progress*, tells the story of an ale-house owner who kept his idiot son as a featured entertainment because of his "foolish words and gestures . . . at which the old man would laugh and so would the guests." I give you Keith Thomas's rather lengthy comment on this sort of deplorable sport because it takes us far in the direction I have been trying to describe:

> It would be a long task to trace the genealogy of the new sensibilities which by the eighteenth century were to make this sort of thing seem increasingly barbarous. It begins with the Tudor conduct-books which reiterated with growing force the humanist maxim that men should not be mocked for faults for which they were not responsible. It develops through the Latitudinarian divines, who saw human nature as essentially benevolent and therefore rejected the Hobbesian view that

the cause of laughter was the misfortunes of others. It culminates in the literary theory of the early eighteenth century, where humor grows kindly and where bizarre quirks of personality are not aberrations calling for satiric attack but amiable eccentricities to be savored and enjoyed.*

And so the common, the crass, and the vulgar—the folk in general—co-opted the grotesque for themselves. If aristocrats wanted to know what they were missing, they only had to open the pages of Rabelais's *Gargantua and Pantagruel*, where laughter derives from a deep appreciation of the grotesque—grotesqueries from the heart of carnival, folk festivals, and peasant revels of all kinds. One can only read that baggy novel—grotesque itself in sheer bulk and heft—and feel how empty life would be without such occasional barbaric excess. From the perspective of those in power, however, the grotesque stood outside the norm, beyond civility—indeed, that's what it means to be malformed, misshapen, abnormal. By the end of the Renaissance, politeness demands one to stifle even the smallest laugh prompted by such unfortunates. In the novels of Charles Dickens, deformities are transformed into pleasant and amusing eccentricities to satisfy the refined taste of Victorian readers. But for those who stand outside the middle class, grossness is the only role it is practical to fulfill, the only form to fill. The marginal, the outsiders, are already misshapen; they are already perceived by the majority as deviants. This makes sense of the social outsider—the Jew or the black—not only as a prime source of humor, but also as a prime target for comics.

The promulgation of statutes, especially statutes about something as fundamental as laughter, erected an even higher wall between those in power and those who live and work outside the boundaries of power. Furthermore, these statutes make very clear that those who persist in laughing do so as outlaws or delinquents. I quote here from the French sociologist Pierre Clastres, on the difficulty of expressing oneself in the face of authorized speech—in the face, that is, of officially declaimed sentences:

*Ibid., p. 81.

The exercise of power ensures the domination of speech: only the masters can speak. As for the subjects: they are bound to the silence of respect, reverence, or terror. Speech and power maintain relations such that the desire for one is fulfilled in the conquest of the other. Whether prince, despot, or commander-in-chief, the man of power is always not only the man who speaks, but the sole source of legitimate speech: an impoverished speech, a poor speech to be sure, but one rich in efficiency, for it goes by the name *command* and wants nothing save the *obedience* of the executant.*

Jokebooks, in their derisive laughter, treated the lower classes as an outlaw group, worthy of not much more than ridicule. Richard Flecknoe, a writer who argued for keeping the theaters open during the Protectorate—someone not unsympathetic, that is, to the cause of merriment—declared in 1657 that the "vulgar were properly the subject of ridiculousness." Jokebooks took particular delight in ridiculing the vernacular speech of rustics. George Puttenham, who wrote books on standards of Elizabethan literary taste, especially disliked "the inferior sort who abuse good speech by strange accents or ill-shapen sounds."** Deformities moved to the interior region. A person must be misshapen, the logic goes, if he or she speaks ill-formed sentences. Such aberrations of grammar and syntax must bespeak a deep deformity—at the level of the soul and the mind: The lower classes were both depraved and dumb.

The theater, the heart of popular entertainment, site of merry scandals and rude performances, received much abuse, like the condemning of performance art today, by the conservative. If only popular forms of entertainment could be stopped—rock and roll, certain kinds of acting, burlesque—standards would miraculously return to society. Philip Stubbes, a Puritan pamphleteer and author of the *Anatomie of Abuses* (1583), not unlike some modern moral crusader, called the theater "a site for promiscuity—it permits the mixing of distinct and exclusive speech types, and above all of jest and earnest." The Lord Mayor of London in 1605 recommended

*Pierre Clastres, *Society against the State: Essays in Political Anthropology*, trans. Robert Hurley (Cambridge, Mass.: MIT Press, 1987), p. 151.

**Thomas, "The Place of Laughter," p. 77.

closing the theater at Blackfriars because actors violated decorum by depicting "worshipped aldermen of the City of London, to their great scandal and to the lessening of their authority."*

By criminalizing laughter, the Puritans forced laughter into taking a revolutionary turn. When the vernacular of the peasant is erased by those in power, the peasant resorts to other means of expression. To laugh under the legislative restrictions of the new political regime is to strike a blow against the state. War broke out: governmental and ecclesiastical authority versus the entire cadre of peasantry. European peasantry had learned well how to take restrictive and repressive statutes of all kinds and turn them upside down through laughter. Carnival served as their college. But Chaucer really immortalized the power of the underdog peasant, who had learned in folk festival how to laugh in a truly topsy-turvy, devilish way—through a release of air in the nether throat, that is, through the great symbol of substratum laughter—through farting.**

From the time of Chaucer all the way through the Renaissance and into the period of Jonathan Swift, the history of farting, naturally enough, merges with the history of laughter, specifically with the history of peasant laughter. At those moments when the church most fervently desired to control laughter, during carnival, farting forged a new definition of the laugh by inverting it and creating an entirely new laugh. The fart brings together the alimentary and respiratory systems in one foul and corrosive act. Even the terms overlap in the sixteenth century: "To break a jest" and "to break wind." Both acts disrupt—"break"—rupturing the ordinary course of events, the "diet" of living. A fart is a chink in the two closed internal systems: the air it releases carries meaning from both the digestive and respira-

*Ibid., p. 79.

**According to the *OED*, the word *gas* was coined during this period by a Dutch chemist, J. B. Van Helmont (1577–1644), based on the Greek χάος (*chaos*). *Gas* was first used as a physiological term, not as a term of chemistry. (The Dutch pronunciation of *g* as a spirant accounts for its being used to represent Greek χ). Van Helmont believed that gas existed in the body as a result of an occult process whereby water reached an ultra-rarified state. For Van Helmont, *gas* is another of those humoral terms. Much later—by the nineteenth century—a *gas* is a slang term for anything funny.

tory systems.* The Falstaffian gut has two avenues of escape: one through the mouth in a laugh and the other, sometimes more deadly and sometimes more invisible, out the anus in a fart.

The fart is fundamentally degrading. It represents the degradation of food, as it decays beyond fecal matter, into invisibility. When the peasant farts, he always degrades himself. How better to disarm the potency of ridicule than to ridicule oneself first? We know this technique from modern humor, in which ethnic minorities exploit their own group's stereotypes. If bigots and racists think of blacks as shiftless and lazy, let's say, then Richard Pryor can evoke great laughter by shuffling across the stage in parody of Stepin Fetchit. Pryor not only evokes laughter by knocking down the stereotypes, but through the sheer genius of his exaggerated performance. Indeed, that is how the stereotype dies—by being taken to its absurd extreme. Out of this seeming act of degradation, Pryor can generate a new respect for himself and for blacks in general. When he farts, the peasant knows he is acting like a boor, and it is in that self-awareness that laughter is born. The peasant gains a recognition, acquires a degree of substantiality, when others laugh at him. Perhaps it takes the vision of a Russian, like Bakhtin, with a deep awareness of the peasant traditions of that country, to encompass the meaning of those seemingly gross acts of farting in public. Bakhtin argues that the individual peasant who farts becomes a symbol for peasantry in general:

> In grotesque realism, therefore, the bodily element is deeply positive. It is presented not in a private, egotistic form, severed from the other spheres of life, but as something universal, representing all the people. As such it is opposed to severance from the material and bodily roots of the world; it makes no pretense to renunciation of the earthy, or independence of the earth and the body. We repeat: the body and bodily life have here a cosmic and at the same time an all-people's character; this is not the body and its physiology in the modern sense of these words, because it is not individualized. The material bodily principle is contained not in the

*In his book *On Food and Cooking*, Harold McGee writes that Saint Augustine saw "involuntary bodily functions, flatulence among them, as unmistakable signs of man's fall from grace: once man failed to obey God, he became unable to obey even himself, and lost control over his physical nature" (p. 257).

biological individual, not in the bourgeois ego, but in the people, a people who are continually growing and renewed. This is why all that is bodily becomes grandiose, exaggerated, immeasurable.

This exaggeration has a positive, assertive character. The leading themes of these images of bodily life are fertility, growth, and a brimming-over abundance. Manifestations of this life refer not to the isolated biological individual, not to the private, egotistic "economic man," but to the collective ancestral body of all the people. Abundance and the all-people's element also determine the gay and festive character of all images of bodily life; they do not reflect the drabness of everyday existence. The material bodily principle is a triumphant, festive principle, it is a "banquet for all the world." This character is preserved to a considerable degree in Renaissance literature, and most fully, of course, in Rabelais.*

Farting by a well-known individual does not stand as a gesture of daintiness or reserve. On the contrary, John Aubrey in his *Lives of the Poets* retails the story of the grossest violation of social decorum in Elizabethan society, which occurred when the earl of Oxford not only embarrassed himself but affronted the queen of England, while "making of his low obeisance, and failing to repress a fart of remarkable proportions." What could be worse than defiling the court with a loud and smelly noise! As mentioned earlier, jestbooks capitalized on this quirky humor of personality by fabricating stories of prodigious farters like the duke of Ormond, the duchess of Marlborough, and other highfalutin names of the day, all of whom produced laughter by breaking the boundaries of social decorum.** When aristocrats farted, they drew laughs because the act revealed the great social distance separating them from the lowly peasants. An aristocratic fart is an act every bit as silly as Prince Charles singing rap. It's incongruent and absurd. It's something that clearly marks aristocrats as declassé, an act they should not be seen or heard performing. An aristocratic fart is a holiday.

*Bakhtin, *Rabelais*, p. 19.

**This genre of literary flatulence spread to America. Mark Twain so much loved the kind of humor revealed in Aubrey's historical gaffe that he recast it with Sir Walter Raleigh as the culprit. Raleigh breaks such profound wind that "it raises an exceeding mightie and distressful stinke, whereat all did laffe full sore," in front of Queen Elizabeth and the brightest lights of the day, including Francis Bacon, Ben Jonson, and William Shakespeare. Twain called his tale "Fireside Conversation in the Time of Queen Elizabeth," or simply "1601."

But Aubrey and his circle remain funny only in context. That is, only so long as those in power have given notice that public farting—inversionary laughter—stands outside accepted norms. Indeed, the festivals in which farting starred as the main attraction, in carnival rituals of all kinds, would also have to be characterized as gross and outlandish, off limits for any respectable, right-minded citizen. Wherever a laugh could be heard, the Puritans searched it out and eliminated its possibility. Royal proclamations in 1541 abolished the ritual of the boy bishop "as superstitious and child-like." The village lords of misrule were similarly outlawed as anathema in a world of "honesty, comeliness and seriousness."* The Inns of Court aimed at getting rid of Christmas revels, along with all forms of Christmas mumming, Maypoles and May Day celebrations, and Shrove Tuesday revels.

A new sensibility had taken hold of the Renaissance, a sensibility that tried to gag that most ornery of archenemies: laughter. In 1655, a particular set of Baptists went to such extremes as to make their members swear a holy oath that they would never make jokes—in public or in private. Other religious groups carried on long debates about what kind of laughter constituted a venial sin. But all were agreed: laughter constituted a sin.

Whereas Aristotle defined the glory of human beings by their singular ability in the animal kingdom to laugh, the Puritans argued that laughter belonged to humans *only* because human beings partake of original sin. And that sense of sin, in the Puritan scheme of the world, can be found not too far under every laugh. The preacher Thomas Granger turns the idea into a solemn admonition: "Whenever a man laugheth, let him but dive to the ground of his laughter, and he shall find some matter of grief and repentence, both in the person or thing laughed at, and in himself."**

As the Renaissance wore on, the Puritans hit harder and harder at

*Thomas, "The Place of Laughter," p. 79.

**Ibid., p. 81.

those pesky little books filled with mostly off-color one-liners and short stories, and jestbooks that one Puritan reformer referred to as "the witless devises of Gargantua." For most Puritans, to laugh at the foibles and faults of other people only revealed the laugher's own weakness, and the true Puritan opposed laughing at virtually any topic: "They held it wrong to portray vice for the sake of entertainment; the laughter of theatre audiences, thought William Prynne, was 'altogether inconsistent with the gravity, modesty and sobriety of a Christian.' They condemned the mystery plays which had mixed ribaldry with God's word; and they declared it immoral to be a professional comedian. 'What mere madness is this?' demanded Christopher Fetherston, 'that a man whom God hath endowed with wit and reason should put on a noddy's coat and feign himself to be a fool.' "*

The Puritans viewed laughter as a sin in great part because laughter turned people away from hard work. To understand how crucial a role laughter played in this period of history, we must take up momentarily the contributions of Puritanism to the rise of capital enterprise in the West. Since the sociologist Max Weber first made the connection, historians have taken for granted the thesis that Puritanism, in its various forms, accelerated the rise of capitalism. What fueled this connection is something we have seen before—decorum and seriousness. The two cannot be separated.

Protestantism in general, and certainly Calvinism, presented believers with the problem of election. How could a person know whether he or she was one of the elect? Not by prayer, necessarily, or good works alone. But certain outward signs might indicate that God had bestowed his favor: for instance, hard work that had been rewarded by financial success. Calvin's theology contained two tenets that allowed for such monetary signs of election. These tenets would contribute to the rise of capitalism: The first required a firm duty to unremitting toil; the other, a concomitant of the first, required the avoidance of expenditures of time or money in diversions. The busyness of business—seriousness—guided human actions. The clock, effi-

*Ibid., p. 79.

ciency, diligence, order, rationality—all those habits of mind that stood opposed to the waste and excess of joking and laughing—became catchwords of a new regime of salvation through labor.

Calvinists believed that people could not earn salvation, however, through striving alone. Yes, they had to work, but that in itself did not guarantee election. Along with that striving, Calvin argued, the elect would eventually manifest outward signs that God had rewarded their particular toil. A certain demeanor, for example, once seen as related to one's state of health, now signified the state of one's soul. A dignified, sober demeanor could emanate only from a state of grace. As the historian Roland Bainton remarks, "Hence the impulse to work, not in order to earn salvation but to be assured of it. And if labor, then, were blessed by prosperity, one might infer a further sign of God's good pleasure."*

In this spirit of intensified capitalist preoccupation, entertainment and amusement only serve to wither the ideal of salvation; a state of grace can be sundered by a laugh, election denied by vulgar behavior like farting. Jokes take one out of the serious business of busyness; they prevent one from amassing capital. The joker is a devil, his beguiling demeanor the key to his fallen nature. By definition, a joke could never be counted among the elect. Indeed, erratic, déclassé behavior signaled to others that a person had definitely not been elected. Stop and listen to him or her, and you, too, might fall from grace—lose your chance at heaven. Laughter became a barometer, then, a measure of one's inclination toward ultimate glory. Certainly, no person would deliberately laugh in public; the elect laughed privately—if at all. To joke, to laugh, to participate in festivals, was to flaunt one's fate, to laugh at hell itself.

Puritans naturally placed high value on decorum, on controlling bodily functions and adopting and maintaining proper manners. Such insistence on the decorous life opened even greater distances between the upper

*Roland H. Bainton, *The Reformation of the Sixteenth Century* (Boston: Beacon Press, 1952), p. 250.

levels of society and a whole range of peasant and artisan classes, who, of course, could never hope to earn the material signs of spiritual election. Remember, outward signs were visible manifestations of an inner state of grace, so that everything in one's life, even the most trivial, routine acts, registered with significance and meaning. The Renaissance introduced new eating instruments like the fork, which made a refined outward manner easier to pull off. Fingers were notoriously unclean; food should never be handled with such gross things. The fork can be construed, in this Puritan scheme of election, as an instrument of spirituality, and the outpouring of manner books in the Renaissance as manuals of devotion. This new sobering, religiously elevated set of manners and gestures was what the Puritans called *civility.**

Norbert Elias, who has traced the history of manners in the West, claims that this concept of *civilité* took hold of social life in England and central Europe in the second quarter of the sixteenth century: "It's individual starting point can be exactly determined. It owes the specific meaning [of *civilité*] to a short treatise of Erasmus of Rotterdamn, *De civilitate morum puerilium* (*On Civility in Children*), which appeared in 1530." Recall, Erasmus had written *The Praise of Folly* in 1511. By 1530, he too, like his close friend Thomas More, had caught the new spirit of sobriety. *The Praise of Folly* was immensely popular, but the more somber work, the *De civilitate*, enjoyed an even greater popularity and went through more than thirty-five printings in the first six years. "In all," Elias says, "more than 130 editions may be counted, 13 of them as late as the eighteenth century."**
It spawned other books like it, pressed into service as schoolbooks for the education of young boys. The book's influence can be measured in part by

*Fernand Braudel, writing about the history of material culture, notes that the individual fork "dates from about the sixteenth century and spread from Venice, from Italy in general and probably Spain . . . an English traveler in 1608 discovered it in Italy, found it amusing and then adopted it, incurring the mockery of his friends who christened him *forciferus*, fork-carrier" (*Capitalism and Material Life, 1400–1800*, trans. Miriam Kochan [New York: Harper and Row, 1974], p. 139). Braudel also points out that Jacopo Bassano painted one of the first forks in any depiction, in his *Last Supper*, in 1559.

**Norbert Elias, *The History of Manners*, vol. 1, trans. Edmund Jephcott (New York: Pantheon Books, 1978), pp. 53–54.

looking at the cognate words it generated, besides the Latin *civilitas* and English *civility*: in French *civilité*; Italian *civilita*; and German *Zivilitat*.

In simple terms, Erasmus aims at providing the appearance of aristocratic bearing for every young boy, in something called "outward bodily propriety," so that each one carries the bearing of the prince. Thus, while the church wanted to hold the inner life to strict guidelines, Erasmus used manners—outward look and deportment—as a key to civility, as a way of shaping the inner life. Gestures come to life from a deep articulation in the soul. By Erasmus's time, both inside and outside had been corraled by the church, which strived for the total control of the person. Erasmus also sought to eradicate those moments when the inner world turns public and makes itself felt and heard—in farting and laughing. Gestures and manners in the secular, political world can be likened to an outward sign of election in the world of religion.

Erasmus dismisses laughter flatly with a few lines, for laughter presents no problem: One simply should not engage in such an uncivilized act. He devotes a good deal of his treatise, then, to a less straightforward issue in which manners are opposed to health. In seeming imitation of scholastic discussions of angels or other highly abstract religious matters, Erasmus raises the questions, Should a well-behaved, young boy "retain the wind by compressing the belly?" In the best of all circumstances, Erasmus says yes, no farting. But he knows one can contract serious illness through exercising that kind of strict control, and so he relents a bit and advises: "Reprimere sonitum, quem natural fert, ineptorum est, qui plus tribuunt civilitati, quam soluti" (Fools who value civility more than health repress natural sounds). A young man, unable to repress his flatulence, should leave the room and not make a scene.

Erasmus then gets quite specific about farting. In fact, he spends so much time talking about farting, one can only conclude that it must have been an enormous problem in polite Renaissance society. The message seems to be that, while it is terribly disruptive to make an unholy noise by releasing it in public, it is more dangerous to hold one's wind:

To contract an illness: Listen to the old maxim about the sound of wind. If it can be purged without a noise that is best. But it is better that it be emitted with a noise than that it be held back.

At this point, however, it would have been useful to suppress the feeling of embarrassment so as to either calm your body or, following the advice of all doctors, to press your buttocks together and to act according to the suggestions in Aethon's epigrams: Even though he had to be careful not to fart explosively in the holy place, he nevertheless prayed to Zeus, though with compressed buttocks. The sound of farting, especially those who stand on elevated ground, is horrible. One should make sacrifices with the buttocks firmly pressed together.

To let a cough hide the explosive sound: Those who, because they are embarrassed, want the explosive wind not be heard, simulate a cough. Follow the law of Chiliades: Replace farts with coughs.

Regarding the unhealthiness of retaining the wind: There are some verses in volume two of Nicharchos's epigrams where he describes the illness-bearing power of the retained fart, but since these lines are quoted by everybody I will not comment on them here.

Bodily control, as Keith Thomas argues, had become a mark of a highly stratified social hierarchy: "The new etiquette was meant to distinguish the elite from the vulgar in a way which I think would not have been apparent in the Middle Ages. It stemmed more from a concern with the preservation of social authority than from any deep psychological fear of the body. It was meant to establish that dignified style which contemporaries thought necessary for the maintenance of social respect."*

The new cult of decorum promulgated during the Renaissance had interesting side effects. For one thing, laughter really helps bring into being the late-seventeenth-century definition of *vulgar*, meaning "coarse," for only the vulgar—the people—could laugh so uproariously and continuously without regard to social decorum, or worse yet, without feeling ashamed of putting their fallen state on display. An account of 1649 observed that those "most apt to laughter were children, women and the common people."** But these were code words, really, for those that God had not chosen to wel-

*Thomas, "The Place of Laughter," p. 80.

**Ibid.

come to heaven—eccentrics and off-beats of all sorts. Laughter really marked the boundary between the upper and lower classes in this period, in the most religious way—defining those who would ultimately ascend into heaven and those who would fall into hell. One might say, more accurately, that laughter forced into existence the idea of vulgarity—lower class, boorish expressions of a devilishly fleshly, sinful life.

# 8

## Sick. Sick. Sick.

*and*

*yet he is*

*not ill*

*The* most well-known essay in the English language remains, after more than two hundred fifty years, Jonathan Swift's "A Modest Proposal." The essay proposes a solution to eighteenth-century Ireland's chronic and serious poverty, which Swift deliberately casts as a pesky issue of public decorum: Homeless women, raggedy infants clutched to their breasts, clog up every street and byway in Dublin with their begging. Unhoused and unfed, they offend the proprieties of civic leaders, and present a model of the most unsightly kind of behavior. The fortunate infants are those who starve to death, while the smart women eventually submit to abortions. But the situation calls for swifter action, for city treasuries can no longer afford to support such derelicts, and without a solution the general population will lose all faith in their government. Worse yet, such a loss of faith could result in unruly and excessive behavior at the fringes: a confusion of categories, followed by a collapse of order. An answer has to be found—a "fair, cheap and easy" answer.

A friend of Swift's—unnamed in the essay, but referred to, significantly, as an American—hatches a devilishly brilliant plan: Let the kids suckle at their mother's breasts for one year—free food!—and then feed those tasty morsels to Irish "persons of quality and fortune." To ensure a steady food supply, he adds a practical note—that more male babies should be served up than female babies. In the dispassionate prose of an instructional manual, Swift dispenses precise information: directions (on how to carve up a small boy); lists (of body parts); details (about weight and average milk consumption); and careful tabulations (numbers of infant males, percentages of those homeless, of those above a certain income, and on and on). Swift exploits words like *reckoning* and *number*, *computation* and *accounting*, to give his proposal the tone of mathematical accuracy and scientific believability.

Indeed, Swift taps into an embryonic genre of eighteenth-century record-keeping. He wants "A Modest Proposal" to read like a contemporary tract on statistics. Though the word was not commonly used until the end of the century, statistics, along with other mercantilist theories, was being formulated as a science during Swift's lifetime. It required only the probability models of calculus to make it complete. Although statistics began in the most mundane way, its history is important for understanding the turn laughter took during this period: The Irish government appointed an English surgeon, Sir William Petty, as physician general of the army and ordered him to prepare a survey of forfeited estates throughout the country. He approached the problem in the most familiar way he knew—by operating on the body politic as if it were the body natural. With his scalpel, he sliced a diverse population into its constituent parts: age, race, sex, income, and so on. That is, Petty dissected the body politic into digestible parts and served them up to expectant government officials: "A Modest Proposal" as serious governmental policies based on the predictability of mathematical computations.

In the narrative that accompanied his survey, *The Political Economy of Ireland*, published after his death in 1691, Petty coined the terrifying phrase "political arithmetic." By reducing people to ciphers, Petty could describe them as a resource, whose labor could then be mined. "People," as Petty sees them, in terms worthy of Swift, "are capital material . . . raw and indigested." His economic views, widely quoted during Swift's day, prepared the way for a new and dreadful form of manipulation. Here is Petty's preface, which so resembles Swift's fleshy irony that, had it not been written in all seriousness by a medical doctor, we might dismiss it as satire: "As students of medicine practice their inquiries upon cheap and common animals, and such whose actions they are best acquainted with, and where there is the least confusion and perplexure of parts; I have chosen Ireland as such a political animal, who is scarce twenty years old." In other words, Petty has chosen to inventory the poor inhabitants of Ireland—those "cheap and common animals."

Sir William Petty was a product of the end of the seventeenth century. All that insistence throughout the century on decorum and order conspired to produce the sort of insidious conclusions that Petty so facilely reached. As Petty makes horrifyingly clear, that inordinate insistence on order and uniformity caused human beings—singular individuals—to disappear. By imposing severe standards of appearance and behavior, the state could control its citizens much more easily and efficiently. Uniformity erased individuality, and in particular wiped out the one characteristic, laughter, that Aristotle insisted separated human beings from all other creatures in the animal kingdom. No surprise, then, that by the time of "A Modest Proposal," in 1729, the idea of uniformity had already worked its way into the language so thoroughly it had produced a new word, *mass*, to refer to an unformed blob of humanity. *Average* and *mean* came to characterize a wide segment of the general population in the new governmental science of the *state* applied by *bureaucrats* (another eighteenth-century coining) to the general and leveled mass of humanity.*

"A Modest Proposal" outraged a good many eighteenth-century read-

*The word *bureaucrats*, officials who govern out of their desk drawers, first describes absentee administrators in Swift's place of birth, Dublin. *Statistics* derives from the Italian word for *state*. A Scotsman, Sir John Sinclair, borrowed the word *Statstik* from German, and replaced the term "political arithmetic" in 1798 with that German adaptation.

ers because Swift had made them aware—shockingly aware—that he was talking about real, live human beings, and individual human lives were easy to overlook in the first decades of the eighteenth century. How could one assert oneself as a person under such reductive, mathematical standards? In other words, how could one break out of the mold that had begun to define life in the eighteenth century, and that had begun to hold it so narrowly in check? In Aristotle's time, as I have already shown, the mean or the average shaped life toward an idealized goal—the *summum bonum*—and marked, for the ideal leader, the middle and wise road between the two margins of deficiency and excess. One could fall into a deficiency of laughter, for instance, and be characterized as an *agelaste*. One might laugh to excess and be classed as a buffoon. Or one could exercise restraint and moderation and display a proper wit and thus achieve the Aristotelean Mean.

But by the early years of the eighteenth century, to run the middle road meant to be average—just all right, but no more, statistically normal. The middle ground today means a C grade; and many students insist they would rather have a D or an F, to know they stink, than feel they are just run-of-the-mill. Who wants bland? With outright laughter outlawed, and with a rise in literacy that began to encompass greater numbers and classes of people, subversion began to be accomplished in more subtle, decorous ways. One can describe irony and satire as humor biting away, not from the edges, the margins and the extremes, but from those "in the know"—from aristocrats themselves—producing a curious kind of silent laughter. Irony and satire in effect can be read as ridicule with class. Irony clothes itself in respectability and thus is particularly suited to the class-minded sensibility of the Enlightenment. Satire instructs just like laughter, carries all the sting of an aggressive joke, but it denotes without the mess and noise of a bona fide joke.

While no one should underestimate the power and force of irony and satire, the exercise of a sharp and potent literate wit does not result in topsy-turvy laughter or in revolutionary laughter. It is laughter of the mind, not the body. It is the laughter of festival and the substratum, but translated to a society that has a dramatically increased interest in and facility with literacy.* It is mind rising above matter. Satire is really a restrained, polite brand of vituperation—criticism held under very careful check. A satirist or ironist displays his or her wit precisely by *not* eliciting gales of laughter and thus seems to avoid violating decorum. But even when irony speaks softly, the stick it wields can deliver painful blows. The ironist has a political agenda, to subvert the status quo as much as any carnival clown or festival fool. Unlike the kings of carnival, however, ironists do not intend to overthrow the reigning order. They merely prod and poke and strike their way toward reform, for as highly literate members of the established order themselves, they have a stake in maintaining the existing social structures by holding fast to relationships among statuses, roles, and offices.

In fact, in a society like that of eighteenth-century Ireland, marked by discrete caste divisions, satire and irony clearly mirror (and thus reinforce) existing power relationships, by creating different levels of understanding among the literate, the highly literate, and—those left out of the joke altogether—the illiterate. Swift really talks to but a small number of perceptive readers, and to virtually no one at the margins of his society. Irony requires not just literacy, but a well-practiced reading proficiency. Its lessons are not broad, blatant ones, such as those we come to expect in carnival, but subtle and slight. In the end, however, Swift borrows his strategy from carnival.

Oh, of course Swift doesn't intend us to buy his proposal. He's only kidding about eating kids. But he had us going for a time, and for that brief moment that we take his arguments seriously, we feel disgusted and repulsed. Swift has plunged to the very bottom of Bakhtin's substratum for his irony: cannibalism—baby cannibalism, at that. Out of that disgust he raises readers' awareness of a problem that plagues his country at the most basic

*The eighteenth century saw the first newspapers, as well as the first magazine. Subscribers got treated to that new, highly carnivalized genre, the novel, serialized in the pages of the *Gentleman's Magazine*.

level—the disappearance of singular human beings. Out of the decomposition of the body, as Bakhtin has argued, comes the resurrection, the reassertion of the importance and the glory of the individual human being.

An accomplished master of irony, like Swift, raises a begrudgingly wry smile and a knowing eyebrow, but only with the most elite readers. The others he leaves behind feeling belittled or angry. The most agile of his readers, however, he coalesces into a coterie of intellectuals, a hip insider's group, the most deeply literate of the literate. As Socrates, the first *eiron*, knew, when irony hits with its sudden shock of recognition, it wakes a reader up like a slap in the face. When readers finally catch on, they feel smart, but only for an instant, realizing in that flash of insight that the author has been slyly manipulating meaning behind their backs. As the smart fades, readers are left feeling dumb. In the end, Swift leaves behind his most interesting creation—a small group of silent laughers—a band of ironists, who from that point on will always read with a hypercritical eye.

Swift has recruited his small cadre of ironists out of a new middle level of readers—the literate masses. This group expanded rapidly, both in London and in New York, in the eighteenth century. Not only did reading habits change, however, but more important, an expanding literacy altered the political culture as well, permitting more and more citizens to participate—or to feel, at least, that they were participating—in the electoral workings of democracy.

The magazine took the lead as one of the principal instruments of political change. Literate peasants and artisans no longer felt the urgent need to upset order through subversive laughter. As readers of magazines, they could now pride themselves on knowing every current idea in the arts and sciences, just like the landed gentry. Even though articles could cover only the general outlines of any given subject, readers still felt themselves a vital part of those in authority and control. That is the transforming power of literacy: Literacy encourages people to analyze and criticize, to reason and debate, rather than to disrupt or even destroy. Hostile jokes give way to heated discussion. The magazine created a community of readers, an expanded coterie of those in the know.

In London, one of the most popular magazines, the *Tatler*, appeared three times a week beginning in 1709. The *Tatler* set as its task to refine taste, to serve as a guidebook, as its introduction points out, where "all questions of good manners are discussed from the standpoint of a more humane civilization, and a new standard of taste is established." Anyone reading the magazine entered a kind of general schooling—in ideas and information, but more important, in proper behavior. And the essence of proper behavior, as we have seen, just happens to be the enemy of laughter—moderation. Richard Steele, the founder of the *Tatler*, comments in the initial issue, that as "the ideal of a gentleman is examined, its essence is found to lie in forbearance." And forbearance meant no loud laughing in public.

The *Tatler* was succeeded by an even more popular magazine called the *Spectator*, which Steele, along with John Addison, also edited. The *Spectator* stepped up publication, appearing daily, from March 1711 to December 1712, and revived in 1714. The *Spectator* took a slightly different attitude toward refined humor. While the magazine featured essays on manners, morals, and literature, its stated aim was "to enliven morality with wit, and to temper wit with morality," and it thus served as an instruction manual on what constituted good wit, a recipe that included generous helpings of restraint. The politician and historian Thomas Macaulay enjoyed the *Spectator*'s witty tone and complimented its editors for providing "perhaps the finest essays, both serious and playful, in the English language."*

In New York, the key, upper-crust magazine was *New-York Magazine; or, Literary Repository.* Like its British counterpart, *New-York Magazine* emphasized in each issue an American brand of "forbearance," what it touted as "the very ideas of justice, truth, benevolence, modesty, humility, mildness, and temperance." It, too, boasted an aristocratic readership,

**Edinburgh Review*, July 1843, p. 119.

counting among its readers the chief justice, John Hay; the vice-president of the United States, John Adams, and no less than the president of the United States himself, George Washington. But that list hides what turns out to be a much more democratic range of readers—from barbers and bakers to butchers and boarding house proprietors. A similar expansive list could be produced for Addison and Steele's magazines, as well. As with the *Spectator* and the *Tatler, New-York Magazine* changed politics; it reduced the numbers of people who felt like outsiders: "The radicalism of the small shopkeepers and urban artisans lost its urgency as those groups began to participate more fully in a political culture that had once been closed to them. . . . The values of the magazine were traditional; it was the participation of the working class that was new."*

Just a century before, governments had passed legislation to shut down festivals and carnivals of all kinds. Now, the power of printing transformed wisecracking laughter into the subtleties of wit, and with the aid of magazines, that refined brand of humor got broadcast throughout a larger and larger section of the middle class. Even that boorish holdover from carnival, the fart, underwent a refinement by literacy into moments—even extended moments—of sometimes strained wit, but wit nonetheless. Two examples will suffice. The first, from Henry Fielding's great novel of landed-class life, *Tom Jones*, occurs in the presence of the novel's most dignified, prim, and proper character, Squire Western's sister.

Miss Western has just delivered a tirade on how contemptible she finds her brother's opinions and ideas, using refined, highly schooled English, but her brother soundly and suddenly undercuts her. In fact, in a bizarrely humorous way, the Squire sends language back to its Edenic state, to a time when word and deed matched perfectly, and sound married sense:

"Thou art one of those wise men," cries she, "whose nonsensical principles have undone the nation; by weakening the hands of our government at

*David Paul Nord, "A Republican Literature: Magazine Reading and Readers in Late-Eighteenth-Century New York," in *Reading in America: Literature and Social History*, ed. Cathy N. Davidson (Baltimore: Johns Hopkins University Press, 1989), p. 115.

home, and by discouraging our friends and encouraging our enemies abroad." "Ho! are you come back to your politics?" cried the Squire: "as for those I despise them as much as I do a f__t." Which last words he accompanied and graced with the very action, which, of all other, was the most proper to it.

My second example returns us to the master of satire and irony, Jonathan Swift. Swift delivers a long digression on flatulence of all kinds, in the form of an encomium to Aeolus, the god of wind, in his satiric work *Tale of a Tub*. Excessive wind comes to symbolize a group of religious zealots that Swift hated, the Enthusiasts. In a revolutionary move that only a ludic genius could pull off, Swift carnivalizes the already carnivalesque image of the fart by reversing the flow of flatulence from mouth to anus. He converts a carnival fart into one, long carnival belch:

It was an invention ascribed to Aeolus himself, from whom this sect is denominated; and who in honour of their founder's memory have to this day preserved great numbers of those barrels, whereof they fix one in each of their temples, first beating out the top. Into this barrel, upon solemn days, the priest enters, where, having before duly prepared himself by the methods already described, a secret funnel is also conveyed from his posterior to the bottom of the barrel, which admits new supplies of inspiration from a northern chink or cranny. Whereupon you behold him swell immediately to the shape and size of his vessel. In this posture he disembogues whole tempests upon his auditory, as the spirit from beneath gives him utterance, which, issuing *ex adytis* and *penetralibus* is not performed without much pain and gripings. And the wind in breaking forth deals with his face as it does with that of the sea.

Swift made fast work of both divine inspiration and the holy kiss of conspiracy from the Middle Ages, that is, of the holiness of air. Indeed, the air that passes *ex adytis* from the priest parodies the Latin theological phrase *ex adyto cordis*, "from the bottom of the heart." Picture the Mass turned radically upside down: the *osculum conspiratio* reversing direction and winding up in fits of farting and belching: Starting with the fools, as I have already observed, Swift and others tried to pump some air back into eighteenth-century laughter by letting the hot air out of religious excess.*

The earl of Shaftesbury, in a book conspicuously titled *Characteristics of Men, Manners, Opinions, and Times* (1711), advocated the use of ridicule to "deflate" (the term is apt) religious extremists of all kinds—from Enthusiasts to Ranters—and lower-class pretensions of all sorts, through detached, ironical humor. A contemporary of Shaftesbury, Anthony Collins, called by T. H. Huxley the "Goliath of Freethinking," sounded this warning in 1713 in his *Discourse of Free-Thinking*:

> No history of any other country in the world can produce a parallel wherein the principle and practice of ridicule were ever so strongly encouraged and so constantly pursu'd, fix'd and rooted in the minds of men, as it was and is in the Church against Puritans and Dissenters. Even at this day the ridicule is so strong against the Dissenters . . . especially in the villages and small country towns, that they are unable to withstand its force, but daily come over in numbers to the Church to avoid being laugh'd at.

Manners, decorum—a refining sense, as the *Tatler* has it, of forbearance—demanded something more subtle and wry, something more intellectual than crude outbursts of laughter. Addison even ruled out cuckoldry as a theme for evoking laughter, exonerating the husband as simply an "innocent, unhappy creature." "By the end of the seventeenth century," Keith Thomas avers, "the doctrine that human weakness was no subject for laughter had taken hold of much middle-class opinion; and it helped to produce the sentimental and humanitarian movements of the eighteenth century. . . . The area of permissible laughter was thus further restricted by doctrines of sympathy which outlawed many traditional forms of humour which had required a suppression of the sensibilities."**

Irony and satire fit perfectly the demands of the new sensibility. The

*In an obscure Restoration play, *The London Cuckolds*, by Edward Ravenscroft, a farting scene takes place halfway through the action. So popular was this play that it was performed annually on Lord Mayor's Day for half a century, until David Garrick refused to endure its grossness any longer.

**Thomas, "The Place of Laughter," p. 80.

watchword was *wit*, itself a refinement of the German *Witz*. *Wit* results from the collision of an important Latin root, *vide*, "to see," and the Sanscrit *veda*, "knowledge." Those same roots also produce words like *wise*, cognate with Middle High German *Witan*, "I know," and *Witz*, which means "joke" and "[good] sense." The idea of the jester as a seer and wise person we have already encountered as a Renaissance court tradition in the fool who speaks the truth. Even outside the court, that tradition holds: A poet like Swift, for example, acts as both the legislator and the soothsayer, providing understanding through wry laughter.

Literacy, whose power Chaucer had exploited to hone oral forms, like *dicacitas* and *facetiae*, into that great literate weapon, the joke, eighteenth-century satirists now used to defuse laughter and to make it much more accessible. Wit instructed and reformed, giving definitive shape to the refined sensibilities of a new middle-class population.

The ironist, however, still belongs at the top of the literate heap. He or she is an author possessed of the highest authority. Swift can only laugh half-heartedly himself because from his perspective he can see two things at once: one, that he is part of the problem; and two, that the government has created a situation so absurd, only an absurd response makes sense.* Swift's money, his authority, his education—his position of religious privilege as dean of Saint Patrick's—place him squarely in the heart of the system that has created the problem in the first place. The expanding middle ground of readers, as I have argued, felt they had moved deeper into that system, and so had more of a proprietary feeling about the status quo. The task of moving ideas off center, of asserting oneself with feeling at the far margins, fell to another, lower class—to the coarse and boorish peasants. This is what George Eliot implies, in one of her essays, when she observes that "the last thing in which the cultivated man can have community with the vulgar is

*A contemporary of Swift's, Immanuel Kant, in his *Critique of Judgment*, goes so far as to say that "in everything that is supposed to excite a lively and convulsive laugh, there must be something absurd."

their jocularity." While she may be right, what a difference in humor—and laughter. Addison and Steele even declared that one could separate a man of wit from the riffraff by his "faint contrived kind of half-laugh."

The vulgar, those most common of folk, had managed to keep the tightly fitting mantle of civility and decorum—the straitlaced jacket of respectability—off their backs: "By the mid-eighteenth century it had become a platitude that only the lower classes had escaped the stifling effect of 'good breeding.' "* Philip Dormer Stanhope, fourth earl of Chesterfield, lord lieutenant of Ireland from 1745 to 1746, wrote almost daily to his son from 1737 onward on matters of etiquette. Some of these epistles later got published as a handbook of good manners. In one of his letters, Chesterfield summarizes the prevailing, ludic attitude that separates aristocracy from the mob: "Frequent and loud laughter is the characteristic of folly and ill manners; it is the manner in which the mob express their silly joy at silly things. . . . There is nothing so illiberal, and so illbred, as audible laughter. True wit, or sense, never yet made anybody laugh . . . how low and unbecoming a thing laughter is: not to mention the disagreeable noise that it makes, and the shocking distortion of the face that it occasions."**

Decorum did not suit hoi polloi; it chafed and choked. Good breeding simply does not offer very fertile ground for laughter. Laughter demands more raggedy circumstances than upper-crust living permits. ("He got to be a joker," the Beatles sing, "he just do as he please.") James Beattie, a poet and self-styled popular philosopher of the late eighteenth century, declared in his *Essays: on Poetry* (1778) that the common people—the vulgar and the average—should command widespread attention for their unbridled potency and power:

> The conversation of the common people though not smooth, nor so pleasing, as that of the better sort, has more of the wildness and strong expression of nature. The common people speak and look what they think,

*Thomas, "The Place of Laughter," p. 79.

**From letter 32 (1748), Earl of Chesterfield, *Letters to His Son on the Fine Art of Becoming a Man of the World* (New York and London: M. Walker Dunne, 1901), p. 57.

bluster and threaten when they are angry, affect no sympathies which they do not feel, and when offended are at no pains to conceal their dissatisfaction. They laugh when they perceive anything ludicrous, without much deference to the sentiments of their company: and, having little relish for delicate humor . . . they amuse themselves with such pleasantry as in the higher ranks of life would offend by its homeliness.*

The upper classes dignified themselves by recognizing limits and exercising restraint. They surrendered their own desires to proper etiquette, to an abstract set of rules. Life at the top is a stylized affair, expressed through a series of carefully articulated, meticulously learned gestures. The lower classes felt most alive, not by channeling their lives through the narrow gauge of rule and law, but by fully unbridling their passions and desires. They disregard, as Beattie points out, "the sentiments of their company."

Bakhtin and others make the point that the eighteenth-century commitment to cognitive reason and abstract rationalism "prevented the Encyclopedists from grasping theoretically the nature of ambivalent festive laughter. The image of the contradictory, perpetually becoming and unfinished being could not be reduced to the dimensions of the Enlighteners' reason."** By the eighteenth century, carnival had lost its streetwise political bite, remaining only as an aesthetic, informing influence on literature, coopted by the reform-minded writers of the day.

In the Enlightenment, irony and satire in great part silenced real bellowing, gutsy laughter. It took an anomaly, an aberration in the pantheon of late-eighteenth-century writers, to preserve the perverse excess that folk carnival once held. It took someone to step beyond the restraint of irony and satire—to disregard reform in favor of revolution—to make a bold declaration for straightforward passion. Just as Chaucer had dipped down into the peasantry for his most vital, most puckish characters, so in the late eigh-

*At roughly the same time, Wordsworth and Coleridge published the first edition of *Lyrical Ballads* (1798), in which they attempted to treat of "low subjects in the language of the common man." The peasant had become a symbol for poetic liveliness and emotional honesty—a commodity, really—that could be exploited when necessary for its various potencies.

**Mikhail M. Bakhtin, *Rabelais and His World*, trans. Helene Iswolsky (Bloomington: Indiana University Press, 1984), p. 118.

teenth century William Blake recognized that that same life force—dramatic, life-affirming power, the power necessary for hearty laughter—could only be found at the level of substratum excess, however perverse and amoral that excess might appear to the rest of the world.

For all the world, Blake writes some strange lines. In a sense, he is the avant-garde, the courageous front man who wrenches from the clutches of the moralists a freer, more passionate way of life. Blake creates the atmosphere for the reassertion of belly laughs. The laughing itself he leaves for someone else. But Blake assures that it will happen.* In essence, he incorporates the grotesque realism of Bakhtin into highly literate poetry. Blake does a great service for the history of laughter, for he breaks the suffocating hold of statistics closing around the citizens of London. He wants to forge individuals once again out of that general mass of humanity. He does it by going back to the most basic of basics—to breath. Blake not only makes possible a new kind of easy breathing, he shows it in action. Instead of reciting his two major works, *Songs of Innocence* and *Songs of Experience*, he sings them to audiences. He places total importance on the power of the human voice.

Infusing poetry with his quirky vision, he heralds Whitman's big-hearted, lusty free verse. And that wide-throated breathing informed humor all the way into the contemporary world, exploding with Blakean energy in someone like Lenny Bruce. Without embellishment, without pretty metaphors, in a wildly original, invigorated, and personal mythology, Blake composes an emancipation proclamation for the human spirit—a proclamation because he desperately wants people to wake up from their mass slumber, to walk the earth as fully enlivened, fully animated individuals. He would have them walk on their hands, so vehemently does he turn the world upside down, so thoroughly does he invert heaven and hell. Everything that looks moral and good actually deadens: "Damn braces; bless relaxes." In the fire of hell burns the only true and real energy.

Blake shocks and surprises every bit as much as Swift when he de-

*To show his commitment to laughter, Blake uses the word *laugh*, or variations of it, one hundred fourteen times in his poetry.

claims, for instance, that "the road of excess leads to the palace of wisdom"; or when he confesses that he would "sooner murder an infant in its cradle than nurse unacted desire"; or when he counsels that "the lust of the goat is the bounty of God." While Blake does not talk directly about laughter, he certainly opens the door to a way of expression, a form that takes its cue from a carnivalesque tradition that generates power enough to destroy all boundaries. "More than any other Romantic poet—if he was indeed a Romantic—" says one reviewer of a recent book on Blake's religion and morality, "Blake has been adopted as the people's bard, the 'Devil's Party,' the 'Contrary State,' the voice of eternal Opposition and Delight."*

What would Blake's poetry sound like if his subject were laughter? That is a legitimate question, since laughter cavorts all through history as the voice of "eternal opposition and delight." Laughter, with its ability to slide easily into excess, surely would make an appropriate subject for someone with Blake's vision, someone who could keep that kind of power intensely alive. And indeed, that's just what the German philosopher Friedrich Nietzsche attempts to do. The philosopher of excess, Nietzsche takes Blake's lead and, fifty years after Blake's death, makes laughter the most vibrant expression, the most powerful assertion of selfhood imaginable. Like Blake, Nietzsche hopes to break those ties that bind people so tightly. Like Blake, he venerates coarseness and horseness, the unfettered animal side of humanity. He loves to hear the whinnying of the Houyhnhnms: "When man neighs with laughter, he surpasses all animals by his vulgarity." But we must read vulgarity here as something positive, as a first step toward the will to power, for Nietzsche, like Blake, loves to turn things over. Nietzsche turns vulgarity inside out. He rescues the lower-class outcast. Carnivalizing of the world is a necessity for breathing.

Again like Blake, Nietzsche stands beyond good and evil—an idea he articulates in a book of the same name—and proceeds, himself, to turn heaven and hell topsy-turvy: "What has so far been the greatest sin here on

*Richard Holmes, "Lord of Unreason," review of *Witness against the Beast: William Blake and the Moral Law*, by E. P. Thompson (New York: New Press, 1994), in the *New York Review of Books*, May 12, 1994, p. 15.

earth? Was it not the word of him who said, 'Woe unto those who laugh here? . . . He did not love enough: else he would have loved us who laugh. But he hated and mocked us: howling and gnashing of teeth he promised us. . . . Laughter I have pronounced holy; you higher men, *learn* to laugh!" Blake and Nietzsche, in their combined assertion of the human spirit, are really two amoral characters. And for Nietzsche, the one thing that takes people beyond traditional morality—that can absolutely and utterly set them free—is unfettered, deforming laughter:

> The hybrid European—all in all, a tolerably ugly plebian—simply needs a costume: he requires history as a storage room for costumes. To be sure, he soon notices that not one fits him very well; so he keeps changing. Let anyone look at the nineteenth century with an eye for these quick preferences and changes of the style masquerade; also for the moments of despair over the fact that "nothing is becoming." It is no use to parade as romantic or classical, Christian or Florentine, baroque or "national," in *moribus et artibus*: it "does not look good." But the "spirit," especially the "historical spirit," finds its advantage even in this despair: again and again a new piece of prehistory or a foreign country is tried on, put on, taken off, packed away, and above all *studied*: we are the first age that has truly studied "costumes"—I mean those of moralities, articles of faith, tastes in the arts, and religions.*

Vulgarity and distortion, the exaggeration of character through caricature, represents, for Nietzsche, the very essence of a vibrant psychic life as well as an aesthetic life. The two may be powerfully connected. At least they are in Nietzsche's system, where art literally informs—gives shape to—a person's inner life. Only through caricature, only by crossing the boundaries of normal appearance, that is, can a person assert his or her individuality in this period: "Caricature is the first sign of a higher psychic life (as in the fine arts)."

Edward Lear, the master of nonsense verse, published his *Book of Nonsense* in 1846 and, because of the popularity of that edition, offered an enlarged edition in 1861. In an article about Victorian laughter, "Fantasy

*Friedrich Nietzsche, *Beyond Good and Evil: Prelude to a Philosophy of the Future*, trans. Walter Kaufman (New York: Random House, 1966), p. 150.

and Nonsense," Gillian Avery points out that Lear's "subjects themselves are eccentric, lonely figures, frequently with some feature such as a grotesquely long nose or a globular figure—the sort of outcast, in short, that Lear in his darker moments felt himself to be."* Only the grotesque lives far enough away from rule and order to be able to rejoice in nonsense—in outcast language and grammar. The opening limerick in Lear's *Book of Nonsense* reveals the overarching aim of this "eccentric, lonely figure":

There was an Old Derry down Derry,
Who loved to see little folks merry;
So he made them a book, and with laughter they shook
At the fun of that Derry down Derry.

One simply cannot avoid this truth, that in the nineteenth century the social order for many had become a prison, the only escape from which seems to have been an assertion through exaggeration, excess, and caricature in general. Whatever seemed monstrous could also liberate. So the nineteenth century saw the appearance of such monsters as Frankenstein's creation, the Wolfman, and Count Dracula. The respectable Doctor Jekyll transforms into the monstrous Mister Hyde. Feral children, raised in the wild by all sorts of animals, from wolves to gazelles, also suddenly emerge from the woods and surprise decorous citizens.

The novelists take up this strategy for letting strange figures loose on the unsuspecting world. Charles Dickens's characters, for instance, have been described as eccentric, marginal, excessive in one way or another. They suffer from being humorous; they have become unbalanced owing to an excess of one of the four humors coursing inside their bodies. And because of their eccentricities, they evoke laughter in their readers. Martin Chuzzlewit, Scrooge, and Sarah Gamp have all moved beyond the middle to enjoy bizarre, even despicable, and always humorous lives at the edges of society.

In story after story—by E. T. A. Hoffmann, James Hogg, Edgar Allan

*Gillian Avery, "Fantasy and Nonsense," in *The Victorians*, vol. 6 of *New History of Literature*, ed. Arthur Pollard (New York: Bedrick, 1987), p. 288. Recall that the mimes on the ancient Greek stage were sometimes depicted with long noses, large stomachs, warts, and hunched backs—all for the sake of a laugh.

Poe, Fyodor Dostoyevsky—characters face their darker, more formidable sides through a confrontation with a double, a hideous look-alike. As Rimbaud puts it, "Je est un autre" (I am an other). Characters live with a formidable doppleganger imprisoned within their beings. Over time, in order to reach some kind of psychic health, that darker element must be set free.

But what could a society do with all those eccentrics, with those "freaks"? There's the rub: We will not understand laughter at the end of the nineteenth century unless we strain to hear it in the context of a profound silencing, for this is an age when monstrous behavior may lead to liberation, but it will almost certainly also end in incarceration. As the age began to criminalize fringe characters, prisons began to proliferate. Punishment became big business. I can do no better to make this point than to quote Michel Foucault on the subject of prison reform during this period:

> It was a time when, in Europe and the United States, the entire economy of punishment was redistributed. It was a time of great "scandals" for traditional justice, a time of innumerable projects for reform. It saw a new theory of law and crime, a new moral or political justification of the right to punish; old laws were abolished, old customs died out. "Modern" codes were planned or drawn up: Russia, 1769; Prussia, 1780; Pennsylvania and Tuscany, 1786; Austria, 1788; France, 1791, Year IV, 1808 and 1810. It was a new age for penal justice.*

Foucault concludes the introduction to his book by pointing out that by the end of the nineteenth century torture had disappeared as something for public display to become hidden from view, incorporated into the normal routine of punishment. The sense of what Foucault calls "carnival" drained out of public executions—and he means carnival quite literally—where death instead of laughter inverted rules, mocked authority, and transformed criminals into heroes. Was that the government's ultimate power—to seize another life? If that was so, if government resorted to snuffing out lives as the most extreme edge of its ferocity, then in fact it held no power. A determined, courageous person, condemned to death but unwilling to

*Michel Foucault, *Discipline and Punish: The Birth of the Prison*, trans. Alan Sheridan (New York: Vintage Books, 1979), p. 7.

cower, could turn a public execution into a public mockery. And Foucault argues that that happened time and again.

In a way, making torture invisible offered protection to those in power. It made the idea of torture more terrifying for the general populace, because it gave every citizen the opportunity to conjure private images of pain and torment. Each person could conceive the most vivid horrors and in the process come to confront the darker side of the soul, to see what he or she, just like those in power, was capable of imagining. People scared themselves to death. In a democratization of sadism the state torturer disappeared: The rabble tortured themselves. Here was "gallows humor," a dark, sick joke played on the general population.

Classic nineteenth-century studies like Charles Baudelaire's *On the Essence of Laughter*, George Meredith's "An Essay on Comedy," and Henri Bergson's *Laughter* situate laughter in the context of social control, as part, one might say, of the larger issue of punishment and prison reform: laughter deeply embedded in the carnival of death. That is, these tracts continue a virtually unbroken line from the seventeenth century, a tradition that permits laughter so long as it serves to secure the middle ground. So, for instance, Bergson writes, "In laughter, we always find an unavowed intention to humiliate, and consequently to correct our neighbor." In its ultimate intent, humiliating laughter tries to pull deviants—those who stumble both physically and metaphorically—back into the center: "Now it is the business of laughter to repress any separatist tendency. Its function is to convert rigidity into *plasticity*, to readapt the individual to the whole, in short to round off the corners wherever they are met."*

George Meredith argues that when the comic spirit sees human beings "self-deceived, or hoodwinked, given to run riot in idolatries, drifting

*Henri Bergson, *Laughter: An Essay on the Meaning of the Comic*, trans. Claudesley Brereton and Fred Rothwell (London: Macmillan), p. 35. (I italicize "plasticity" to emphasize that laughter reaches *solutions*. In this case, the solution borders on the therapeutic—to reform the misguided.) In America, in the sixties, when *tripping* took on its drug-related metaphoric connotation, Ken Kesey gave friends and strangers free rides by adding tabs of LSD to punch bowls at parties to which he had so generously passed out invitations. Kesey nicknamed his crew "the Merry Pranksters." Jesters make people trip. By the sixties, tripping represented a way out of what Bergson calls "the whole," and LSD offered one of the hippest solutions.

into vanities, congregating in absurdities, planning short-sightedly, plotting dementedly . . . whenever they offend sound reason, fair justice; are false in humility or mined with conceit, [it] casts an oblique light on them, followed by volleys of silvery laughter." Here, in this kind of laughter, Meredith says, we find "the ultimate civilizer."

Laughter, then, in a curious way, takes on its old, familiar shape from carnival, in never-ending battles between civility and disorder—Fat going toe-to-toe against Skinny, excess going head-to-head against curtailment, the joker trying desperately to score against the straight man. Laughter in this period had to joke its way out of prison, out from under the surveillance and grip of governmental controls. It struggled valiantly and mightily, but it might not have succeeded without the help of the final figure in the late-nineteenth-century triumvirate of the psyche: Sigmund Freud. Blake set the parameters, Nietzsche filled in the philosophical rigor, and Freud added the last important ingredient, namely, the pursuit of pure pleasure.

To discuss Freud's theories of wit and joking fully would take an entire book in itself, since his theories are not only complicated but sometimes even contradictory. But we certainly cannot leave the history of laughter at the end of the nineteenth century without at least touching on Freud's seminal work on jokes [*Witz*] and laughter, *Jokes and Their Relation to the Unconscious*, which was published in 1905. No one had analyzed jokes per se—the modern, aggressive joke, that is—until the father of psychoanalysis and individuality, Sigmund Freud, gave them serious consideration. For him, jokes take on the same psychic importance, say, as dreams: "The processes of condensation, with or without the formation of substitutes, of representation by nonsense and by the opposite, of indirect representation, and so on, which, as we found, play a part in producing jokes, show a very far-reaching agreement with the processes of the 'dream-work.'" **

*George Meredith, "An Essay on Comedy," in *Comedy*, ed. Wylie Sypher (Garden City, N.Y.: Doubleday, Anchor, 1956), p. 72.

**Sigmund Freud, *Jokes and Their Relation to the Unconscious*, trans. James Strachey (New York: W. W. Norton, 1963), p. 159. Gershon Legman, *The Rationale of the Dirty Joke: An Analysis of Sexual Humor* (New York: Grove Press, 1968), is another important book for the study of jokes, but more as a catalog of themes than as an analysis of intent.

But Freud did more than elevate jokes to a position of high seriousness, a subject for polite, intellectual conversation. With Freud, finally, a monumental change takes place in the history of attitudes toward laughter. As far back as the fifth century B.C., Plato had pointed out the mixed emotions—the feelings of both pain and pleasure—that people experience in ridiculing their neighbors. Freud's description of aggressive joke-telling, in which this very process takes place, also maps well onto Chaucer's "Miller's Tale." But Freud does something more. While he wrote extensively on aggressive humor, exploring theories of incongruity and naivete associated with humor, of childish innocence in the adult, his greatest contribution by far was to return to joke-telling the notion of unadulterated pleasure.

Freud's analysis of the crucial social circumstances involved in telling jokes, which he explains in *Jokes and Their Relation to the Unconscious*, grows naturally out of the ideas he explores in an earlier work, *Civilization and Its Discontents*, where civilization constantly plays a massive, aggressive joke on everyone: constricting desires even as people seek to maximize their own pleasure. Freud's schema for his famous division of the psyche—into id, ego, and superego—really inscribes in one person that familiar combat between pleasure and authority that lies at the heart of laughter.

That psychic battle replicates the dramatic *agon* of carnival. Indeed, in modern life it is given expression in our most popular form of delivering laughter—stand-up comedy. The stand-up comic creates jokes to blow holes in the thick walls of civilization, to the delightful howls of an audience repressed and constrained by those walls, having to work daily behind them. By virtue of being on the stage, the comedian has been granted a temporary visa out of the most restrictive aspects of civilization. The audience secretly wishes it could be like the comic—so free, so easy, so uninhibited.

Freud finds in jokes representative stages of a person's development toward maturity. For the earliest stages of the joke, Freud points to the play of the child, who finds pleasure in recognizing what is already familiar. Then, as the child internalizes a sense of self, he or she begins to play less and less, especially where play violates rules and transgresses authority. The child's response to this new situation, in which he or she keeps encountering a series of no's, is to create a transitional comic form, one that skirts and hedges prohibitions—and this Freud calls the jest. The jest gets its point across without overtly violating the rules.

While not an out-and-out joke, the jest permits the superego—the critical, rational judge—to shut down long enough for some significant play to take place. Jesting is one of the socially acceptable ways for the mature psyche to regain its childish sense of play. For that reason, the content of jokes matters little. What counts is the joke's conceptual force, its power to satisfy the discontents of civilization: to relieve temporarily the pressures of civilized life.

Jokes work, as I have said, because they make possible the temporary suspension of the superego—the stern judge who continually forbids us to follow our hearts' desires. The great economy of the joke, for Freud, lies in the way that jokes both create problems—obstacles, Freud calls them, a "psychical damming up"—and remove those problems "by the act of recognition." Recognition here might be the punch line, the salutary realization of a witty solution to the obstacle created in the joke's narrative. "The enjoyment of recognition," Freud theorizes, "is joy in power, a joy in the overcoming of a difficulty. . . . Recognition is pleasurable in itself—i.e., through relieving psychical expenditure—and the games founded on this pleasure make use of the mechanism of damming up only in order to increase the amount of such pleasure."*

I call Freud the father of stand-up comedy because, through jokes, he articulated an acceptable way for the discontent, or marginal malcontent, to break the law, to upset the status quo, with impunity. In this way, the comic has affinities with the outlaw. Every comic is a social scofflaw who could

*Freud, *Jokes and the Unconscious*, pp. 121–22.

be charged with breaking and entering—with breaking society's rules and restrictions, and with entering people's psyches. What the joker steals are secure, familiar ways of thinking and feeling. But the joker's a remarkably cordial, remarkably generous thief, leaving behind a valuable treasure called pleasure.

At the turn of the century, pleasure became big business. Nowhere was this more true than in America, which could be construed as one grand pleasure palace. The gears of industry were already roaring—producing goods, producing gadgets—and soon the roar of the twenties, too, the mighty roar of pleasure, would join the din. Freud's ideas on humor found a much more compatible home in this country than in Europe. The prototype of all amusement parks opened in New York in 1900, the same year Freud published his *Interpretation of Dreams*. The first carousel, in Central Park, started spinning at the end of the nineteenth century; George Ferris unveiled his wheel of fun at the Chicago World's Fair in 1893.* The pursuit of pleasure truly became the national pastime, as big a business as the business of criminal correction—the two not as disparate as they seem.

At the turn of the century, more and more people, as Foucault and others have demonstrated, found themselves in prison for breaking the law. In the name of pleasure, people paid money for thrills they got by breaking certain natural laws, gravity, for example, in rides like the roller coaster or the loop-the-loop. At gaming tables, people defied the law of averages, and they navigated fun houses where the laws of physics had temporarily been repealed. For a few hours, even a day, ordinary working stiffs could let loose; they could act crazy—scream and yell and laugh like deviants and freaks without being stigmatized—in Luna Park, Steeplechase Park, or Dreamland, just a short ride from the heart of Manhattan, on that little spit of land known as Coney Island.

Freud repositioned the joker as a person who operates from some freakish sideshow—from the fringes of the pleasure palace—and who

*Baseball teams and football teams—virtually every uniformed, organized sport, in fact—took to the field during this same period.

breaks the law without having to pay the price. Indeed, the joker may be the only person in society who generates pleasure for his audience by breaking the law. Freud really collapses the prison and the park, civilization merging with discontent.

By 1830, books had begun to appear with the phrase "the middle class" in their titles, as a signal that in America in particular a new phenomenon had been born. The middle class meant respectability and acceptance—seventeenth-century sensibility rewritten this time with a powerful new ingredient. Decorum and manners had been restated within the context of a process of professionalization. The emerging middle class in its search for respectability caused entire occupations, like undertaking, nutrition, and car repair, to be reconceptualized and represented as professions. To that end, schools and licensing organizations emerged to make certain that people who now engaged in these jobs had been properly trained and certificated. To take only one example, undertakers became quasi-scientists called morticians.

The children of middle-class parents went to professional schools, earned degrees, entered professions, hung out licenses, and on and on. This had the not-so-surprising effect of further criminalizing everyone and every idea hanging out there at the fringes. And so, as we have seen, the numbers of prisons in England and America increased dramatically during this period. In the woodsy edges of civilization, in the sylvan fringes, where monsters and freaks lurked, laughter found a comfortable home.

That is the legacy of humor bequeathed to the modern world. The laughter of ridicule from the biblical and ancient world, tainted with sin from the Puritans, moved to the edge in the nineteenth century, and always, always just dying to assert its connection to the world of peasantry and subvert the normal order. And, God, what fun, what playful, childish fun—to crack someone's head wide open with a joke. In America, jokers couldn't wait to get their hands on that big, wide target, the middle class.

For me, all these historical streams came together in the late 1950s, when a singular genius named Lenny Bruce brought about a revolution in comedy. Bruce immediately played into the hands of authority. He refused subtlety and charm and went directly for the jugular of every mainstream, middle-class idea, from Eisenhower to Eisenhower jackets, from Brylcream to Brillo, from the way people thought to the way people dressed. Throughout his life he battled every form of authority on every level—nightclub owners, the police, and the courts—and spent the last days of his nightclub career performing routines about the injustices he had suffered at the hands of those who made and enforced the law. The material came from his own life, molded out of his hassles with the law, his many busts for uttering four-letter words on stage or for using or holding drugs. In the end, I believe the authorities silenced him.*

Bruce died of an overdose, but he was too savvy about drugs to kill himself with an overdose of heroin. Too smart, that is, unless someone sold him something much more pure than he was used to, or gave him heroin laced with something lethal. He complained continually about narcs planting drugs on him or in his car or in the club. Undercover cops could have sold him something to kill him off. Certainly, a good number of people in positions of authority found him an absolute horror. They would rather he shut up. Their lives would be easier if he would remain silent. To top it off, he thumbed his nose and made fun of his enemies in his routines. I can only conjecture about the details. The awful truth is that Lenny Bruce is dead.

Like some hip Kaspar Hauser or Wild Boy of Aveyron, Bruce—who looked indeed as if he could have been raised in the woods by animals—appeared on the scene, alien and strange, a fringe character. He thought differently. He had been arrested for something, no one was quite sure for what, but the word on the street had it that he'd been impersonating a priest of some nonexistent church and soliciting funds for his flock. He smoked

*An ad for Lenny Bruce's records on the Reprise label in *Ramparts* magazine just shortly after his death read, "It's safe to listen now. He's dead."

dope, like those weird jazz musicians (like those *black* jazz musicians); he wore dark glasses (what the hell was he hiding?) and bizarre Nehru jackets (he even had to *dress* weirdly). He used foul language, hip talk, and in his act went beyond the president to take on the pope himself! Nothing was sacred: The entire world cracked apart as soon as he blessed it with one of his zany jokes, as if life were one grand carnival. Bruce stepped onto the stage and the evening turned Mardi Gras.

He even broke out of the parameters Freud had established for the joker, for Bruce never assumed the stage persona of an outlaw—an outspoken big mouth who joked the pants off the emperor. Rather, his life offstage perfectly matched his life onstage. He lived as a joker, a comic. Bruce did not become King of Carnival on prescribed holidays: He showed a new way to live by living it. A performance onstage by Lenny Bruce meant only that he had an audience, a venue, and some backer with enough money to pay him for the evening. After all, he had to eat. But I have spent enough evenings with Bruce to know that he lived his routines. I'm describing something quite different from the comedian who's "always on," like Robin Williams, being goofy and acting crazy no matter where. That kind of clowning takes ego and nerve. But Bruce always took whomever he was with back behind the scenes and revealed to them the truth. He had a mission: to tell a new story, to narrate the world differently. Here was the revolution he handed audiences, showing them carnival as a continuous way of life, the world upside down as the normal state of affairs. And if he could do it, so could anyone else. This was no act. Unlike Shelly Berman or Mort Sahl, he assembled no character up there on the stage. He was all Lenny Bruce.

What license he took, then, giving voice to whatever cockamamy idea or bit of idea happened to cross his mind, as if his internalized censor, the dependable superego, had gone on vacation. Here was a man firmly treading, as William Blake called it, "the road of excess." It was anyone's guess if he would wind up at Blake's destination, "the palace of wisdom." But as time went on, larger and larger audiences attested to the fact that he had not only reached the palace, but had taken up comfortable residence inside. And they knocked at his door to be let in. Because, my God, he seemed to take Freud so damned seriously—telling jokes, spritzing, doing shticks, and all the time laughing that insider's laugh of his. Pleasure! That's what he wanted. Maybe that's all that he wanted. Like some hedonist, he knocked over every idol, trampled on every icon, in his rush for that nightful of pleasure. And for holding onto such a selfish attitude, he would be hounded by the law, condemned, and finally destroyed.

Only someone who stood at the margins of the margins could have the nerve to pull off such a trick—to have so much fun at *everyone's* expense. Even being a performer in this country should require work, and audiences should see evidence of it. Everyone wants to see some sweat. Everyone in this country—Christian and non-Christian alike—knows that we all toil by the sweat of the brow. But Bruce broke even that rule. He performed relaxed and cool—the Zen of zaniness. Like a loosely connected puppet, he bobbed and bounced, slouching in his S-curve, looking not just a bit whacked out on some exotic drug. Any moment he threatened to fall fast asleep in front of a room full of people—people who had paid a lot to see . . . Lenny Bruce himself. Thin and pale, at times he looked for all the world like some specter, some apparition. It was easy for his detractors to call him "sick."

The name stuck so well that newspapers and popular magazines credited Bruce with ushering in a whole generation of so-called sick comics: Mort Sahl, Bob Newhart, Shelly Berman to a degree, Elaine May and Mike Nichols, and later, the most gifted of the next generation, Richard Pryor. Walter Winchell called Bruce "America's number one vomic." One wonders how long Winchell had to listen to Bruce, how many routines he had to sit through, before his stomach began to turn. *Time* magazine called Bruce "the most successful of the new sickniks," and ran a show business article on the sickies, featuring Lenny Bruce as their most diseased leader:

> They joked about father and Freud, about mother and masochism, about sister and sadism. They delightedly told of airline pilots throwing out a few passengers to lighten the load, of a graduate school for dope addicts, of

parents so loving they always "got upset if anyone else made me cry." They attacked motherhood, childhood, sainthood. And in perhaps a dozen nightclubs across the country—from Manhattan's Den to Chicago's Mister Kelley's to San Francisco's hungry i—audiences paid stiff prices to soak it up. For the "sick" comedians, life's complexion has never looked so green. *

Herb Caen, the enormously popular writer for the *San Francisco Chronicle* who covered the hipper entertainment scene for the newspaper, was the first person to argue that the patient had been misdiagnosed:

They call Lenny Bruce a sick comic—and sick he is. Sick of the pretentious phoniness of a generation that makes his vicious humor meaningful. He is a rebel, but not without a cause, for there are shirts that need unstuffing, egos that need deflating and precious few people to do the sticky job with talent and style. Sometimes you feel a twinge of guilt for laughing at one of Lenny's mordant jabs—but that disappears a second later when your inner voice tells you, with pleased surprise, "But that's true." The kind of truth that might not have dawned on you if there weren't a few Lenny Bruces around to hammer it home.**

Lots of people found Bruce sick, of course, because of the very irreverence that Herb Caen so much admired. If Lenny Bruce wouldn't see the value of wholesome middle-class life, if he couldn't support mainstream values and dreams, then he must be ill, since robust health emanates from the heart of the heart of the body politic. Those who fully participate in normalcy fully participate in health; those who don't must by definition be sick. But Bruce compounded the sickness because he seemed to get so much damned pleasure from the bits and shticks he so zanily performed on the stage. Guilt did not plague him. He truly enjoyed making people laugh by forcing them to see the absurdities in everyday life—in politics, in social arrangements, in sexual arrangements and relationships. He let his audiences

*"The Sickniks," *Time*, July 13, 1959. Sputnik was the most well-known "nik" during the time. *Nik* was added to many words in the fifties, the most famous probably the beats, to produce *beatniks*, to which many San Francisco beat-scene poets objected. The suffix was perhaps added to make the beats sound more pink or red; and this may be true of the sick comics of the fifties as well—a kind of linguistic blacklisting.

**Quoted in Albert Goldman, *Ladies and Gentlemen, Lenny Bruce* (New York: Ballantine Books, 1974), p. 299.

see how mundane ideas stifled them. Better yet, he let them see that they did not have to accept the status quo; he led them behind the stage to see all the plywood sets, the make-up, and the costumes. All of reality turned out to be nothing more than a construction, and a flimsy one at that. And, here, ladies and gentlemen, let me introduce you to the construction company: those 2 to 4 percent of America's elite who own 90 percent of the wealth in this country. *Mad*, that satiric magazine of the fifties with its quirky hero, Alfred E. Neuman—"What, me worry?"—had come alive on the stage. But the majority of the critics balked: No one, they assumed, could possibly be having that much fun. Or read another way, it's simply perverse for anyone to be having that much pleasure—and certainly perverse to be sucking so many others in along with him.

He hooked me with a vengeance. I had a long and exciting relationship with Bruce, which began in 1956 when I was a freshman at UCLA.* A friend said to me that I should go over to a particular strip joint—a burlesque house—in Hollywood called the Highland House, on Yucca and Highland avenues. They had this comedian, he said, who came out between the shows and with a black jazz musician—Eric Miller—did . . . well, not exactly stand-up routines and, well, not exactly impersonations either, although he had some terrific voices, but he thought something different, something unexplainable, and something certainly not describable, was happening to comedy on that stage; and he knew I would absolutely love it.

So I went. What I saw startled and delighted and shocked me so much that I went every night for the next thirty or forty nights in a row. I stopped attending classes and slept in the daytime, so I could spend my evenings in a dark and dank strip joint in Hollywood. I became such a regular that one night Bruce came to the apron of the stage and asked me to meet him back-

*I hesitate calling it a friendship, or even an acquaintance. Lenny Bruce lived in his own world, deep inside his own imagination. I was more like a participant-observer, a witness at a wild experiment. Think of being invited to a Thanksgiving dinner only to find the host believes it's Halloween, and you'll have a sense of how I felt around him: slightly outside of things, slightly awkward, but always ready for a treat or a trick. It just depended on his mood.

stage after the show. He wanted to know what the hell I was doing in a place like that. I told him I loved the show, that I couldn't stop coming to see him. He wanted me to come talk. And so, after the shows, I would go out with him and Eric Miller, or some of the other musicians, hang out and talk about comedy, discuss his routines, and drink into the early morning hours. As a kid I had wanted to be a stand-up comic; I had worked out a few routines with a friend, and together we performed them at bar mitzvahs and weddings and fraternity parties. With Bruce, I had entered a new phase of comedy—I knew that—and I was hungry to get all I could. I count that four or five weeks with him as my college education. No class I took, no book I read, no lecture I heard, showed me how to look at the world with such a radical vision; no one else taught me how to turn ideas around and to look at them from the opposite side or from the bottom up. No one but Lenny Bruce.

Bruce not only turned the world upside down, it seemed, but inside out as well. He did routines about a character named Father Flotsky, a prison chaplain whom Bruce rendered in the voice of Barry Fitzgerald. In one part of the routine, Father Flotsky tries to get a gun away from an inmate by promising all kinds of bribes without success, and finally offers him the prison's most treasured prize—the vibrator. In three or four minutes, Bruce destroyed every hokey, B-grade prison movie ever made (knocking over a few sexual taboos, to boot), sending up in particular a cheesy prison movie made in 1954, *Riot in Cell Block Number Nine*. He made it impossible to watch another one of those movies without seeing through it and laughing out loud. He did the same with radio. His Lone Ranger and Tonto pushed issues of power, of whites and Indians, of colonization, of the possibility of love between a cowboy and an Indian. In an instant, he rewrote the Wild West.

Long before people popularly accepted ideas of political and sexual liberation, Bruce made his audiences think about them. And after the initial shock, many of those people sitting out there said, He may be right. That's how I felt—shocked and surprised—when Bruce brought Moses and Jesus back to earth only to use them in an exposé of the hypocrisy of organized religion, of evangelical healing, decades before Jim and Tammy Faye Bakker reached the front pages of the national newspapers. He took the unspoken, off-limits theme of homoeroticism running just below the surface of the film *The Defiant Ones*, a movie about a white man (Tony Curtis) and a black man (Sidney Poitier) chained together who escape from a roadside work gang, and made it the theme of an extended critique of race and sex. He wasn't just talking about homoeroticism, made more taboo by situating it between a white man and a black man—he actually acted out that doubly tabooed subject. There on the stage, in living flesh, Bruce came out chained to Eric Miller. *The Defiant Ones* came to life before a startled audience, except the dialogue had changed; the issues had radically altered; the affect took a different slant. Bruce had carnivalized race, turned the issues upside down, brought his own meaning to bigotry. And again, he moved the ideas beyond a mere act. I drank with Lenny Bruce and Eric Miller. They were friends—off the stage. In bars, they talked about bigotry and racism; in restaurants, they laughed off the defiant stares they got.

I first saw Lenny Bruce do that bit in 1958. The movie had just been released. In the film, Curtis plays a bigot, and he has to confront his own prejudices to ensure his survival while shackled to his fellow prisoner. *The Defiant Ones* captured the attention of American movie-goers: Hollywood had finally dealt with serious racial issues. The Academy of Motion Pictures nominated it for Best Picture, Best Actor (both Curtis and Poitier), Best Supporting Actor (Theodore Bikel), Best Supporting Actress (Cara Williams), and Best Director (Stanley Kramer). It won Oscars for Best Cinematography and Screenplay. Who could mess with such a gem? But Bruce rewrote the movie. Here's the movie we should have gotten, his routine announced, and here's the theme up front: These two guys hate each other, kind of hate each other, maybe because they've been told to—and these two guys love each other, really love each other, though they can't tell each other.

Lenny Bruce knew that, if civil rights were to be taken seriously, blacks and whites would have to discuss their deepest, most stereotypical prejudices frankly and openly, with an acknowledgment not only of huge issues but also of silly prejudices on both sides. So Bruce tells Miller he will teach him how to say "watey-melon" correctly, if Miller will only tell him that one secret that all black people seem to know: What does "gwine" actually mean? Like, "I gwine down to de lebby." If Miller will only reveal that secret, Bruce promises to tell all about the secret ingredients of "Jew food," like *kishke* and *kugel.*

By the end of the routine, I felt a strange kind of relief. The secret was out: White folks did make fun, privately, of blacks eating watermelon. Blacks did find Jewish food weird. Bruce had confessed—made a public declaration—for everyone in the audience. He made it easier for everyone to breathe. And it was clear, absolutely clear, that Lenny Bruce and Eric Miller were friends—close friends—that they truly enjoyed each other. The old *bête noire* raised its head again—those two guys took great pleasure in making everyone laugh.

So, there was Lenny Bruce, inventing in some significant way a new genre of comedy, making us all laugh—sometimes against our own wills—with a series of strange, wonderfully surreal routines. It was underground humor. Without uttering a word—just by being on stage with Eric Miller—Bruce corralled his audience into a conspiracy of subversion. With his jabbing wit, he surprised and sometimes even repulsed audiences. Bruce talked revolution in 1956, and lots of people didn't like to hear it, didn't want to hear it. Remember, the Selma March had not yet taken place; the civil rights movement had not yet taken shape in this country. The war in Vietnam was still a hushed secret. The free speech movement was at least six or seven years away.

But without Lenny Bruce, without this wild man of laughter, all of that political activism would have taken longer to burst forth. He put ideas in the air; he planted seeds of change. To listen to Bruce meant to experience both pleasure and pain: If you found him funny, you just might have to change your life. I am convinced that, without talking specifically about

Vietnam, Lenny Bruce helped generate a viable antiwar movement in this country. His laughter hit so hard and so forcefully at the truth. By turning history—contemporary, daily history—topsy-turvy, Bruce offered people a way of discovering the lies behind governmental policies. He did what all good festivals, in their purest form, always tried to do: He placed the little people—the average Joes and Josephines—back in control.

Lenny Bruce performed initially against the backdrop of scantily dressed women, who did their bumping and grinding on a stage in the glow of myriad purple lights. He pulled off his routines, that is, in burlesque houses, places where audiences expected only mindless activity, and wrapped his subversive patter around the house itself. Bruce chose the Highland House; he knew it as a place where all guards were partially down already, where the women were engaged in their own subversion of traditional mores. They removed their clothes. Bruce imitated them by divesting reality of its respectable attire. Both Bruce and the strippers ended up at the same place—the bare, naked truth. The strippers titillated, aroused, but mostly, because of obscenity laws, stopped short of total nudity. But Bruce went all the way; and eventually after all his testing and taunting of the law, the police shut him down, arrested him. He had taken it all off, and that was against the law.*

I realize now that what we in the audience witnessed was Bakhtin's carnival in mid-twentieth-century incarnation. The image of gyrating pelvises—of a substratum carnivalizing spirit that held out the hope of regeneration—lingered behind Bruce's every word. Bruce knew those women; he worked them into his routines. That's the milieu in which he grew up. His mother, Sally Marr, taught what she called "exotic dancing" most of her life, and in the fifties she landed at the most well-known burlesque house in

*How fitting that *burlesque*, initially a literary term, should originate in Swift's time, to mean "derisive imitation," or sometimes even "grotesque realism." It takes on its specific sexual charge, however, only in America, where the carnivalizing of sex becomes something of a theatrical tradition, a form of popular entertainment. Burlesque—and vaudeville in general—produced some of America's greatest comics: Milton Berle, Georgie Jessel, Henny Youngman, Jack Benny, along with scores of others. Sex and humor went gloriously together, but not until Lenny Bruce did the joking catch up to the powerful fascination of people gazing at the naked human body.

Hollywood, the Pink Pussycat. Lenny Bruce chose to perform at a burlesque house because he knew those women in their own way worked against bourgeois standards of good taste. Together he and the strippers offered a model of standing naked—in flesh and word. In the end, then, Bruce gave us folk festival—spectacle—for the noncommitted generation of the fifties. Just as Blake had done centuries before, Bruce sounded an alarm; and he did it through Nietzschean laughter, a laughter that extolled flesh and tolled the future.

Of course Bruce had not read Bakhtin. (He may not even have read Blake or Nietzsche.) But he believed in people—in their ultimate dignity—so much so that he had instinctively reinterpreted Bakhtin onto the stage of a burlesque theater. Not only did Bruce's theater pieces dignify flesh at a substratum level, they also glorified humanity by showing people their lives stripped of all the corruption and hypocrisy that kept them in half light.

I'm glad I got to see the man and his work. Lenny Bruce always managed to get the last laugh: He was a "topper." I bet he's laughing even now.

# *epilogue*

*Project* yourself back to 1940, in, let's say, New York City. Friends have been talking to you about a new motion picture—the first talkie from this filmmaker, the first talkie long after talkies have made their debut—a new motion picture in a grand culmination, it appears to the naked eye, of a technological revolution in entertainment and fun.* You don't know exactly what to expect, but the entire city—who knows, perhaps the entire nation—holds some opinion about the star of this movie. And so you enter the auditorium knowing that anything might happen—anything might happen because Hollywood has been emphatically proclaiming the possibilities inside the movie house as virtually limitless. Every image on the screen is a miracle, another highly stylized and dazzling little world, not unlike the surreal reality of jokes.

The room darkens. As the screen flickers to life, the main character wobbles side-to-side into view. You remember him in his tired black derby and shabby frock coat, in pants at least two sizes too large. You recall the cane he deftly handles in his right hand, the frequent wrinkle of his nose, and the twitch of his tiny brush of a moustache. But tonight something is radically different. A war's raging in Europe, and tonight this guy's not just wearing a military uniform. He's wearing the uniform, it seems, of the enemy! This is comedy *and* motion pictures: The status quo is not welcome in the movie theater. So tonight Charlie Chaplin has no choice: he can look no other way but shocking.

Who the hell is this nervy character, this seeming traitor? W. C. Fields praised him begrudgingly as a "goddamned ballet dancer." "The greatest actor of us all," said another contemporary Hollywood star. "A tramp in the city," one postmodern critic, Frederic Morton, called him. He could turn into almost anything anyone wanted. That poor soul of a genius even elic-

*The words *film* and *movie* both move into the language around the same time—around 1910, just at the height of Coney Island's mesmerizing power.

ited a comment from the formidable mind of Hannah Arendt, who saw in Chaplin a political champion "who could not fail to arouse the sympathy of the common people who recognized in him the image of what society had done to them."* On this particular night in 1940 he has taken on the biggest political enemy that the common people have ever faced. On this night, he is Hitler—No, he is Charlie Chaplin embodying the Ur-dictator, Adnoid Hynkel—in a film of his own creation titled *The Great Dictator.*** (Actually, Chaplin plays two roles in this film: the dictator and one who might be considered his exact opposite—a poor Jewish barber.)

Chaplin the clown, the burlesque, miming, acrobatic dancer, had turned the Menace of Europe upside down. How very unsettling: Audiences didn't know whether they could risk a laugh. Wasn't it dangerous, after all, to laugh in the Fuhrer's face? Wasn't there a taunting children's song to that effect? Didn't that mean Hitler could retaliate, then, and do anything he damned well pleased? No wonder audiences seemed as nervous as those who listened to Lenny Bruce a decade or two later, unsure whether to laugh or leave as Bruce, in one of his more sexually evocative routines, uttered the phrase "to come" over and over. When the audience squirmed and tittered, Bruce told them it was only words—nothing more. Chaplin used the same strategy. The dictator is always only words (*dictare* means "to say"): Henchmen execute his sentences. Everyone finally laughs. What a powerful release. In 1940 New York, in 1960 Hollywood, they all finally laugh: Everything rises and evaporates—dictators and dirty words.

With film, Chaplin could climb inside the persona of Hitler—he could *become* Hitler, wear the dictator like a clown suit, and by so doing declaw and defang the Emperor of Evil. How had he learned so much about laughter? Obviously, Chaplin had not found the technique by reading Bakhtin, nor by studying the history of European folk festival. The history of evoking laughter through inversion Chaplin seemed to know by instinct. He also

*Quoted in Norman Manea, *On Clowns: The Dictator and the Artist* (New York: Grove Press, 1992), p. 33.

**Chaplin plays with a title not unlike "A Modest Proposal." A proposal for eating children cannot be considered "modest." No dictator can be truly "great."

knew that if laughter really had power, it should have the power to deny even the most potent evil. And so he put it to the test by confronting the visage of Adolf Hitler and demonstrating that the ultimate dictator could most easily be eliminated through a series of exaggerated gestures—through a laugh. Moreover, Chaplin knew why. The dictator—that is, the most serious of the serious—always threatens to become a parody of himself. A little push can send him sailing into silliness, a fall that can happen to any of us. We all feel tempted to laugh when we catch a glimpse of ourselves being stuffy or overly serious. Chaplin held up a fun-house mirror, distorting the image of Adolf Hitler into a grotesquerie. He separated the comic part of Hitler from the serious, and caricatured the former for greater effect. After Chaplin showed that separation to audiences, they could never see Hitler as an integrated character again. Hitler would always appear in their mind's eye as a jerk—a scary jerk, but a jerk nonetheless. Chaplin took Aristotle's admonition not to ridicule our neighbors and turned it to advantage. If ridicule can destroy our neighbors, why not use it to deride our enemies out of existence?

No, Chaplin did not prevent the war. But he could, in a series of frames on the screen—through the illusion of reality—convert the image of Hitler into a comic mannequin. This he did primarily through gesture. If movies did nothing else, they made audiences sophisticated students of gesture: keen observers of hand and face and body movements. The screen took on gargantuan proportions; close-ups offered a Bakhtinian view of grotesque realism. When Chaplin moved across the screen, he trailed the entire history of comics—from ancient mimes to vaudeville stars—behind him. And when audiences laughed, they released the force of the entire history of laughter.

Through laughter, Chaplin altered audiences' perceptions. After Chaplin, movie audiences could never see a goose step or a *Sieg Heil* the same way again. They could never again sit through newsreel footage of Nazis marching in parade without seeing through the Third Reich. He showed Nazis for what they were: a high proportion of gesture and rant. In order to stop the Holocaust—the extermination of millions of Jews and Gypsies and homosexuals—the world first had to believe that the butchering *could* be stopped.

Did Chaplin influence Lenny Bruce? I don't know if Bruce ever sat through a Chaplin movie, but just as Blake and Freud and Nietzsche profoundly affected attitudes toward laughter, so did Chaplin. And Bruce, standing in the middle of that stream of history, got swept up by it. That's the way, I think, laughter works. A laugh released in 1966 has been building up since people first started laughing. So yes, Chaplin influenced Bruce. But so did Plato and Aristotle and Hippocrates influence Bruce—and Chaplin, too. Chaplin's two roles, dictator and Jewish barber—victimizer and victim—really embody the history of laughter. The joker always acts out both Carnival and Lent, both pleasure and pain.

After Chaplin, after Nietzsche—after Blake even—every laugh is pointedly political: Every laugh assaults head-on whatever dictator, whatever inhumane law, currently holds the people by the throat. Chaplin is both clown and dictator, just as Hitler is both dictator and clown.* What Chaplin exploits is the absolutely absurd comic side of the great dictator's ravings. But he uncovered the same streak in himself. The genius of Chaplin—and the frightening irony of it all—is that Chaplin the joyful buffoon recognized that at the bottom of his desire to make people laugh lay the dictatorial, fascist part of himself. That's why he could play the role so well on the screen. The joker loves—no, the joker needs—to be in control. Chaplin wrote *The Great Dictator*, directed it, and acted in it. Chaplin also wrote the music for most of his movies. He also owned and operated his own studios in Hollywood. He loved control. And he loved laughter.

Let me make this point more strongly by returning for a moment to the story of Sarah and Abraham that I began in chapter 1. After Sarah weans

*See Norman Manea, *On Clowns: The Dictator and the Artist*, for a hint at this connection between clown and dictator. Manea draws on his years in a concentration camp for this connection. "Existence under terror distracts your perceptions," Manea says, "and frequently tempts you to make risky and farfetched associations" (p. 53). Chaplin makes the associations for us, and removes the risk. The terror remains.

Isaac, the couple commemorate the event by holding a feast. Ishmael, a son born of Abraham and an Egyptian maid named Hagar, attends the celebration. Sarah observes Ishmael laughing at her son, Isaac, in mockery.* Perhaps he is mocking the true heir to Abraham. Whatever the reason, the scene presents in the two sons of Abraham the two sides of laughter: ridicule and joy. Indeed, the two never seem far apart, especially in social situations when even a hint of competition is present. Chaplin represents those same two sides, updated and politically charged, in *The Great Dictator*, and brings to bear on the political realities of fascism the rich and ambivalent history of laughter in his film.

Some people hated Lenny Bruce. Some people—some of the same people, I suspect—later came to hate Richard Pryor. Some probably even hate Lily Tomlin or Paula Poundstone. Audiences find every comic both lovable and detestable, both witty and nasty. If comics want their bits to work well, they must act like dictators. Like dictators, comics come across as know-it-alls, presenting their little stories emptied of all complexities. In their desire to make people laugh, they manifest a wholesale need to direct and control. True, unlike the dictator, the joker lays his victims out only metaphorically, slaying them with elaborate jokes and punchy one-liners. Yet perhaps it might be said that the comic and the commandant require each other, that being a joker or a dictator is only a matter of degree or emphasis. Mel Brooks won an Oscar for his screenplay *The Producers* mainly for his carnivalizing send-ups of the Nazis in the play within the movie *Springtime for Hitler*.

Movies, and particularly comic movies, lend themselves to violence. I don't mean just the early Russian epics like *Battleship Potemkin* or *Alexander Nevsky*, or other spectacles like *Birth of a Nation* or *Greed*, but also the early Hollywood comedies that came slapping and banging and falling from the Keystone Kops. Their herky-jerky movements on the silent screen

*Some controversy surrounds the Hebrew word here: some commentators have it as "play"; but most have translated it as "mockery" or "derision."

would have thrilled Hobbes with their inelastic action—Henri Bergson, too, who locates the comic in the opposition between the mechanical and the living, the rigid and the supple: "automatism in contrast with free activity."* And all those falls and pratfalls would have appealed in a big way, I suspect, to Freud.

By necessity, film is a violent medium. Filming and editing, both mechanical intrusions, interrupt the fluent narrative of the story. Even the best of editing violates the continuous flow we call reality.** The editor slices and splices. The camera-person lines up a shot; directors shoot movies. Someone screams out, "Cut!" It makes sense that contemporary film does violence and special effects (a violent assault on normal perception) best of all—a natural conclusion, and maybe the only conclusion, from such an aggressive medium.

In this context, Chaplin's attraction to movie-making seems all the more natural, and his subject, Hitler, just right. The joker may well be the dictator who has found a way to put his or her will to a beneficial social use. That's one of the vital historical lessons here, that the dictator and the joker call each other into being, and that audiences feel most like laughing when they feel most suffocated.†

These connections may explain our current fascination with comics and laughter.‡ We live in a time when scores and scores of people admit to feeling neglected, marginal, forgotten, and worst of all, powerless—feeling they have no voice or that no one cares to listen. To attend a club anytime is to have a comic defuse the world's ills and problems with humor—if only

*Henri Bergson, *Laughter: An Essay on the Meaning of the Comic*, trans. Claudesley Brereton and Fred Rothwell (London: Macmillan, 1921), p. 31.

**One can see reality violated most violently and most clearly in animated cartoons like "Tom and Jerry" and "The Roadrunner."

†William Kunstler, the radical lawyer, commented recently that, during the trial of the Chicago Seven, Abbie Hoffman turned Judge Julius Hoffman's courtroom into a "festival of life": One day he waltzed in with a Viet Cong flag, on another he stood up and recited the long list of those killed in Vietnam, and so on. The dictatorial, angry Judge Hoffman, Kunstler added, saw respect for the law turned upside down (KCRW, "The Politics of Culture," October 11, 1994).

‡Montreal even boasts an International Museum of Humor, which opened in the fall of 1993 and grew out of the city's annual Just for Laughs Festival.

for a short time. These days, however, comics speak more and more for those who stand outside the threshold of power. Hence the proliferation in recent years of ethnic minorities taking the stage themselves. How much more powerful for a marginalized person to stand up and make fun of himself or herself, instead of some proxy like Mort Sahl or even Lenny Bruce, who in the end can talk only secondhand about black or Chicano problems. Not only do the new comics defuse those problems momentarily for a whole ethnic minority, but they also become role models as they get up in front of an audience—no small feat in itself—and make everyone laugh. That's power, after all. I think that sense of power explains as well the rise of female comedians. Women like Gracie Allen and Mary Livingston served as dumb pals—straight women—to their stand-up comic husbands (George Burns and Jack Benny), who refused to let their jokes stray from the confines of the kitchen: domestic fun in the style of Lucille Ball and Desi Arnez.

Jackie "Moms" Mabley, who worked the black nightclubs in the thirties, with a little help from the likes of Pigmeat Markham, Dusty Fletcher, and even Stepin Fetchit, may have been an exception. Mel Watkins, in his comprehensive book on African-American humor, describes Mabley doing what she did best, delivering sexually suggestive, openly hilarious little stories, standing alone in front of a microphone dressed, as one journalist recalls, "in an outfit Phyllis Diller might wear if she was black":

> She would do her famous shuffle, sing some comical parody of a popular song, tell stories, or just stand there, and the audience would howl. The stories most often focused on some folksy experience she shared with the audience or the obsessive quest for a young man, a gambit that became her trademark. . . . Mabley was brilliant at establishing a mood of comforting affiliation with her audience; on stage she could literally become the grandmother that most everyone knew at one time or another.*

But "Moms" Mabley performed most of her life in Harlem. Although she did many bits about Southern racism, she played mainly to black audiences. Mabley spoke boldly and frankly and refused to act like a well-bred

*Mel Watkins, *On the Real Side* (New York: Simon and Schuster, 1994), p. 391.

lady. She continually broke social constraints. Stand-up women comics, with her vitality, like Paula Poundstone, Elaine Booser, and Sandra Bernhardt, appear with some regularity today. And their appearance attests, in part, to the transforming power of laughter. Listen to their routines: You'll hear a humor fairly free of violence. In fact, many of the jokes deflate the pumped-up macho image of men. As Lily Tomlin says, "Macho does not mean mucho."

In a way, women and men seem to have traded comic places. As women comics have moved out of the kitchen and onto the stage, their male counterparts have beat a retreat to the safety of high school—or even junior high—and most often to the school's gym or locker room. Steven Stark, a commentator on National Public Radio, notices signs of early adolescence rising in films, sitcoms, cartoons, and even in the TV news. Talk show hosts like Howard Stern and Don Imus "sit in a playhouse-like radio studio with a bunch of guys and horse around for hours talking about sex or sports . . . all the while laughing at the gang's consciously loutish, subversive jokes. To the extent that women participate, they are often treated to a barrage of sexual and scatological humor. It's no wonder the audience for both shows is predominantly male."*

Stark finds the most blatant examples of immaturity in "Late Show with David Letterman" and "Seinfeld." Late-night TV, he says, has always been dominated by men, but in recent years he notices a difference—it has regressed to a boy's world:

> One of Letterman's contributions to late-night entertainment has been to take its humor out of the nightclub-act tradition . . . and place it firmly in that prankish, subversive, back-of-the-classroom seventh-grade realm that has become so culturally prominent. Although Letterman rarely greets women guests with filthy jokes (you can't do that on network television), he often treats them with the exaggerated deference and shyness typical of fourteen-year-old boys.

Like a group of fourteen-year-olds, the men on *Seinfeld* seem not to hold regular jobs, the better to devote time to "the gang." One woman,

*Steven Stark, "Where the Boys Are," *Atlantic Monthly* 274, no. 2 (September 1994): 18.

Elaine, is allowed to tag along with the boys, much like those younger sisters who are permitted to hang out with their brothers. It's not simply that everyone in Seinfeld's gang is unmarried and pushing fortysomething. It's that given their personas, it's difficult to imagine any of them having a real relationship with any woman but his mother.*

At the beginning of this book, I suggested that to understand the history of laughter one would have to learn to read using a kind of inversion and indirection, probing deeper than between the lines in an attempt to reach meaning somewhere underneath the lines. I also raised the following questions: If laughter really works—if it really does its topsy-turvy job—shouldn't those who have lived at the bottom of the heap for so many centuries, or who have stood beside the heap, finally move somewhere closer to the top and center? Shouldn't we eventually hear from them?

Historically, the odds against women standing up there on the stage, taking on the firmly entrenched and the powerful, have been high, for several sociological reasons. Here is Mahadev Apte, an anthropologist who has written about humor, outlining the disadvantages that have effectively prevented women from telling jokes publicly—and often privately:

> Women's humor reflects the existing inequality between the sexes not so much in its substance as in the constraints imposed on its occurrence, on the techniques used, on the social settings in which it occurs, and on the kind of audience that appreciates it. . . . These constraints generally, but not universally, stem from the prevalent cultural values that emphasize male superiority and dominance together with female passivity and create role models for women in keeping with such values and attitudes.**

Passivity and the sharp, aggressive expression of wit simply do not mix. Nancy Walker has written one of the few books about women's humor, and while she confines her comments primarily to the expression of humor

*Ibid. Stark continues, "Compare this situation comedy with the one that was roughly its cultural predecessor, *Cheers*, which appeared in the same time slot. On that show, too, the men didn't spend much time at work, but they did hang out in a traditional domain of adults (the tavern), and the hero, Sam Malone, spent many of his waking hours chasing women. Seinfeld is better known for sitting in a diner eating french fries with his pals. One of his most celebrated 'risque' episodes was about—what else?—masturbation" (pp. 19–20).

**Mahadev L. Apte, *Humor and Laughter: An Anthropological Approach* (Ithaca: Cornell University Press, 1985), p. 69.

in literature, they still reveal the strong social bias against women telling jokes: "American women writers, from colonial times to the present, have repeatedly articulated their awareness of the cultural prejudices against a display of female wittiness." She goes on to say that, by the midnineteenth century, what one writer calls the "'cult of domesticity' was so firmly intrenched that womanly wit had difficulty maneuvering around the image of ideal womanhood—an image that denigrated woman's intellect in favor of her emotional and intuitive nature: 'Anti-intellectualism was implicit in the cult which exalted women as creatures who did not use logic or reason, having a surer, purer road to the truth—the high road of the heart.'"*

Joking and laughter have come a long way from Gracie Allen to Roseanne Barr. So has the world—we hope. The power of laughter—and I think the feminist movement has produced more joking than, say, the antiwar movement ever did—has helped a bit to bring about changes in attitude. At any rate, from here on out, we could write a quite different book tracing the history of laughter. We wouldn't have to read so obliquely, so much under the covers. Lenny Bruce gave us new ears. Now all we have to do is listen. And we should, for we can learn a lot from this new, above-ground ethnic and female laughter.

It's a Promethean image, peasants and minorities—the disenfranchised of all kinds—seizing from the gods the mighty Olympian flames. The Titans, Prometheus and Epimetheus, the smart brother and the dumb one—they should now feel like an old, familiar team—the joker and the straight man both love to play with fire. But so is motion picture technology a Promethean dare, in its attempt to harness fire—to domesticate light. And motion pictures have become our principal artful form of entertainment as America moves closer and closer toward fulfilling its destiny as pleasure palace. Film is the most subtle of practical jokes, the grandest of illusions, a medium that tempts the most enterprising jokers—from Chaplin to Hal Roach, from

*Nancy A. Walker, *A Very Serious Thing: Women's Humor and American Culture* (Minneapolis: University of Minnesota Press, 1988), pp. 26, 27.

Woody Allen to Mel Brooks, from Steven Spielberg to Penny Marshall—to try their tricks on us.

The United Nations Building in New York has this line chiseled into its facade: "Prometheus teacher in every act brought the fire that hath proved to mortals a means to mighty ends." For this book, Prometheus' theft of fire must also stand as a seizing from the gods of fiery laughter. Such a bold act carnivalizes everyone's imagination by bringing a piece of the heavens down to earth. Such Titanic nerve reverses normal expectations. Prometheus: the most impudent of practical jokers.* In some versions of the myth, in fact, Prometheus steals fire from the one who knows fiery, caustic laughter better than any other mythological character—Hephaistos.

Fire is actually about speed: Scientists describe it as rapid oxidation, a ravenous consumption of oxygen—$O_2$. So, too, is laughter about speed, and invigoration through the rapid intake of air—the ancient art of pneumatology. Through such "sudden glory" we reach solutions to problems instantaneously; we feel joy and exhilaration we might otherwise never have gotten. In that way, laughter empowers. In that way, laughter is indeed the "means to mighty ends."

*I choose this word *impudent* deliberately. Derived from Latin *pudere*, "to be ashamed" (the prefix *im* turns it negative: "unashamed"), the gerund *pudendus* yields *pudenda*, "genitals." To act *impudently* is to act unashamedly from the substratum, from the crotch. The word Freud uses for dirty joke, *Zote* (from "unclean hair," "pubic hair") is etymologically connected to the word for female genitalia. One can only wonder about the potency of shaggy dog stories and of "letting one's hair down."

I have described the closed-off body reaching perfection by the end of the seventeenth century; it knows no shag, no pudenda. All protrusions have been eliminated, all orifices sealed. By the eighteenth century—a time when toilet facilities move inside many homes—only the peasant shits, farts, belches, and screws. Everyone else blushes and flushes.

# bibliography


Abartis, Caesarea. 1977. *The Tragicomic Construction of Cymbeline and the Winter's Tale.* Salzburg Studies in English Literature. Jacobean Drama Series, 73. Salzburg, Austria.

Abrahams, Roger D. 1968. "Trickster, the Outrageous Hero." In *Our Living Traditions: An Introduction to American Folklore*, ed. Tristram P. Coffin, pp. 170–78. New York: Basic Books.

———, and Alan Dundes. 1969. "On Elephantasy and Elephanticide." *Psychoanalytic Review* 56:228.

———. 1972. "Joking: The Training of the Man of Words in Talking Abroad." In *Rappin' and Stylin' Out: Communication in Urban Black America*, ed. Thomas Kochman, pp. 215–40. Urbana: University of Illinois Press.

———. 1985. *Afro-American Folktales: Stories from Black Traditions in the New World*. New York: Pantheon Books.

Adolf, Helen. 1947. "On Medieval Laughter." *Speculum* 22:251–53.

Adrados, Francisco R. 1975. *Festival, Comedy, and Tragedy.* Trans. Christopher Holme. Leiden: E. J. Brill.

Aers, David. 1980. *Chaucer, Langland, and the Creative Imagination*. London: Routledge and Kegan Paul.

Ahlberg, Janet, and Allan Ahlberg. 1978. *The Old Joke Book*. London: Fontana Lion Books.

Alford, F. 1981. "The Joking Relationships in American Society." *American Humor: An Interdisciplinary Newsletter* 8:1–8.

Alleau, R., ed. 1964. *Dictionnaire des jeux*. Paris: Tchou.

Allen, Philip S. 1910. "The Mediaeval Mimus." *Modern Philology* 7:329ff.

Amarasingham, L. R. 1973. "Laughter as Cure: Joking and Exorcism in a Singhalese Curing Retreat." Doctoral dissertation, Cornell University, Ithaca, New York.

Amsler, Mark E. 1980. "Literary Theory and the Genre of Middle English Literature." *Genre* 13 (Fall): 389–96.

Andreas, James. 1979. "Festive Liminality in Chaucerian Comedy." *Chaucer Newsletter* 1:3–6.

Apte, Mahadev L. 1985. *Humor and Laughter: An Anthropological Approach*. Ithaca: Cornell University Press.

Apuleius, Lucius. 1951. *The Golden Ass*. Trans. Robert Graves. New York: Farrar, Straus and Giroux.

Arden, Heather. 1980. *Fools' Play: A Study of Satire in the "Sottie."* Cambridge: Cambridge University Press.

Arieti, Silvano. 1976. *Creativity: The Magic Synthesis*. New York: Basic Books.

Armin, Robert. [1600] 1973. *Foole upon Foole*. Ed. A. F. Lippincott. Salzburg, Austria: University of Salzburg Press.

Armstrong, Martin Donisthorpe. 1928. *Laughing: An Essay.* New York: Harper and Company.

Ashley, Kathleen M., ed. 1990. *Victor Turner and the Construction of Cultural Criticism: Between Literature and Anthropology.* Bloomington: Indiana University Press.

Ashton, J., ed. 1883. *Humour, Wit, and Satire of the Seventeenth Century.* London: Chatto and Windus.

Auden, W. H. 1962. "Notes on the Comic." In *The Dyer's Hand*. New York: Random House.

Auerbach, Erich. 1953. "Sermo Humilis." In *Literary Language and Its Public in Late Latin Antiquity and in the Middle Ages*. New York: Doubleday, Anchor Books.

———. 1953. *Mimesis: The Representation of Beauty in Western Literature*. Trans. Willard Trask. Garden City, N.Y.: Doubleday, Anchor Books.

Austin, James C. 1978. *American Humor in France: Two Centuries of French Criticism of the Comic Spirit in American Literature*. Ames: Iowa State University Press.

Austin, J. L. 1962. *How to Do Things with Words*. New York: Oxford University Press.

Austin, Mary. 1924. "The Sense of Humor in Women." *New Republic* 26 (November): 10–13.

Auty, Susan G. 1975. *The Comic Spirit of Eighteenth-Century Novels*. Port Washington, N.Y.: Kennikat Press.

Babcock, Barbara, ed. 1978. *The Reversible World*. Ithaca: Cornell University Press.

Babcock-Abrahams, Barbara. 1975. "'A Tolerated Margin of Mess': The Trickster and His Tales Reconsidered." *Journal of the Folklore Institute* 11:147–86.

Bainton, Roland H. 1952. *The Reformation of the Sixteenth Century.* Boston: Beacon Press.

Baker, D. C. 1982. "'De Arte Lacrimandi': A Supplement and Some Connections." *Medium Aevum* 52 (2): 222–25.

Bakhtin, Mikhail M. 1968. *Speech Genres and Other Late Essays*. Ed. Caryl Emerson and Michael Holquist and trans. Vern W. McGee. Austin: University of Texas Press.

———. 1978. "Rabelais et Gogol." In *Esthetique et theorie du roman*, trans. Doria Olivier. Paris: Hachette.

———. 1981. *The Dialogic Imagination*. Ed. Michael Holquist and trans. Caryl Emerson and Michael Holquist. Austin: University of Texas Press.

———. 1984. *Problems of Dostoyevsky's Poetics*. Ed. and trans. Caryl Emerson. Minneapolis: University of Minnesota Press.

———. 1984. *Rabelais and His World*. Trans. Helene Iswolsky. Bloomington: Indiana University Press.

Barber, C. L. 1963. *Shakespeare's Festive Comedy: A Study of Dramatic Form and Its Relation to Social Custom*. New York: Meridian Books.

Barnstone, Tony, Willis Barnstone, and Xi Haixin, trans. 1992. *Laughing Lost in the Mountains: Poems by Wang Wei*. Boston: University Press of New England.

Barolsky, Paul. 1978. *Infinite Jest: Wit and Humor in Italian Renaissance Art*. Columbia: University of Missouri Press.

Baron, Robert A. 1978. "Aggression-Inhibiting Influence of Sexual Humor." *Journal of Personality and Social Psychology* 3(2): 189–97.

Barreca, Regina, ed. 1988. *Last Laughs: Perspectives on Women and Comedy*. Studies in Gender and Culture, vol. 2. New York: Gordon and Breach Science Publishers.

———. 1990. *They Used to Call Me Snow White: Women's Strategic Use of Humor*. New York: Viking Press.

———. 1991. *They Used to Call Me Snow White . . . but I Drifted: Women's Strategic Use of Humor*. New York: Penguin Books.

Barron, M. L. 1950. "A Content Analysis of Intergroup Humor." *American Sociological Review* 15:88–94.

Basso, Keith H. 1979. *Portraits of the 'Whiteman': Linguistic Play and Cultural Symbols among the Western Apache*. Cambridge: Cambridge University Press.

Bataille, Georges. 1968. "Writings on Laughter, Sacrifice, Nietzsche, Un-Knowing." Trans. Annette Michelson. *October* (Spring): 36.

———. 1989. *The Tears of Eros*. Trans. Peter Connor. San Francisco: City Lights Books.

Bateson, Gregory. 1952. "The Position of Humor in Human Communication." In *Cybernetics, Eighth Conference*, ed. Heinz von Foerster. New York: The Josiah Macy Jr. Foundation.

———. 1969. "The Position of Humor." In *Motivation in Humor*, ed. Jacob Levine. New York: Atherton Press.

———. 1972. "A Theory of Play and Fantasy." In *Steps to an Ecology of Mind*. New York: Ballantine Books.

Baudelaire, Charles. 1955. "On the Essence of Laughter." In *The Mirror of Art*, trans. and ed. Jonathan Mayne, pp. 133–53. New York: Phaidon.

Bausinger, Hermann. 1958. "Schwank und Witz." *Stadium Generale* 11: 699–710.

Beattie, James. 1778. *Essays: On Poetry and Music, as They Effect the Mind; On Laughter and Ludicrous Composition; on the Utility of Classical Learning*. Edinburgh: W. Creech and E. Dilly.

Beatts, Anne. 1975. "Can a Woman Get a Laugh and a Man Too?" *Mademoiselle*, November, pp. 140ff.

———. 1976. "Why More Women Aren't Funny." *New Woman*, March/April, pp. 22–28.

Bedier, Joseph. 1925. *Las fabliaux: Etudes de littérature populaire et d'histoire littéraire du Moyen Age*. 5th ed. Paris: Champion.

Ben-Amos, Dan. 1973. "The Myth of Jewish Humor." *Western Folklore* 32:112–31.

Benjamin, Walter. 1969. *Illuminations*. Ed. Hannah Arendt and trans. Harry Zohn. New York: Schocken Books.

———. 1979. "A Small History of Photography." In *One-way Street and Other Writings*, trans. E. Jephcott and K. Shorter, pp. 243–44. London: New Left Books.

———. 1979. *Reflections*. Ed. Peter Demetz and trans. E. Jephcott. New York: Harcourt Brace Jovanovich.

Bennetts, Leslie. 1987. "The Pain behind the Laughter of Moms Mabley." *New York Times*, August 8, sec. 2.

Benson, Larry D., and Theodore M. Andersson, eds. 1971. *The Literacy Context of Chaucer's Fabliaux*. Indianapolis: Bobbs-Merrill.

Benson, Robert. 1980. *Medieval Body Language: A Study of the Use of Gesture in Chaucer's Poetry*. Anglistica 21. Copenhagen.

Berek, Peter. 1978. "'As We Are Mock'd with Art': From Scorn to Transfiguration." *Studies in English Literature* 8:289–305.

Berger, Arthur Asa. 1976. "Anatomy of the Joke." *Journal of Communication* 26 (3): 113–15.

———. 1993. *An Anatomy of Humor*. New York: Transaction Publishers.

———. 1994. *Blind Men and Elephants: Perspectives on Humor*. New York: Transaction Publishers.

Berger, Peter L., and Thomas Luckmann. 1967. *The Social Construction of Reality: A Treatise in the Sociology of Knowledge*. Garden City, N.Y.: Doubleday, Anchor Books.

———. 1969. "Christian Faith and the Social Comedy." In *Holy Laughter: Essays on Religion in the Comic Perspective*, ed. M. Conrad Hyers, pp. 123–33. New York: Seabury Press.

Berger, Phil. 1984. "The New Comediennes." *New York Times Magazine*, July 29, pp. 27ff.

Bergler, E. 1956. *Laughter and the Sense of Humor*. New York: Intercontinental Medical Book Corporation.

Bergmann, Merrie. 1986. "How Many Feminists Does It Take to Make a Joke? Sexist Humor and What's Wrong with It." *Hypatia* 1:63–82.

Bergson, Henri. 1921. *Laughter: An Essay on the Meaning of the Comic*. Trans. Claudesley Brereton and Fred Rothwell. London: Macmillan.

Berlyne, D. E. 1959. "Laughter, Humor, and Play." In *Handbook of Social Psychology*, ed. G. Lindzey and E. Aronson, 3:705–852. Reading, Mass.: Addison-Wesley.

Bermant, Chaim. 1986. *What's the Joke: A Study of Jewish Humor through the Ages*. London: Weidenfeld and Nicholson.

Bermel, Albert. 1990. *Farce: A History from Aristophanes to Woody Allen*. Carbondale: Southern Illinois University Press.

Bernstein, Michael André. 1983. "When the Carnival Turns Bitter: Preliminary Reflections upon the Abject Hero." *Critical Inquiry* 10 (December): 283–305.

———. 1992. *Bitter Carnival: Ressentiment and the Abject Hero*. Princeton: Princeton University Press.

Bier, Jesse. 1968. *The Rise and Fall of American Humor*. New York: Holt, Rinehart and Winston.

Billington, Sandra. 1984. *A Social History of the Fool*. New York: St. Martin's Press.

Blair, Walter. 1960. *Native American Humor, 1800–1900*. San Francisco: Chandler.

Blair, Walter, and Hamlin Hill. 1978. *America's Humor: From Poor Richard to Doonesbury*. New York: Oxford University Press.

Blair, Walter, and Raven I. McDavid Jr. 1983. *The Mirth of a Nation: America's Great Dialect Humor*. Minneapolis: University of Minnesota Press.

Bledstein, Burton J. 1978. *The Culture of Professionalism: The Middle Class and the Development of Higher Education in America*. New York: W. W. Norton.

Bloch, R. Howard. 1983. *Etymologies and Genealogies: A Literary Anthropology of the French Middle Ages*. Chicago: University of Chicago Press.

———. 1983. "The Fabliaux, Fetishism, and Freud's Jewish Jokes." *Representations* 4 (Fall): 1–26.

———. 1986. *The Scandal of the Fabliaux*. Chicago: University of Chicago Press.

Bloomfield, Morton W. 1952. *The Seven Deadly Sins*. Ann Arbor: Michigan State College Press.

———. 1972. "The Gloomy Chaucer." In *Veins of Humor*, ed. Harry Levin, pp. 57–68. Harvard English Studies 3. Cambridge: Harvard University Press.

Bone, Robert. 1970. *The Negro Novel in America*. New Haven: Yale University Press.

Born, Lester Kruger. 1928. "The Perfect Prince: A Study in Thirteenth and Fourteenth Century Ideals." *Speculum* 3:420–504.

Boskin, Joseph. 1979. *Humor and Social Change in Twentieth Century America.* Boston: Trustees of the Public Library of the City of Boston.

Boston, Richard. 1974. *An Anatomy of Laughter.* London: Collins.

Bosworth, John. 1898. *An Anglo-Saxon Dictionary.* Enlarged by T. Northcote Toller. Oxford: Clarendon Press.

Bowen, Barbara C. 1984. "Roman Jokes and the Renaissance Prince, 1455–1528." *Illinois Classical Studies* 9:137–48.

———. 1986. "Renaissance Collections of Facetiae, 1344–1490: A New Listing." *Renaissance Quarterly* 39 (Summer): 1–15.

———. 1986. "Renaissance Collections of Facetiae, 1499–1528: A New Listing." *Renaissance Quarterly* 39 (Winter): 263–75.

Bowman, John R. 1982. "Getting Even: Notes on the Organization of Practical Jokes." In *The Paradoxes of Play,* ed. John Loy. West Point, N.Y.: Leisure Press.

Brant, C. S. 1948. "On Joking Relationships." *American Anthropologist* 50:160–62.

———. 1972. "A Preliminary Study of Cross-Sexual Joking Relationships in Primitive Society." *Behavior Science Notes* 7:313–29.

Braudel, Fernand. 1974. *Capitalism and Material Life, 1400–1800.* Trans. Miriam Kochan. New York: Harper and Row.

Bremmer, Jan, and Herman Roodenburg, eds. 1992. *A Cultural History of Gesture.* Ithaca: Cornell University Press.

Brewer, Derek W. 1972. "Afterword: Notes towards a Theory of Medieval Comedy." In *Medieval Comic Tales,* trans. Peter Rickard et al., pp. 140–49. Totowa, N.J.: Rowman and Littlefield.

Bricker, Victoria Riefler. 1973. *Ritual Humor in Highland Chiapas.* Austin: University of Texas Press.

Bristol, Michael D. 1983. "Carnival and the Institutions of Theater in Elizabethan England." *English Literary History* 50:637–55.

———. 1985. *Carnival and Theater: Plebeian Culture and the Structure of Authority in Renaissance England.* New York: Methuen.

Brody, Morris. 1950. "The Meaning of Laughter." *Psychoanalytic Quarterly* 19: 192–201.

Brooke, Nicholas. 1979. *Horrid Laughter in Jacobean Tragedy.* London: Open Books.

Brown, Michele, and Ann O'Connor, eds. 1988. *Hammer and Tongues: A Dictionary of Women's Wit and Humour.* London: Grafton Books.

Brown, Peter. 1969. *Augustine of Hippo.* Berkeley: University of California Press.

Bruere, Martha Bensley, and Mary Ritter Beard. 1935. *Laughing Their Way: Women's Humor in America.* New York: Macmillan.

Brukman, Jan. 1975. "Tongue Play: Constitutive and Interpretive Properties of Sexual Joking Encounters among the Koya of South India." In *Sociocultural Dimensions of Language Use*, ed. Mary Sanches and Ben G. Blount, pp. 253–67. New York: Academic Press.

Brunvand, Jan Harold. 1972. "The Study of Contemporary Folklore: Jokes." *Fabula* 13:1–19.

Bunkers, Suzanne L. 1985. "Why Are These Women Laughing? The Power and Politics of Women's Humour." *Studies in American Humor*, n.s., 4, 1, no. 2 (Spring/Summer): 82–93.

Burckhardt, Jacob. 1958. *The Civilization of the Renaissance in Italy.* Vol. 1. New York: Harper and Row.

Burke, Peter. 1978. *Popular Culture in Early Modern Europe*. New York: New York University Press.

Burlin, Robert B. 1977. *Chaucerian Fiction*. Princeton: Princeton University Press.

Burt, Sir Cyril. 1945. "The Psychology of Laughter." *Health Education Journal* 3: 15–34.

Busby, O. M. 1923. *Studies in the Development of the Fool in Elizabethan Drama*. New York: Oxford University Press.

Bushnell, Donald D. 1937. *The Cathartic Effects of Laughter.* New York: Simon and Schuster.

Butler, Mary Marguerite. 1969. *Hrotsvitha: The Theatricality of Her Plays*. New York: Philosophical Library.

Callahan, William A. 1993. "Chuckling across Boundaries: Laughter and Politics in China and the West." Doctoral dissertation, East/West University, Hawaii.

Camille, Michael. 1992. *Image on the Edge: The Margins of Medieval Art*. Cambridge: Harvard University Press.

Cantor, Joanne R. 1976. "What Is Funny to Whom? The Role of Gender." *Journal of Communication* 26 (3): 164–72.

———. 1976. "Humor on Television: A Content Analysis." *Journal of Broadcasting* 20:501–10.

Carlson, Richard S. 1975. *The Benign Humorists*. New York: Archon Books.

Casanowicz, L. M. 1894. *Paranomasia in the Old Testament*. Boston: Norwood.

Castle, Terry. 1986. *Masquerade and Civilization: The Carnivalesque in Eighteenth-Century English Culture and Fiction*. Palo Alto: Stanford University Press.

Cazamian, Louis. 1930. *The Development of English Humor.* New York: Macmillan.

Chambers, E. K. 1903. *The Mediaeval Stage*. Oxford: Oxford University Press.

Chapman, A. J. 1975. "Humorous Laughter in Children." *Journal of Personality and Social Psychology* 31:42–49.

Chapman, A. J., and N. J. Gadfield. 1976. "Is Sexual Humor Sexist?" *Journal of Communication* 25:141–53.

Charles, L. H. 1945. "The Clown's Function." *Journal of American Folklore* 58:25–34.

Charney, Maurice. 1978. *Comedy High and Low: An Introduction to the Experience of Comedy.* New York: Oxford University Press.

Chenu, M. D. 1926–27. "Auctor, Actor, Autor." *Archivum Latinitatis Medii Aevi. Bulletin du Cange* 3–4:81–86.

Chiaro, Delia. 1992. *The Language of Jokes: Analysing Verbal Play.* London: Routledge.

Christensen, J. B. 1963. "Utani: Joking, Sexual License, and Social Obligations among the Luguru." *American Anthropologist* 65:1314–27.

Clastres, Pierre. 1987. *Society against the State: Essays in Political Anthropology.* Trans. Robert Hurley. Cambridge: MIT Press.

Cleland, R. S. 1957. "An Investigation of the Relation between Creative Humor and Authoritarianism." Doctoral dissertation, University of Florida, Gainesville.

Cohen, J., ed. 1967. *The Essential Lenny Bruce.* New York: Bell Publications.

Cohen, Sandy. 1985. "Racial and Ethnic Humor in the United States." *Amerikastudien* 30:203–11.

Cohen, Sarah Blacher, ed. 1979. *Comic Relief: Humor in Contemporary American Literature.* Chicago: University of Illinois Press.

Cohn, R. 1951. "Forced Crying and Laughing." *Archives of Neurology and Psychiatry* 66:738.

Clubb, Merrel D. 1932. "A Plea for an Eclectic Theory of Humor." *University of California Chronicle* 34:340–56.

Colie, Rosale. 1966. *Paradoxica Epidemica: The Renaissance Tradition of Paradox.* Princeton: Princeton University Press.

Collier, Denise, and Kathleen Beckett. 1980. *Spare Ribs: Women in the Humor Biz.* New York: St. Martin's Press.

Colonna, Enza. 1978. "Viterbo: Il linguaggio comico nel medioevo." *Quaderni Medievali* 6:203–16.

Cook, Albert. 1949. *The Dark Voyage and the Golden Mean: A Philosophy of Comedy.* Cambridge: Harvard University Press.

Cooke, Thomas D. 1978. *The Old French and Chaucerian Fabliaux: A Study of Their Comic Climax.* Columbia: University of Missouri Press.

Cooke, Thomas D., and Benjamin L. Honeycutt, eds. 1974. *The Humor of the Fabliaux.* Columbia: University of Missouri Press.

Cooper, Lane. 1922. *An Aristotelian Theory of Comedy.* New York: Harcourt, Brace.

Cornford, Francis Macdonald. 1961. *The Origin of Attic Comedy.* Ed. Theodore H. Gaster. New York: Doubleday, Anchor Books.

Corrigan, Robert W. 1965. *Comedy: Meaning and Form.* San Francisco: Chandler Press.

Coser, Rose Laub. 1959. "Some Social Functions of Laughter." *Human Relations* 12:171–82.

———. 1960. "Laughter among Colleagues: A Study of the Social Functions of Humor among the Staff of a Mental Hospital." *Psychiatry* 23:81–95.

Cote, Richard G. 1986. *Holy Mirth.* Whitinsville, Mass.: Affirmation Books.

Cowan, Louise, ed. 1984. *The Terrain of Comedy.* Dallas: Dallas Institute of Humanities and Culture.

Cox, Harvey. 1969. *The Feast of Fools.* New York: Harper and Row.

Cox, James. 1979. "Toward Vernacular Humor." *Virginia Quarterly Review* 46:311–30.

Cox, Samuel S. 1880. *Why We Laugh.* New York: Harper.

"Coyotes and Clowns." 1987. *Las Palabras: A Quarterly Newsletter of the Millicent Rogers Museum* 8 (3): 1–4.

Craig, Patricia, ed. 1990. *The Penguin Book of British Comic Stories.* New York: Viking Penguin.

Craik, T. W. 1964. *The Comic Tales of Chaucer.* London: Methuen.

Cray, Ed. 1964. "The Rabbi Trickster." *Journal of American Folklore* 77:331–45.

Crossan, John. 1976. *Raid on the Articulate: Comic Eschatalogy in Jesus and Borges.* South Bend, Ind.: Notre Dame University Press.

Crossley-Holland, Kevin. 1979. *The Exeter Book Riddles.* London: Penguin Books.

Culler, Jonathan. 1988. *On Puns: The Foundation of Letters.* London: Oxford University Press.

Cunningham, Bonnie, ed. 1974. *The Puffin Joke Book.* London: Puffin Books.

Curtius, Ernst Robert. 1953. *European Literature and the Latin Middle Ages.* Trans. Willard Trask. Princeton: Princeton University Press.

Darwin, Charles. 1904. *The Expression of the Emotions in Man and Animals.* London: Murray.

David, Alfred. 1976. *The Strumpet Muse: Art and Morals in Chaucer's Poetry.* Bloomington: Indiana University Press.

Davies, Christie. 1982. "Ethnic Jokes, Moral Values, and Social Boundaries." *British Journal of Sociology* 33:383–408.

———. 1987. "Language, Identity, and Ethnic Jokes about Stupidity." *International Journal of the Sociology of Language* 65:39–52.

———. 1988. *Jokes Are about People*. Bloomington: Indiana University Press.

———. 1991. "Exploring the Thesis of the Self-Deprecating Jewish Sense of Humor." *Humor: International Journal of Humor Research* 4:189–209.

———. 1992. *Ethnic Humor around the World: A Comparative Analysis*. Bloomington: Indiana University Press.

Da Vinci, Leonardo. 1956. *Treatise on Painting*. Ed. Philip McMahon. Princeton: Princeton University Press.

Davis, Jay M., and Amerigo Farina. 1970. "Humor Appreciation as Social Communication." *Journal of Personality and Social Psychology* 15:175–78.

Davis, Jessica M. 1978. *Farce*. London: Methuen.

Davis, Murray S. 1993. *What's So Funny? The Cosmic Conception of Culture and Society.* Chicago: University of Chicago Press.

Davis, Natalie Zemon. 1971. "The Reasons of Misrule: Youth Groups and Charivari in Sixteenth-Century France." *Past and Present* 50:41–75.

———. 1975. *Society and Culture in Early Modern France*. Palo Alto: Stanford University Press.

Dearborn, G. V. N. 1900. "The Nature of the Smile and the Laugh." *Science* 9:851–56.

De Doulet, Jules. 1845. *Dictionnaire des mystères, moralités, rites, figures, et cérémonies singulières*. In *Nouvelle encyclopedie theologique*, ed. J. P. Migne. Nouvelle ser., 43. Paris.

Deleuze, Gilles. 1977. "Nomad Thought." In *The New Nietzsche*, ed. David B. Allison. New York: Dell Publishing.

Deloria, Vine Jr. 1969. *Custer Died for Your Sins: An Indian Manifesto*. New York: Macmillan.

Derrida, Jacques. 1963. *Dissemination*. Trans. Barbara Johnson. Chicago: University of Chicago Press.

———. 1987. *The Archaeology of the Frivolous: Reading Condillac*. Trans. John P. Leavy Jr. Lincoln: University of Nebraska Press.

Des Pres, Terrence. 1991. *Writing into the World: Essays, 1973–1987*. New York: Viking Penguin.

Detienne, Marcel, and Jean-Pierre Vernant. 1991. *Cunning Intelligence in Greek Culture and Society.* Trans. Janet Lloyd. Chicago: University of Chicago Press.

Dinshaw, Carolyn L. 1980. "Dice Games and Other Games in *Le Jeu de Saint Nicolas*." *PMLA* 95, no. 5 (October): 802–11.

Diot, Rolande. 1986. "Sexus, Nexus, and Taboos versus Female Humor: The Case of Erica Jong." *Revue Francaise D'Etudes Americaines* 30 (November): 491–99.

Dodds, Eric R. 1951. *The Greeks and the Irrational.* Berkeley: University of California Press.

Dolgopolova, Z., ed. 1982. *Russia Dies Laughing: Jokes from Soviet Russia.* London: Andre Deutsch.

Donaldson, Ian. 1970. *The World Upside-Down: Comedy from Jonson to Fielding.* Oxford: Oxford University Press.

Doran, John. 1966. *The History of Court Fools.* New York: Haskell House.

Douglas, Mary. 1966. *Purity and Danger: An Analysis of the Concepts of Pollution and Taboo.* London: Routledge and Kegan Paul.

———. 1968. "The Social Control of Cognition: Some Factors in Joke Perception." *Man* 3:361–76.

———. 1975. "Jokes." In *Implicit Meanings: Essays in Anthropology*, pp. 90–114. London: Routledge and Kegan Paul.

Draiter, Emil. 1978. *Forbidden Laughter: Soviet Underground Jokes.* Los Angeles: Almanac Publishing House.

Dresner, Zita Zatkin. 1982. "Twentieth-Century American Women Humorists." Doctoral dissertation, University of Maryland, College Park.

Dudden, Arthur Power, ed. 1987. *American Humor.* New York: Oxford University Press.

Duncan, Edgar Hill. 1972. "Short Fiction in Medieval English: A Survey." *Studies in Short Fiction* 9, no. 1 (Winter): 1–29.

———. 1973. "Short Fiction in Medieval English, Part 2: The Middle English Period." *Studies in Short Fiction* 9, no. 3 (Summer): 227–43.

Dundes, Alan. 1971. "A Study of Ethnic Slurs: The Jew and the Polack in the United States." *Journal of American Folklore* 86:202.

———. 1977. "Jokes and Covert Language Attitudes: The Curious Case of the Wide-Mouth Frog." *Language in Society* 6:144–47.

———. 1987. *Cracking Jokes: Studies of Sick Humor Cycles and Stereotypes.* Berkeley: Ten Speed.

———, ed. 1973. *Mother Wit from the Laughing Barrel.* Jackson: University Press of Mississippi.

Dundes, Alan, and Robert A. Georges. 1962. "Some Minor Genres of Obscene Folklore." *Journal of American Folklore* 75:221–26.

DuVal, John Tabb, trans. 1993. *Fabliaux, Fair and Foul.* New York: Pegasus Books.

Dworkin, Susan. 1987. "Roseanne Barr: The Disgruntled Housewife as Stand-up Comedian." *Ms.*, July/August, pp. 106–8.

Eastman, Max. 1921. *The Sense of Humor.* New York: Hamish Hamilton.

———. 1937. *The Enjoyment of Laughter.* New York: Hamish Hamilton.

Eco, Umberto. 1983. *The Name of the Rose.* Trans. William Weaver. New York: Harcourt Brace Jovanovich.

———. 1984. *Semiotics and the Philosophy of Language.* Bloomington: Indiana University Press.

Eggebroten, Anne. 1984. "Laughter in the *Second Nun's Tale:* A Redefinition of the Genre." *Chaucer Review* 19:55–60.

Eimerl, Sarel. 1962. "Can Women Be Funny? Humor Has Nothing to Do With Sex . . . or Does It?" *Mademoiselle*, November, p. 151.

Eisenbud, J. 1964. "The Oral Side of Humor." *Psychoanalytic Review* 51:57–73.

Elias, Norbert. 1978. *The History of Manners: The Civilizing Process.* Vol. 1. Trans. Edmund Jephcott. New York: Pantheon Books.

———. 1982. *Power and Civility.* Trans. Edmund Jephcott. New York: Pantheon Books.

Ellison, Ralph. 1986. "An Extravagance of Laughter." In *Going to the Territory.* New York: Random House.

Ellman, Maud. 1993. *The Hunger Artists: Starving, Writing, and Imprisonment.* Cambridge: Harvard University Press.

Ellul, Jacques. 1985. *The Humiliation of the Word.* Trans. Joyce Main Hanks. Grand Rapids, Mich.: William B. Eerdmans.

Elsbree, Langdon. 1972. "The Purest and Most Perfect Form of Play: Some Novelists and the Dance." *Criticism* 14, no. 4 (Fall): 361–72.

Emerson, Joan. 1969. "Negotiating the Serious Import of Humor." *Sociometry* 32:169–81.

Empson, William. 1958. *Seven Types of Ambiguity.* New York: Meridian Books.

Enck, J. J., E. R. Forter, and A. Whitley, eds. 1960. *The Comic in Theory and Practice.* New York: Appleton-Century-Crofts.

English, James F. 1986. "The Laughing Reader: A New Direction for Studies of the Comic." *Genre* 19 (Summer): 129–54.

Enright, D. J. 1986. "Present Laughter." *Times Literary Supplement*, September 26, p. 1079.

———. 1987. "Awfully Funny." *Times Literary Supplement*, December 18–24, pp. 1399–1400.

Erasmus. 1958. *The Praise of Folly*. Trans. John Wilson. Ann Arbor: University of Michigan Press.

Esar, Evan. 1952. *The Humor of Humor*. New York: Horizon Press.

———. 1978. *The Comic Encyclopedia*. New York: Doubleday.

Escarpit, Robert. 1967. *L'humour*. Paris: P.U.F.

Epsy, Willard. 1972. *The Game of Words*. New York: Grosset and Dunlap.

Falk, Robert Paul, ed. 1975. *The Antic Muse: American Writers in Parody*. New York: Grove Press.

Faral, Edmond. 1964. *Les jongleurs en France du Moyen Age*. Paris: Champion.

Farb, Peter. 1974. *Word Play: What Happens When People Talk*. New York: Alfred A. Knopf.

Fauset, Jessie. 1925. "The Gift of Laughter." In *The New Negro*, ed. Alain Locke. New York: Albert and Charles Boni.

Fehl, Philip P. 1979. "Farewell to Jokes: The Last *Capricci* of Giovanni Domenico Tiepolo and the Tradition of Irony in Venetian Painting." *Critical Inquiry* 5, no. 4 (Summer): 761–91.

Feinberg, Leonard. 1971. *Asian Laughter*. New York: Weatherhill.

Feldman, Gayle. 1990. "The Best-Seller Blues: Hard Lessons from a Cosby Book." *New York Times Book Review*, June 10.

Felheim, Marvin, ed. 1962. *Comedy: Plays, Theory, and Criticism*. New York: Harcourt, Brace and World.

Ferguson, Margaret. 1975. "Saint Augustine's Region of Unlikeness: The Crossing of Exile and Language." *Georgia Review* 29:842–64.

Feurerstein, Georg. 1993. *Holy Madness*. New York: Arkana Press.

Fine, Gary Alan. 1976. "Obscene Joking across Culture." *Journal of Communication* 26:134–40.

Fineman, Jael. 1991. *The Subjectivity Effect in Western Literary Tradition: Essays Toward the Release of Shakespeare's Will*. Cambridge: MIT Press.

Fiorentino, Poggio. 1930. *Facetiae Erotica of Poggio Fiorentino*. New York: Privately printed.

Finucci, Valeria. 1992. "Jokes on Women: Triangular Pleasures in Castiglione and Freud." *Exemplaria* 4, no. 1.

Fisher, Seymour, and Rhoda L. Fisher. 1981. *Pretend the World Is Funny and Forever: A Psychological Analysis of Comedians, Clowns, and Actors*. Hillsdale, N.J.: Lawrence Erlbaum.

Fitzgerald, Robert, trans. 1975. *The Iliad.* Garden City, N.Y.: Doubleday, Anchor Books.

Fleet, F. R. 1890. *A Theory of Wit and Humor.* London: Remington and Co.

Flieger, Jery Aline. 1985. "The Purloined Punchline: Joke as Textual Paradigm." In *Lacan and Narration: The Psychoanalytic Difference in Narrative Theory*, ed. Robert Con Davis. Baltimore: John Hopkins University Press.

Flugel, J. C. 1954. "Humor and Laughter." In *Handbook of Social Psychology*, ed. Gardner Lindzey, 2:709–34. Cambridge, Mass.: Addison-Wesley.

Fortenbaugh, W. W. 1975. *Aristotle on Emotion.* New York: Barnes and Noble.

Foster, Edward E. 1968. "Humor in the *Knight's Tale.*" *Chaucer Review* 3:88–94.

Foucault, Michel. 1977. "What Is an Author?" In *Language, Counter-Memory, Practice*, ed. D. F. Bouchard, pp. 113–39. Ithaca: Cornell University Press.

———. 1979. *Discipline and Punish: The Birth of the Prison.* Trans. Alan Sheridan. New York: Vintage Books.

Foxx, Redd, and Norma Miller. 1977. *The Redd Foxx Encyclopedia of Black Humor.* Pasadena, Calif.: Ward Ritchie Press.

Frank, Roberta. 1972. "Some Uses of Paranomasia in Old English Scriptural Verse." *Speculum* 47 (April): 207–26.

Freedman, Jim. 1977. "Joking, Affinity, and the Exchange of Ritual Services among the Kiga of Northern Rwanda: An Essay on Joking Relationship Theory." *Man* 12:154–65.

Freud, Sigmund. 1928. "Humor." *International Journal of Psychoanalysis* 9:1–6.

———. 1963. *Jokes and Their Relation to the Unconscious.* Trans. James Strachey. New York: W. W. Norton.

Fry, William F. Jr. 1963. *Sweet Madness: A Study of Humor.* Palo Alto: Pacific Books.

Frye, Northrop. 1944. "The Nature of Satire." *University of Toronto Quarterly* 14 (October): 75–89.

———. 1948. "The Argument of Comedy." In *English Institute Essays*, ed. D. A. Robertson Jr. New York: Columbia University Press.

———. 1964. *Theories of Comedy*, ed. Paul Lauter. Garden City, N.Y.: Doubleday, Anchor Books.

———. 1981. *The Great Code: The Bible and Literature.* New York: Harcourt Brace Jovanovich.

Fuller, R. G. C., and A. Sheehy-Skeffington. 1974. "Effects of Group Laughter on Responses to Humorous Material: A Replication and Extension." *Psychological Reports* 35:531–34.

Furrow, Melissa M. 1985. *Ten Fifteenth-Century Comic Poems.* New York: Garland Publishing.

Gaignebet, Claude. 1975. "Le cycle annuel des fêtes à Rouen au milieu de XVIe siècle." In *Les fêtes de la Renaissance* 3:569–78. Paris: Editions du Centre National de la Recherche Scientifique.

Galligen, Edward L. 1984. *The Comic Vision in Literature*. Athens: University of Georgia Press.

Gallop, Jane. 1979. "Why Does Freud Giggle When the Women Leave the Room?" Paper read at the meeting of the Northeast Modern Language Association, Women and Humor session, Hartford, Connecticut.

Galnoor, Itzhak, and Steven Lukes, eds. 1985. *No Laughing Matter: A Collection of Political Jokes*. London: Routledge and Kegan Paul.

Ganim, John M. 1987. "Carnival Voices and the Envoy to the *Clerk's Tale*." *Chaucer Review* 22 (2): 112–27.

Garrett, Robert Max. 1909. "De Arte Lacrimandi." *Anglia* 32:269–94.

Garrison, Webb B. 1960. *Laughter in the Bible*. St. Louis: Bethany Press.

Gay, Peter. 1990. *Reading Freud: Explorations and Entertainments*. New Haven: Yale University Press.

Geertz, Clifford. 1973. "Deep Play: Notes on the Balinese Cockfight." In *The Interpretation of Cultures: Selected Essays*, pp. 412–53. New York: Basic Books.

Georges, Robert A. 1969. "Toward an Understanding of Storytelling Events." *Journal of American Folklore* 82:313–28.

Gilbert, Sandra, and Susan Gubar. 1979. *The Madwoman in the Attic: The Woman Writer and the Nineteenth-Century Literary Imagination*. New Haven: Yale University Press.

Gilliatt, Penelope. 1990. *To Wit: Skin and Bones of Comedy*. New York: Charles Scribner's Sons.

Ginzberg, Louis. 1968. *The Legends of the Jews*. Philadelphia: Jewish Publication Society of America.

Girling, F. K. 1957. "Joking Relationships in a Scottish Town." *Man* 57:102.

Goffman, Erving. 1959. *The Presentation of Self in Everyday Life*. New York: Doubleday, Anchor Books.

———. 1967. *Introduction Ritual: Essays on Face to Face Behavior*. New York: Doubleday, Anchor Books.

Goldberg, Isaac. 1938. *What We Laugh At—and Why*. Girard, Kansas: Haldeman-Julius Publications.

Goldman, Albert. 1974. *Ladies and Gentlemen, Lenny Bruce!!* From the journalism of Lawrence Schiller. New York: Ballantine Books.

Goldsmith, Robert Hillis. 1963. *Wise Fools in Shakespeare*. East Lansing: Michigan State University Press.

Good, Edwin. 1965. *Irony in the Old Testament*. London: S.P.C.K.

Goody, J. R., and Ian Watt. 1968. "The Consequences of Literacy." In *Literacy in Traditional Societies*, ed. J. R. Goody. London: Cambridge University Press.

Gopnik, Adam. 1993. "The Outsider." *New Yorker*, October 25, pp. 86–93.

Gower, John. 1901. *Confessio amantis*. In *The English Works of John Gower*, ed. G. C. Macaulay. Oxford: Clarendon Press.

Grant, Mary. 1924. *The Ancient Rhetorical Theories of the Laughable: The Greek Rhetoricians and Cicero*. Madison: University of Wisconsin Press.

Grassi, Joseph A. 1986. *God Makes Me Laugh*. Wilmington: M. Glazier.

Grassvogel, David I. 1959. "The Depths of Laughter: The Subsoil of a Culture." *Yale French Studies* 23:63–71.

Graux, Charles. 1877. "Chorikos éloge du duc Aratios et du gouveneur Stephanos." *Revue de Philologie*, pp. 55–84.

Gravely, Norma J. 1978. "Sexist Humour as a Form of Social Control . . . or, Unfortunately . . . the Joke Is Usually on Us." In *Selections on the Status of Women in American Society*, ed. R. Winegarten. Austin: University of Texas Press.

Gray, Donald J. 1966. "The Uses of Victorian Laughter." *Victorian Studies* 10 (2): 145–76.

Gray, Frances. 1994. *Women and Laughter.* Charlottesville: University of Virginia Press.

Green, Julien. 1985. *God's Fool: The Life and Times of Francis of Assisi*. Trans. Peter Heinegg. San Francisco: Harper and Row.

Green, Martin, and John Swan. 1992. *The Triumph of Pierrot: The Commedia dell'Arte and the Modern Imagination*. New York: Macmillan.

Green, Rayna. 1977. "Magnolias Grow in Dirt: The Bawdy Lore of Southern Women." *Southern Exposure* 4:29–33.

Green, Thomas A., and W. J. Pepicello. 1978. "Wit in Riddling: A Linguistic Perspective." *Genre* 2 (Spring): 1–13.

Greenberg, A. 1972. "Form and Function of the Ethnic Joke." *Keystone Folklore Quarterly* 27:144–61.

Greenway, John, ed. 1966. *The Anthropologist Looks at Myth*. Austin: University of Texas Press.

Gregory, J. C. 1924. *The Nature of Laughter.* London: Kegan Paul, Trench.

Greig, J. Y. T. 1923. *The Psychology of Laughter and Comedy.* London: Allen and Unwin.

Grimes, William. 1993. "Encapsulating That Elusive Thing Called Humor." *New York Times*, August 24, sec. B, p. 1.

Grinberg, M., and S. Kinser. 1985. "Les combats de carnaval et de carême." *Annales E. S. C.* 38 (1): 65–98.

Groch, A. S. 1974. "Joking and Appreciation of Humor in Nursery School Children." *Child Development* 45:1098–1102.

Grotjahn, Martin. 1966. *Beyond Laughter: Humor and the Subconscious.* New York: McGraw-Hill.

Gruber, Wilhelm E. 1981. "The Wild Men of Comedy: Transformations in the Comic Hero from Aristophanes to Pirandello." *Genre* 14 (Summer): 207–27.

Gruden, Robert. 1974. "Renaissance Laughter: The Jests in Castiglione's *Il Cortegiano.*" *Neophilologus* 58:199–204.

Gruner, Charles R. 1978. *Understanding Laughter: The Workings of Wit and Humor.* Chicago: Nelson-Hall.

Gulliver, P. H. 1957. "Joking Relationships in Central Africa." *Man* 57:225–38.

Gurewitch, Morton. 1975. *Comedy: The Irrational Vision.* Ithaca: Cornell University Press.

Gutman, Jonathan, and Robert F. Priest. 1969. "When Is Aggression Funny?" *Journal of Personality and Social Psychology* 12:60–65.

Habicht, Werner. 1959. *Die Gebärde in englischen Dichtungen des Mittelalters.* München: Verlag der Bayerischen Akademie der Wissenschaften.

Haidu, Peter. 1977. "Repetition: Modern Reflections on Medieval Aesthetics." *Modern Language Notes* 92:875–87.

Hall, Audrey S., and William Quinn. 1982. *Jongleur: A Modified Theory of Oral Transmission.* Washington, D.C.: University Press of America.

Hall, Frank. 1974. "Conversational Joking: A Look at Applied Humor." *Folklore Annual of the University Student Association* 6:26–45.

Hammond, P. B. 1964. "Mossi Joking." *Ethnology* 3:259–67.

Hancher, Michael. 1980. "How to Play Games with Words: Speech-Act Jokes." *Journal of Literary Semantics* 9:1–20.

Handelman, Don, and B. Kapfirer. 1973. "Forms of Joking Activity: A Comparative Approach." *American Anthropologist* 74:484–517.

Handelman, Susan A. 1982. *The Slayers of Moses: The Emergence of Rabbinic Interpretation in Modern Literary Theory.* Albany: State University of New York Press.

Hanford, James Holly. 1926. "The Progenitors of Golias." *Speculum* 1:38–57.

Harris, Joel C., ed. *The World's Wit and Humor: An Encyclopedia of the Classic Wit and Humor of All Nations.* Metuchen, N.J.: Scarecrow Press.

Hartman, Geoffrey. 1981. *Saving the Text*. Baltimore: Johns Hopkins University Press.

Haskell, Molly. 1991. "Making Art of Angst." Review of *Woody Allen: A Biography*, by Eric Lax. *New York Times Book Review*, May 12, p. 1.

Haskins, Charles Homer. 1926. "The Spread of Ideas in the Middle Ages." *Speculum* 1:19–30.

Haskins, Jim. 1977. *The Cotton Club*. New York: Random House.

———. 1984. *Richard Pryor: A Man and His Madness*. New York: Beaufort Books.

Hastings, James, ed. 1923. *Encyclopedia of Religion and Ethics*. New York: Charles Scribner's Sons.

Hawkes, Terrence. 1980. "Comedy, Orality, and Duplicity: *A Midsummer Night's Dream* and *Twelfth Night*." In *Shakespearean Comedy*, ed. Maurice Charney. New York: New York Literary Forum.

Hazlitt, W. Carew. 1890. *Studies in Jocular Literature*. London: Elliot Stock.

Hearn, Francis. 1976. "Toward a Critical Theory of Play." *Telos* 30 (Winter): 145–60.

Hearne, Vicki. 1993. "Can an Ape Tell a Joke?" *Harper's*, November, pp. 58–69.

Heilbrun, Carolyn. 1979. "Woman as Outsider." In *Reinventing Womanhood*, pp. 37–70. New York: W. W. Norton.

Heller, L. G. 1974. "Toward a General Typology of the Pun." *Language and Style* 7:271–82.

Henkle, Roger B. 1980. *Comedy and Culture: England, 1820–1900*. Princeton: Princeton University Press.

Herondas. 1981. *The Mimes of Herondas*. Trans. Guy Davenport. San Francisco: Grey Fox Press.

Hertzler, Joyce O. 1970. *Laughter: A Socio-Scientific Analysis*. New York: Exposition Press.

Hess, Linda, and Skukdev Singh, trans. 1983. *The Bijak of Kabir.* San Francisco: North Point Press.

Hilbert, Richard. 1977. "Approaching Reason's Edge: Nonsense as the Final Solution to the Problem of Meaning." *Sociological Inquiry* 47:25–31.

Hill, W. W. 1943. *Navajo Humor.* General Series in Anthropology. Menasha: George Banta.

Hirshey, Gerri. 1989. "The Comedy of Hate." *Gentleman's Quarterly*, August, pp. 226 ff.

Hoa, N. D. 1955. "Double Puns in Vietnamese: A Case of 'Linguistic Play.'" *Word* 11:237–44.

Hobbes, Thomas. 1907. *The Leviathan; or, The Matter, Form and Power of a Commonwealth, Ecclesiastical and Civil.* London: Routledge.

Hockett, C. F. 1967. "Where the Tongue Slips, There Slip I." In *Honor Roman Jakobson*, 2:910–36. The Hague: Mouton.

———. 1977. *The View from Language: Selected Essays, 1948–1974.* Athens: University of Georgia Press.

Holland, Norman N. 1959. *The First Modern Comedies: The Significance of Etherege, Wycherly, and Congrave.* Cambridge: Harvard University Press.

———. 1968. *The Dynamics of Literary Response.* New York: Oxford University Press.

———. 1980. "Why Ellen Laughed." *Critical Inquiry* 7:345–71.

———. 1982. *Laughing: A Psychology of Humor.* Ithaca: Cornell University Press.

Holliday, Carl. 1975. *The Wit and Humor of Colonial Days, 1607–1800.* Williamstown, Mass.: Corner House.

Howard, J. H. 1962. "Peyote Jokes." *Journal of American Folklore* 75:10–14.

Howe, Irving. 1951. "The Nature of Jewish Laughter." *New American Mercury* 72:211–12.

Huet, Marie-Helene. 1993. *Monstrous Imagination.* Cambridge: Harvard University Press.

Hugh-Jones, Siriol. 1961. "We Witless Women." *Twentieth Century*, July, pp. 16–25.

Hughes. Derek. 1986. "Providential Justice and English Comedy, 1660–1700: A Review of the External Evidence." *Modern Language Review* 81:273–92.

Hughes, Langston. 1966. *The Book of Negro Humor.* New York: Dodd, Mead.

Hughes, Langston, and Arna Bontemps, eds. 1958. *The Book of Negro Folklore.* New York: Dodd, Mead.

Hugo, Victor. 1888. *The Man Who Laughs.* Boston: Little Publishers.

Huizinga, Johan. 1955. *Homo Ludens: A Study of the Play Element in Culture.* Boston: Beacon Press.

———. 1955. *The Waning of the Middle Ages.* London: Penguin Books.

Hunningher, Benjamin. 1961. *The Origin of the Theater: An Essay.* New York: Hill and Wang.

Hurwood, Bernhardt J., trans. 1968. *The Facetiae of Giovanni Francesco Poggio Bracciolini.* New York: Award Tandem Books.

Hutcheson, Francis. 1750. *Reflections on Laughter.* Glasgow: Privately published.

Hvidberg, Fleming Friis. 1962. *Weeping and Laughter in the Old Testament: A Study of Canaanite-Israelite Religion.* Leiden: E. J. Brill.

Hyde, Lewis. 1983. *The Gift: Imagination and the Erotic Life of Property.* New York: Vintage Books.

Hyers, M. Conrad, ed. 1969. *Holy Laughter: Essays on Religion in the Comic Perspective.* New York: Seabury Press.

Hynes, William, and Thomas Steele. 1981. "St. Peter: Apostle Transformed to Folk Trickster." *Arche* 6:1–18.

Illich, Ivan. 1985. *$H_2O$ and the Waters of Forgetfulness.* Dallas: Dallas Institute for the Humanities.

Ingram, Allan. 1986. *Intricate Laughter in the Satire of Swift and Pope.* New York: St. Martin's Press.

Jackson, John Hughlings. 1958. "An Address on the Psychology of Joking." In *Selected Writings of John Hughlings Jackson.* New York: Basic Books.

Jacobs, M. 1960. "Humor and Social Structure in an Oral Literature." In *Culture in History: Essays in Honor of Paul Radin,* ed. S. Diamond, pp. 180–89. New York: Columbia University Press.

Jacobson, E. 1946. "The Child's Laughter." *Psychoanalytic Study of the Child* 2:39–60.

Jaeger, C. Stephen. 1985. *The Origins of Courtliness: Civilizing Trends and the Formation of Courtly Ideals, 939–1210.* Philadelphia: University of Pennsylvania Press.

Jagendorf, Zvi. 1984. *The Happy End of Comedy: Jonson, Moliere, and Shakespeare.* Newark: University of Delaware Press.

Jeanson, Francis. 1950. *Signification humaine du rire.* Paris: Editions du Seuil.

Jefferson, Margo. 1994. "Seducified by a Minstrel Show." *New York Times,* March 22, "Arts and Leisure," p. 1.

Jefferson, Gail. 1979. "A Technique for Inviting Laughter and Its Subsequent Acceptance Declination." In *Everyday Language: Studies in Ethnomethodology,* ed. George Psathas, pp. 74–96. New York: Irvington Publishers.

Johnson, Ragnar. 1975. "The Semantic Structure of the Joke and Riddle: Theoretical Positioning." *Semiotica* 14 (2): 142–74.

———. 1977. "Two Realms and a Joke: Besociation Theories of Joking." *Semiotica* 16 (3): 195–221.

———. 1978. "Jokes, Theories, Anthropology." *Semiotica* 17 (2): 22–40.

Jones, W. H. S. 1946. *Philosophy and Medicine in Ancient Greece.* Bulletin of the History of Medicine, no. 8. Baltimore: Johns Hopkins University Press.

Jong, Erica. 1980. "You Have to Be Liberated to Laugh." *Playboy,* April, p. 208.

Jordan, Robert M. 1967. *Chaucer and the Shape of Creation.* Cambridge: Harvard University Press.

Joubert, Laurent. 1980. *Treatise on Laughter.* Trans. Gregory David de Rocher. Tuscaloosa: University of Alabama Press.

Jusserand, J. J. 1895. "Les contes à rire et la vie des réclusis au XIIe siècle d'après Aelred, abbé de Rievaulx." *Romania* 29:122.

Kadushin, Max. 1952. *The Rabbinic Mind.* New York: Block.

Kallen, Horace M. 1968. *Liberty, Laughter, and Tears.* De Kalb: Northern Illinois Press.

Kantorowicz, Ernst H. 1957. *The King's Two Bodies: A Study in Medieval Political Theology.* Princeton: Princeton University Press.

Kao, George, ed. 1946. *Chinese Wit and Humor.* New York: Coward-McCann.

Katzenellenbogen, Adolf. 1946. *Allegories of the Virtues and Vices in Medieval Art from the Early Christian Times to the Thirteenth Century.* Trans. Alan Crick. New York: W. W. Norton.

Kaufman, Gloria, ed. 1992. *Sketches: A Patchwork of Feminist Humor and Satire.* Bloomington: Indiana University Press.

Kaufman, Gloria, and Mary Kay Blakely, eds. 1980. *Pulling Our Own Strings: Feminist Humor and Satire.* Bloomington: Indiana University Press.

Kaufmann, Walter. 1956. *Existentialism from Dostoyevsky to Sartre.* New York: Meridian Books.

Kay, W. David. 1977. "Erasmus's Learned Joke: The Ironic Use of Classical Learning in the *Praise of Folly.*" *Texas Studies in Language and Literature* 19:248–67.

Kayser, W. 1963. *The Grotesque in Art and Literature.* Trans. Ulrich Weisstein. Bloomington: Indiana University Press.

Keller, Hans. 1957. "Lachen und Weinen." *Germanisch-Romanische Monakscheft,* n.s., 7:309–27.

Kelling, G. W. 1971. "An Empirical Investigation of Freud's Theory of Jokes." *Psychoanalytic Review* 58:473–85.

Kelly, L. G. 1971. "Punning and the Linguistic Sign." *Linguistics* 66: 5–11.

Kendrick, Laura. 1988. *Chaucerian Play: Comedy and Control in the Canterbury Tales.* Berkeley: University of California Press.

———. 1988. *The Game of Love: Troubadour Wordplay.* Berkeley: University of California Press.

Kennedy, John G. 1970. "Bond of Laughter among the Tarahumara Indians: Towards the Rethinking of Joking Relationship Theory." In *The Social Anthropology of Ralph Leon Beals,* ed. Walter Goldschmidt and Harry Hoijer, pp. 36–38. Berkeley: University of California Press.

Kenner, Hugh. 1981. "The Jokes at the Wake." *Massachusetts Review* 22 (4): 722–33.

———. 1990. *Historical Fictions*. San Francisco: North Point Press.

Kenney, W. Howland. 1979. *Laughter in the Wilderness: Early American Humor to 1783*. Kent, Ohio: Kent State University Press.

Keough, William. 1990. *Punchlines: The Violence of American Humor.* New York: Paragon.

Kerényi, Carl. 1962. *The Religion of the Greeks and Romans.* New York: E. P. Dutton.

Kermode, Frank. 1991. *The Uses of Error.* Cambridge: Harvard University Press.

Kern, Edith. 1980. *The Absolute Comic.* New York: Columbia University Press.

Kimmins, Charles W. 1928. *The Springs of Laughter.* London: Neill & Co.

Kincaid, James R. 1971. *Dickens and the Rhetoric of Laughter.* Oxford: Clarendon Press.

King, A. R. 1979. "North American Indian Clowns and Creativity." In *Forms of Play of Native North Americans*, ed. Edward Norbeck and Claire R. Farrer, pp. 143–51. New York: West Publishers.

Kinser, Samuel. 1986. "Presentation and Representation: Carnival at Nuremberg, 1450–1550." *Representations* 13 (Winter): 1–41.

———. 1990. *Rabelais' Carnival: Text, Context, Metatext.* Berkeley: University of California Press.

Kirshenblatt-Gimblett, Barbara, ed. 1976. *Speech Play: Research and Resources for the Study of Linguistic Creativity.* Philadelphia: University of Pennsylvania Press.

Kittel, Gerhard. 1949. *Theologisches Wörterbuch zum Neun Testament.* Trans. and ed. A. R. Coates. London: A. C. Black.

Klapp, O. E. 1949. "The Fool as Social Type." *American Journal of Sociology* 55:157–62.

———. 1962. *Heroes, Villains, and Fools.* Englewood Cliffs, N.J.: Prentice-Hall.

Klein, Julia. 1984. "The New Stand-up Comics: Can You Be a Funny Woman without Making Fun of Women?" *Ms.*, October, pp. 116–88.

Klein, Stewart. 1983. "The Queens of Comedy." *Harper's Bazaar*, Autumn, p. 166.

Knoepflmacher, U. C. 1971. *Laughter and Despair.* Berkeley: University of California Press.

Koepping, Klaus-Peter. 1985. "Absurdity and Hidden Truth: Cunning Intelligence and Grotesque Body Image as Manifestations of the Trickster." *History of Religions.*

Koestler, Arthur. 1964. *The Act of Creation.* London: Hutchinson.

———. "Humor and Wit." 1910. *Encyclopedia Britannica* 9:5–11.

Kofsky, Frank. 1974. *Lenny Bruce: The Comedian as Social Critic and Secular Moralist.* New York: Monad Press.

Kolve, V. A. 1966. *The Play Called Corpus Christi*. Palo Alto: Stanford University Press.

Korsmeyer, Carolyn. 1977. "The Hidden Joke: Generic Uses of Masculine Terminology." In *Feminism and Philosophy*, ed. Mary Vetterling-Braggin, Frederick A. Elliston, and Jane English. Totowa, N.J.: Littlefield, Adams.

Kravitz, S. 1977. "London Jokes and Ethnic Stereotypes." *Western Folklore* 26:275–301.

Kreitler, H., and S. Kreitler. 1970. "Dependence of Laughter on Cognitive Strategies." *Merrill-Palmer Quarterly* 16:163–77.

Kris, Ernst. 1971. "Ego Development and the Comic." In *Psychoanalytic Explorations in Art*, pp. 204–16. New York: Schocken Books.

Kronenberger, Louis. 1952. *The Thread of Laughter.* New York: Alfred A. Knopf.

Kundera, Milan. 1981. *The Book of Laughter and Forgetting*. New York: Alfred A. Knopf.

———. 1982. *The Joke*. New York: Harper and Row.

———. 1984. *The Unbearable Lightness of Being*. New York: Harper and Row.

Kurath, Hans, and Sherwood M. Kuhn. 1954. *Middle English Dictionary.* Ann Arbor: University of Michigan Press.

La Capra, Dominique. 1983. "Bakhtin, Marxism, and the Carnivalesque." In *Rethinking Intellectual History*, pp. 291–324. Ithaca, N.Y.: Cornell University Press.

Lachmann, Renate. 1987. *Bakhtin and Carnival.* Minneapolis: Center for Humanities Studies, University of Minnesota.

Ladurie, Emmanuel Le Roy. 1979. *Carnival in Romans*. Trans. Mary Feeney. New York: George Braziller.

La Gaipa, J. J. 1968. "Stress, Authoritarianism, and the Enjoyment of Different Kinds of Hostile Humor." *Journal of Psychology* 70:3–8.

Langer, Suzanne. 1953. *Feeling and Form: A Theory of Art.* New York: Charles Scribner's Sons.

Latour, M. 1956. *Le problème du rire et du réel.* Paris: Hachette.

Leacock, Stephen. 1935. *Humor: Its Theory and Technique with Examples and Samples*. New York: Dodd, Mead.

———. 1938. *Humor and Humanity: An Introduction to the Study of Humor.* New York: Thornton and Butterworth.

Legman, G. 1968. *The Rationale of the Dirty Joke: An Analysis of Sexual Humor.* New York: Grove Press.

———. 1982. The *Rationale of the Dirty Joke: No Laughing Matter.* New York: Breaking Point.

Le Goff, Jacques. 1985. *The Medieval Imagination*. Trans. Arthur Goldhammer. Chicago: University of Chicago Press.

Lehman, Benjamin H. 1941. *Studies in the Comic*. Berkeley: University of California Press.

Leonard, Frances McNeely. 1981. *Laughter in the Courts of Love: Comedy in Allegory, from Chaucer to Spenser.* Norman, Okla.: Pilgrim Books.

Levin, Harry. 1987. *Playboys and Killjoys: An Essay on the Theory and Practice of Comedy.* New York: Oxford University Press.

Levine, Jacob. 1961. "Regression in Primitive Clowning." *Psychoanalytic Quarterly* 30:72–83.

———. 1969. *Motivation in Humor.* New York: Atherton Press.

Levine, Jacob, and F. C. Redlich. 1955. "Failure to Understand Humor." *Psychoanalytic Quarterly* 24:560–72.

Levine, Joan B. 1976. "The Feminine Routine." *Journal of Communication* 26 (3): 173–75.

Levine, Lawrence W. 1987. *Black Culture and Black Consciousness: Afro-American Folk Thought from Slavery to Freedom*. New York: Oxford University Press.

———. 1994. "Laughing Matters." Review of *On the Real Side*, by Mel Watkins. *New York Times Book Review*, February 27, p. 1.

Levine, Robert. 1982. "Wolfram Von Eschenbach: Dialectical 'Homo Ludens.'" *Viator* 13:177–201.

Levy, H. L. "'As myn auctour seyth.'" *Medium Aevum* 12:25–39.

Lewis, C. S. 1967. *Studies in Words*. 2d ed. Cambridge: Cambridge University Press.

Lewis, Paul. 1981. "Mysterious Laughter: Humor and Fear in Gothic Fiction." *Genre* 14 (Fall): 309–27.

Limon, Jose E. 1989. "Carne, Carnales, and the Carnivalesque: Bakhtinier Batos, Disorder, and Narrative Discourses." *American Anthropologist* 16:471–86.

Lipking, B. 1970. "Traditions of the *Facetiae* and Their Influence in Tudor England." Doctoral dissertation, Columbia University, New York.

Lloyd, Ernest L. 1938. "The Respiratory Mechanism in Laughter." *Journal of General Psychology* 19:179–89.

Longobard, P. G. 1975. "Comprehension of Joke Humor in Schizophrenia." Doctoral dissertation, University of Wisconsin, Madison.

Loomans, Diane, and Karen Kolberg. 1993. *The Laughing Classroom: Everyone's Guide to Teaching with Humor and Play.* Tiburon, Calif.: H. J. Kramer.

Lott, Eric. 1993. *Blackface Ministrelsy and the American Working Class*. New York: Oxford University Press.

Lowe, John. 1987. "Hurston, Humor, and the Harlem Renaissance." In *The Harlem Renaissance Re-examined*, ed. Victor A. Kramer, pp. 283–313. New York: AMS Press.

Ludovici, Anthony. 1932. *The Secret of Laughter.* London: Constable.

Lynn, Kenneth. 1958. *The Comic Tradition in America.* New York: Doubleday.

McCullough, Joseph B. 1985. "Shades of Red and Black: A Consideration of Modern Humor by Women." *Amerikanstudien* 30 (2): 191–201.

McDougall, William. 1903. "The Theory of Laughter." *Nature* 67:318–19.

———. 1922. "A New Theory of Laughter." *Psyche*, n.s., 2.

McGhee, Paul E. 1974. "Development of Children's Ability to Create the Joking Relationship." *Child Development* 45:552–56.

———. 1976. "Sex Differences in Children's Humor." *Journal of Communication* 26:176–89.

———. 1979. "The Role of Laughter and Humor in Growing Up Female." In *Becoming Female: Perspectives on Development*, ed. Claire B. Kopp, pp. 183–206. New York: Plenum Press.

———. 1979. *Humor: Its Origin and Development.* San Francisco: W. H. Freeman.

———. 1972. *The Psychology of Humor.* New York: Academic Press.

McGhee, Paul E., and Jeffrey H. Goldstein, eds. 1983. *Handbook of Humor Research.* Vol. 2. New York: Springer-Verlag.

McGhee, Paul E., and P. Grodzitsky. 1973. "Sex-Role Identification and Humor among the School Children." *Journal of Communication* 84:189–93.

McGlashan, Alan. 1976. *Gravity and Levity.* London: Chatto and Windus.

McGuigan, Cathleen, and Janel Huck. 1984. "The New Queens of Comedy: Women Comics Aren't Putting Themselves Down When They Do Stand Up." *Newsweek*, April 30, p. 58.

McPeek, James A. S. 1951. "Chaucer and the Goliards." *Speculum* 26:332–36.

Macaulay, Ronald K. S. 1983. "The Social Significance of Scottish Dialect Humor." Paper delivered at WHIM Conference on Linguistic Humor, University of Arizona, Tucson.

Macionis, John. 1989. *Sociology.* 2d ed. New York: Prentice-Hall.

Makarius, L. 1970. "Ritual Clowns and Symbolic Behavior." *Diogenes* 69:44–73.

Maltin, Leonard. 1978. *The Great Movie Comedians: From Charlie Chaplin to Woody Allen.* New York: Crown.

Manea, Norman. 1992. *On Clowns: The Dictator and the Artist.* New York: Grove Press.

Marc, David. 1989. *Comic Visions: Television Comedy and American Culture*. Boston: Unwin Hyman.

Martin, Linda, and Kerry Segrave. 1986. *Women in Comedy*. Secaucus, N.J.: Citadel Press.

Mast, G. 1973. *The Comic Mind*. New York: Bobbs-Merrill.

Mathewson, Louise. 1920. *Bergson's Theory of the Comic in the Light of English Comedy*. University of Nebraska Studies in Language, Literature, and Criticism, 5. Lincoln, Nebraska.

Maurice, Arthur B. 1910. "Feminine Humorists." *Good Housekeeping* 50 (January): 34–39.

Mauron, Charles. 1964. *Psycho-critique du genre comique*. Paris: Corti.

Mayer, P. 1951. "The Joking of 'Pals' in Gusii Age-Sets.'" *African Studies* 10:27–41.

Mehlman, Jeffrey. 1975. "How to Read Freud on Jokes: The Critic as Schadchen." *New Literary History* 6, no. 2 (Winter): 439–61.

Mellencamp, Patricia. 1986. "Situation Comedy, Feminism, and Freud: Discourses of Gracie and Lucy." In *Studies in Entertainment: Critical Approaches to Mass Culture*, ed. Tania Modleski. Bloomington: Indiana University Press.

Mellinkoff, Ruth. 1973. "Riding Backwards: The Theme of Humiliation and Symbol of Evil." *Viator* 4:153–76.

Menard, Philippe. 1969. *Le rire et le sourire dans le roman courtois en France au Moyen Age, 1150–1250*. Publications Romances et Francaises, 105. Geneva.

Mendel, Werner M., ed. 1970. *A Celebration of Laughter*. Los Angeles: Mara Books.

Menon, V. K. Krishna. 1931. *A Theory of Laughter*. London: Allen and Unwin.

Merchant, W. M. 1972. *Comedy*. London: Methuen.

Meredith, George. 1956. "An Essay on Comedy." In *Comedy*, ed. Wylie Sypher. Garden City, N.Y.: Doubleday, Anchor Books.

Metcalf, Fred, ed. 1986. *The Penguin Dictionary of Modern Humourous Quotations*. London: Penguin Books.

———. 1992. *The Penguin Dictionary of Jokes*. London: Penguin Books.

Middleton, Russell, and John Moland. 1959. "Humor in Negro and White Subcultures: A Study of Jokes among University Students." *American Sociological Review* 24:61–69.

Mikhail, E. H. 1972. *Comedy and Tragedy: A Bibliography of Critical Studies*. Troy, N.Y.: Whitson Publishing.

Miller, F. C. 1967. "Humor in a Chippewa Tribal Council." *Ethnology* 6:263–71.

Miller, Jacqueline T. 1987. *Poetic License: Authority and Authorship in Medieval and Renaissance Contexts*. New York: Oxford University Press.

Milner, G. B. 1972. "Homo Ridens: Towards a Semiotic Theory of Humor and Laughter." *Semiotica* 5:1–30.

Minnix, Kathleen. 1993. *Laughter in the Amen Corner: The Life of Evangelist Sam Jones*. Athens: University of Georgia Press.

Mitchell, Carol A. 1977. "The Sexual Perspective in the Appreciation and Interpretation of Jokes." *Western Folklore* 36 (4): 303–29.

———. 1978. "Hostility and Aggression toward Males in Female Joke Telling." *Frontiers* 3, no. 3 (Fall): 19–23.

———. 1985. "Some Differences in Male and Female Joke-Telling." In *Women's Folklore, Women's Culture*, ed. Jordan Rosan and Susan J. Kalcik, pp. 163–86. Philadelphia: University of Pennsylvania Press.

Mitchell, William E., ed. 1992. *Clowning as Critical Practice: Performance Humor in the South Pacific*. Pittsburgh: University of Pittsburgh Press.

Monnot, Michel. 1982. *Selling America: Puns, Language, and Advertising*. New York: University Press of America.

Monuro, D. H. 1951. *Argument of Laughter*. New York: Cambridge University Press.

Moreau, R. E. 1941. "The Joking Relationship (Utani) in Tanganyika." *Tanganyika Notes and Records* 12:1–10.

———. 1943. "Joking Relationships in Tanganyika." *Africa* 14:386–400.

Morreall, John. 1983. *Taking Laughter Seriously*. Albany: State University of New York Press.

Morris, Linda Ann Finton. 1978. "Women Vernacular Humorists in Nineteenth-Century America: Ann Stephens, Frances Whitcher, and Marietta Holley." Doctoral dissertation, University of California, Berkeley.

Mulkay, Michael. 1988. *On Humor: Its Nature and Place in Modern Society*. New York: Basil Blackwell.

Murdoch, Iris. 1977. *The Fire and the Sun: Why Plato Banished the Artists*. Oxford: Clarendon Press.

Myers, Henry A. 1935. "The Analysis of Laughter." *Scientific Review* 43: 452–63.

Nash, Walter. 1985. *The Language of Humour: Style and Technique in Comic Discourse*. English Language Series, no. 16. London: Longman.

Neitz, Mary Jo. 1980. "Humor, Hierarchy, and the Changing Status of Women." *Psychiatry* 43 (August): 211–23.

Nelson, William. 1969. "The Boundaries of Fiction in the Renaissance: A Treaty between Truth and Falsehood." *English Literary History* 36: 30–58.

———. 1973. *Fact or Fiction: The Dilemma of the Renaissance Story Teller*. Cambridge: Harvard University Press.

Neu, Jerome. 1987. "A Tear Is an Intellectual Thing." *Representations* 19 (Summer): 35–61.

Neumann, Siegfried. 1969. "Volkprosa mit Komischen Inhalt: Zur Problematik ihres Gehalts und ihrer Differenzierung." *Fabula* 9:137–48.

Nevo, Ruth. 1964. "Towards a Theory of Comedy." *Journal of Aesthetics and Art Criticism* 21:98–208.

Nicoll, Allardyce. 1931. *Masks, Mimes, and Miracles: Studies in the Popular Theatre*. London: George G. Harrap.

Nietzsche, Friedrich. 1966. *Beyond Good and Evil: Prelude to a Philosophy of the Future*. Trans. Walter Kaufmann. New York: Random House.

Nohain, Jean. 1965. *Histoire du rire à travers le monde*. Paris: Hachette.

Norris, W. Yates. 1964. *The American Humorist: Conscience of the Twentieth Century.* Ames: Iowa State University Press.

Novak, William, and Moshe Waldoks, eds. 1981. *The Big Book of Jewish Humor.* New York: Harper and Row.

Nykrog, Per. 1957. *Les fabliaux: Etude d'histoire litteraire et de stylistique medievale*. Copenhagen: Munksgaard.

Obrdlik, Antonin J. 1942. "'Gallows Humor': A Sociological Phenomenon." *American Journal of Sociology* 47:709–16.

O'Connell, W. E. 1960. "The Adaptive Functions of Wit and Humor." *Journal of Abnormal and Social Psychology* 61:263–70.

———. 1964. "Resignation, Humor, and Wit." *Psychoanalytic Review* 51:49–56.

———. 1968. "Humor and Death." *Psychological Reports* 22:391–402.

———. 1969. "Creativity in Humor." *Journal of Social Psychology* 78:237–41.

———. 1969. "The Social Aspects of Wit and Humor." *Journal of Social Psychology* 79:183–82.

Oehlschlaeger, Fritz. 1993. *Old Southwest Humor from the St. Louis Reveille, 1844–1850*. Columbia: University of Missouri Press.

Ogilvy, J. D. 1963. "Mimi, Scurrae, Histriones: Entertainers of the Early Middle Ages." *Speculum* 38:603–19.

Ollbrechts-Tyteca, Lucie. 1974. *Le comique du discours*. Brussels: University of Brussels.

Olson, Glending. 1982. *Literature as Recreation in the Later Middle Ages*. Ithaca: Cornell University Press.

Olson, Paul A. 1986. *The Canterbury Tales and the Good Society.* Princeton: Princeton University Press.

Oring, Elliott. 1981. *Israeli Humor: The Content and Structure of the Chizbat of the Palmah*. Albany: SUNY Press.

———. 1984. *The Jokes of Sigmund Freud: A Study in Humor and Jewish Identity.* Philadelphia: University of Pennsylvania Press.

———. 1992. *Jokes and Their Relations.* Lexington: University Press of Kentucky.

Owens, Charles A. Jr. 1977. *Pilgrimage and Storytelling in the Canterbury Tales: The Dialectic of "Ernest" and "Game."* Norman: University of Oklahoma Press.

Owst, G. R. 1926. *Preaching in Medieval England.* Cambridge: Cambridge University Press.

Pagnol, Marcel. 1962. *Notes sur le rire.* Monte Carlo: Pastorelle.

Paredes, A. 1973. "Folk Medicine and the Intercultural Jest." In *Introduction to Chicano Studies*, ed. L. I. Duran and H. R. Bernard, pp. 261–75. New York: Macmillan.

Parker, Richard G. 1991. *Bodies, Pleasures, and Passions: Sexual Culture in Contemporary Brazil.* Boston: Beacon Press.

Parsons, E. C., and R. L. Beals. 1934. "The Sacred Clowns of the Pueblos and Mayo-Yaqui Indians." *American Anthropologist* 36:491–514.

Partridge, Eric, ed. 1970. *A Dictionary of Slang and Unconventional English.* 7th ed. New York: Macmillan.

Patrides, C. A. 1989. "Homer: The Invention of Reality." *Michigan Quarterly Review* 28, no. 3 (Summer): 305–22.

Paulos, John Allen. 1980. *Mathematics and Humor.* Chicago: University of Chicago Press.

———. 1988. *Innumeracy: Mathematical Illiteracy and Its Consequences.* New York: Hill and Wang.

Payne, F. Anne. 1981. *Chaucer and Menippean Satire.* Madison: University of Wisconsin Press.

Paz, Octavio. 1962. *Magia de la risa.* Mexico: Universidad Veracruzana.

Pearson, H. 1962. *Lives of the Wits.* New York: Harper and Row.

Pedler, F. J. 1940. "Joking Relationships in East Africa." *Africa* 13:170–73.

Pelton, Robert D. 1980. *The Trickster in West Africa: A Study of Mythic Irony and Sacred Delight.* Berkeley: University of California Press.

Peto, Endre. 1946. "Weeping and Laughing." *International Journal of Psychoanalysis* 27:129–33.

Petrarca, Francesco. 1943. *Renim memorandum libri.* Ed. Giuseppe Billanovich. Firenze: Sansoni.

Philips, Susan. *Teasing, Punning, and Putting People On.* Working Papers In Sociolinguistics, 28. Austin: Department of Anthropology, University of Texas.

Piddington, Ralph. 1933. *The Psychology of Laughter: A Study in Social Adaptation*. London: Figurehead.

Plessner, Helmuth. 1961. *Lachen und Weinen*. Bern: Francke Verlag.

Pliny the Elder. 1952. *Natural History*. Vols. 7, 16. Ed. H. Rockham. Cambridge: Harvard University Press.

Polhemus, Robert M. 1980. *Comic Faith: The Great Tradition from Austen to Joyce*. Chicago: University of Chicago Press.

Pope-Hennessy, John. 1968. "The Virgin with the Laughing Child." In *Essays on Italian Sculpture*, pp. 72–77. London: Thames and Hudson.

Powell, Chris, and George E. C. Paton, eds. 1988. *Humor in Society: Resistance and Control*. New York: St. Martin's Press.

Prange, A. J., and M. M. Vitols. 1963. "Jokes among Southern Negroes: The Revelation of Conflict." *Journal of Nervous and Mental Diseases* 136:162–67.

Priestly, J. B. 1925. *English Comic Characters*. London: Bodley Head.

———. 1929. *English Humour*. London: Longmans, Green.

Rabinowitz, Isaac. 1972. "'Word' and Literature in Ancient Israel." *New Literary History* 4, no. 1 (Autumn): 119–39.

Radcliffe-Brown, A. R. 1940. "On Joking Relationships." *Africa* 13:195–210.

———. 1949. "A Further Note on Joking Relationships." *Africa* 19:133–40.

Radcliff-Umstead, Douglas. 1986. *Carnival Comedy and Sacred Play: The Renaissance Drama of Giovan Maria Cecchi*. Columbia: University of Missouri Press.

Radin, Paul. 1956. *The Trickster: A Study in American Indian Mythology*. London: Routledge and Kegan Paul.

Rahner, Hugo. 1949. "Der spielende Mensch." *Eranos-Jahrbuch* 16:29.

———. 1967. *Men at Play*. New York: Herder and Herder.

Rainer, Peter. 1975. "Interview: Five Women Comedy Writers Talk about Being Funny for Money." *Mademoiselle*, November, p. 86.

Randall, Lilian M. C. 1966. "Humor and Fantasy in the Margins of an English Book of Hours." *Apollo* 84:482–88.

———. 1972. "Games and Passion in Pucelle's *Hours of Jean d'Evreux*." *Speculum* 42:246–57.

Ransom, Daniel. 1985. *Poets at Play: Irony and Parody in the Harley Lyrics*. Norman, Okla.: Pilgrim Books.

Raskin, Victor. 1985. *Semantic Mechanisms of Humor*. Boston: D. Reidel.

———. 1985. "Jokes." *Psychology Today*, October, pp. 34–39.

———. 1985. "Telling Good Humor from Bad: Limitations of the Linguistics of Humor." In *The Fifth International Conference on Humor*, ed. Desmonde MacHale. Dun Looghire, Ireland: Boole.

Rather, Lois. 1971. "Were Women Funny? Some Nineteenth Century Humorists." *American Book Collector* 21 (5): 4–10.

Raulin, Jules Marie. 1900. *Le rire et les exhilarants*. Paris: J. B. Baillière et fils.

Rebolledo, Tey Diana. 1985. "Walking the Thin Line: Humor in Chicana Literature." In *Beyond Stereotypes: The Critical Analysis of Chicana Literature*, ed. Maria Herrera-Sobek, pp. 91–107. Binghamton: Bilingual Press.

Redfern, Walter. 1984. *Puns*. Oxford: Basil Blackwell.

Reich, A. 1950. "The Structure of the Grotesque-Comic Sublimation." In *The Yearbook of Psychoanalysis*, 6:194–207. New York: International Universities Press.

Reich, Hermann. 1903. *Der Mimus*. Berlin: Weidmann.

Reik, Theodore. 1962. *Jewish Wit*. New York: Gamut.

Repplier, Agnes. 1936. *In Pursuit of Laughter.* Boston: Houghton Mifflin.

Resnick, I. M. 1987. "Risus Monasticus: Laughter and Medieval Monastic Culture." *Revue Benedictine* 97:90–100.

Reynolds, V. 1958. "Joking Relationships in Africa." *Man* 58:29–30.

Rheingold, Harriet L. 1967. "The Social and Socializing Infant." In *Concept of Development*, ed. H. W. Stevenson. Monograph of the Society for Research and Child Development.

Richler, Mordecai. 1983. *The Best of Modern Humor.* New York: Alfred A. Knopf.

Rieu, E. V., trans. 1945. *The Odyssey.* Baltimore, Md.: Penguin Books.

Rigby, Peter. 1968. "Joking Relationships, Kin Categories, and Clanship among the Gogo." *Africa* 38:133–55.

Rinder, Irwin D. 1965. "A Note on Humor as an Index of Minority Group Morale." *Phylon: The Atlanta University Review of Race and Culture* 26, no. 2 (Summer): 117–21.

Robertson, Nan. 1985. "Milan Kundera Accepts the Jerusalem Prize." *New York Times*, May 10, p. 24.

Robbins, Rossell Hope, trans. 1960. *The Hundred Tales*. New York: Crown Publishers.

Robinson, Fred Miller. 1992. *Comic Moments*. Athens: University of Georgia Press.

Robinson, Edward, trans. 1959. *A Hebrew-English Lexicon of the Old Testament.* Oxford: Oxford University Press.

Rocher, Gregory de. 1978. "Le rire au temps de la Renaissance: Le *Traite du Ris* de Laurent Joubert." *Revue Belge de Philologie et d'Histoire* 56:629–40.

———. 1979. *Rabelais's Laughers and Joubert's "Traite du Ris."* Tuscaloosa: University of Alabama Press.

Rodway, Allan. 1975. *English Comedy: Its Role and Nature from Chaucer to the Present Day.* Berkeley: University of California Press.

Rohrich, Lutz. 1977. *Der Witz: Figuren, Formen, Funktionen.* Stuttgart: Carl Ernst Palschel Verlag.

Rollins, Alice Wellington. 1884. "The Humor of Women." *Critic and Good Literature*, n.s., 26 (June 28): 301–2.

———. 1884. "Women's Sense of Humor." *Critic and Good Literature*, n.s., 13 (March 29): 145–46.

Rosaldo, Renato. 1987. "Politics, Patriarchs, and Laughter." *Cultural Critique* 6:65–86.

Rosenberg, Bernard, and Gilbert Shapiro. 1958. "Marginality and Jewish Humor." *Midstream* 4:70–80.

Rosenthal, F. 1956. *Humor in Early Islam.* Philadelphia: University of Pennsylvania Press.

Ross, Thomas W., ed. 1972. *Chaucer's Bawdy.* New York: Dutton.

———. 1983. *A Variorum Edition of the Works of Geoffrey Chaucer: The Miller's Tale.* Norman: University of Oklahoma Press.

Rourke, Constance. 1931. *American Humor: A Study of the National Character.* New York: Harcourt, Brace.

Roy, Bruno. 1975. "L'humor érotique au XVe siècle." In *L'érotisme au Moyen Age*, ed. Bruno Roy. Montreal: Presses de l'Universite de Montreal.

Rubin, Louis D. Jr., ed. 1973. *The Comic Imagination in American Literature.* New Brunswick, N.J.: Rutgers University Press.

Rubinstein, Henri. 1983. *Psychosomatique du rire.* Paris: R. Laffont.

Rudolf, Georg. 1981. *The Theatrical Notation of Roman and Pre-Shakespearean Comedy.* Bern: Francke Verlag.

Ruggiers, Paul, ed. 1977. *Versions of Medieval Comedy.* Norman: University of Oklahoma Press.

Russell, Leonard, ed. 1941. *English Wits.* London: Hutchinson.

Russo, Mary. 1986. "Female Grotesques: Carnival and Theory." *Feminist Studies/ Critical Studies*, ed. Teresa de Lauretis. Bloomington: Indiana University Press.

Sacks, Harvey. 1973. "On Some Puns with some Intimations." In *Sociolinguistics*, ed. R. W. Shuy, pp. 135–44. Washington, D.C.: Georgetown University Press.

———. 1974. "An Analysis of the Course of a Joke's Telling in Conversation." In *Explorations in the Ethnology of Speaking*, ed. Richard Bauman and Joel Scherzer, pp. 337–53. New York: Cambridge University Press.

———. 1978. "Some Technical Considerations of a Dirty Joke." In *Studies in the Organization of Conversational Interaction*, ed. J. Schenkein, pp. 249–70. New York: Academic Press.

Sagarin, Edward. 1962. *The Anatomy of Dirty Words*. New York: Lyle Stuart.

Saint, Denis E. de. 1965. *Essai sur le rire et le sourire des Latins*. Paris: Société des Belles Lettres.

Sakuma, Makoto. 1974. *Laughter as a Weapon*. Tokyo: Seijo University.

Salemi, Joseph S. 1983. "Selections from the Facetiae of Poggio Brocciolini." *Allegorica* 8, nos. 1 and 2 (Summer/Winter): 77–183.

Salingar, Leo. 1974. *Shakespeare and the Traditions of Comedy.* New York: Cambridge University Press.

Samarin, William J. 1969. "The Forms and Functions of Nonsense Languages." *Linguistics* 50:70–74.

Sanborn, Kate. 1885. *The Wit of Women*. New York: Funk and Wagnalls.

Sangree, M. L. 1972. "Laughter in Small Groups." Doctoral dissertation, State University of New York at Buffalo.

Sapir, Edward. 1932. "Two Navaho Puns." *Language* 8:217–19.

Saward, John. 1975. "The Fool for Christ's Sake in Monasticism East and West." *Theology and Prayer.* Vol. 3. Oxford: Oxford University Press.

Schaeffer, Neil. 1981. *The Art of Laughter.* New York: Columbia University Press.

Schechter, William. 1970. *The History of Negro Humor in America*. New York: Fleet Press.

Schiller, Paul. 1938. "A Configurational Theory of Jokes and Puzzles." *Journal of General Psychology* 18:217–34.

Schilling, Bernard N. 1965. *The Comic Spirit: Boccaccio to Thomas Mann*. Detroit, Mich.: Wayne State University Press.

Schlauch, Margaret. 1966. "English Short Fiction in the Fifteenth and Sixteenth Centuries." *Studies in Short Fiction* 3, no. 4 (Summer): 393–435.

Schless, Howard H. 1961. "The Comic Element in the Wakefield Noah." In *Studies in Medieval Literature*, ed. MacEdward Leach. Philadelphia: University of Pennsylvania Press.

———. 1976. "Dante: Comedy and Conversion." *Genre* 9 (77): 415.

Schmitt, Jean-Claude, ed. 1984. "Gesture." *History and Anthropology* 1:1–228.

Schneidau, Herbert N. 1976. *Sacred Discontent: The Bible and Western Tradition*. Berkeley: University of California Press.

Schnitz, Neil. 1983. *Of Huck and Alice: Humorous Writing in American Literature*. Minneapolis: University of Minneapolis Press.

Schoeck, Helmut. 1966. *Envy: A Theory of Social Behavior.* New York: Harcourt, Brace and World.

Schutz, Charles. 1977. *Political Humor: From Aristophanes to Sam Ervin.* Cranberry, N.J.: Fairleigh Dickinson University Press.

Schweiger, Werner Rudolph. 1964. *Der Witz.* Bern: Francke Verlag.

Screech, Michael A., and Ruth Calder. 1920. "Some Renaissance Attitudes to Laughter." In *Humanism in France*, ed. A. H. T. Levi. London: Manchester University Press.

Sebeok, Thomas A., ed. 1984. *Carnival!* Berlin: Mouton.

Segal, Daniel. 1984. "Playing Doctor, Seriously: Graduation Follies at an American Medical School." *International Journal of Health Services* 14 (3): 379–96.

Segal, Eric. 1968. *Roman Laughter: The Comedy of Plautus.* Cambridge: Harvard University Press.

Seitel, Peter. 1977. "Blocking the Wind: A Haya Folktale and an Interpretation." *Western Folklore* 36, no. 3 (July): 189–207.

Sellers, Pat. 1987. "Funny Ladies: Stand-Up's Newest Standouts." *Cosmopolitan*, September, pp. 290–93.

Serres, Michael. 1982. *The Parasite.* Trans. Lawrence R. Schehr. Baltimore: Johns Hopkins University Press.

Sessions, William H. 1967. *More Quaker Laughter.* London: William Sessions.

Seward, Samuel Swayze. 1930. *The Paradox of the Ludicrous.* Palo Alto: Stanford University Press.

Sewell, Elizabeth. 1952. *The Field of Nonsense.* London: Chatto and Windus.

Sharman, Anne. "'Joking' in Padhola: Categorical Relationships, Choice, and Social Control." *Man* 4:103–17.

Sheppard, Alice. 1976. "Humor and Sex-Role Stereotypes." Paper presented at the International Conference on Humor and Laughter, Cardiff, Wales.

———. 1985. "Funny Women: Social Change and Audience Response to Female Comedians." *Empirical Studies of the Arts* 3:179–95.

———. 1986. "From Kate Sanborn to Feminist Psychology: The Social Context of Women's Humor, 1885–1985." *Psychology of Women Quarterly* 10:155–70.

Shershow, Scott Cutler. 1986. *Laughing Matters: The Paradox of Comedy.* Amherst: University of Massachusetts Press.

Sherzer, Joel. 1978. "Oh! That's a Pun and I Didn't Mean It." *Semiotica* 22:269–85.

———. 1985. "Puns and Jokes." In *Handbook of Discourse Analysis*, vol. 3, ed. Teun A. Van Dijk. London: Academic Press.

Shultz, T. R., and F. Horibe. 1974. "Development of the Appreciation of Verbal Jokes." *Developmental Psychology* 10:13–20.

Sidis, Boris. 1919. *The Psychology of Laughter.* New York: Appleton.

Simmons, D. C. 1963. "Protest Humor: Folkloristic Reaction to Prejudice." *American Journal of Psychiatry* 120:567–70.

Sinclair, Keith Val. 1978. "Comic Audigier in England." *Romania* 104: 257–59.

Skeels, D. 1954. "A Classification of Humor in Nez Perce Mythology." *Journal of American Folklore* 67:57–63.

Slater, E., and F. H. Freshfield. 1899. "The Sense of Humor in Men." *Cornhill* 3d ser., 6:347–52.

Sloane, David E. E., ed. 1983. *The Literary Humor of the Urban Northeast, 1830–1890.* Baton Rouge: Louisiana State University Press.

Smith, Sarah Stansbury. 1983. "'Game in Myn Hood': The Traditions of a Comic Proverb." *Studies in Iconography* 9:1–11.

Sochen, June, ed. 1991. *Women's Comic Visions.* Detroit: Wayne State University Press.

Sorell, W. 1972. *Facets of Comedy.* New York: Grosset and Dunlap.

Spade, Paul Vincent. 1975. *The Medieval Liar: A Catalogue of the Insolubilia Literature.* Toronto: Pontifical Institute.

Spalding, Henry D. 1980. *A Treasury of Italian Folklore and Humor.* New York: Jonathan David Publishers.

Spanchkeren, Kathryn Van. 1985. "A Funny Thing Happened on the Way to the Apocalypse: Laurie Anderson and Humor in Women's Performance Art." *Studies in American Humor*, n.s., nos. 1 and 2 (Spring/Summer): 94–104.

Specter, Michael. 1994. "Odessa, Where Reality Is a Laugh a Minute." *New York Times*, April 3, sec. E, p. 3.

Spencer, Herbert. 1911. *On the Physiology of Laughter: Essays on Education and Kindred Subjects.* London: Dent.

Speroni, Charles, ed. 1964. *Wit and Wisdom of the Italian Renaissance.* Berkeley: University of California Press.

Starkman, Miriam, ed. 1962. *Swift: Gulliver's Travels and Other Writings.* New York: Bantam Books.

Steadman, John M. 1972. *Disembodied Laughter: Troilus and the Apotheosis Tradition.* Berkeley: University of California Press.

Stearns, Frederic R. 1972. *Laughing: Physiology, Pathophysiology, Psychology, Pathopsychology, and Development.* Springfield, Ill.: Charles C. Thomas.

Stebbins, Robert A. 1990. *The Laugh Makers: Stand-up Comedy as Art, Business, and Life-Style.* Montreal: McGill–Queen's University Press.

Steegmuller, Francis. 1988. "The Abbé Geliani: 'The Laughing Philosopher.'" *American Scholar* 57: 589–97.

Stein, Charles W., ed. 1984. *American Vaudeville: As Seen by Its Contemporaries.* New York: Alfred A. Knopf.

Steinem, Gloria. 1978. "If Men Could Menstruate." *Ms.*, October, p. 110.

Steiner, Rudolf. 1981. *The Being of Man and His Future Revolution.* Trans. Pauline Wehrle. London: Rudolf Steiner Press.

Sterling, Philip. 1965. *Laughing on the Outside: The Intelligent White Reader's Guide to Negro Tales and Humor.* New York: Grosset and Dunlap.

Stern, Alfred. 1949. *Philosophie du rire et des pleurs.* Paris: Presses Universitaires de France.

———. 1958. "Why Do We Laugh and Cry?" In *Frontiers in Science*, ed. Edward Hutchings. New York: Basic Books.

Stevens, Philip Jr. 1978. "Bachama Joking Categories: Toward New Perspectives in the Study of Joking Relationships." *Journal of Anthropological Research* 34:47–71.

Steward, J. 1931. "The Ceremonial Buffoon of the American Indian." *Papers of the Michigan Academy of Science, Arts, and Letters* 14:187–207.

Stewart, Susan. 1959. *Nonsense: Aspects of Intertexuality in Folklore and Literature.* Baltimore: Johns Hopkins University Press.

Stillman, Deanna, and Ann Beatts. 1976. *Titters: The First Collection of Humor by Women.* New York: Collier.

Stimpson, Catharine R. 1987. "The 'F' Word: Why Can't We Say It In Public?" *Ms.*, July/August, pp. 80 ff.

Stoddard, Karen M. 1976. "'Women Have No Sense of Humor' and Other Myths: A Consideration of Female Stand-Up Comics, 1960–1976." *American Humor: An Interdisciplinary Newsletter*, Fall, p. 11.

Stone, Leo. 1954. "On the Principal Obscene Word of the English Language." *International Journal of Psycho-Analysis* 5:30–56.

Storer, Edward, trans. 1923. *The Facetiae of Poggio and Other Medieval Story-Tellers.* London: George Routledge.

Strauss, Leo. 1952. *Persecution and the Art of Writing.* Glencoe, Ill.: Free Press.

Strohm, Paul. 1980. "Middle English Narrative Genres." *Genre* 13 (Fall): 379–88.

Stukeley, William. 1723. *Of the Spleen: Its Description and History.* London.

Suchier, Walther, ed. 1955. *Joca Monachorum: Das Mittelalteinische Gespräch Adrian und Epictitus nebst verwandten Texten.* Tübigen: M. Niemeyer.

Sudnow, David, ed. 1972. *Studies in Social Interaction.* New York: Free Press.

Suleiman, Susan Rubin. 1990. *Subversive Intent: Gender, Politics, and the Avant-Garde.* Cambridge: Harvard University Press.

Sully, James. 1903. *An Essay on Laughter: Its Forms, Its Causes, Its Development, and Its Value*. London: Longmans Green.

Susman, A. 1941. "Word Play in Winnebago." *Language* 17:342–44.

Susskind, Norman. 1964. "Love and Laughter in the *Romans Courtois*." *French Review* 37:651–57.

Swain, Barbara. 1932. *Fools and Folly during the Middle Ages and the Renaissance*. New York: Columbia University Press.

Swaley, Marie C. 1961. *Comic Laughter: A Philosophical Essay*. New Haven: Yale University Press.

Sykes, A. J. M. 1966. "Joking Relationships in an Industrial Setting." *American Anthropologist* 68:188–93.

Sypher, Wylie, ed. 1956. *Comedy*. Garden City, N.Y.: Doubleday, Anchor Books.

Talhouet, J. de. 1923. *Le rire et l'origine des idées*. Rennes: G. Vator.

Tallman, R. S. 1974. "A Generic Approach to the Practical Joke." *Southern Folklore Quarterly* 38:259–74.

Tanner, Roy L. 1986. *The Humor of Irony and Satire in the Tradiciones Peruanas*. Columbia: University of Missouri Press.

Tatlock, J. S. P. 1945. "Medieval Laughter." *Speculum* 21:289–94.

Taussig, Michael. 1993. *Mimesis and Alterity: A Particular History of the Senses*. New York: Routledge.

Tave, Stuart M. 1960. *The Amiable Humorist*. Chicago: University of Chicago Press.

Taylor, Archer. 1977. *English Riddles from Oral Tradition*. Berkeley: University of California Press.

Telushkin, Rabbi Joseph. 1992. *Jewish Humor: What the Best Jewish Jokes Say about Jews*. New York: Morrow.

Thomas, Keith. 1977. "The Place of Laughter in Tudor and Stuart England." *Times Literary Supplement*, January 21, pp. 76–83.

Thompson, E. P. 1972. "'Rough Music': Le Charivari Anglais." *Annales ESC* 27:285–312.

Thomson, Arthur Malcolm. 1966. *Anatomy of Laughter*. London: Epworth Press.

Thomson, D. F. "The Joking Relationship and Organized Obscenity in North Queensland." *American Anthropologist* 37:460–90.

Thomson, P. 1972. *The Grotesque*. London: Methuen.

Tietze-Conrat, E. 1957. *Dwarfs and Jesters in Art*. Garden City, N.Y.: Phaidon Press.

Titier, M. 1975. "Some Aspects of Clowning among the Hopi Indians." In *Themes in Culture*, ed. Mario D. Zamora, J. M. Mahar, and H. Orinstein, pp. 326–36. Quezon City, Philippines: Kayumanggi.

Torrance, Robert M. 1978. *The Comic Hero*. Cambridge: Harvard University Press.

Toth, Emily. 1981. "Female Wits!" *Massachusetts Review* 22, no. 4 (Winter): 783–93.

———. "A Laughter of Their Own: Women's Humor in the United States." In *Critical Essays on American Humor*, ed. William Bedford Clark and W. Craig Turner, pp. 199–215. Boston: G. K. Hall.

———. "Forbidden Jokes and Naughty Ladies." *Studies in American Humor*, n.s., 4, nos. 1 and 2 (Spring/Summer): 7–17.

Towsen, J. H. 1976. *Clowns*. New York: Hawthorn Books.

Trachtenberg, S. 1975. "The Economy of Comedy." *Psychoanalytic Review* 62:557–78.

"The Trickster." 1979. Special issue of *Parabola* 4, no. 1.

Trotter, Elizabeth Stanley. 1922. "Humor with a Gender." *Atlantic Monthly*, December, pp. 784–87.

Trueblood, Elton. 1964. *The Humor of Christ*. New York: Harper and Row.

Tucker, Susie. 1959. "Laughter in Old English Literature." *Neophilologus* 43:222–26.

Turner, Victor W. 1967. "Betwixt and Between: The Liminal Period in *Rites de Passage*." In *The Forest of Symbols: Aspects of Ndembu Ritual*, pp. 93–111. Ithaca: Cornell University Press.

———. 1969. *The Ritual Process: Structure and Anti-Structure*. Chicago: Aldine Publishing.

———. 1977. *Dramas, Fields, and Metaphors: Symbolic Action in Human Society*. Ithaca: Cornell University Press.

———. 1977. "Variations on a Theme of Liminality." In *Secular Ritual*, ed. Sally Moore and Barbara G. Meyerhoff, pp. 35–37. Amsterdam: Van Gorcum.

Ulmer, Gregory. 1989. *Teletheory: Grammatology in the Age of Video*. New York: Routledge.

Utley, Frances Lee. 1969. "The Urban and the Rural Jest (with an Excursus on the Shaggy Dog)." *Journal of Popular Culture* 2:563–77.

Vasey, George. 1877. *The Philosophy of Laughter and Smiling*. London: J. Burns.

Vecsey, Christopher, and William J. Hymes. 1979. "Trickster Myths: A Working Bibliography." Paper prepared for the American Academy of Religion, Consultation on Trickster Myths.

Vincent-Casey, Mireille. 1986. "L'envie au Moyen Age." *Annales: Economies, Sociétés, Civilisations* 35:253–71.

Waddell, Helen. 1929. *The Wandering Scholars*. Boston: Houghton.

Walker, Nancy. 1981. "Wit, Sentimentality, and the Image of Women in the Nineteenth Century." *American Studies* 22, no. 2 (Fall): 5–22.

———. 1981. "Do Feminists Ever Laugh? Women's Humor and Women's Rights." *International Journal of Women's Studies* 4, no. 1 (January/February): 1–9.

———. 1984. *The Tradition of Women's Humor in America.* Huntington Beach, Calif.: American Studies Publishing.

———. 1988. *A Very Serious Thing: Women's Humor and American Culture.* Minneapolis: University of Minnesota Press.

Walker, Nancy, and Zita Dresner, eds. 1988. *Redressing the Balance: American Women's Literary Humor from Colonial Times to the 1980s.* Jackson: University Press of Mississippi.

Wallace, Ronald. 1979. *The Last Laugh: Form and Affirmation in the Contemporary American Novel.* Columbia: University of Missouri.

———. 1984. *God Be with the Clown: Humor in American Poetry.* Columbia: University of Missouri Press.

Walle, Alf H. "Getting Picked Up without Being Put Down: Jokes and the Bar Rush." *Journal of the Folklore Institute* 13:201–17.

Wallis, W. D. 1922. "Why Do We Laugh?" *Scientific Monthly* 15:343–47.

Walsh, James Joseph. 1928. *Laughter and Health.* New York: D. Appleton.

Ward, Benedicta. 1982. *Miracles and the Medieval Mind.* Philadelphia: University of Pennsylvania Press.

Washburn, R. W. 1929. "A Study of the Smiling and Laughing of Infants in the First Year of Life." *General Psychology Monographs* 6:397.

Weber, Carlo. 1970. "A God Who Laughs." In *A Celebration of Laughter*, ed. Werner Mendel, pp. 119–33. Los Angeles: Mara Books.

Weber, Samuel. 1987. "The Divaricator: Remarks on Freud's Witz." *Glyph* 1–26.

———. 1982. *The Legend of Freud.* Minneapolis: University of Minnesota Press.

———. 1987. "Laughing in the Meanwhile." *Modern Language Notes* 102, no. 4 (September): 691–706.

Webster, G. 1960. *Laughter in the Bible.* St. Louis: Bethany Press.

Weimann, Robert. 1978. *Shakespeare and the Popular Tradition in the Theater*, ed. Robert Schwartz. Baltimore: Johns Hopkins University Press.

Weinberg, Bernard. 1961. *History of Literary Criticism: The Italian Renaissance.* Chicago: University of Chicago Press.

Weinstein, Sharon. 1974. "Don't Women Have a Sense of Comedy They Can Call Their Own?" *American Humor: An Interdisciplinary Newsletter* 1, no. 2 (Fall): 9–12.

Weisstein, Naomi. 1973. "Why We Aren't Laughing . . . Anymore." *Ms.*, November, pp. 43–51 ff.

Weldon, Fay. 1984. *Down among the Women.* Chicago: Academy Chicago Publishers.

Wells, John Edwin, ed. 1967. *A Manual of the Writings in Middle English, 1050–1400*, revised by J. Burke Severs and Albert Harding. New Haven: Connecticut Academy of Arts and Sciences.

Welsford, Enid. 1966. *The Fool: His Social and Literary History*. Gloucester, Mass.: Peter Smith.

Werge, Thomas. 1991. "Did You Hear the One About . . . ? *Notre Dame Magazine*, Spring, pp. 16–22.

Wertheim, Arthur Frank. 1979. *Radio Comedy*. New York: Oxford University Press.

Whicher, George F. 1949. *The Goliard Poets: Medieval Latin Songs and Satires*. N.p.

White, Allon. 1993. *Carnival, Hysteria, and Writing: The Collected Essays and Autobiography of Allon White*. New York: Oxford University Press.

White, Beatrice. 1960. "Medieval Mirth." *Anglia* 78, no. 3:284–301.

White, C. M. N. 1957. "Joking Relationships in Central Africa." *Man* 245:187.

———. 1958. "A Note on Luvale Joking Relationships." *African Studies* 17:28–33.

White, E. B., and Katharine S. White, eds. 1948. *A Subtreasury of American Humor*. New York: Modern Library.

Whitman, Cedric. 1964. *Aristophanes and the Comic Hero*. Cambridge: Harvard University Press.

Wilder, Marshall P., ed. 1908. *The Wit and Humor of America*. 10 vols. New York: Funk and Wagnalls.

Willeford, William. 1969. *The Fool and His Sceptre: A Study in Clowns and Jesters and Their Audience*. London: E. Arnold.

William, Riggin. 1981. *Picaros, Madmen, Naifs, and Clowns: The Unreliable First Person Narrator*. Norman: University of Oklahoma Press.

Williams, John A., and Dennis A. Williams. 1991. *If I Stop I'll Die: The Comedy and Tragedy of Richard Pryor*. New York: Thunder's Mouth Press.

Williams, Paul V. A., ed. 1979. *The Fool and the Trickster*. Totawa, N.J.: Rowman and Littlefield.

Wilson, Barbara, and Rachel Da Silva, eds. 1982. *Backbone 4: Humor by Northwest Women*. Seattle: Seal Press.

Wilson, C. P. 1979. *Jokes: Form, Content, Use, and Function*. London: Academic Press.

Wilt, Judith. 1980. "The Laughter of Maidens, the Cackle of Matriarchs: Notes on the Collision between Comedy and Feminism." In *Women and Literature*, ed. Janet Todd. New York: Holmes and Meier.

Wimsatt, W. K., ed. 1969. *The Idea of Comedy*. Englewood Cliffs, N.J.: Prentice-Hall.

Winnick, Charles. 1963. "A Content Analysis of Orally Communicated Jokes." *American Image* 20:261–91.

Winnicott, D. W. 1987. *The Child, the Family, and the Outside World.* Menlo Park, Calif.: Addison-Wesley.

Wisse, R. R. 1971. *The Schlemiel as Modern Hero.* Chicago: University of Chicago Press.

Wolfe, Susan S. 1980. "Ingroup Lesbian Feminist Political Humor." Paper delivered at the meeting of the Midwest Modern Language Association, Minneapolis, Minnesota, November.

Wolfenstein, Martha. 1954. *Children's Humor: A Psychological Analysis.* Glencoe, Ill.: Free Press.

———. 1956. "Children's Understanding of Jokes." *Psychoanalytic Study of the Child* 8:162–73.

Wolff, H. A., C. E. Smith, and H. A. Murray. 1934. "The Psychology of Humor: A Study of Responses to Race-Disparagement Jokes." *Journal of Abnormal and Social Psychology* 28:341–65.

Wood, Fredrik T. 1939. "The Comic Elements in the English Mystery Plays." *Neophilologus* 26:39 ff.

Woolf, Virginia. 1947. "Lewis Carroll." In *The Moment and Other Essays.* London: Hogarth Press.

Wright, Thomas. 1968. *Anglo-Saxon and Old-English Vocabularies.* 2 vols. 2nd ed. Edited and collated by Richard P. Wulcker. Darmstadt: Wissenschaftliche Buchgesellschaft.

Wright, Thomas. 1865. *A History of Caricature and Grotesque in Literature and Art.* London: Virtue Brothers.

Young, Gayle. 1983. *English Prose Jestbooks in the Huntington Library: A Chronological Checklist.* San Marino: Huntington Library.

———. 1986. "Ice Age Cro-Magnon Man Finally Gets Some Respect." *Los Angeles Times*, November 23, p. 2.

Young, R., and M. Frye. 1966. "Some Are Laughing, Some Are Not—Why?" *Psychological Reports* 18:747–54.

Young, Robert. 1879. *Analytical Concordance to the Holy Bible.* London: Lutterworth Press.

Zall, Paul M. 1963. *A Hundred Merry Tales and Other English Jestbooks of the Fifteenth and Sixteenth Centuries.* Lincoln: University of Nebraska Press.

Zenner, W. P. "Joking and Ethnic Stereotyping." *Anthropological Quarterly* 43:93–113.

Zhao, Y. 1988. "The Information-Conveying Aspect of Jokes." *Humor.* Vols. 1–3. Berlin: Mouton.

Zijderveld, Anton C. 1968. "Jokes and Their Relation to Social Reality." *Social Research* 35:286–311.

———. 1983. "The Sociology of Humour and Laughter." *Current Sociology* 31, no. 3 (Winter): 1–103.

Zillman, D., and S. H. Stocking. 1976. "Putdown Humor." *Journal of Communication* 26:154–63.

Zippen, David. 1966. "Sex Differences and the Sense of Humor." *Psychoanalytic Review* 53:45–55.

Zucker, Wolfgang. 1967. "The Clown as the Lord of Disorder." *Theology Today* 24:306–317.

# *index*